T. R. MALTHUS
PRINCIPLES OF POLITICAL ECONOMY
VARIORUM EDITION
VOLUME I

T. R. MALTHUS
PRINCIPLES OF POLITICAL ECONOMY

VARIORUM EDITION

EDITED BY
JOHN PULLEN

ASSOCIATE PROFESSOR OF ECONOMICS,
UNIVERSITY OF NEW ENGLAND
NEW SOUTH WALES

VOLUME I

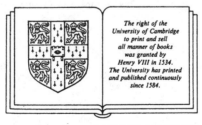

The right of the
University of Cambridge
to print and sell
all manner of books
was granted by
Henry VIII in 1534.
The University has printed
and published continuously
since 1584.

CAMBRIDGE UNIVERSITY PRESS

CAMBRIDGE
NEW YORK   PORT CHESTER
MELBOURNE   SYDNEY

FOR THE ROYAL ECONOMIC SOCIETY, 1989

CAMBRIDGE UNIVERSITY PRESS
Cambridge, New York, Melbourne, Madrid, Cape Town, Singapore, São Paulo

Cambridge University Press
The Edinburgh Building, Cambridge CB2 8RU, UK

Published in the United States of America by Cambridge University Press, New York

www.cambridge.org
Information on this title: www.cambridge.org/9780521303590

First published 1989
This digitally printed version 2008

A catalogue record for this publication is available from the British Library

Library of Congress Cataloguing in Publication data
Malthus, T. R. (Thomas Robert), 1766–1834.
Principles of political economy.
Includes index.
1. Economics. 2. Classical school of economics.
I. Pullen, John, 1933–   . II. Title.
HB161.M25   1987   330.15′3   86–32742

ISBN 978-0-521-30359-0 hardback (Volume I)
ISBN 978-0-521-07591-6 paperback (Volume I)

ISBN 978-0-521-32362-8 hardback (Volume II)
ISBN 978-0-521-07593-0 paperback (Volume II)

CONTENTS

Contents

Volume II

ACKNOWLEDGEMENTS

This variorum edition has received assistance over a long period of time from many persons and institutions. Five in particular have played a major part. In the beginning Mr Piero Sraffa assisted and encouraged the study of the Manuscript Revisions, and the project in its early stages benefited greatly from the guidance of Associate Professor B. L. J. Gordon and Professor G. S. L. Tucker. More recently Professor Donald Winch and Mrs Patricia James made a large number of indispensable contributions to both the content and the presentation. To them and to the many colleagues and correspondents who have provided information and advice over the years the variorum edition is deeply indebted. Acknowledgements are also due to Mr A. H. Finkell, Librarian, Marshall Library of Economics, Cambridge, and to Mr A. E. B. Owen, Keeper of Manuscripts, Cambridge University Library, for advice on particular aspects of the Manuscript Revisions; and to the Library of the University of New England, Australia, in particular the Inter-Library Loan Department, for assistance in obtaining rare books and articles. Permission to make use of unpublished or copyright material has been kindly granted by the British Library; Cambridge University Library; the Houghton Library, Harvard University; the Library of the University of Illinois at Urbana-Champaign; the publishing firm of John Murray; and New College Library, Edinburgh University Library. Research for the project has been financially supported by the University of New England, and the Australian Research Grants Committee; and publication costs have been subsidised by the Royal Economic Society.

SYMBOLS

Principles	Unless otherwise stated, '*Principles*' refers to T. R. Malthus, *Principles of Political Economy*.
Principles 1.267 or 1.267	Page 267 of the first edition of the *Principles*.
Principles 2.267 or 2.267	Page 267 of the second edition of the *Principles*.
Manuscript Revisions or MR	The manuscript notes made by Malthus in a copy of the first edition of the *Principles*, now held in Cambridge University Library.
a, b, c, ...	These Roman letters in the margins of Volume I of this variorum edition indicate the lines in which alterations occurred or commenced in either the Manuscript Revisions or the second edition of the *Principles*. The details of the alterations are given in Volume II alongside the appropriate identification number; for example, 1.267a, 1.267b, 1.267c. These identification numbers are also used to identify comments made by the present editor on the alterations.
α, β, γ, ...	These Greek letters in the margins of Volume I refer to comments made by the present editor on passages in the *Principles* that were *not* altered. These editorial comments are given in Volume II, alongside the appropriate identification number; for example, 1.272α, 1.273β. The comments identified by Greek letters are in general concerned with bibliographical matters, as distinct from the comments identified by Roman letters whose main purpose is to summarise and explain the alterations.
[4]	In Volume II of this variorum edition, a number in square brackets following an abbreviated passage from edition 1 of the *Principles* (for example, 1.14b, 1.19b) indicates the number of lines of the text of edition 1 over which that passage extends.
* † ‡ §	Footnotes in either the first edition of the *Principles*, or the second edition of the *Principles*, or the Manuscript Revisions.
1 2 3 ...	Footnotes by the editor of this variorum edition.
Ed.	Indicates a footnote added to ed. 2 of the *Principles* by the editor (John Cazenove) of ed. 2.

EDITORIAL PROCEDURES IN THIS
VARIORUM EDITION

The procedure followed in preparing this variorum edition has been, as a general principle, to record every alteration in every word, letter, and number. No attempt has been made to identify and exclude alterations that are doctrinally insignificant. As a result, some of the alterations listed in Volume II below appear to be quite trivial, but it was thought preferable to err on the side of including some trivia than to omit alterations which might prove to be significant. However, a few exceptions were made to this general principle. The following alterations have not been recorded: (1) the use of letters instead of numerals, for example, 'three hundred' for '300', 'secondly' for '2dly'; (2) the use of different symbols, for example, '£' for 'l', and 'III' for 'iii'; (3) the use of abbreviations, for example, 'Sect.' for 'Section', 'Hen. VII' for 'Henry VII', 'ch.' for 'chap.', 'Id.' for 'Ibid', 'p.' for 'page'; (4) the use of capitals, where no ambiguity or change of meaning is involved, for example, 'Note' for 'note', 'Demand and Supply' for 'demand and supply'; (5) spelling alterations where both variants were acceptable in Malthus' time, for example, 'shew' and 'show'.

Punctuation alterations between the two editions have not been specifically recorded in this variorum edition except when they change, clarify or obscure the meaning; or when they are part of a recorded alteration. Misprints and mistakes in ed. 1 have been recorded even if they were not corrected in MR or ed. 2. Likewise misprints and mistakes that occurred in ed. 2 have been recorded. Spellings which are obsolete now but which were acceptable variants in the nineteenth century have not been regarded as misprints or mistakes and have not been recorded; for example, 'raisons' for 'raisins', 'spunge' for 'sponge'.

In most instances, the alterations between the two editions of the *Principles* are identifiable by a sequential comparison of the two texts. However in some instances the process of identification is more difficult, because passages have been transposed from one context in ed. 1 to another context (more or less distant from the first) in ed. 2.[1]

All the Manuscript Revisions appear to be in Malthus' hand with the exception of nine sides of the interleaved sheets which from the style of the handwriting and the relative absence of corrections appear to have been written

---

[1] For example, a new paragraph was introduced into *Principles* 2.280, and sentences were added to it from *Principles* 1.308, 1.311, and 1.312, with some alterations in each of the transposed sentences. See 1.307l.

by an amanuensis.[1] Fortunately, Malthus' handwriting is usually quite clear. After one has become accustomed to certain peculiarities, decipherment does not present serious difficulties, provided that the flow of ideas is uninterrupted. But on many of the interleaved and supplementary sheets, statements have been altered several times. New sentences have been written between the lines, and these new sentences have in turn been deleted wholly or partially and replaced by further words placed between the lines, so that one is confronted with two or three alternative versions, which are not always legible or intelligible. Because of the difficulties involved in deciphering and presenting these alternative versions, only the final version has been recorded in Volume II of this variorum edition, except in a few cases where an earlier and legible version is thought to have some substantive interest. In most cases the later versions contain only stylistic variations.

In some cases the marginal notes have been recorded in this variorum edition by listing the words deleted and inserted. But in cases where a number of deletions and insertions occur within the same passage, it was thought better to record, not the individual deletions and insertions, but the new meaning that Malthus intended to convey. This method of recording should enable the reader to compare the different versions at a glance without the labour of reconstructing the new meaning.

In recording in Volume II the Manuscript Revisions, the original punctuation has been retained, except where the sense appears to require an alteration, or where the original punctuation might impede understanding. Abbreviations which would have been printed in full if published have been so given; for example, 'should' for 'sh'd', 'quantity' for 'q^y'. Otherwise, the original spelling is retained, with errors noted.

The procedure adopted in presenting in Volume II the details of the alterations is, first, to present the ed. 1 version[2] alongside its identification number. This is then followed by the new version, if any, in MR alongside the symbol 'MR'; and then by the new version, if any, in ed. 2 alongside its identification number. See for example 1.64f. A combined symbol – for example, 'MR/2.16' in 1.21a – means that exactly the same alteration occurred in both MR and ed. 2. If there is an MR entry but no ed. 2 entry (see, for example, 1.91j) this means that an alteration occurred at that point in MR but not in ed. 2. If there is an ed. 2 entry, but no MR entry (see, for example, 1.65d) this means that an alteration occurred at that point in ed. 2 but not in MR.

In recording the alterations between the two editions of the *Principles*, a decision had to be made on whether to use the first edition or the second edition

---

[1] See 1.261b.

[2] Where the altered passage in ed. 1 is extensive, it is abbreviated by the use of ellipsis, and is followed by a number in square brackets indicating the number of lines of the text of ed. 1 over which that passage extends. See above, p. ix, Symbols.

as the base. There are precedents for using the last edition revised by an author as the authoritative base for a variorum study, but in this case because of the omissions and additions made by the editor we cannot be sure of the extent to which the second edition of the *Principles* is an authoritative version of Malthus' last thoughts. The first edition therefore seemed to be the appropriate choice. This choice was reinforced by the decision to incorporate the Manuscript Revisions in this variorum edition. As Malthus made the revisions using the first edition as the base, it seemed appropriate to present them in that way. Also when the three versions are listed in their chronological order (ed. 1, MR, ed. 2), it is easier to appreciate the chronological developments. A further reason for choosing the first edition of the *Principles* as the base for this variorum edition is that it provides an opportunity to reprint for the first time the full text of the first edition, including the 70-page 'Summary of the Contents of the Foregoing Work' which Malthus regarded as 'useful' (see 1.523a), but which was not included in the second edition.

Volume II of this variorum edition contains, in addition to the details of the alterations, some editorial comments on the alterations. These comments provide further bibliographical information on the sources cited by Malthus in the two editions and in MR. They also attempt to explain the meaning, and to assess the significance, of some of the alterations, making use of some of Malthus' other works published after 1820 where they throw light on the alterations. These editorial comments are offered as contributions to an understanding of the development of Malthus' thought, but do not pretend to be either comprehensive or definitive. Many of the alterations remain unexplained and unassessed.

INTRODUCTION TO THE VARIORUM EDITION

The first edition of Malthus' *Principles of Political Economy* was published in 1820. His correspondence and manuscripts show that he was eager to produce a second edition, and that during the rest of his life he recorded many alterations which he wished to incorporate.[1] However the second edition was published only posthumously in 1836, with the assistance of an anonymous editor; and since then the study of Malthus' *Principles* has been impeded by the difficulties involved in reconciling the two editions. Some students of Malthus' work have been unaware of the existence or the extent of the differences between the two editions, with the predictable result that those who use only the first edition frequently disagree in their interpretations of Malthus with those who use only the second. Moreover those who are aware of the existence of the two editions, and who attempt to heed the differences, do not have an easy task. The first edition has never been reprinted in its entirety, and is extremely rare.[2] Even when the two editions can be placed side by side on the scholar's desk, the task of identifying and interpreting the differences is far from easy. The difficulties are exacerbated by the fact that, on his own admission, the editor of the posthumous second edition made alterations to the text, but except in a few instances did not identify them. Consequently some of the differences between the two editions reflect the editor's rather than Malthus' views.

This variorum edition is designed to overcome, or at least mitigate, these difficulties that impede the study of Malthus' *Principles*. It reproduces the 1820 edition in full, identifies the differences between the two editions, and includes a commentary that attempts to clarify and explain the differences wherever possible. This variorum edition also contains the unpublished manuscript notes – referred to hereafter as the Manuscript Revisions or MR – made by Malthus in preparing the second edition, and now held in Cambridge University Library.

---

[1] The title page of the second edition carries the statement: 'with considerable additions from the author's own manuscript'.

[2] Parts of the first edition are reprinted in *The Works and Correspondence of David Ricardo*, edited by Piero Sraffa with the collaboration of M. H. Dobb, Vol. II, *Notes on Malthus's Principles of Political Economy*, Cambridge University Press for the Royal Economic Society, 1951. The second edition has been reprinted several times. Ricardo (1772–1823), one of the leading figures in classical political economy, was a correspondent, critic and close personal friend of Malthus.

Introduction

MALTHUS' WORKS BEFORE 1820

Before proceeding to an account of the events surrounding the publication of the first edition of the *Principles* it would be appropriate to note briefly Malthus' works before 1820, and to situate his *Principles* in the context of his earlier literary endeavours. The first edition of the *Principles* was not the work of a young man – he was fifty-four years of age when it was published – nor of a man who had only recently come to the study of political economy.

Thomas Robert Malthus was born in 1766, one of seven children of an affluent landowning middle-class family living south of London in the county of Surrey.[1] His father, Daniel Malthus (1730–1800), was described as 'a gentleman of good family and independent fortune, attached to a country life, but much occupied in classical and philosophical pursuits, and with a strong bias towards foreign literature'.[2] Daniel Malthus travelled widely in England and Europe, and was an admirer of Jean-Jacques Rousseau who once visited the Malthus home. Malthus was educated in the homes of private tutors, the most notable being the radical Gilbert Wakefield (1756–1801), and attended the Dissenting Academy at Warrington in the north of England, established for the education of the sons of Protestant Dissenters. In 1784 he became an undergraduate at Jesus College at the University of Cambridge, and in 1788 graduated as Ninth Wrangler (i.e. ninth in order of merit in his year). In 1789 he was ordained a minister of the Church of England and received an appointment as curate at Okewood in Surrey.[3] In 1793 he was elected to a Fellowship of Jesus College, but in accordance with the prevailing rules he had to resign when he married in 1804. In 1805 he was appointed Professor of History and Political Economy at the newly established East India College, at Haileybury, in Hertfordshire, north of London. He was the first person in England to bear the title of Professor of Political Economy. The purpose of the College was to educate young men destined for careers in the service of the East India Company, and Malthus retained his position in the College until his death in 1834.

Malthus' first known work was a political pamphlet written in 1796 entitled: *The Crisis, a View of the Present Interesting State of Great Britain, by a Friend*

---

[1] For further biographical details of Malthus, see in particular Patricia James, *Population Malthus. His Life and Times*, London, Routledge and Kegan Paul, 1979; and also James Bonar, *Malthus and His Work*, 2nd ed., London, 1924; [William Empson], 'Life, Writing and Character of Mr Malthus', *Edinburgh Review*, Vol. LXIV, 1837, pp. 469–506, and [William Otter], 'Memoir of Robert Malthus', in T. R. Malthus, *Principles of Political Economy*, ed. 2, 1836, pp. xiii–liv. Empson (1791–1852) was a colleague of Malthus at the East India College. Otter (1768–1840), Bishop of Chichester (1836–40), was a friend of Malthus from University days; his eldest daughter married Malthus' son.

[2] Otter, 'Memoir of Robert Malthus', p. xxi.

[3] See *Notes and Queries*, 11th Series, Vol. IV, 1911, p. 126; quoted by James Bonar, 'Life of Thomas Malthus', Appendix XI, typescript held in the Rare Book Room, Library of the University of Illinois at Urbana-Champaign.

Introduction

to the Constitution. Malthus failed in an attempt to have the pamphlet published, and the MS. has now been lost. From the comments of his contemporaries, and from the brief extracts that they quoted,[1] it appears to have been essentially a plea for the revival of what Malthus called 'true Whig principles'. Its two main objects were to protest against the administration of the Prime Minister, William Pitt, and to arbitrate between political extremists. Malthus placed his hope in 'the returning sense and reason of the country gentleman, and middle classes of society'.[2] The pamphlet also contained a strong plea for religious toleration, and argued for adequate (but not excessive) outdoor relief for the elderly and needy. This emphasis on the need for moderation in politics and on the role of the middle classes was to become a dominant characteristic of Malthus' political economy. Malthus' father approved of the pamphlet, and was disappointed that it could not be published: 'what you have done appears to me to be extreamly [sic] well done and to be perfectly adapted to the occasion. ... I can't reconcile myself to your not publishing your pamphlet.' The radical nature of its contents, and by implication the tendency to radicalism in both father and son, are evident in Daniel's comment: 'I am sure it will never do you discredit, though I cannot answer that it will get you a Deanery.'[3]

Malthus' first published work, and his most famous, was *An Essay on the Principle of Population*, 1798. It went through six editions in his lifetime (1798, 1803, 1806, 1807, 1817 and 1826), with further clarifications and developments being added in successive editions. There is a tendency amongst some commentators on Malthus to treat the *Essay on Population* and the *Principles of Political Economy* as separate and unconnected compartments of Malthus' thought, as if the former dealt with demography alone, and the latter with political economy alone. As a consequence of this tendency, attempts are sometimes made to assess his views on population on the basis of the *Essay* alone, without considering the important statements on population contained in the *Principles*, in particular in ed. 1, Chapter VII, Section II, 'Of the Increase of Population considered as a Stimulus to the continued Increase of Wealth'. Likewise, attempts are sometimes made to assess his views on economic issues such as demand and public works on the basis of the *Principles* alone, without considering his comments on these issues in the *Essay*. There is no justification in Malthus' writings for this compartmentalised approach. On the contrary, it is more appropriate to situate the *Essay* within the general framework of the *Principles*, and to regard the *Essay* as a more

---

[1] Extracts from 'The Crisis', with commentaries were published by Empson, 'Life, Writing and Character', pp. 479–82, and Otter, 'Memoir of Robert Malthus', pp. xxxv–xxxvii. Further details of 'The Crisis' are contained in a letter of Malthus' father of 14 April 1796. See Bonar, *Malthus and His Work*, pp. 413–14, and 'Life of Thomas Malthus', Ch. V, pp. 4–5.

[2] Empson, 'Life, Writing and Character', p. 479.

[3] See Bonar, *Malthus and His Work*, pp. 413–14. As Bonar noted, the evidence of this letter conflicts with Otter's view ('Memoir of Robert Malthus', p. xxxv) that Malthus 'refrained from printing it at his father's request'.

Introduction

intensive and extensive treatment of one particular aspect of the *Principles*. Chronologically the *Essay* preceded the *Principles* but logically it is part of the *Principles*. The successive editions of the *Essay* can be seen not as separate intellectual exercises, but as steps in the evolution of Malthus' thought, and as a preparation for and complement to the *Principles*.

During 1799 Malthus travelled in the north of Europe with a group of university friends. These travels appear to have played an important role in the development of his ideas on population in particular and on political economy in general. His diaries reveal his keen interest in the demographic and economic conditions of the countries he was visiting, and also his attempt to construct a reasoned analysis of the causes of these conditions.[1] In the summer of 1802, in the brief interval in the Napoleonic Wars afforded by the Peace of Amiens, he travelled in France and Switzerland. The journey was inspired more by social than intellectual considerations – in particular, the company of a pretty and athletic cousin whom he subsequently married – but his correspondence shows that the development of his economic ideas was stimulated by his observations of economic conditions in the places he visited.[2]

In 1800, between the first and second editions of the *Essay*, Malthus published a small pamphlet dealing with the extraordinary increase in food prices that occurred in 1799–1800. Entitled *An Investigation of the Cause of the Present High Price of Provisions*, it attributed the increase in food prices to the excessive spending power generated by the Poor Laws, and foreshadowed his future arguments for a less generous scale of poor relief. In a letter of 28 November 1800 to George Turner, a friend from his student days at Cambridge, Malthus explained that he had composed this twenty-eight page pamphlet in only two days, and that he had written it in the hope that it would have some immediate impact on current political debates. He added that it had been well received – a second edition was published in 1800 – and suggested that it might have influenced a recent government report.[3]

---

[1] See Patricia James, ed., *The Travel Diaries of T. R. Malthus*, Cambridge University Press for the Royal Economic Society, Cambridge, 1966.

[2] See Eugenio Masè-Dari, *Tre Lettere Inedite di R.T. [sic] Malthus*, Modena, 1929. In the letter of 12 September 1802, Malthus said of his future wife: 'In Chamouni [sic] Miss Eckersall has acquired a deathless name, and is to be handed down to posterity by the Historian of the Alps, as the first lady that ever reached the summit of Mount Breven, a mountain of very con[siderable] height opposite Mont Blanc, and hitherto untrodden by female foot.' On 16 January 1803 he described her as 'The Heroine of the Breven'.

[3] Malthus to Turner: 'I sat up till two o'clock ... to finish it that it might come out before the meeting of parliament. You will see that it was written in a hurry, but such as it is, it has obtained some little notice. A friend of mine gave it to the Chancellor, who called it the best that had appeared on the subject, and immediately sent it to Mr. Pitt. I know not the opinion of the latter about it; but whether from that or from some other source, you will see that in the first report of the committee of the House of Commons, now just published, much of the same kind of reasoning has been adopted.' (Letter of 28 November [1800], published in the *Economic Journal*, 1897, Vol. VII, pp. 270–1.) For further details of this letter and pamphlet, see James, *Population Malthus*, pp. 86–92. The 'just

Introduction

Malthus' continuing concern with the problem of the poor is evident in his remarks on the Poor Laws in the second (1803), third (1806) and fourth (1807) editions of the *Essay*, and in a forty-page pamphlet entitled, *A Letter to Samuel Whitbread, Esq. M.P. on his Proposed Bill for the Amendment of the Poor Laws*, London, 1807. This was a criticism of Whitbread's Bill, and a reply to the criticisms of Malthus made by Whitbread in his speech (and subsequent pamphlet) on the Bill. Malthus particularly objected to Whitbread's proposal to provide cottages for the poor; he believed that such a policy would encourage improvident marriages, and would result in an over-supply of labour, low wages, starvation, and premature death.[1]

The *Edinburgh Review*, Vol. XI, January 1808, pp. 429–48, contained an article entitled 'Spence on Commerce', which was a review of William Spence, *Britain Independent of Commerce*, 1807. It has been attributed to Malthus,[2] and contains a number of themes that were to appear in Malthus' later thoughts. For example, its statement that 'the internal commerce of a country is of infinitely greater consequence than its external;' (p. 447) could be compared with his statement in 1827 to the Select Committee on Emigration that 'I think the home trade much more important than the foreign.'[3] Also, its statements on the importance of consumption, on the dangers of an excessive accumulation of

---

published' report was most probably: Great Britain. Parliament. House of Commons. *Parliamentary Papers*. 'First Report from the Committee appointed to consider the present High Price of Provisions.' 1800, ordered to be printed 24 November 1800. The Committee argued that, if poor relief is given in the form of money or bread, the demand for bread will increase and the shortage of bread will be worsened. One of the recommendations of the Committee was therefore that 'as large a Portion as possible of this [Parish] Relief should be given neither in Money nor in the Sort of Bread usually consumed in each Parish, but in some other wholesome Substitute ...' (p. 10). See *House of Commons Sessional Papers of the Eighteenth Century*, ed. Sheila Lambert, Vol. 131, Scholarly Resources Inc., 1975.

[1] The *Letter to Samuel Whitbread* was dated 27 March 1807; a second edition was also published in 1807. For further details, see James, *Population Malthus*, pp. 136–41.

[2] See W. E. Houghton, ed., *The Wellesley Index to Victorian Periodicals 1824–1900*, 3 vols., University of Toronto Press and Routledge and Kegan Paul, 1966–79, Vol. 1, p. 442. The attribution to Malthus is based on a list of authors of articles in the *Edinburgh Review* compiled by Henry Brougham, and on a statement in *Memoirs and Correspondence of Francis Horner, M.P.*, edited by his brother Leonard Horner, 2 vols., 2nd ed., Boston and London, 1853, Vol. I, p. 446. Also a probable attribution to Malthus is given by F. W. Fetter, 'The Authorship of Economic Articles in the *Edinburgh Review*, 1802–47', *Journal of Political Economy*, Vol. LXI, 1953, p. 246. But Bernard Semmel believes the article was probably not written by Malthus. See B. Semmel, 'Malthus and the Reviews', pp. 14–15, in *Occasional Papers of T.R. Malthus*, Burt Franklin, New York, 1963. In support of Semmel's view, it is strange that Malthus did not refer to the article either in *Principles* 1.354 and 2.316 when he commented on James Mill's reply to Spence, or in any of his other works and correspondence. On the other hand, Horner's statement to Francis Jeffrey of 17 February 1808 that 'Malthus has begun to contribute' implies that an article by Malthus had recently been submitted and published. It is unlikely that Horner's statement referred to Malthus' article on Newenham in the *Edinburgh Review* of July 1808 because that article was not read by Jeffrey, the editor of the *Review*, until just before 21 April 1808. See the letter of that date from Jeffrey to Malthus, in Henry Cockburn, *Life of Lord Jeffrey with a Selection from his Correspondence*, 2 vols., Edinburgh, 1852, Vol. II, p. 125; quoted by James, *Population Malthus*, pp. 149–50.

[3] See below, Introduction, p. liv.

capital, and on the reciprocity of the causes of growth,[1] foreshadow similar ideas in the *Principles*.

In July 1808 and April 1809, Malthus published two articles on the Irish problem: 'Newenham and Others on the State of Ireland', *Edinburgh Review*, Vol. XII, July 1808, pp. 336–55; and 'Newenham on the State of Ireland', *Edinburgh Review*, Vol. XIV, April 1809, pp. 157–70. In these reviews of the works of Thomas Newenham (1762–1831) and others, Malthus displayed sympathy for the plight of the Irish, and argued strongly for Irish emancipation. His analysis of the economic distress in Ireland identified a number of causes; notably, the want of capital and above all of demand; the 'monopolizers of England', who had secured a prohibition on the import of Irish woollen goods; and the excessive growth of the Irish population. These themes were to reappear more formally in the *Principles* of 1820, in his analysis of the causes of the progress of wealth.

In 1811 Malthus published two articles on monetary matters. The period 1810–11 saw a considerable increase in the price of gold and a decrease in the gold value of paper currency. The Bullion Committee was set up by the House of Commons in February 1810, and in its report of June 1810 attributed the high price of gold bullion to the excessive issue of bank notes by the Bank of England, after the Bank Restriction Act of 1797 had empowered the Bank to issue notes without the obligation of redeeming them in gold. Ricardo had been asked by the *Edinburgh Review* to review the *Bullion Report* and the literature that preceded and followed it, but declined, preferring to present his views in a pamphlet entitled, *Reply to Mr Bosanquet's Practical Observations on the Report of the Bullion Committee*, January 1811.[2] Malthus was then approached, and accepted. His article on 'Depreciation of Paper Currency', in the *Edinburgh Review*, Vol. XVII, February 1811, was a review of six pamphlets on the currency question, including two by Ricardo – his *Reply to Mr Bosanquet's Practical Observations*, and his earlier *The High Price of Bullion a Proof of the Depreciation of Bank Notes*, 1810. Malthus agreed with Ricardo that the essential cause of the high price of bullion was the excessive issue of paper money, but criticised Ricardo for placing exclusive emphasis on the supply of the currency, and ignoring the demand for currency. Ricardo replied to Malthus in an appendix to the fourth edition of his *High Price of Bullion* which appeared in April 1811.

It was at this stage that the correspondence between Malthus and Ricardo began, and soon grew into a friendship that was to play an important part in the

---

[1] For example, 'consumption must exist somewhere, or there could be no production'; 'the enriching effects that can arise from a great consumption, without the aid of many land proprietors'; 'there are limits to the accumulation of capital, though we do not know where to place them'; 'production generates consumption, as well as consumption production', *Edinburgh Review*, January 1808, pp. 434–35.
[2] See Sraffa, 'Note on the Bullion Essays', p. 10, in Ricardo, *Works*, Vol. III.

development of their respective systems and in the early development of the science of political economy. Malthus' first letter to Ricardo on 16 June 1811 began: 'One of my principal reasons for taking the liberty of introducing myself to you, next to the pleasure of making your acquaintance, was, that as we are *mainly* on the same side of the question, we might supersede the necessity of a long controversy in print respecting the points in which we differ, by an amicable discussion in private.'[1] It appears that Ricardo had drafted an introductory letter to Malthus before he received Malthus' letter, and that by a remarkable coincidence he had also used the phrase 'amicable discussion in private'.[2] After Ricardo's reply of 18 June 1811 their first meeting was arranged for 22 June, the first of many such meetings at which they exchanged views and discussed their differences. The depth of their friendship is evident in Malthus' statement in reply to a suggestion that there might have been some jealousy between Ricardo and himself: 'I never loved any body out of my own family so much. Our interchange of opinions was so unreserved, and the object after which we were both enquiring was so entirely the truth, and nothing else, that I cannot but think we sooner or later must have agreed';[3] and also in Ricardo's statement shortly before his death in his last letter to Malthus on 31 August 1823: 'And now my dear Malthus I have done. Like other disputants after much discussion we each retain our own opinion. These discussions however never influence our friendship; I should not like you more than I do if you agreed in opinion with me.'[4] From their first exchange of letters in June 1811 until the publication of Malthus' *Principles* in April 1820, seventy-three letters from Ricardo to Malthus and sixty-one letters from Malthus to Ricardo have been recorded.[5] They did not originally intend that the views exchanged in their correspondence should appear in print. However in the ensuing years their correspondence covered a wide range of issues – for example, rent, profits, corn laws, value – and many of the ideas expressed in their letters reappeared in their publications.

Malthus' next publication – his second on monetary problems – was 'Pamphlets on the Bullion Question', in the *Edinburgh Review*, Vol. XVIII, August 1811. Ostensibly a review of six pamphlets on the bullion controversy, this article gave Malthus the opportunity to develop his earlier ideas more fully. In preparing the article he sought to consult Ricardo on some points, but deliberately excluded from the article the finer points of their controversy. On 14 August 1811 he wrote to Ricardo that the review 'will be quite of a general nature, and will have

---

[1] In Ricardo, *Works*, Vol. VI, pp. 21–23. [2] Ibid., pp. 23–28.

[3] Empson, 'Life, Writing and Character', p. 499. Empson added that this was 'the only time that we ever saw an approach to anger on the countenance of Mr Malthus'.

[4] Ricardo, *Works*, Vol. IX, p. 382.

[5] See Ricardo, *Works*, Vol. VI, p. xiv, and Vol. XI, p. x. A further nineteen letters have been recorded from Ricardo to Malthus, and fifteen from Malthus to Ricardo, before Ricardo's death on 11 September 1823.

nothing to do with our controversy which appears to me to be too nice a question for the generality of readers to be interested about'.[1]

At about this time Malthus' work on political economy suffered a number of interruptions due to the rowdy and undisciplined behaviour of the students at the East India College, who were admitted at the age of fifteen under the patronage of the Directors of the East India Company, and could not easily be expelled. Their commotions and riots received widespread adverse publicity, and the College was threatened with closure. It apparently fell to Malthus amongst the College staff to defend the College against its critics. In April 1813 he published *A Letter to the Right Honourable Lord Grenville occasioned by some Observations of His Lordship on the East India Company's Establishment for the Education of their Civil Servants*, in which he argued that the general and specialised education given at the College provided a more suitable training for future administrators in India than the alternative of a public school and university education. Although the East India Company's Charter was renewed in 1813 for another twenty years, and although the College course became formally recognised as a pre-requisite for appointment in India, the disturbances continued, and in January 1817 Malthus published another pamphlet entitled, *Statements respecting the East India College, with an appeal to facts in refutation of the charges lately brought against it in the Court of Proprietors*, which incorporated material from the 1813 pamphlet, but which presented a much more vigorous defence of the College. The College survived the crisis, and although one cannot be certain of the extent to which the survival was due to Malthus, it is certain that his participation caused him considerable inconvenience, and delayed his other literary pursuits and publications. On 22 December 1815 he wrote to Ricardo: 'I should have written before but have been overwhelmed with College business and able to do nothing, on account of these foolish disturbances, and the necessity [of] constant councils, Reports &c: The term is ended now, and I can breath again; but I have latterly done little to my Edition [ed. 5 of the *Essay on Population*]'; and again on 28 December 1815: 'I have been so much interrupted already by College business, that I have made very little progress in my edition since I saw you, and I find it will require altogether more time than I expected ... I much fear that I shall be called upon to write something about the College, which will be very inconvenient to me.'[2] The one redeeming feature of the disturbances and the threatened closure of the College is that they elicited from Malthus a declaration of his pedagogical views, which might not otherwise have been revealed.

In 1814–15 Malthus published two pamphlets on the Corn Law controversy. The first, entitled *Observations on the Effects of the Corn Laws, and of a Rise or Fall in the Price of Corn on the Agriculture and General Wealth of the Country*, was published in the

---

[1] In Ricardo, *Works*, Vol. VI, p. 48.   [2] Ibid., pp. 341, 346–47.

spring of 1814. Parliamentary discussions were about to take place on the revision of the Corn Laws, and although Malthus obviously intended to make a contribution to the discussions, it was not his intention, in this pamphlet, to present a personal opinion either for or against the Corn Laws:

> It is not however my intention, on the present occasion, to express an opinion on the general question. I shall only endeavour to state, with the strictest impartiality, what appear to me to be the advantages and disadvantages of each system, in the actual circumstances of our present situation, and what are the specific consequences, which may be expected to result from the adoption of either.[1]

In presenting this impartial survey, Malthus criticised Adam Smith's arguments in favour of export bounties on corn on the grounds that bounties violate 'the great principles of supply and demand',[2] but he also confessed to his own past error in not giving due weight to the opposing arguments. The *Observations* was apparently well received; a second edition was published in 1814, and a third in 1815.

In his second pamphlet on the Corn Laws, entitled *The Grounds of an Opinion on the Policy of Restricting the Importation of Foreign Corn: intended as an Appendix to 'Observations on the Corn Laws'*, London, 1815, Malthus abandoned the impartial approach of the *Observations*, and presented his own 'deliberate, yet decided, opinion in favour of some restrictions on the importation of foreign corn'.[3] This view was in accordance with that of Lord Liverpool's Tory government, and in opposition to that of Malthus' Whig friends, who viewed it with dismay.[4] Despite mob riots in London, and a large number of petitions to Parliament, the Corn Law of 1815 was passed, preventing the import of corn when the price was below 80s. a quarter. Malthus' colleague, William Empson, later recalled the reluctance with which Malthus gave his support to the Corn Law. Malthus realised the enormity of supporting this exception to the general principle of free trade, and 'he was not on this occasion as sure as usual of the soundness of the judgment which he had pronounced'.[5] Nevertheless he believed that it was his duty to point out that no great advantages would result from the repeal of the Corn Law, and that 'under the actual circumstances of our present situation, it is our wisest policy to grow our own average supply of corn'.[6] He was convinced that his support for the Corn Law was motivated by a genuine concern for the general welfare, but it was interpreted differently. As Patricia James has said, his support for the Corn Law made him appear 'the ally of the agricultural interest against the community, an apostate from the basic tenets of economic liberty'; and it became 'even easier than it had been before' to see him as 'an ogre who wanted large families of little children to be starved into extinction'.[7]

---

[1] Malthus, *Observations*, pp. 3–4.   [2] Ibid., p. 3.   [3] Malthus, *Grounds*, p. 2.
[4] See James, *Population Malthus*, p. 264.
[5] Empson, 'Life, Writing and Character', pp. 496–7; quoted by James, *Population Malthus*, p. 269.
[6] Malthus, *Grounds*, p. 47.   [7] James, *Population Malthus*, pp. 264, 269.

Introduction

Another pamphlet was published by Malthus in 1815, viz. *An Inquiry into the Nature and Progress of Rent* ... As this was essentially a preview of the *Principles*, Chapter III, 'On the Rent of Land', it is discussed below under 'The writing of the first edition of the *Principles*'. It was brought forward for early publication in 1815 in the form of a separate pamphlet because of its relevance to the Corn Law controversy.

After the pamphlets of 1815, Malthus' publisher, John Murray, apparently proposed a new (fifth) edition of the *Essay on Population*. On 1 October 1815 Malthus wrote to Ricardo: 'I am now thinking about a new edition of the *Essay* which Murray wishes to have finished before anything else is done', and outlined the changes he proposed to make.[1] He wrote in a similar vein on 13 October 1815 to Pierre Prévost.[2] By the end of the year some progress had apparently been made; in a letter of 28 December 1815 to Ricardo, he referred to the new chapters that Ricardo had seen and asked Ricardo to mention any passages which struck him as 'objectionable';[3] but, as noted above, in his letters of 22 and 28 December 1815 to Ricardo he complained of the delays that had occurred because of continuing student disturbances at the College.[4] He wrote in a similar vein to Ricardo on 9 February 1816: 'I have almost determined to extend my new edition to another volume; but I have been doing nothing at it lately, having been compelled to be thinking of drawing up something about the College'[5] – presumably the *Statements respecting the East India College*, 1817. The strain of College problems evidently proved to be too great, and on 28 April 1816 he advised Ricardo that he had given up 'the idea of a new edition this season'.[6] His attentions in the middle of 1816 seem to have been devoted mainly to his defence of the College,[7] but later in 1816 he was able to return to his work on the *Essay*. On 8 September 1816 he reported to Ricardo that although he was 'still a good deal engaged in College matters', he was 'now beginning to think seriously' of his new edition. He had abandoned the idea of another (third) volume and had 'nearly determined' to omit almost completely the questions of bounties and restrictions.[8] Further progress had apparently been made by the end of 1816, because on 26 December 1816 Malthus, in sending an urgent request to Murray to publish the *Statements respecting the East India College*, expressed his regret that

---

[1] In Ricardo, *Works*, Vol. VI, p. 289. John Murray (1778–1843) was one of the founders and the publisher of the *Quarterly Review*. Letters from Ricardo and Malthus to Murray are held in the archives of the firm of John Murray, Albemarle Street, London.

[2] See G. W. Zinke, 'Six Letters from Malthus to Pierre Prévost', *Journal of Economic History*, Vol. II, 1942, p. 175; and Ricardo, *Works*, Vol. II, p. vii. Prévost (1751–1839), professor of physics at Geneva, translated Malthus' *Essay on Population* into French.

[3] In Ricardo, *Works*, Vol. VI, p. 346.

[4] In late 1815 the College experienced its most serious riots, when fourteen disguised students attacked two College servants. See James, *Population Malthus*, pp. 231–2.

[5] In Ricardo, *Works*, Vol. VII, p. 21.   [6] Ibid., p. 30.

[7] Letter to Ricardo of 6 August 1816, ibid., p. 51.   [8] Ibid., p. 68.

the *Statements* would cause an 'interruption to our other business'.[1] However, after the publication of the *Statements* he was able to report to Ricardo on 26 January 1817: 'I am busy about my new edition which is after all to be three volumes', adding that there were some points on which he wanted to consult Ricardo.[2] Then on 20 February 1817, after a delay of at least eighteen months since the new edition of the *Essay* had been proposed by Murray, Malthus wrote to Murray urging him 'to make considerable exertions' in order that the new edition could be published in the spring. In a tone of almost frantic urgency he admonished Murray: 'It is really therefore very desireable that matters should be hastened forward as fast as possible, and that no delay that is avoidable should be allowed.'[3] Murray, who must have been an even-tempered person, obligingly responded to Malthus' importunate demands, and published the new edition of the *Essay* in June 1817. In the Preface Malthus said that the new edition contained important additions which 'consist in a considerable degree of the application of the general principles of the Essay to the present state of things',[4] thus emphasising his belief that the problems of political economy should always be considered and evaluated in the light of their practical applications. One of the important additions was an extension to the Appendix which first appeared in the third edition and in which Malthus had replied to critics. The extended Appendix concluded with the statement:

By these alterations I hope and believe that the work has been improved without impairing its principles. But I still trust that whether it is read with or without these alterations, every reader of candour must acknowledge that the practical design uppermost in the mind of the writer, with whatever want of judgment it may have been executed, is to improve the condition and increase the happiness of the lower classes of society.[5]

The fifth edition of the *Essay* was reviewed by J. B. Sumner in the *Quarterly Review*, Vol. XVII, No. XXXIV, July 1817, Art. IV, 'Malthus on Population', pp. 369–403. John Bird Sumner (1780–1862), Bishop of Chester 1828, Archbishop of Canterbury 1848, was the author of *A Treatise on the Records of Creation*, 1816, which argued that the pressure of population gives rise to more good than evil, and therefore that Malthus' principle of population can be reconciled with the concept of divine benevolence. Malthus in the fifth edition of the *Essay* praised Sumner's *Treatise*, describing it as a 'masterly developement and

---

[1] Murray archives.   [2] In Ricardo, *Works*, Vol. VII, pp. 123–24.   [3] Murray archives.
[4] The Preface is dated 7 June 1817. A letter from Malthus to Murray of 11 June 1817 contains instructions for the despatch of complimentary copies. The additions were published also as a separate volume entitled *Additions to the Fourth and Former Editions of an Essay on the Principle of Population*, 1817. Malthus asked Ricardo for his comments on the *Additions*: 'By the by you have never told me, in return for my criticism on your work, how much you think me wrong in my Additions.' (Letter of 12 October 1817 in Ricardo, *Works*, Vol. VII, p. 194.) Ricardo's reply was given in his letter of 21 October 1817 (ibid., pp. 201–3), with a response by Malthus on 3 December 1817 (ibid., p. 214). The *Additions* was reviewed, together with Ricardo's *Principles*, in the *British Critic*, N.S., Vol. VIII, 1817, pp. 354–71.
[5] Malthus, *Essay*, ed. 5, Vol. III, p. 428.

completion'[1] of the views he had briefly outlined in the *Essay*, but he generously did not remind Sumner and others that such a reconciliation had been presented more concisely and even more persuasively in the final two chapters of the first edition (1798) of the *Essay*, the two chapters which he omitted from subsequent editions in deference to the criticism of 'some distinguished persons in our church'.[2]

A copy of the *Quarterly* containing Sumner's review was sent by Murray to Malthus, who commented: 'It is ably done, and I am quite satisfied, though I cannot quite agree with him in his critique respecting a different arrangement.'[3] Malthus would have been particularly gratified by Sumner's statement that 'it was soon found a much easier matter to disbelieve Mr. Malthus than to refute him', and by Sumner's comment on Malthus' reply to Godwin's perfectibilist utopia:

A visionary notion of theoretical perfectibility could only be met by a practical statement of the evils, moral and physical, which beset human nature. Society has no greater enemy than the man who would substitute theory for experience; and no sincerer friend than the man who appeals to experience to refute him.[4]

THE WRITING OF THE FIRST EDITION OF THE *PRINCIPLES*

Malthus' most important contribution to economic thought – his *Principles of Political Economy* – appears to have had its origins in a long-standing but unsuccessful proposal to publish a work on Adam Smith. From a letter[5] of 16 December 1804 to the publishers Cadell and Davies, we know that in 1804 or perhaps earlier he conceived the idea of publishing a new edition of Adam Smith's *Wealth of Nations*.[6] Eight years later the project was still in mind but apparently still not close to completion; on 3 September 1812, he wrote again to Cadell and Davies saying that the work would 'consist of foot notes where only short remarks were required, [with] an additional volume of longer notes and dissertations, – to be finished in about two years'.[7] However he suffered a

---

[1] Ibid., p. 425.
[2] See Otter, 'Memoir of Robert Malthus', p. lii. On Malthus' deletion of these two theological chapters, Empson said ('Life, Writing and Character', p. 500): 'as they were unsatisfactory to some of his private friends, he left them to their fate, to perish with his reply to the perishable theories of Condorcet and Godwin. They contain, however, the principle of the answer which he continued to give, as often as he was applied to for a philosophical solution of the problem of human life.'
[3] Letter of 1 December 1817 from Malthus to Murray in Murray archives.
[4] Sumner, 'Malthus on Population', op. cit. p. 396.
[5] Quoted by James, *Population Malthus*, pp. 165–66.
[6] Adam Smith (1723–90), *An Inquiry into the Nature and Causes of the Wealth of Nations*, London, 1776.
[7] See Theodore Besterman, ed., *The Publishing Firm of Cadell and Davies. Select Correspondence and Accounts. 1793–1836*, Oxford University Press, London, 1938, pp. 163–64. See also the footnote in Ricardo, *Works*, Vol. VI, pp. 159–60; and James, *Population Malthus*, pp. 245–49. Malthus' plan for an additional volume of notes might have been derived from the volume of notes by Germain

disappointment in 1813 when he became aware of the impending publication of an edition of the *Wealth of Nations* by David Buchanan on precisely the same plan, and was forced to abandon his project.[1] In a letter of 10 November 1813 to Francis Horner he said: 'Under these circumstances I am not sure whether it may be necessary for me to change my plan and to publish only a volume of essays instead of a new edition of Smith.' He evidently remained in a state of indecision for many months; in a letter of 9 August 1814 to Macvey Napier he gave his engagement 'respecting a new Edition of Adam Smith's Wealth of Nations' as a reason for not undertaking further work.[2] But a definite decision to abandon the Adam Smith project must have been made soon after, for his friend John Whishaw wrote on 28 October 1814 to Horner: '[Malthus] seems to have relinquished the plan of editing Adam Smith (in consequence of being forestalled by Buchanan); and seems disposed to publish a volume or two of essays on distinct branches of political economy.'[3]

This new plan must have been mentioned by Whishaw to John Murray, because the Murray archives contain an 'Extract' of a letter to Malthus dated 3 January 1815, which reads in part: 'If I understand Mr. Whishaw correctly – it is your intention to publish a Volume of detached remarks upon the more interesting topics of political Economy meaning to incorporate in that Volume the two tracts on "Rent" and on "Bullion".' The 'Extract' proceeds to make Malthus an offer of £1000 for the copyright of this proposed volume, together with the copyright of some of Malthus' pamphlets. It stipulates that the volume should be of the same size as 'the second Volume of Buchanan's recently published edition of Smith's Wealth of Nations', and suggests that the volume be published 'perhaps at the meeting of Parliament next year'.[4] This liberal offer from Murray was referred to by Malthus on 5 January 1815 in a letter to another

---

Garnier included as the fifth volume in his translation of the *Wealth of Nations*. See below, Vol. II, 1.46α.

[1] David Buchanan (1779–1848), journalist, newspaper editor and writer on political economy. His edition of Adam Smith's *Wealth of Nations* was published first in 1814, with a second edition in 1817. Malthus referred to Buchanan's edition in complimentary terms in *Principles* 1.137. See below, 1.137b.

[2] British Library, Add. MSS 34611, f. 107. Macvey Napier (1776–1847), Scottish lawyer and prominent Whig, was editor of the *Supplement to the fourth, fifth and sixth editions of the Encyclopædia Britannica*, editor of the seventh edition of the *Encyclopædia Britannica*, and succeeded Francis Jeffrey in 1829 as editor of the *Edinburgh Review*.

[3] In Ricardo, *Works*, Vol. VI, p. 159. Francis Horner and John Whishaw were close friends of Malthus. Horner (1778–1817), a lawyer and writer on political economy, was one of the founders of the *Edinburgh Review* in 1802, and was chairman of the Bullion Committee in 1810. John Whishaw (1764–1840), a lawyer and eminent Whig, had met Malthus at Cambridge. He assisted Malthus with proof-reading. See below, Introduction, p. xxxiii, fn. 4.

[4] Quoted by James, *Population Malthus*, p. 270. The tract on 'Rent' referred to by Murray was presumably *An Inquiry into the Nature and Progress of Rent* ..., 1815, but as Patricia James has noted, the tract on 'Bullion' is a mystery. If Malthus ever published such a tract, it has yet to be discovered. By the 'second Volume' of Buchanan's edition of the *Wealth of Nations*, Murray presumably meant the fourth volume consisting of Buchanan's Notes.

bookseller, Rowland Hunter, with whom Malthus apparently had discussed possible future publications. Malthus said: 'I believe I mentioned to you when I was in Town, that having given up the Edition of Adam Smith, ... I wished to make my other plan approach in some degree to it in point of profit.'[1] But James Mill and, more surprisingly, Ricardo, were not immediately informed of this change of plan. On 24 November 1814, Mill wrote to Ricardo: 'What is Mr. Malthus doing with his notes on Adam Smith? I see Buchannans [sic] book is out.';[2] and on 13 January 1815 Ricardo wrote to Malthus: 'I hope your notes on Adam Smith are in great forwardness, and that they will soon follow the smaller publications which you are now preparing.'[3] Both of these letters imply that Malthus' notes on Adam Smith were, at that time, substantial in volume and almost ready for publication.

Malthus had been lecturing on political economy at the East India College, Haileybury, since 1806 and his lectures probably consisted to a large extent of commentaries on Adam Smith. An examination paper set by Malthus in 1808 contains three questions that explicitly refer to the views of Adam Smith, and the other twenty-one questions appear to refer to particular topics treated in the *Wealth of Nations*.[4] The Inverarity Manuscript shows that Malthus' students undertook a detailed analysis of the *Wealth of Nations*.[5] It is very likely that some of this lecture material would have been included in his proposed edition of the *Wealth of Nations*. It is also likely that when he was forestalled by Buchanan he conceived the alternative plan of publishing an extended version of this lecture material in the form of a volume of 'essays on distinct branches of political economy', or 'detached remarks upon the more interesting topics of political economy'; and that after further adaptations in response to current events and controversies, these essays and remarks became the basis of his *Principles of Political Economy*.

As already noted, when the controversial *Grounds of an Opinion* was published in February 1815, it was accompanied almost simultaneously by another pamphlet, *An Inquiry into the Nature and Progress of Rent, and the Principles by which it is regulated*. This was a very different work from the *Grounds*. Whereas the *Grounds* announced a practical policy intended for immediate application in the real

---

[1] Quoted by James, *Population Malthus*, p. 271. This letter states that the approach to Murray had been by Malthus himself; it does not refer to Whishaw's role in the negotiations.
[2] In Ricardo, *Works*, Vol. VI, p. 159.   [3] Ibid., p. 169.
[4] A copy of this examination paper was provided by Patricia James from the collection of examination papers of the East India College for 1808 held in the Bodleian Library, Oxford.
[5] The Inverarity Manuscript held in the Marshall Library of Economics, Cambridge, consists of questions and notes written by a student of Malthus, J. D. Inverarity, on interleaved sheets in a copy of the *Wealth of Nations*. It dates from 1830, but suggests that this exegetical approach to the *Wealth of Nations* had been Malthus' standard pedagogical method. See J. M. Pullen, 'Notes from Malthus: the Inverarity Manuscript', *History of Political Economy*, Vol. XIII, No. 4, Winter 1981, pp. 794–811.

world, and was written in a readily comprehensible style, the *Inquiry* was much more abstract and philosophical, and its reasoning far from simple. Indeed, Malthus admitted that the *Inquiry* was not really suited to, and not originally intended for, publication in the 'ephemeral' form of a pamphlet. He described its contents as 'the substance of some notes on Rent, which with others on different subjects relating to political economy, I have collected in the course of my professional duties at the East India College'. He added that it had been his intention to publish it 'at some time or other', but that he felt obliged to publish it now as a pamphlet because of its close connection with the Corn Law controversy that was currently under public discussion.[1] This suggests that the material in the *Inquiry*, which had been developed in the course of his lecturing, would have formed part of the separate volume of editorial notes in his planned edition of the *Wealth of Nations*; and that following the abandonment of the latter plan he intended to publish it in the separate volume of essays on 'distinct branches of political economy'. The fact that he was prepared to bring forward the material on rent for immediate publication in response to a current economic issue, even though it was to be in the ephemeral and unsuitable form of a pamphlet, testifies to his concern with the practical applications of theory. This concern was evident even in his undergraduate days, and was apparently shared with his father. In response to his father's urgings to study the practical applications of mathematics Malthus said: 'I am by no means, however, inclined to get forward without wishing to see the use and application of what I read. On the contrary I am rather remarked in college for talking of what actually exists in nature, or may be put to real practical use.'[2]

His misgivings about the suitability of publishing a treatment of the difficult question of rent in the form of a pamphlet proved to be well founded. On 6 February 1815, only a few days after the *Inquiry* had been published, Malthus sent a 'corrected copy' to Murray, with a proposal to divide it into sections, in the belief that this would 'tend to render the subject clearer and more intelligible to the generality of readers'.[3] Murray prepared proof sheets of 'the new arrangement', and Malthus returned them with a letter of 13 February 1815 asking for additional copies of the *Inquiry* 'as soon as the new arrangement ... is printed

---

[1] Malthus, *Inquiry into ... Rent*, 'Advertisement'.
[2] In a letter of 13 January 1786 Malthus' father had said: 'I hate to see a girl working curious stitches upon a rag.' See Otter, op. cit., p. xxvii; Bonar, *Malthus and His Work*, p. 409; and Bonar, 'Life of Thomas Malthus', Ch. IV, p. 42. However Malthus did not push the methodological principle of '*cui bono?*' to extremes; he argued that 'it would surely be most unwise to restrain inquiry, conducted upon just principles, even where the immediate practical utility of it was not visible.' (*Principles* 1.12.)
[3] Murray archives. Although 'the generality of readers' appear to have found the *Inquiry* difficult, Empson described it as 'a masterly performance, of which Mr Ricardo always spoke in the highest terms' ('Life, Writing and Character', p. 495). Empson recognised that Malthus' contribution on rent had been foreshadowed by James Anderson, and simultaneously presented by Edward West.

off'.[1] Murray must have suggested that a new arrangement into sections would not be sufficient to meet the criticisms of the complexity of the *Inquiry*, and that a more drastic simplification of the contents was required, but in his letter of 13 February 1815 Malthus argued that the difficulty of the subject precluded further simplification:

I cannot do any thing essential towards writing the tract to the meanest capacities without casting it quite anew, and running the risk of spoiling the whole, which would not be worth while. The fact is that the subject tho it may appear quite easy before it is considered is one of the most curious and difficult in the whole range of political economy, involving the great question of the *produit net* of the Economists. Sir James Mackintosh writes me word, that he sees no other fault in it, than that of its being too philosiphical [sic] for the form in which it is published. Perhaps it would have been better if the Appendix [i.e. the *Grounds of an Opinion*, published about a week after the *Inquiry*] had come out first. I hope *that* is considered as intilligible [sic].[2]

There is no record of a second edition of the *Inquiry*. The printed pages of the first edition were incorporated, with substantial alterations and additions, in Malthus' manuscript of Chapter III, 'On the Rent of Land', in the *Principles*,[3] but despite this further elaboration his ideas on rent remained one of the more difficult and least convincing aspects of his political economy.

Further intimations that Malthus was moving towards the idea of publishing a separate work on political economy are to be found in a letter of 9 March 1816 in which Ricardo reported to Hutches Trower that Malthus 'is yet doubtful whether he shall add an additional volume to his Essay on Population [in the fifth edition], or whether he shall publish a separate and independent work, containing his present views on the interesting subjects of Agriculture and Manufactures, and the encouragement which is afforded them by natural and artificial causes';[4] and also in the reminiscences of a Haileybury student who said that Malthus in 1816–17 was at work on the fifth edition of the *Essay*, and was 'full of the ideas to be embodied in his crowning work on Political Economy published in 1820'.[5]

After the publication of the fifth edition of the *Essay on Population* in June 1817, Malthus appeared to channel his efforts more directly towards the publication of his *Principles*. His proximate motivation was undoubtedly the publication of Ricardo's *Principles*,[6] which gave Malthus an additional and strong stimulus, and indeed an obligation, to publish a work on political economy. Ricardo had

---

[1] Murray archives. [2] Murray archives.
[3] Empson, 'Life, Writing and Character', p. 495, stated: 'The substance of this Essay [on rent] has been transferred to the Principles of Political Economy.' On the manuscript of ed. 1 of the *Principles*, see below, pp. xxxviii–xxxix.
[4] In Ricardo, *Works*, Vol. VII, pp. 26–27. Hutches Trower (1777–1833), a stockbroker, was a friend of Ricardo and one of his main correspondents.
[5] Quoted by James, *Population Malthus*, p. 243.
[6] David Ricardo, *On the Principles of Political Economy and Taxation*, John Murray, London, 1817; 2nd ed., 1819; 3rd ed., 1821; reprinted in Ricardo, *Works*, Vol. I.

devoted an entire chapter to a criticism of Malthus' views on rent (Chapter XXIX in ed. 1, 'Mr. Malthus's Opinions on Rent'), and Malthus would obviously have been expected to reply in print. Not long after the publication of Ricardo's *Principles* on 19 April 1817 Malthus expressed his desire to answer Ricardo; in a letter to Ricardo of 12 October 1817 he said 'I am meditating another volume, but hardly know what to call it', and in another letter of 3 December 1817 he said 'I am meditating a volume as I believe I have you told you, and I want to answer you, without giving my work a controversial air. Can you tell me how to manage this.'[1] By early 1818 the meditating had progressed to writing. In a letter of 30 March 1818 to Pierre Prévost in Geneva Malthus said: 'I am at present engaged in a volume on those subjects in Political Econ^y the principles of which do not yet appear to be quite settled, & in this I shall advert frequently to Mr Ricardo's work. I shall not however be ready for the press till next Spring [1819].'[2] By August 1818 the work had advanced to the stage where Malthus read some of the manuscript to Ricardo, but progress was slow.[3] On 21 October 1818 he complained to Ricardo of interruptions:

I am going on with my volume, though slowly, and with more interruptions than I intended or expected. I boggle ever at the title; and it [is] not till after some delay and difficulty, that I have at length determined upon "The Principles of Political Economy considered, with a view to their practical application". I could not find any term like tracts or essays which I liked. Will the title do? what do you say? – But though I have at length determined on what I am going to write about, I doubt whether I shall finish this spring.[4]

Despite Malthus' doubt about finishing the *Principles* by the spring of 1819, Murray announced in the *Monthly Literary Advertiser* of 10 November 1818 that Malthus' *Principles* was 'in the Press', and Ricardo in a letter of 18 November

---

[1] In Ricardo, *Works*, Vol. VII, pp. 194, 215. Malthus' habit of referring anonymously to publications he wished to criticise – see below, p. lxi, fn. 3 – is further evidence of his distaste for controversy. Ricardo in a letter to Trower of 26 January 1818 attested to Malthus' 'great version to controversy' (*Works*, Vol. VII, p. 247). However this interpretation of the aim and spirit of Malthus' *Principles* differs from that of Torrens. In a review of Malthus' *Principles*, Torrens said: 'The very ingenious Author states, in his introduction, that it has been his wish to avoid giving to his Work a controversial air. Throughout the greater part of the book, however, his leading object seems to be to controvert the opinions of Mr. Ricardo.' ([R. Torrens], *The Traveller*, 21 April 1820, 'Notice of Mr. Malthus's New Work'). Empson, who must have come to know and understand Malthus very well, summarised Malthus' attitude to controversy in the following terms: 'Mr Malthus was not fond of storms, as the petrel is said to be, for their own sake. But it will be seen, on looking at the date and nature of his pamphlets, that he usually turned out in one. At these times, the opportunity of being useful was excitement enough: and his spirit rose with the occasion.' ('Life, Writing and Character', p. 496.)

[2] In Ricardo, *Works*, Vol. II, p. vii; and Zinke, 'Six letters', p. 178.

[3] In a letter to Malthus of 20 August 1818, Ricardo said, 'I am sorry that you have not made any great progress in the work that you are about. . . . I differed very little from the opinions expressed in that part of your MS which you read to me, but I wish to have an opportunity of judging of your system as a whole, and therefore shall be glad when it comes in its printed form.' (Ricardo, *Works*, Vol. VII, p. 284.)

[4] In Ricardo, *Works*, Vol. VII, p. 312. On the title of the *Principles*, see below, p. xxxvi.

Introduction

1818 to Murray concerning the forthcoming second edition of his *Principles*, asked: 'If Mr. Malthus is going to publish I submit to you whether I should not wait to see his book, as I know that I shall be attacked in it.'[1] But Ricardo must have then been informed by Murray that Malthus' *Principles* would be delayed. On 28 December 1818 Ricardo advised James Mill of the delay and offered the following explanation: 'His book is delayed, I believe, partly at Murray's suggestion of the time of year now fixed upon being the most favourable time for publication, and partly I think, from doubts which he cannot help entertaining of the correctness of his opinions.'[2] Later, in the Introduction to the *Principles*, Malthus explained the main reason for the delay in the following terms:

I have so very high an opinion of Mr. Ricardo's talents as a political economist, and so entire a conviction of his perfect sincerity and love of truth, that I frankly own I have sometimes felt almost staggered by his authority, while I have remained unconvinced by his reasonings. I have thought that I must unaccountably have overlooked some essential points, either in my own view of the subject, or in his; and this kind of doubt has been the principal reason of my delay in publishing the present volume.[3]

Whatever the reason for the delay in the publication of Malthus' *Principles*, Ricardo did not wait to see it, but proceeded to publish the second edition of his *Principles* on 27 February 1819.

Seventeen months were to elapse between the announcement on 10 November 1818 that Malthus' *Principles* was 'in the Press', and its actual publication in April 1820. On 8 July 1819 Ricardo told Trower that Malthus 'calculates on publishing his book by the end of the year',[4] but by September 1819 the work was apparently still a long way from publication; in his letter of 10 September 1819 to Ricardo, Malthus said:

But though I have been lately finishing the beginning, I have by no means arrived at the end. I think I have a fourth or a fifth to write yet; and having composed the different parts at different times and not in their natural order, I have still much to put out and put in, before it will be fit to send to the press. I can hardly expect to be out before February or March.[5]

---

[1] Ricardo, *Works*, Vol. II, p. vii; Vol. VII, p. 329.
[2] Ricardo, *Works*, Vol. II, pp. vii–viii; Vol. VII, pp. 379–80. James Mill (1773–1836), utilitarian philosopher, historian, economist, supporter of Ricardo, advocate of Say's Law, and critic of Malthus. Without Mill's persistent urgings, Ricardo's *Principles* would probably never have been written.
[3] *Principles* 1.23. This main reason for the delay was also explained to Ricardo in Malthus' letter of 10 September 1819, which contains the further reason: 'We have been now returned to the College [after the summer vacation] above a month, nearly indeed six weeks, and I have been delayed and led away as usual by thoughts relating to the subjects of our discussions.' (In Ricardo, *Works*, Vol. VIII, pp. 64–66.)
[4] Ricardo, *Works*, Vol. VIII, p. 47.
[5] In Ricardo, *Works*, Vol. VIII, p. 66. On 21 September 1819 Ricardo replied: 'I am glad that you are proceeding merrily with your work. I now have hopes it will be finished. You have been very indolent, and are not half so industrious, nor so anxious as I am, when I have any thing in hand.' (*Works*, Vol. VIII, p. 73.)

Introduction

As usual he had underestimated the difficulty of the task and overestimated the time he would have available to devote to it.

However the progress report that Malthus sent to his publisher on 21 September 1819 was much more optimistic: 'I am going on well with my volume and hope to begin printing the middle of November or at the latest the beginning of December. I am making a copious analysis, which I think will be very useful, and on the whole I am sanguine as to its success.'[1] In a letter of 26 September 1819 Malthus, replying to Murray's suggestion that some of his earlier pamphlets be republished, revealed a determination to expedite the *Principles* – 'it would [be] a very inconvenient interruption to me now to prepare the pamphlets you allude to for the press;' – and also his confidence in the success of the *Principles*; he hoped that 'if left to itself' it would have 'an extensive sale'.[2]

On 14 October 1819 Malthus advised Ricardo that he hoped 'to begin printing the middle or end of next month', and added: 'I fear I shall have too large a volume when it is finished, although I cannot include taxation and some other subjects which I wish to discuss. I am making an analysis like Sismondi's which will take up a good deal of room.'[3] This time there was to be no delay. Printing must have started as planned around the end of November, because by 9 December 1819 Malthus was correcting the proofs, and had accepted an offer from John Whishaw to 'superintend the press'.[4] But as it was not the custom for the printer to require that the full manuscript be submitted before starting to print, a further three months passed before Malthus advised Murray, on 4 March 1820, that he would be sending the last section to Mr Roworth, the printer, on 7 March. Malthus added that he would 'immediately begin printing the Summary, which is [?drawn] out, and only wants a little looking over'.[5]

An exchange of letters between Ricardo and J. R. McCulloch during the period November 1819 to April 1820 shows that Malthus' critics were anxiously

---

[1] Murray archives. The 'copious analysis' was the 'Summary of the Contents of the Foregoing Work' which Malthus included in the first edition of the *Principles*, pp. 523–92. See below, 1.523a.

[2] Murray archives.

[3] In Ricardo, *Works*, Vol. VIII, pp. 108–9. On 9 November 1819 Ricardo replied: 'I am glad to hear that your book will be so soon in the press, but I regret that the most important part of the conclusions from the principles which you endeavour to elucidate, will not be included in it, I mean taxation.' (*Works*, Vol. VIII, p. 130.) On 12 November 1819 Ricardo told Trower that he believed Malthus' work was 'actually in the press'. (*Works*, Vol. VIII, pp. 159–60.)

[4] The proofs were to be sent first to Whishaw and then to Malthus. Whishaw had previously corrected the proofs of the fifth edition, 1817, of Malthus' *Essay on Population*. In a letter of 12 December 1816 to Murray, Malthus said: 'I meant to have told you that Mr Whishaw has kindly undertaken to correct the proofs; but as there is now no great hurry in the printing, I still think it would be adviseable to send the sheets to me after he has seen them, as there are often errors, which none but the author himself can be aware of, and it was with this view that I wished to have another copy by me with the marginal corrections.' (Murray archives.) Malthus' letter of 3 February 1815 to Murray indicates that Whishaw also proof-read the *Inquiry into . . . Rent*, 1815, and the *Grounds of an Opinion*, 1815. (Murray archives.)

[5] Murray archives. The letter also indicated that the Summary was modelled on Sismondi's 'Table Analytique'; and discussed details of its presentation. See below, 1.523a.

awaiting the publication of his *Principles*. McCulloch wrote to Ricardo on 5 December 1819 saying that he considered Malthus' reputation as an economist to be 'very much overrated'; that he should like to reduce Malthus 'to his just magnitude'; and that Malthus' *Principles* ought to be 'handled pretty roughly'.[1] In a reply to McCulloch on 18 December 1819 Ricardo said that he would make up his mind on Malthus' abilities as an economist after reading the work which was 'now in the press'.[2] In a further letter to McCulloch of 28 February 1820 Ricardo speculated on the contents of Malthus' *Principles* and said that it had been 'in the press a very long time, and must now be nearly ready for publication'.[3] McCulloch replied that he was 'anxious to see Mr. Malthus work', and repeated that Malthus 'deserves to be very roughly handled'.[4] On 29 March 1820 Ricardo reported to McCulloch that Malthus had shown him a chapter of the *Principles*, but that Malthus' criticisms could be 'easily disposed of'.[5] In his reply of 2 April 1820 McCulloch asked Ricardo to send his opinions on Malthus' work when it was published.[6]

Malthus' *Principles* was finally published early in April 1820. In a letter to Murray of 31 March 1820 he said he was disappointed that he had not received the proofs of the Summary as quickly as he had expected, and that the *Principles* could not now be published at the beginning of April. He asked Murray on what day it would '*really* be published' as he would like to call on Murray 'to arrange a few presents'.[7] Publication must have occurred within days, because in a letter to Murray of 16 April 1820 Malthus asked for copies to be sent to various persons.[8] On 30 April 1820 he asked Murray 'how we are going on', and re-affirmed his confidence in the experiential validity of his ideas: 'I do not expect sudden conversions; but I have a strong persuasion that the principles which I have laid down, will be found so conformable with experience that they will gradually prevail like those of the Essay on Population.'[9] The final reference in the Murray archives to the publishing of the first edition of the *Principles* occurs in a letter from Malthus on 26 January 1821. Murray had apparently told Malthus that the *Quarterly Review*, of which Murray was the publisher, was looking for someone to review the *Principles*. Malthus recommended John Cazenove, who had previously declined Malthus' invitation to review the *Principles* 'on the grounds of modesty and want of time', but who was subsequently reported to Malthus to be 'making remarks' on the *Principles* 'for his own satisfaction and amusement'.[10]

---

[1] In Ricardo, *Works*, Vol. VIII, p. 139.   [2] Ibid., p. 142.   [3] Ibid., p. 160.
[4] Ibid., p. 167.   [5] Ibid., p. 173.
[6] On 8 April 1820 Ricardo agreed to McCulloch's request, and sent his opinions on 2 May 1820. See Ricardo, *Works*, Vol. VIII, pp. 176–78.
[7] Murray archives.   [8] Ibid.   [9] Ibid.
[10] Murray archives. Malthus dated the letter 26 January 1820, but it is franked 27 January 1821. Its contents also indicate that '1820' must have been an error. On Cazenove, see below, Introduction,

Introduction

From the foregoing it is evident that in the writing of his *Principles* Malthus was influenced to a large extent by Ricardo – not only by the need to answer Ricardo's *Principles*, but also through the debates that occurred in their frequent meetings and correspondence. In his Introduction to the *Principles* Malthus acknowledged the extent of Ricardo's influence. He stated that he wished to avoid giving his *Principles* 'a controversial air', but as one of his 'professed objects' in writing the *Principles* was 'to discuss controverted opinions', he recognised the impossibility of freeing his work entirely from controversy. As Ricardo was his major disputant, it was inevitable that 'a considerable portion' of his attention should be devoted to Ricardo's *Principles*. He apologised for the inclusion of this degree of controversy, but deemed it justified because of Ricardo's ability and authority, and because of 'the interests of the science of which it treats'. (*Principles* 1.22–23.)

However, the introduction gives further insights into Malthus' aims and motives, and shows that Ricardo was not the only influence operating on Malthus' *Principles*. Malthus' statement that 'The treatise which we already possess [i.e. Adam Smith's *Wealth of Nations*] is still of the very highest value;' (*Principles* 1.5) indicates that although throughout the *Principles* and indeed in his lectures he was prepared to criticise Adam Smith, he saw his role as essentially transmitting the Adam Smith tradition as he perceived it, and that he wished to situate his own contributions within the context of Adam Smith's work. Thus, although the desire to answer Ricardo was an important influence on the writing of Malthus' *Principles* – and the large number of references to Ricardo is further evidence of the extent of the influence – it would appear that Malthus did not regard his *Principles*, and did not wish his *Principles* to be regarded, merely or mainly as an answer to Ricardo. If his intention had been merely to answer Ricardo, it would have been more appropriate to prepare an annotated edition of Ricardo's *Principles* incorporating his own notes on Ricardo, along the lines he had once proposed for Adam Smith.[1] From the general format and tone of

---

p. lxi. Murray was the publisher, not the editor of the *Quarterly Review* – except for several later numbers which he jointly edited – but it seems that he was more active than the editor, William Gifford, in finding books for review and appropriate reviewers. See Samuel Smiles, *A Publisher and His Friends. Memoir and Correspondence of the late John Murray . . .*, John Murray, London, 1891, Vol. I, p. 154. However, no review of the *Principles* was published in the *Quarterly Review*; it was only mentioned very briefly in one paragraph (pp. 297–98) in the *Quarterly Review*, Vol. XXIV, No. XLVIII, January 1821, Art. I, 'Freedom of Commerce', pp. 281–302. This article has been attributed possibly to M. Fletcher. See F. W. Fetter, 'The Economic Articles in the *Quarterly Review* and their Authors, 1809–52. I and II', *Journal of Political Economy*, Vol. 66, 1958, pp. 53, 159. Malthus' *Principles* was reviewed in *The Traveller*, 21 April, 26 April and 1 May, 1820 [by Robert Torrens]; *The Scotsman*, No. 171, 29 April 1820, p. 143 [by J. R. McCulloch]; *The British Critic*, Vol. XIV, August 1820, pp. 117–38, and September 1820, pp. 275–93; *The Monthly Review*, Vol. 95, 1821, pp. 60–76; and *The Eclectic Review*, Vol. XVI, 1821–22, pp. 69–85. There was also a brief notice in the *Monthly Magazine and British Register*, Vol. 49, 1820, p. 558.

1 Ricardo himself had at one stage thought to answer Malthus by means of an annotated edition of Malthus' *Principles*. See letter of 24 November 1820 from Ricardo to Malthus. (Ricardo, *Works*, Vol. VIII, p. 301.)

Introduction

Malthus' *Principles*, and from the large number of references to writers other than Ricardo, Malthus' aim in writing the *Principles* was obviously much broader than a mere critique of Ricardo. This broader aim is evident in his statement that 'One of the specific objects of the present work is to prepare the general rules of political economy for practical application, ...'[1]

Although Malthus intended the *Principles* to be more than a refutation of Ricardo, he did not intend it to be a complete and systematic treatise on political economy. He stated that 'The present period, therefore, seems to be unpropitious to the publication of a new systematic treatise on political economy'; that 'it is obviously more advisable that the different subjects which admit of doubt should be treated separately'; and that the disputed areas of the science should be publicly discussed for some time before any attempt is made to establish 'a consistent whole'. (*Principles* 1.5.) Some modern writers have unfairly criticised the *Principles* for not being a systematic treatise, but at least some of Malthus' contemporaries were aware that it was conceived only as a series of dissertations on disputed points. The *British Critic* reviewed the *Principles* very favourably, for example, 'Mr. Malthus's book ... is worth its weight in gold', and concluded with the statement: 'We cherish the hope that he will some day favour the public with a complete system of political economy, arranged in a strictly scientific form, and embracing a review of all that his predecessors have attempted or achieved in this arduous field of investigation' (pp. 292–93); and the *Monthly Review* (op. cit., p. 62) noted that Malthus' *Principles* was not 'an attempt to frame a new and complete treatise'. The same point was emphasised some years later by Joseph Garnier who also drew attention to the fact that the title of the *Principles* is a misnomer: 'Malgré son titre, le livre sur les Principes n'est point un traité complet, mais seulement une collection de dissertations relatives à des questions sur lesquelles il avait plus spécialement fixé son attention, et qu'il discutait particulièrement avec Ricardo et J.-B. Say.'[2] The alternative title 'tracts', or 'essays', which Malthus mentioned and rejected in his letter of 21 October 1818 to Ricardo, quoted above, would have been more accurate.

MALTHUS' WORKS AFTER 1820 AND PREPARATIONS FOR EDITION 2 OF THE *PRINCIPLES*

From a statement by William Empson, a colleague of Malthus at the East India College, we know that Malthus was engaged in the preparation of a second

---

[1] *Principles* 1.21. See below, Vol. II, 1.16α.
[2] 'Malthus', *Dictionnaire de l'Économie Politique*, publié sous la direction de MM. Ch. Coquelin et Guillaumin, Paris, 1852, Tome II, p. 127.

Introduction

1818 to Murray concerning the forthcoming second edition of his *Principles*, asked: 'If Mr. Malthus is going to publish I submit to you whether I should not wait to see his book, as I know that I shall be attacked in it.'[1] But Ricardo must have then been informed by Murray that Malthus' *Principles* would be delayed. On 28 December 1818 Ricardo advised James Mill of the delay and offered the following explanation: 'His book is delayed, I believe, partly at Murray's suggestion of the time of year now fixed upon being the most favourable time for publication, and partly I think, from doubts which he cannot help entertaining of the correctness of his opinions.'[2] Later, in the Introduction to the *Principles*, Malthus explained the main reason for the delay in the following terms:

I have so very high an opinion of Mr. Ricardo's talents as a political economist, and so entire a conviction of his perfect sincerity and love of truth, that I frankly own I have sometimes felt almost staggered by his authority, while I have remained unconvinced by his reasonings. I have thought that I must unaccountably have overlooked some essential points, either in my own view of the subject, or in his; and this kind of doubt has been the principal reason of my delay in publishing the present volume.[3]

Whatever the reason for the delay in the publication of Malthus' *Principles*, Ricardo did not wait to see it, but proceeded to publish the second edition of his *Principles* on 27 February 1819.

Seventeen months were to elapse between the announcement on 10 November 1818 that Malthus' *Principles* was 'in the Press', and its actual publication in April 1820. On 8 July 1819 Ricardo told Trower that Malthus 'calculates on publishing his book by the end of the year',[4] but by September 1819 the work was apparently still a long way from publication; in his letter of 10 September 1819 to Ricardo, Malthus said:

But though I have been lately finishing the beginning, I have by no means arrived at the end. I think I have a fourth or a fifth to write yet; and having composed the different parts at different times and not in their natural order, I have still much to put out and put in, before it will be fit to send to the press. I can hardly expect to be out before February or March.[5]

---

[1] Ricardo, *Works*, Vol. II, p. vii; Vol. VII, p. 329.

[2] Ricardo, *Works*, Vol. II, pp. vii–viii; Vol. VII, pp. 379–80. James Mill (1773–1836), utilitarian philosopher, historian, economist, supporter of Ricardo, advocate of Say's Law, and critic of Malthus. Without Mill's persistent urgings, Ricardo's *Principles* would probably never have been written.

[3] *Principles* 1.23. This main reason for the delay was also explained to Ricardo in Malthus' letter of 10 September 1819, which contains the further reason: 'We have been now returned to the College [after the summer vacation] above a month, nearly indeed six weeks, and I have been delayed and led away as usual by thoughts relating to the subjects of our discussions.' (In Ricardo, *Works*, Vol. VIII, pp. 64–66.)

[4] Ricardo, *Works*, Vol. VIII, p. 47.

[5] In Ricardo, *Works*, Vol. VIII, p. 66. On 21 September 1819 Ricardo replied: 'I am glad that you are proceeding merrily with your work. I now have hopes it will be finished. You have been very indolent, and are not half so industrious, nor so anxious as I am, when I have any thing in hand.' (*Works*, Vol. VIII, p. 73.)

all. In addition there are 18 loose sheets that are not interleaved between the pages of the 1820 text. For this variorum edition, the term 'supplementary sheets' is used in referring to these 18 sheets. They consist of 10 single and 8 double sheets with 50 sides of writing in all. In most cases, they can be related to particular pages in either the 1820 or the 1836 edition.

An interesting aspect of these Manuscript Revisions is that not all of them appeared as alterations in the second edition of the *Principles*. Some were carried forward into the second edition without any change; others were carried forward in a slightly altered version; in some other cases, the meaning was incorporated into larger changes in the second edition; but a large number were omitted from the second edition. One possible explanation of these omissions is that Malthus altered his views again, decided to omit from the second edition some of the entries he had made in the Manuscript Revisions, and recorded these decisions in documents which were available to the editor of the second edition but which subsequently have been lost. A second possible explanation is that Malthus might never have intended to publish all the Manuscript Revisions; some might have been merely working notes or *aides-mémoires*. A third possible explanation is that the editor of the posthumous second edition took it upon himself to omit some of the Manuscript Revisions.

As well as a large number of alterations in the Manuscript Revisions being omitted from the second edition, a large number of alterations in the second edition do not occur in the Manuscript Revisions. The Manuscript Revisions, as they now stand, contain only a small proportion of the total alterations in the second edition. They are not sufficiently extensive to have been the 'author's own manuscript' which the editor of the second edition referred to on the title page, and which he used in preparing the second edition. This is also obvious from the fact that 38 of the entries in the Manuscript Revisions are in the form of an incomplete introductory phrase; for example, 1.19c, 'while to proceed straight forward &c:'. This suggests that, because of limited space in the margins of the *Principles*, Malthus had completed the statements elsewhere. The editor of the second edition must have had access to all or most of these completions because 28 of the 38 incomplete statements appear in a completed form in the second edition. Only one of the completed statements appears amongst the interleaved and supplementary sheets. The conclusion must therefore be that the final manuscript that went to the publisher of the second edition was a very different document from the Manuscript Revisions as they exist now. Nevertheless the Manuscript Revisions provide an indication of the development of some of Malthus' ideas after 1820, and the fact that they contain ideas that do not appear in ed. 2 of the *Principles* makes them, as it were, an intermediate 'edition' of the *Principles*.

The Manuscript Revisions, as described here, should be distinguished from another Malthus manuscript held by the library of the University of Cambridge, viz. the manuscript of part of the first edition of the *Principles*. It contains the Introduction and the first three chapters of the *Principles*. There are many differences between this manuscript of the first edition, and the published first edition, but they are mainly of a minor nature.[1]

Malthus' correspondence provides information about his preparations for the second edition of the *Principles*, about the other publications and activities in which he became engaged after 1820, and about the influence of his personal circumstances on his writings. In a letter to Ricardo of 26 October 1820 he said 'I am preparing a new edition and shall be glad of any corrections and suggestions which you will give me, both in reference to those parts which relate to you, and any others.'[2] On 10 January 1821 the *Monthly Literary Advertiser* carried a list of Murray's 'works preparing for immediate publication'. It included Malthus' *Principles*, described as 'A New Edition, corrected and enlarged, 2 vol. 8vo ... similar to the last Edition of the Essay on Population.'[3] The appearance of this announcement implies that, by early 1821, Malthus had taken some significant steps towards the preparation of ed. 2, and that Murray at that stage had agreed to publish it; but it seems, from a letter of Malthus to Pierre Prévost, that at the end of March 1821 the new edition was by no means ready for 'immediate publication'.[4]

Murray's confidence in the outcome of a second edition seems to have altered in April 1821. According to Malthus' letter of 27 March 1821 to Prévost, Murray was, at the end of March, very optimistic about the prospects for Malthus' publications. As well as a new edition of the *Principles*, Murray had apparently thought that a new (sixth) edition of the *Essay on Population* might probably be wanted in the course of the year. But one month later on 26 April 1821 Malthus reported to Prévost that Murray was of the opinion that 'the times are not favourable to book-selling', and had advised him to defer the new edition of his *Principles* until Christmas 1821.[5]

In early 1821 Malthus was involved in a study of Ricardo's comments on his

---

[1] One exception however could be the following footnote which occurs on the sheet numbered 39 in the manuscript but which does not occur in the published first edition: 'If Mr. Ricardo's theory be true, we ought to tax the wages of labour directly, which we have hitherto carefully and I think justly avoided.' This footnote refers to a statement in which Malthus said that if the 'Economists' (i.e., the Physiocrats) were correct in thinking that land is the sole source of wealth, then all taxes should be laid on land. (See *Principles* 1.20.) In the footnote Malthus draws an inference for fiscal policy from his interpretation of Ricardo's theory of value. If labour is the sole source of wealth, then all taxes should be laid on labour.

[2] In Ricardo, *Works*, Vol. VIII, p. 285.

[3] See ibid., p. 341. The 'last edition' of the *Essay on Population* was the fifth edition, 1817, 3 vols, 8vo. The announcement called forth an uncomplimentary remark by J. R. McCulloch: 'I see Malthus is taking to his old trick of bookmaking – His book instead of being lengthened ought to have been curtailed by one third – .' (Letter of 22 January 1821, in Ricardo, *Works*, Vol. VIII, p. 341.)

[4] See letter of 27 March 1821, in Zinke, 'Six letters', p. 181: 'I am preparing a new edition and may perhaps say something on Mr. Say's letters in an Appendix.'

[5] See Zinke, 'Six letters', p. 181. The sixth edition of Malthus' *Essay* was not published until 1826.

Introduction

Principles. Ricardo started to write these 'notes on Malthus', as he called them, soon after the publication of Malthus' *Principles.* They were finished by 16 November 1820, and were in Malthus' possession for at least three months early in 1821. They were also seen by McCulloch, Trower and James Mill. Ricardo appeared to change his mind several times on whether they should be published. At one stage he proposed to publish them as an appendix to a new edition that he would make of Malthus' *Principles*; later he thought to publish them as an appendix to the third edition of his own *Principles*; but he finally decided not to publish. The Notes lay unnoticed for almost a century, but after being discovered in 1919 they were published by J. H. Hollander and T. E. Gregory[1] in 1928, and re-published as Vol. II of Ricardo's *Works* in 1951.

From the sheer extent of Ricardo's Notes, and from the fact that they were discussed by Malthus and Ricardo in conversation and correspondence, it might be expected that they exerted a major influence on Malthus, and accounted for many of the alterations in the second edition of the *Principles.* But that does not appear to have been the case. Only about one-fifth of Ricardo's 315 Notes appear to have elicited responses from Malthus in MR or ed. 2. In a few instances, Malthus appeared to accept the criticisms made by Ricardo on some points of doctrine, and corrected his text accordingly.[2] In several other instances, Malthus omitted or corrected his interpretations of Ricardo's views after Ricardo in his Notes denied having held such views.[3] However, in many of his responses, Malthus merely clarified his own position, without showing any inclination to accept Ricardo's criticisms. In some cases Malthus' response took the form of a stronger expression of his own view, and even a movement away from an attempted reconciliation by Ricardo. Thus the majority of Ricardo's Notes appear to have had little influence on Malthus, especially if the extent of influence is measured by the number of instances where Malthus relinquished his own views and accepted Ricardo's as a result of Ricardo's criticisms in the Notes.[4] Even some of Ricardo's longest Notes and some of his strongest criticisms

---

[1] David Ricardo, *Notes on Malthus' 'Principles of Political Economy'*, edited with an introduction and notes by J. H. Hollander and T. E. Gregory, Baltimore, The Johns Hopkins Press, 1928. For a detailed account of the writing of Ricardo's Notes and the discovery of the manuscript, see the introduction by Sraffa and Dobb in Ricardo, *Works*, Vol. II, p. ix–xv.

[2] For example, Note 12, on the definition of 'real value' (see 1.62c); Note 300 on Malthus' use of the expression 'domestic and foreign labour' (see 1.489e); and Notes 42, 43, 44 on a mean between corn and labour as a measure of value. Ricardo's criticism probably influenced Malthus' decision to reject this measure of value and to omit entirely the relevant Section from MR and ed. 2 (see 1.126a).

[3] For example, Note 310 on Ricardo's theory of profits (see 1.512c), and Note 36 on the invariability of gold as a measure of value. Note 36 was probably the reason why Malthus omitted an entire Section from ed. 2. See 1.108a.

[4] See Sraffa and Dobb: 'The changes [in the second edition of Malthus' *Principles*] are extensive, but in general they do not appear to be carried out with a view to meeting Ricardo's criticisms' (in Ricardo, *Works*, Vol. II, p. xiii).

Introduction

of Malthus were apparently ignored and left unanswered in Malthus' revisions in MR and ed. 2.[1]

There are a number of possible reasons why Ricardo's Notes had such little influence on Malthus. (1) Some of the Notes did not call for a response, being merely a summary of Malthus' views or a statement of agreement with Malthus. (2) It is also possible that some of the Notes, or some parts of them, were added after Malthus had seen the Notes in 1821. (3) Although the tone of some of the Notes implies that Ricardo intended to publish them, and although this was possibly mentioned to Malthus, it appears that, as already noted, Ricardo finally decided not to publish the Notes. If this latter intention was communicated to Malthus, it could explain why Malthus did not respond more fully to the Notes. If Malthus had suspected that Ricardo's Notes would one day be published, and that Ricardo would thus be given, as it were, the last word in their debate, his response to the Notes might have been quite different. (4) The practical difficulty of obtaining a copy of Ricardo's Notes must also have impeded a more detailed response. If Ricardo's Notes had been published in the early 1820s, Malthus would have been given not only a motive and a justification for responding fully, but also the opportunity to analyse the Notes in detail at his leisure. We do not know whether Malthus copied the Notes, or arranged for them to be copied, while they were in his possession. If he did not retain a copy, it is likely that when the Notes were returned to Ricardo, they ceased forthwith to occupy Malthus' attention. It would have been virtually impossible for him to recall the details of the Notes and to make further responses in later years. (5) Malthus' decision not to respond more fully to Ricardo's Notes could have been motivated by a desire to avoid controversy. As already stated, his distaste for public controversy influenced the structure of the first edition of the *Principles*, and it would be reasonable to assume that it also influenced the preparation of the second edition. (6) Even if Malthus could have responded fully to Ricardo's Notes without giving his work a controversial air, there is another important reason why he probably did not wish to incorporate detailed responses. If he had included in the second edition detailed responses to Ricardo's 315 Notes, its character would have been changed from a general to a polemical treatise. His debate with Ricardo could then have been interpreted as the *main* theme of his *Principles*, and could have detracted from its generality. (7) Finally, it must be said that the most likely reason why Malthus ignored most of Ricardo's critical Notes was that he quite simply believed that they were wrong, and that he had adequately responded to Ricardo's errors already.

In the first half of 1821, while occupied with Ricardo's Notes and with the

---

[1] For example, see Ricardo's criticism of Malthus' theory of rent and Ricardo's emphasis on the role of demand in Notes 50, 51, 54, 67, 74, 77, 78, 81.

preparation of the second edition of his *Principles*, Malthus became engaged in another publishing project, the first of ten publications which he produced after the first edition of the *Principles* and which, while interesting and important in their own right, delayed the preparation of the second edition. In July 1821 an article entitled 'Godwin on Malthus' appeared in the *Edinburgh Review*, Vol. XXXV, Art. VI, pp. 362–77. It was a critical review of William Godwin, *Of Population. An Enquiry concerning the Power of Increase in the Numbers of Mankind. Being an Answer to Mr Malthus's Essay on that Subject*, London, 1820. There is no doubt that Malthus was the author of this anonymous article. On 28 September 1821 Ricardo wrote to Malthus: 'I have read a very good critique on Godwin in the Edin. Review, and I am quite sure that I know the writer. It is very well done, and most satisfactorily exposes Godwin's ignorance as well as his disingenuousness', to which Malthus replied on 9 October 1821: 'I am glad you approve of the Review in the Edinburgh. If you have discovered the author dont betray the secret.'[1]

The debate between Malthus and Godwin had begun with Malthus' attack on Godwin's perfectibilist visions in the first edition of the *Essay on Population* in 1798, but had subsequently lapsed. Godwin was probably stimulated to re-open the debate when Malthus in the fifth edition of the *Essay* in 1817 omitted one of the chapters dealing with Godwin and replaced it with a discussion of Robert Owen.[2] In *Of Population* Godwin strongly criticised Malthus' arguments, in particular the accuracy of Malthus' statistics on population growth and the nature of the remedies proposed by Malthus for over-population. Malthus' reactions were equally strong. In a letter of 12 March 1821 to Simonde de Sismondi he said: 'I have lately been attacked, after a delay of twenty years, by my old antagonist Mr Godwin; but it is a very poor and feeble performance, and the only resemblance of an argument in it is founded upon a miscalculation'.[3] Although the main part of the *Edinburgh Review* article was a calm analysis of Godwin's arguments, other parts had an uncharacteristically abusive and aggressive tone; for example Godwin's work was described as 'the poorest and most old-womanish performance that has fallen from the pen of any writer of name, since we first commenced our critical career'.[4]

At a date prior to 27 September 1821 Malthus had committed himself to bringing out a new edition of his *Principles*, and thought he would be able to complete it in March or early April 1822; but in late 1821 his work was interrupted by the sickness and death of his only brother, whom he 'tenderly

---

[1] Ricardo, *Works*, Vol. III, pp. 84, 94. See also Ricardo's letter to Trower of 4 October 1821 (ibid., pp. 89–90). For further details see Fetter, 'The Economic Articles', p. 250.
[2] See James, *Population Malthus*, pp. 376–82.   [3] In Ricardo, *Works*, Vol. VIII, p. 376.
[4] It is possible that Francis Jeffrey, the editor of the *Edinburgh Review*, made some additions to Malthus' MS., particularly in the opening paragraphs, as was his custom.

Introduction

'tenderly loved'.[1] The work was to be further delayed when in October 1821 he accepted an invitation from Macvey Napier to write an article on population for the *Supplement to the Encyclopædia Britannica*.[2] As noted below, he worked concurrently on this article and on the second edition of the *Principles* throughout 1822. This double commitment undoubtedly impeded the completion of both projects. In addition, the task of preparing the second edition seems to have proved far more difficult than he expected. The resulting delay caused him anxiety, both because of his desire to publish the second edition as soon as possible, and because of his desire to fulfil his commitment to Macvey Napier. In a letter of 23 December 1822 to Prévost he said:

I am now greatly pressed for an article on Population in the Encyclopædia Britannica, which I unwarily promised; while I am very anxious to get out as soon as I possibly can another edition of my last work, in which there will be some new views on a *standard of value* which require a good deal of care and consideration.[3]

He added that his work had been impeded by further engagements 'of a private nature', which as Patricia James has noted probably included the serious student disturbances that occurred at the East India College in the autumn of 1822.[4] Because of these other commitments and engagements it was not until the beginning of February 1823 that a manuscript[5] of the second edition was lodged with Murray. On 24 February 1823 he wrote to Murray:

I am sure that you must have quite forgotten everything about the *Principles of Political Economy* which I left with you three weeks ago, or I must have had a proof sheet by this time. It would be very desireable on many accounts to have it out early in May. But this will certainly not be done unless we make more haste. I should be in Town I believe at the end of the week or the beginning of next, and will then call, and shall hope to find matters in progress.[6]

However a second edition of the *Principles* was not published in 1823. Instead, early in 1823, Malthus published *The Measure of Value Stated and Illustrated, with an application of it to the alterations in the value of the English currency since 1790*. The reason for this change of plan is not clear; in particular, it is not known whether the decision to publish the *Measure of Value* instead of a second edition of the *Principles*

---

[1] See letter of 12 February 1822 from Malthus to Macvey Napier, in British Library, Add. MSS 34613, f.28. Malthus' brother, Sydenham, died on 26 December 1821.
[2] See letters of Malthus to Macvey Napier of 27 September 1821, 8 October 1821, and 12 February 1822, in British Library, Add. MSS 34612, f.445; 34612, f.453, 454; 34613, f.28. See also J. H. Hollander, 'Letters of Malthus to Macvey Napier', *Economic Journal*, Vol. 7, 1897, pp. 265–71. Malthus added on 12 February 1822: 'I had besides particular reasons, latterly, for wishing it [the new edition of the *Principles*] to appear with as little delay as possible', but he did not specify the reasons.
[3] See Zinke, 'Six Letters', p. 188; and Ricardo, *Works*, Vol. II, p. xii.
[4] James, *Population Malthus*, pp. 326–27.
[5] This first MS. of the second edition has not survived as a separate document. Presumably it was absorbed, in whole or part, in the Manuscript Revisions and in ed. 2 of the *Principles*.
[6] Murray archives.

was made by Malthus or by Murray. In a letter to Macvey Napier of 10 May 1823 Malthus said that the *Measure of Value* 'is not in the form, in which I intended it should appear;'[1] and in the *Measure of Value* he stated: 'It was my intention to have done this much more fully than in the present treatise' (p. 61). Presumably the fuller form he would have preferred was a second edition of the *Principles*. In explanation of this change of plan, he said: 'having been interrupted by unforeseen circumstances, and being unwilling to delay any longer the publication of this essential part of my proposed plan, I have determined to submit it to the public in its present form' (*Measure of Value*, p. 61), but he did not identify these 'unforeseen circumstances'. It is possible that the death of Ricardo took away some of Malthus' enthusiasm for a second edition, and contributed to the long delay before its eventual publication. However, this factor could not have influenced the decision to publish *The Measure of Value* early in 1823 instead of a second edition of the *Principles*, as Ricardo did not die until 11 September 1823.

The *Measure of Value* could be described as the least successful of Malthus' publications. It was an attempt to prove that the quantity of labour commanded in exchange is the only measure of the 'natural value' of commodities,[2] and that the value of labour is invariable.[3] If he had been content to argue that the quantity of labour commanded is a useful and approximate measure of value, few economists would have disagreed, even if index numbers measuring general purchasing power had been in existence. But his view that labour commanded is the sole measure and an invariable measure of value found little support amongst his contemporaries, who saw his argument as unconvincing or tautologous. De Quincey, for example, described the *Measure of Value* as a 'blunder' and while commending Malthus for his views on population said that his treatment of value merely exposed his 'intellectual infirmities'.[4] Samuel Bailey described the table used by Malthus in his attempt to prove that the value of labour is invariable, as 'certainly one of the most curious productions in the whole range of political economy', and concluded that 'the formidable array of figures in the table yields not a single new or important truth'.[5]

---

[1] See British Library, Add. MSS 34613, f.148.

[2] 'it is the quantity of *labour* which a commodity will command, and not the quantity of any other commodity, which can represent the conditions of its supply, or its natural value'. (*Measure of Value*, p. 18.)

[3] His argument for 'the necessary constancy of the value of labour' (p. 32) was summarised in his 'Table illustrating the invariable Value of Labour and its Results.' (p. 35.) As this table is also in the Manuscript Revisions (see below, 1.1211), it supports the view that at least some of the material in *The Measure of Value* was originally written as part of the Manuscript Revisions and originally destined to be part of the second edition of the *Principles*.

[4] [T. de Quincey], 'Measure of Value', *London Magazine*, December 1823, pp. 586–88. Contrasting Malthus' powers of logic with Ricardo's, De Quincey added: 'Of all the men of talents, whose writings I have read up to this hour, Mr. Malthus has the most perplexed understanding. He is not only confused himself, but is the cause that confusion is in other men.' (p. 587)

[5] [Samuel Bailey], *A Critical Dissertation on the Nature, Measure and Causes of Value*, 1825, pp. 142, 150.

Introduction

In early 1823, at about the same time as he published the *Measure of Value*, Malthus published the article on 'Population' in the *Supplement to the Fourth, Fifth and Sixth Editions of the Encyclopædia Britannica*. This *Supplement* was published progressively in six volumes, each of two parts, between 1815 and 1824. Malthus' article appeared in Part I of Volume VI in April 1823. It was apparently not the first contribution Malthus had been asked to make to the *Supplement*. When Macvey Napier was appointed editor of the *Supplement* in 1814, he approached Malthus with a proposal, the exact nature of which is uncertain but which presumably offered Malthus an important contributory role. In the letter to Napier of 9 August 1814, referred to above, Malthus reluctantly declined the offer because of other commitments: 'I cannot but feel flattered with your proposal; and were I quite at leisure should not be disinclined perhaps to accede to it. But my engagements in the East India College, together with one which I have formed respecting a new Edition of Adam Smith's Wealth of Nations entirely preclude me from undertaking what you propose. Wishing you every success in the useful work you have commenced ...'[1] As Malthus had just published his *Observations on the Corn Laws* in the spring of 1814, it is possible that Napier had asked Malthus to write the article on 'Corn Laws and Trade'. It was eventually written by J. R. McCulloch.

Seven years later Napier evidently asked Malthus to write the articles on the 'Poor' and 'Population'. Malthus' response on 27 September 1821 was hesitant:

I am very far from being disengaged at present, but think that I could undertake an article on Population, though I cannot promise one on the Poor – at least before I decide, I should wish to know more specifically when it is likely to be wanted. From the actual state of the work, is it probable that it will be wanted as soon as next spring? During that part of next year I expect to be a good deal engaged, and shall probably not be able to undertake more than what I am about ...'[2]

As we have already seen, the work that Malthus was 'about' in September 1821 was his proposed second edition of the *Principles*. He soon after made up his mind not to write the article on the 'Poor'; on 8 October 1821 he wrote to Napier: 'As I shall not be tolerably disengaged before April next, I shall certainly not have time for more than the Article on Population, and will therefore decide at once against undertaking the Article on the Poor, that I may not delay your application in some other quarter.'[3] This implies that Malthus had made a commitment to Napier to write the article on 'Population', a commitment which he soon regretted. Malthus' colleague at the East India College, Sir James Mackintosh, took credit for securing Malthus' involvement. On 8 January 1822 Mackintosh wrote to Napier: 'Malthus at first hesitated about the article

---

[1] British Library, Add. MSS 34611, f.107. In the first sentence, 'perhaps' appears to be an insertion.
[2] British Library, Add. MSS 34612, f.445.   [3] Ibid., f.453, f.454.

Introduction

"Population," but I prevailed on him to undertake it. He has undisturbed leisure and uninterrupted health.'[1]

On 12 February 1822 Malthus wrote to Napier to say that he had decided not to continue with the article on 'Population' because the delays in meeting his prior commitment to publish a second edition of the *Principles* meant that he would be unable to meet Napier's due date.[2] Napier apparently extended the due date until August 1822, and pressed Malthus not to abandon the project; on 11 March 1822, Malthus agreed to continue with it, but again with considerable hesitation:

> It would altogether have suited me better in the actual circumstances in which I am placed, not to write the Arcticle [sic] in the Encyclopædia; but I should be extremely sorry to cause you any real vexation or disappointment; ... It has not been from any disinclination to write the article that I have hesitated, but from a real difficulty in regard to time and other ingagements [sic] ...[3]

By 28 August 1822 Malthus was able to inform Napier: 'I have got my promised article on Population for your Supplement in such a state of forwardness, that I think I can finish it in about a week ...', but at the same time he asked Napier whether the article should be held back pending receipt of the official returns of the last American census. He also added, with a hint of annoyance, that the writing of the article had interrupted his summer vacation 'which we generally spend in a little tour'.[4] The letter of 23 December 1822 to Prévost, cited above, indicates that the article had still not been completed, but finally on 7 January 1823 Malthus sent Napier 'the remaining part of the article',[5] and early in May 1823 received copies of the published article together with his fee of eighty guineas.[6]

Despite Malthus' reluctance to undertake the article on population, and despite the pressure of his concurrent commitment to a second edition of his *Principles*, the article was a very scholarly and finished product. Patricia James has described it as 'almost as clear and forceful as the first *Essay* of 1798', and has judged it to be, because of the nature of the *Encyclopædia Britannica* and the constraint of limited space, 'the most concise and well-written of all his works'.[7] It summarised the main arguments of the *Essay on Population* and adduced further evidence in their support from current population statistics. In addition, although the article was not explicitly polemical, Malthus took the opportunity to explain more clearly the nature and operation of the various checks, no doubt in reply to the misinterpretations that he perceived amongst his critics.

---

[1] *Selections from the Correspondence of the late Macvey Napier, Esq.*, ed. by his son Macvey Napier, London, Macmillan, 1879, p. 33.
[2] British Library, Add. MSS 34613, f.28.   [3] Ibid., f.34.   [4] Ibid., f.96.
[5] Ibid., f.121.
[6] Letters of 10 May and 19 May 1823 from Malthus to Napier, British Library, Add. MSS 34613, f.148, f.160.
[7] James, *Population Malthus*, pp. 321, 401.

Introduction

The early part of 1823 was probably the most prolific period of Malthus' publishing career. As we have seen he published at that time the *Measure of Value*, and the article on 'Population' in the *Encyclopædia Britannica*, and was presumably continuing his preparations for a second edition of the *Principles*. In addition, in April 1823 he published an article in the *Quarterly Review* entitled 'Tooke – On High and Low Prices'.[1] This was a review of Thomas Tooke's *Thoughts and Details on the High and Low Prices of the last Thirty Years*, London 1823. Although Malthus did not entirely agree with Tooke's conclusions, he described Tooke's work 'as a very valuable contribution to the science of political economy', and in particular commended his methodology. Referring to Tooke's 'large and interesting collection of facts', Malthus said:

> This mode of treating his subject we consider as peculiarly judicious. At all times an extensive collection of facts relative to the interchange of the various commodities of the commercial world ... cannot but be of great importance to the science of political economy; but it is more particularly required at the present moment, when it must be acknowledged that some of our ablest writers in this science have been deficient in that constant reference to facts and experience, on which alone it can be safely founded, or further improved.[2]

This emphasis on the importance of observed facts in political economy reflects the empirical side of Malthus' own methodology, and reminds us that he was a professor of history as well as political economy. His perception of the role of the study of economic history in the development of economic theory and the formulation of economic forecasts, is clearly expressed in the statement: 'the sole use of political economy is its application to practice and ... no theories are entitled to confidence in reference to the future, which will not give a satisfactory solution of past phenomena'.[3] Of the many other issues touched on by Malthus in the course of this review, perhaps the most important were: his insistence that all values are determined by supply and demand; his reassertion that labour commanded is the best measure of value; his vigorous renewal of the attack on Say's Law; and his view that the Bank Restriction Act was not significantly responsible for the recent increase of prices. The review also contained a nice example of the anonymity game played by nineteenth-century reviewers. Malthus, writing anonymously as was the custom, referred the reader to the discussion of the history of corn prices given 'by Mr. Malthus ... in his work of Political Economy' (see *Principles* 1.267–80), and, with a delicately-balanced combination of self-praise and self-criticism, added: 'but he [i.e. Malthus] has not, as we should have expected, from his usual and laudable habits of attending to facts and experience, called the particular attention of his reader to the general

---

[1] *Quarterly Review*, Vol. XXIX, No. LVII, Art. VIII, pp. 214–39. For the evidence of Malthus' authorship see Fetter, 'The Economic Articles', p. 160. Malthus commented on the second edition (1824) of Tooke's work in the second edition of his *Principles*. See below, 1.294h.

[2] *Quarterly Review*, April 1823, p. 214.   [3] Ibid., p. 231.

conclusion which unavoidably follows from them',[1] i.e. Tooke's conclusion that the effect of the seasons on corn prices is more significant than is usually recognised.

Later in 1823 Murray evidently asked Malthus to become a regular reviewer for the *Quarterly*. As both publisher of the *Quarterly* since its inception in 1809 and Malthus' publisher since 1815, Murray must have been convinced of Malthus' suitability for that role. In fact his wish to appoint Malthus as a reviewer for the political economy department dated from the preparatory days of the *Quarterly* in 1808.[2] However, in a letter of 7 October 1823, Malthus declined the offer: 'My avocations altogether are such that they would not allow me to undertake any regular department in a Review; but if any work occurs likely to give rise to remarks which may contribute to the progress of a science in which I take a considerable interest, I shall be happy to avail myself of your obliging offer.'[3] Malthus contributed to the *Quarterly* on only one further occasion – his article on 'Political Economy' in 1824 – although a 'note' that he sent to the *Quarterly* later in 1824 was not published.[4]

Malthus' article on 'Political Economy' was published in the *Quarterly Review*, Vol. XXX, No. LX, January 1824, Art. I, pp. 297–334. According to Empson, Malthus considered this article 'one of the best things which he had ever done in Political Economy'.[5] It was a review of the article 'Political Economy' by J. R. McCulloch in the *Supplement to the Encyclopædia Britannica*, Vol. VI, Part I, Edinburgh, 1823. Malthus attempted to show that the 'new school of political economy', as represented by Ricardo and McCulloch, had diverged from the school represented by Adam Smith and himself. He was particularly critical of McCulloch's view, in support of the labour-employed theory of value, that the increase in the value of aged wines is due to the 'labour' of nature. Malthus' article in the *Quarterly Review* was in turn criticised in the *Westminster Review* (by J. S. Mill)[6] who argued that 'because certain Political Economists differ somewhat from Mr. Malthus he dubs them the "new school"', and that the difficulty of reconciling Mr. Malthus and Adam Smith is insuperable.[7] Mill staunchly defended McCulloch's article in the *Encyclopædia*, saying that it 'deservedly ranks among the ablest productions of one of the first political economists of the age; and ... is one of the best elementary treatises of which the science has yet to boast'.[8]

---

[1] Ibid., p. 137.　　[2] See Fetter, 'The Economic Articles', p. 55.
[3] Murray archives; cited in Fetter, ibid.
[4] See letter of 15 September 1824 to Murray in Murray archives, quoted in Fetter, ibid. Malthus also expressed a passing interest in reviewing James Mill's *Elements of Political Economy* and the fifth edition of Say's *Traité d'Économie Politique*. See letter of 5 October 1827 to Murray in Murray archives, quoted in Fetter, ibid.
[5] Empson, 'Life, Writing and Character, p. 496.
[6] 'Political Economy', *Westminster Review*, Vol. III, January 1825, pp. 213–32.
[7] Ibid., p. 216–17.　　[8] Ibid., p. 213.

Introduction

Malthus had earlier tried to persuade Napier that the article on 'Political Economy' in the *Encyclopædia* should not have a Ricardian bias and should not be written by McCulloch. On 27 September 1821 he wrote to Napier: 'I think that the general adoption of the new theories of my excellent friend Mr Ricardo into an *Encyclopædia*, while the question was yet "sub judice" was rather premature. The more I consider the subject the more I feel convinced, that the main part of his structure will not stand'; and on 8 October 1821 he wrote in even stronger terms:

An article of the kind you speak of on Political Economy would I think be very desireable; but no one occurs to me at this moment with sufficient name and sufficient impartiality to do the subject justice. I am fully aware of the merits of Mr Maculloch and Mr Mill, and have a great respect for them both; but I certainly am [of] opinion, after much and repeated consideration, that they have adopted a theory which will not stand the test of experience. It takes a partial view of the subject, like the system of the French Economists; and like that system, after having drawn into its vortex a great number of very clever men, it will be unable to support itself against the testimony of obvious facts, and the weight of those theories, which though less simple and captivating, are more just, on account of their embracing more of the causes which are in actual operation in all economical results.[1]

However McCulloch at that time enjoyed rightly or wrongly a position of considerable eminence in political economy, certainly a position superior to that of Malthus. He was the principal writer of political economy articles for the *Edinburgh Review*, whereas Malthus, having contributed five articles to the *Edinburgh Review* in 1808–11, but having opposed the *laissez-faire* principles of the *Edinburgh Review* and supported the Corn Law in his 1815 pamphlet *Grounds of an Opinion*, was subsequently invited to contribute only one further article – his 1821 article on Godwin. Apart from Ricardo, or perhaps James Mill, McCulloch would have been generally regarded at that time as the best person to write an authoritative article on 'Political Economy'. In the view of some of the members of the Political Economy Club, meeting on 14 October 1823 after Ricardo's death, Malthus had 'a considerable name' in political economy, but he 'entertained opinions on many points, and those some of the most important, which are generally considered as unsound ...'[2] It was McCulloch who was asked to give the Ricardo Memorial Lectures from April to June 1824.

Malthus was worried by the fact that his *Quarterly Review* article, being a criticism of McCulloch, was due to appear in close proximity to McCulloch's course of lectures. As was the case with most of the numbers of the *Quarterly Review*, the 'January 1824' number was not published in the specified month. A letter of 18 February 1824 from Malthus to Murray shows that Malthus was still correcting the proofs of his article,[3] and a further letter of 9 April 1824 indicates

---

[1] British Library, Add. MSS 34612, f.445, f.453.
[2] Diary of J. L. Mallet, quoted by James, *Population Malthus*, pp. 361–62.
[3] Murray archives.

that Murray was proposing to defer the article to the next number, i.e. Vol. XXX, No. LXI, dated April 1824, but published in December 1824. Malthus objected:

> I would much prefer my article coming out in the present number, as I fear that the impression it might make will be essentially weakened by delay ... I should have been sorry that it had come out just at the moment of the first lecture; but as it will now be delayed till the end of the course, it may be thought that it ought to have been a review of that course; but as I cannot attend it, that will be impossible. If the insertion of it is deferred however, I should like to see it again, though it cannot be essentially altered.[1]

Whether out of respect for Malthus' preferences or for other reasons, the article was not deferred to the next number, but its publication was nevertheless delayed – the 'January 1824' number did not appear until August 1824.[2]

In 1824 and 1827 Malthus appeared as a witness before two Select Committees of the House of Commons, and his recorded replies to questions are an important supplement to his published works. His first appearance was on 10 May 1824 before the Select Committee on Artizans and Machinery which had been appointed to consider the laws preventing the emigration of artisans, the laws preventing combinations of workmen, and the laws preventing the exportation of machinery.[3] The circumstances under which he was asked to appear before the Committee are not clear. Certainly he did not profess to be an expert witness on these three topics; on the contrary, in reply to questions, he informed the Committee that he had not directed any particular attention to the second and third topics. On the first topic, emigration of artisans, his responses were quite definite. He thought the laws preventing emigration were ineffective and should be repealed. On the Combination Laws, he was again clearly in favour of repeal, provided that in combining to raise wages, workmen are restrained from using force and intimidation. By implication, therefore, he was not opposed in principle to combinations of workmen, and apparently regarded such combinations as an expression, not a denial, of the concept of *laissez-faire*. It is also interesting to note that Malthus believed that the abolition of the Combination Laws would tend to raise wages, and that by implication such an increase was desirable.

On the third topic, the export of machinery, the Select Committee probably did not find Malthus' replies very satisfactory. The Committee had been set up with the overall purpose of abolishing the laws that restricted commerce, but Malthus' views on the export of machinery proved to be rather circumspect. He agreed that 'upon the whole, and under the actual circumstances' the laws

---

[1] Ibid.

[2] See H. Shine and H. C. Shine, *The Quarterly Review under Gifford*, University of North Carolina Press, Chapel Hill, 1949, p. 87. Unpunctuality was a feature of the *Quarterly Review* from its inception. See S. Smiles, *A Publisher and His Friends*, Vol. I, pp. 156–57.

[3] Great Britain. Parliament. House of Commons. *Parliamentary Papers*. 'Reports of Minutes of Evidence from the Select Committee on Artizans and Machinery. Sixth Report.' 1824.

Introduction

prohibiting the export of machinery were 'perhaps' injurious to the public interest, and that 'in the actual state of things' no evil was likely to arise from the exportation of machinery, but he added that 'there might be peculiar and special circumstances' under which the prohibition would not be injurious. On this topic therefore he refused to give unqualified assent to the principle of free trade.

In the course of his examination on the exportation of machinery Malthus also expressed certain reservations about the principle of division of labour, stating that 'there are limits to the advantages derived from the division of labour, they would not continue to increase just in proportion to the extent of capital, or to the extent of demand for the particular goods'. This is one of the few instances where Malthus' views on the division of labour have been recorded, in contrast with Adam Smith's extended treatment of the subject.

Malthus was elected as one of the ten Royal Associates of the Royal Society of Literature, a position from which he received an annual pension of one hundred guineas for a period of seven years, and which obliged him 'to communicate with the Society, once a year at least' on his nominated subject of 'Political Economy and Statistics'.[1] He made two such communications, in 1825 and 1827. The first was a paper entitled 'On the Measure of the Conditions necessary to the Supply of Commodities', read on 4 May 1825, and published in 1827 and 1829.[2] It was an attempt to show that the natural and necessary conditions of the supply of commodities not subject to monopoly – by which he meant their natural and necessary costs of production – can be measured only by the quantity of labour which they will ordinarily and on average command. It was essentially a repetition of the arguments in the *Measure of Value*, 1823, and was equally unconvincing. He appears to have been preoccupied with this question of value in 1825. The records of the Political Economy Club show that two questions on the measurement of value were proposed by Malthus and discussed at the meeting of 5 December 1825.[3]

Early in 1826 Malthus published the sixth edition of the *Essay on Population*, the last edition to be published in his lifetime. His letters show that he was correcting the proofs in September 1825 and that by the end of December 1825 he had only to correct the Index. The new edition was presented in two volumes, as in the third and fourth editions, instead of three volumes as in the fifth. The change was Murray's decision and did not please Malthus. In a letter to Murray of 20 September 1825, after he had seen the early proofs, he accepted the new format: 'I was at first a little surprised to hear that you intended to reduce the three volumes to two; but I concluded that you understood these matters best, and upon reflection, I considered it an advantage that it might be afforded cheaper',

---

[1] Malthus was also a Fellow of the Royal Society. See James, *Population Malthus*, pp. 356–60.
[2] *Transactions of the Royal Society of Literature*, Vol. I, Part I, 1829, Art. XIV, pp. 171–80.
[3] See below, Introduction, p. lviii.

Introduction

but in a letter to Murray of 25 December 1825, after he had seen the full proofs, he expressed disappointment: 'I fear that the compression of the former edition into two volumes, with the necessary additions, will make the new edition not so agreeable to look at or read, as the last. The main text is very well but the Appendix and index are rather too small.'[1]

The alterations in the sixth edition were summarised by Malthus in the 'Advertisement', dated 2 January 1826, to that edition (pp. xv–xvi). They were mainly statistical, resulting from new information on the population of European countries, and indicate his concern to support his theories with current empirical evidence. There were also a few additional notes, and a half-page extension to the Appendix, Vol. II, p. 498, in which he stated his reasons for not including in the sixth edition a reply to William Godwin's *Of Population*, 1820.[2] Although the alterations were not extensive, they were evidently time-consuming. In the letter of 25 December 1825 to Murray, Malthus said the alterations had 'taken more time than room', and assured Murray that he could 'very justly say' that the new edition contained 'Additions, as well as corrections'.[3]

Following the publication of the sixth edition of the *Essay* early in 1826, Malthus presumably directed his literary efforts during the remainder of 1826 to a work of 261 octavo pages entitled *Definitions in Political Economy, preceded by an inquiry into the rules which ought to guide political economists in the definition and use of their terms; with remarks on the deviation from these rules in their writings*, which was published in January 1827. In a letter to Murray of 10 November 1826, Malthus apologised for the delay in correcting the proofs; he had been 'particularly engaged' in preparing questions for examinations that were soon to commence at the East India College.[4] This hurried note and similar statements in other correspondence give the clear impression that Malthus' literary output continually suffered from the pressure of his lecturing and administrative duties.

The Preface of the *Definitions* opened with a remark which is surely no less true today: 'The differences of opinion among political economists have of late been a frequent subject of complaint.' It stated that 'one of the principal causes' of these differences was 'the different meanings in which the same terms have been used by different writers', and that the object of the *Definitions* was to draw attention to this problem. Despite Malthus' excellent systemizing intentions it is doubtful whether the *Definitions* succeeded in reducing the terminological confusion. J. M. Keynes later described it as 'a minor work of no great interest (except, perhaps, his attack on Ricardo's definition of *Real Wages*)'.[5] However, there is no doubt that

---

[1] Murray archives.
[2] As noted above, p. xlii, he replied anonymously to Godwin's *Of Population* in the *Edinburgh Review*, 1821.
[3] Murray archives.   [4] Ibid.
[5] J. M. Keynes, *The Collected Writings of John Maynard Keynes*, Macmillan for the Royal Economic Society, London, Vol. X, 1972, p. 92.

it is an intensively analytical work which must have involved a considerable expenditure of time and effort. Malthus' close familiarity with the state of contemporary economic literature is apparent in his detailed critical appraisal of definitions used by the Physiocrats, Adam Smith, Say, Ricardo, James Mill, McCulloch and Samuel Bailey. More importantly, his attempt in Chapter I to enunciate 'Rules for the Definition and Application of Terms in Political Economy' is a significant early contribution to economic semantics, and his definitions of sixty economic concepts are a commendable effort of codification. It is possible that this exercise in methodology was Malthus' response to those who had accused him of misusing terms; Robert Torrens, for example, referred to 'The very inaccurate and unphilosophical language which Mr. Malthus employs when alluding to our monetary system.'[1] Malthus' concern with the philology of political economy, and his confidence in his own use of terms, can be seen in his letter of 5 October 1827 to Murray:

It is rather strange that the Definitions have not been anywhere reviewed, although as far as I can learn, all who have read them have approved, and thought that they would be particularly useful in introducing a greater degree of attention to the language of the science without which there is little hope of any essential progress in it. Had the work been more open to just criticism, it would have been attacked fast enough.[2]

The *Definitions* had in fact been reviewed, and attacked, [by J. R. McCulloch] in *The Scotsman* on 10 March 1827. The review began:

Whatever others may think of Mr Malthus' late speculations, it is pleasing to observe, that they have in no degree fallen in his own estimation. The book before us is intended to show that whatever has been done by others during the last twenty years has been ill-done; and that those who wish to study Political Economy in its purity, unmixed with error or alloy of any sort, must resort to the writings of Mr Malthus.

And it concluded by questioning Malthus' qualifications for the office of 'Dictator in the Economical Republic'.[3]

Malthus was of course not alone in his concern for definitions. His idea of publishing a list of definitions might have been derived from the list given by Simonde de Sismondi in *De la richesse commerciale*, 2 Tomes, Geneva, 1803, Vol. I, pp. 342–48, 'Postscriptum. Définitions des mots scientifiques employés dans cet ouvrage'; or from Charles Ganilh, *Dictionnaire d'économie politique*, Paris, 1826; or most probably from the 'Épitome des principes fondamentaux de l'économie

---

[1] Robert Torrens, *An Essay on the External Corn Trade* ..., London, 1815, p. x; quoted by Sraffa in Ricardo, *Works*, Vol. VI, p. 205.

[2] Murray archives. However, Malthus also admitted: 'I am very ready to include myself among those political economists who have not been sufficiently attentive to this subject [i.e. the definition and use of terms].' (*Definitions*, p. 202.)

[3] A much more complimentary review was published by J.-B. Say in *Revue Encyclopédique*, Vol. XXX, 1827, pp. 494–96, although Say defended himself against Malthus' criticisms. The *Definitions* was reviewed also in the *North American Review*, Vol. XXVIII, No. 63, April 1829, pp. 368–88, and [by G. Poulett Scrope] in the *Quarterly Review*, Vol. XLIV, January 1831, Art. I, 'The Political Economists', pp. 1–52.

Introduction

politique' contained in J.-B. Say, *Traité d'économie politique*, 2nd ed., 1814, and subsequent editions. Malthus quoted from the 'Épitome' of the fourth edition, 1819, of Say's *Traité* and expressed his indebtedness to Say for some of the definitions.[1] Also his interest in semantics was probably stimulated by similar interest shown by other members of the Political Economy Club. On 7 June 1824 Torrens initiated discussion on the definitions of profits and wages; and on 9 January 1826 Senior initiated discussion on the definition of capital. In turn the publication of Malthus' *Definitions* might have stimulated Torrens to discuss definitions of eight economic terms at the meeting of the Political Economy Club on 14 January 1828.[2]

Malthus' second appearance before a Select Committee of the House of Commons occurred on 5 May 1827 when he gave evidence to the Select Committee on Emigration from the United Kingdom. On this occasion his evidence, published in the Committee's Third Report[3] in 1829, was much more extensive; he answered 249 questions, compared with only 66 in 1824. The Chairman of the Select Committee was R. J. Wilmot-Horton (1784–1841), MP, who was a fervent advocate of emigration as a cure for poverty. Malthus' correspondence with Wilmot-Horton shows that he was very reluctant to give evidence. In several letters in early 1827 he asked to be excused, saying that 'I have no facts, or results of personal inquiries to communicate, and my opinions on the subject of Emigration are already before the public ...' and 'it really appeared to me that the only evidence I could give was not of the right kind for a Committee of the House of Commons.'[4] But Wilmot-Horton obviously thought that Malthus' evidence would lend strong support to the argument for emigration, and did not accede to his request to be excused. When the Committee's Report was published it gave a prominent place to Malthus' evidence; for example, the Report stated (pp. 38–39): 'Mr. Malthus admits that if it can be shown that the expense of removing such labourers [for whose labour no real demand exists] by Emigration is less than that of maintaining them at home, no doubt can exist of the expediency of so removing them; and this, independent of any question of repayment.' The Committee was particularly pleased to note that the science of political economy, as represented by Malthus, supported the views of practical men: 'The testimony which was uniformly given by the *practical witnesses* – has been confirmed in the most absolute manner by that of Mr. Malthus; and Your Committee cannot but express their satisfaction at finding that the experience of facts is thus strengthened throughout by general reasoning

---

[1] Malthus, *Definitions*, pp. 251, 261. Say claimed priority in the formal presentation of principles (*Revue Encyclopédique*, Vol. XXX, 1827, p. 496).

[2] *Political Economy Club*, Vol. VI, London, 1921, pp. 30–31.

[3] Great Britain. Parliament. House of Commons. *Parliamentary Papers*. 'Third Report from the Select Committee on Emigration from the United Kingdom.' 1827.

[4] Quoted by James, *Population Malthus*, p. 392.

and scientific principles' (p. 9). However, the Committee appear to have exaggerated Malthus' support for emigration as a cure for the poverty caused by over-population. A careful reading of his evidence indicates that he regarded emigration as at best only a partial and temporary cure, not a permanent cure, because the vacuum created by emigration would soon be filled up. This view is brought out even more clearly in his subsequent correspondence with Wilmot-Horton.[1]

Malthus' evidence before the Committee is perhaps more important for its insights into his views on the relationship between wages and effective demand than for his views on emigration. In supporting the policy of emigration as a temporary cure, he argued that low wages resulting from over-population would not necessarily mean high profits for manufacturers, and that higher wages at home resulting from the emigration of surplus population would not necessarily mean lower profits. In his replies to Questions 3279–3292 he argued that higher wages are consistent with higher profits, and that home trade, which is much more important than foreign trade, depends to a large extent on high wages; for example, 'I think that the home demand of the country depends very much upon the condition of the labouring classes; that is, that the extent of the effectual demand for the manufactures and commodities consumed at home depends essentially upon the good condition of the labouring classes.' (Q. 3282)

Malthus' second paper to the Royal Society of Literature was read on 7 November 1827, but was not published until 1829. It was entitled 'On the meaning which is most usually and most correctly attached to the term "Value of a Commodity"', and its aim was to show that when the term 'value of a commodity' is used without referring to some other commodity in which it is to be estimated, the term is 'generally understood to refer, and can only refer correctly, to the conditions of its supply, or the natural and necessary costs of its production' (p. 74).[2] The paper appears to have been intended as a development of the themes treated in his *Definitions in Political Economy* published earlier in 1827. While one can appreciate Malthus' concern to establish a set of generally accepted meanings for the basic concepts of political economy, his approach in this paper was somewhat arbitrary. It no doubt suited his own topological framework to define the value of a commodity in this way, but he gave no evidence to support his view that this was the way value was 'generally understood'. Also his attempt to prove the superiority of his particular definition of value was both unconvincing and self-contradictory. In the *Definitions* (p. 235) he defined value as the 'relation of one object to some other, or others in exchange ...', and in this paper (p. 74) he affirmed that the universal characteristic of

---

[1] Ibid., pp. 396–98. Malthus' correspondence with Wilmot-Horton is in the Catton Collection, Central Library, Derby.
[2] *Transactions of the Royal Society of Literature*, Vol. I, Part II, 1829, Art. VIII, pp. 74–81.

Introduction

value is 'scarcity compared with the demand', but in formally defining the value of a commodity as 'the natural and necessary costs of its production' he appeared to lose sight of the essential relativity of the notion of value, and the essential role of demand in its determination. Moreover, in choosing to adopt this particular definition of value, he did not adhere to the rules of definition which he himself had so admirably formulated in his *Definitions*, and as a result what was no doubt intended as an exercise in economic semantics verged on logomachy.

No publications by Malthus have been recorded for 1828 and 1829. His final publication appeared in 1830 at the age of sixty-four. Entitled *A Summary View of the Principle of Population*, it was a reprint of about two-thirds of the article on 'Population' in the *Supplement to the Encyclopædia Britannica*, 1823, with several small additions. The 'Advertisement' contained in the *Summary View* (pp. iii–iv) noted that 'no work has been so much talked of by persons who do not seem to have read it, as Mr. Malthus's Essay on Population', and reminded the reader that in order to correct the frequent misrepresentations of his views, Malthus had added an Appendix to the third edition (1806) of the *Essay*. The 'Advertisement' quoted Malthus' 1806 hope that with the help of the Appendix 'those who have not had leisure to read the whole work ... may not, from the partial and incorrect statements which they have heard, mistake the import of some of my opinions, and attribute to me others which I have never held'. The 1806 Appendix was reprinted in the fourth (1807) edition of the *Essay*, and given an important extension in the fifth (1817) edition in response to further critics, and another less-important extension in the sixth (1826) edition. The 'Advertisement' to the *Summary View* went on to note that 'the discussion of the subject still continues, and the same misrepresentations have been revived', and explained that this new 1830 work was intended to perform the same service as the Appendix to the *Essay* had previously done. It would provide a concise exposition of Malthus' views, so that those 'who have any wish to consider the subject fairly' would be able to ascertain what Malthus actually said, 'by a very slight sacrifice of time and expense'. The 'Advertisement' did not say who was currently reviving the misrepresentations of Malthus, but it is clear from Malthus' correspondence that the person alleged to be responsible was Michael Thomas Sadler (1780–1835), business man, Tory MP and ardent advocate of factory reform, who had criticised Malthus' principle of population in *Ireland; its Evils and their Remedies, being a refutation of the errors of the Emigration Committee and others, touching that country. To which is prefixed a synopsis of an original treatise about to be published on The Law of Population developing the real principle on which it is universally regulated*, London, 1828; 2nd ed., 1829. The foreshadowed *Law of Population* was published early in 1830. Sadler's criticism was based on 'Sadler's Law' which stated that fecundity is inversely proportional to numbers and prosperity; in other words, that nature provides an automatic check to population growth. Sadler's criticisms of the *Emigration Committee Report*, which had given such prominence to Malthus' evidence in 1827, might have provided Malthus with an additional reason for publishing the *Summary View*. On 18 January 1830 Malthus wrote to Napier, the editor who had persuaded Malthus to write the article on 'Population' for the *Supplement to the Encyclopædia Britannica*:

> It has been suggested to me by some friends that, as the subject of population is reviving on account of Mr Sadlers strange work, which he has published, and the further large one which he has promised, it would be desireable to have some short and *cheap* account of the principle of population, or answer to the main arguments against it, in circulation in order that the great mass who talk about it, may have easy means of getting better information on the subject than they appear to have at present.

The letter also indicates that he had little regard for Sadler's views ('I own that I don't feel inclined to take much trouble with such an opponent – as Mr Sadler'), and that he intended his response to Sadler to be anonymous ('without my appearing to come forward personally as an opponent of Mr Sadler'), thus showing once again his distaste for public controversy. It further appears from this letter that Malthus at first thought to republish the Appendix of the *Essay on Population* as a separate work, adding to it parts of his 'Population' article from the *Supplement*. He requested permission from the proprietors of the *Encyclopædia* to use the 'Population' article in this way, and a note added to this letter indicates that Napier wrote to Malthus on 25 January 1830 granting permission.[1] Later the same day, 18 January 1830, he wrote to his publisher, John Murray, suggesting that the Appendix in the *Essay on Population* be republished, and that it be preceded by part of the *Encyclopædia* article on 'Population', as 'a short sketch of the Principle of Population before coming to the answers of objectors'. He asked for Murray's opinion of the following proposed title, indicating his intention to publish anonymously:

> A short sketch of the Principle of Population, with answers to the objections to it, taken principally from the Appendix to the last Edition of the Essay, and the Article on *Population* in the Supplement to the Encyclopædia Britannica. with the permission of Mr Murray, the Proprietors of the Encyclopædia, and Mr Malthus., by a friend.[2]

However, when the *Summary View* appeared later in 1830, it was not anonymous and did not contain the Appendix to the *Essay on Population*. It is not clear why, or on whose decision, these intentions were changed. The 'Advertisement' to the *Summary View* stated that 'this appendix is to be found in the fifth and sixth editions, and may easily be consulted'. In view of the misunderstandings of Malthus' ideas that have continued to the present day, it is a matter of

---

[1] British Library, Add. MSS 34613, f.276.

[2] Murray archives. The letter also indicates that Murray had intended, at that stage, to publish 'in a cheap form' another edition of the *Essay on Population* and that Malthus had intended to add a preface and notes to the Appendix. This cheap edition, which would have been the seventh, was not published in Malthus' lifetime. Perhaps Murray realised that even a cheap edition of the full *Essay* would not sell when the smaller and cheaper *Summary View* became available.

Introduction

considerable regret that the valuable Appendix to the *Essay* was not included in the 'short and cheap' *Summary View* in 1830 as Malthus originally intended, and has been omitted from modern reprints of the *Essay*. Malthus' belief that this Appendix, written in response to earlier critics, would serve also as a response to later critics, indicates that in his estimation it contained important developments of his arguments, and was of more than passing interest.

During this post-1820 period Malthus' membership of the Political Economy Club undoubtedly played a significant role in the development of his ideas and in his preparation of ed. 2 of the *Principles*. He was one of the twenty original members of the Club founded in London in 1821. Amongst the other original members were Thomas Tooke, the prime mover in the Club's formation, David Ricardo, James Mill, and Robert Torrens. Members elected later during Malthus' lifetime included John Cazenove (proposed by Malthus), Nassau Senior, John Ramsay McCulloch, Robert Wilmot-Horton, Samuel James Loyd, Perronet Thompson, and John Lewis Mallet, who preserved in his diary details of the Club's meetings and discussions. According to Mallet, 'On most occasions Ricardo and Mill led on one side, and Malthus and Cazenove on the other, Torrens and Tooke occasionally differing with both, and Prinsep being a sort of disturbing force.'[1] The Club met monthly between December and June, and discussed questions proposed in advance by members. Malthus attended most of the meetings from the first on 30 April 1821 until the meeting of 4 December 1834 just before his death. He proposed the following eight questions: (1) 'Can there be a general glut of commodities?' Discussed 25 June 1821 and 3 December 1821. (2) 'On what does the demand for labour depend?' Discussed 13 January 1823. (3) 'What would be the practical effects of measuring Prices, and the rate of Profits on a medium which was subject to frequent and considerable variations in its relation to Labour?' Discussed 5 December 1825. (4) 'What do we refer to when we say a commodity is steady in its value?' Discussed 5 December 1825. (5) 'What would be the effect on the Wealth and Capital of a country of an increasing taste for menial servants and attendants compared with material products foreign and domestic?' Discussed 6 March 1826. (6) 'What are the circumstances which determine the differences in the value of Money in different countries, and how are these differences in value to be estimated?' Discussed 2 June 1828. (7) 'Do the low prices of Exportable Commodities, as far as they are independent of improvements in the processes of production, arise from Foreign and Domestic competition?' Discussed 6 March 1834. (8) 'Is there any valid apology for the American Tariff?' Discussed 6 March 1834. The first five questions are quite predictable, reflecting themes frequently treated by Malthus. The last three questions, concerned with foreign exchange and foreign trade, are somewhat surprising, as these topics were not treated at length in his published

---

[1] *Political Economy Club*, pp. 420–21. See also James, *Population Malthus*, pp. 354–56.

works. The eight questions indicate the mixture of the theoretical and the practical in Malthus' intellectual interests. In addition to the discussions on the questions proposed by himself, Malthus participated over the fourteen years of his membership in discussions on a wide range of topics; such as, the effect of machinery on the demand for labour, the extinction of the national debt, the causes of exchange value, the relationship between wages and profits, primogeniture, the definition of wages and capital, and the Factory Acts. On all of these themes alterations are to be found in ed. 2 of the *Principles*.

To summarise, in the fifteen years between the publication of his *Principles* in 1820 and his death in 1834, Malthus published no fewer than ten works; viz. the article on Godwin in the *Edinburgh Review* (1821); two articles in the *Quarterly Review*, on Tooke (1823) and 'Political Economy' (1824); an article on 'Population' in the *Encyclopædia Britannica* (1823); a partial reprint of that article in the *Summary View* (1830); *The Measure of Value* (1823); *Definitions in Political Economy* (1827); two lectures on value read to the Royal Society of Literature (1825 and 1827); and the sixth edition of the *Essay on Population* (1826). In addition he participated regularly in the debates of the Political Economy Club, gave evidence before two Select Committees, and continued to perform his lecturing and examining duties at the East India College. It is not surprising therefore that the publication of the second edition of the *Principles* was delayed, especially when these other activities were conducted in personal circumstances that became increasingly trying.[1] The year 1821 saw the death of his only brother, Sydenham (see above, p. xliii), and the deaths of a cousin, a sister, and two nephews. In 1822 there were further student riots at the East India College. In 1823 Malthus and other members of the staff sent a letter to the Principal of the College objecting to proposed changes in the College system. The future of the College was under threat, and became the subject of enquiry at a special Court of Proprietors in 1824. In 1825 Malthus' youngest child, Lucy, aged seventeen, died. Malthus' son, Henry, was also in poor health, and for his sake the family spent the winter of 1827–28 in Bordeaux. Malthus also appears to have taken charge of a prodigal nephew, Edward Bray, who accompanied them to Bordeaux to avoid being arrested. In 1830 Malthus himself was unwell, and had to consult his physician. His wife was also unwell. After a partial recuperation, he became very ill again, and probably spent some part of the winter of 1830–31 at a convalescent resort. It is conceivable that this combination of family worries, personal ill-health, and teaching duties placed him under considerable strain – he was already fifty-four years of age in 1820 – and while he was able to produce a number of smaller works after 1820, he could no longer muster the physical

---

[1] This brief summary of Malthus' personal circumstances is based on James, *Population Malthus*, passim, where further details can be found.

or psychological reserves necessary to bring the second edition of his *Principles* to finality.

Nevertheless he never seems to have abandoned hope of the second edition. We have seen that his correspondence of 1820–23 contains frequent references to his eagerness to publish a second edition, but that the *Measure of Value* was published in 1823 instead, for reasons that were not made clear. On 5 October 1827 he raised once again with Murray the question of a second edition of the *Principles*:

I am thinking of a new edition of the Political Economy as it has been long out [of] print, and I understand often asked for. There will be much new matter relating to Taxation, the Level of the Precious Metals, and other subjects. And I wished to consult you whether it would be most adviseable to publish these conjointly or seperately [sic].[1]

The statement that there will be 'much new matter' implies that by 1827 Malthus had in mind a new edition that differed considerably from the first edition of 1820, and from the revised edition that he had sent to Murray in 1823. Murray's reply is not known, but when Malthus raised the matter again early in 1834 Murray evidently no longer wished to be involved with the *Principles*. On 27 January 1834 Malthus wrote to Murray:

From what you said to me when I had the pleasure of seeing you the other day, I inferred that you meant to give up the copy right of my Political Economy. I write a line to ascertain whether I have understood you correctly, as it is necessary that I should be quite certain on the subject in making any proposal to another bookseller.[2]

After Malthus' death on 29 December 1834, his son Henry Malthus wrote a letter to Murray which implied that the publication of the second edition was well in hand: 'Would you have the goodness to inform me of your intentions with regard to the publication of the second edition of my father's work on Pol. Econ: ... I am anxious ... to know *when* you think of publishing; and to arrange with Mr. Cazenove about correcting the press.'[3] Henry Malthus had apparently misunderstood Murray's intentions, because the second edition was eventually published in 1836, not by Murray but by William Pickering, who must have been more optimistic than Murray about its commercial feasibility.[4]

Malthus' continuous involvement during the period 1820–34 in the preparation of the second edition can be seen also from the internal evidence of the alterations in both the Manuscript Revisions and the second edition. Several entries in the Manuscript Revisions can be dated in the 1821–23 period, because of references they contain to published works.[5] An alteration in the name of the

---

[1] Murray archives. [2] Ibid.
[3] Ibid. It is significant that the original says '*when*', not 'whether'.
[4] See 1.i b. There was no proper review of ed. 2 of the *Principles*. The article by Empson in the *Edinburgh Review*, 1837 ('Life, Writing, and Character') had the title of ed. 2 as its heading, but was really a biography.
[5] See 1.73b, 1.101d, 1.261h.

reigning monarch, and some scribbled notes on the back of a dated letter from Sydney Smith indicate that Malthus had made entries in the Manuscript Revisions after June 1830.[1] Also, watermarks on ten of the loose sheets suggest that Malthus was probably working on the Manuscript Revisions over many years.[2] In ed. 2, there are references to a number of books, articles and government reports published during the period 1820–34. These publications were by Torrens 1820 and 1821, Ricardo 1821, James Mill 1821, Say and Storch 1823, Tooke 1824, Say 1826, Thompson 1826, West 1826, Malthus (*Definitions in Political Economy*) 1827, Say 1828, Jones 1831, [McCulloch] *Edinburgh Review* 1831, *First Report . . . as to the Employment of Children in Factories* 1833, and *Report from the Select Committee on Agriculture* 1833.[3] Thus there is documentary evidence to show that Malthus was gathering information for inclusion in the second edition over the entire fifteen year period from 1820 to 1834. Even as late as 1833, in his sixty-eighth year, he was reading voluminous government reports, and selecting evidence from them for the second edition of his *Principles*.

THE IDENTITY AND ROLE OF THE EDITOR OF THE SECOND EDITION

In the second edition of the *Principles* there are three contributions by persons other than Malthus whose identities are not stated in the text. These unidentified persons are (1) the editor of the second edition, (2) the author of the 'Advertisement to the Second Edition' (2.vii–xii), and (3) the author of the 'Memoir of Robert Malthus' (2.xiii–liv). The author of the Memoir is known to have been William Otter.[4] The most likely editor of the second edition of Malthus' *Principles* would appear to be John Cazenove (1788–1879). He had been a friend and supporter of Malthus, and was said at one stage to be involved in 'correcting the press' of the second edition. He was a recognised economist, being a member of the Political Economy Club and the author of a number of works on economics.[5] It is probable that Cazenove was also the author of the Advertisement. The last

---

[1] See below, Vol. II, p. 115, fn. 3; and Vol. II, p. 212.

[2] Five of the interleaved sheets have watermark dates (1816, 1818, 1819, 1822, 1831) and five of the supplementary sheets have watermark dates (1828 in each case). See 1.91e, 1.101d, 1.118d, 1.261b, 1.280a, and 1.122l.

[3] See below, Vol. II, Index, for references to these publications. In addition, Malthus referred obliquely to a number of authors and publications, introducing his remarks with statements such as, 'It has been thought by some very able writers . . .' Some of those oblique references can be identified probably as publications in the period 1820–34. See below, Vol. II, p. 469, Works Cited. There is also an oblique reference to the Reform Act, 1832. See 1.438a.

[4] Empson said of the second edition of Malthus' *Principles*: 'A most interesting addition to the present volume is a Memoir of the Author by the Bishop of Chichester . . ., the friend of the author for half a century' ('Life, Writing and Character', p. 472).

[5] For further details, see J. M. Pullen, 'The Editor of the Second Edition of T. R. Malthus' *Principles of Political Economy*', *History of Political Economy*, Vol. X, No. II, 1978, pp. 286–97, parts of which are reproduced here with permission.

Introduction

paragraph of the Advertisement states that 'some discrepancies', 'some needless repetitions', and some 'verbal inaccuracies' might 'have escaped the Editor's notice' (2.xii). In other words, the author of the Advertisement admits the possibility that the editor's work might be defective. It is unlikely that such an admission would have been made if the author of the Advertisement and the editor were not the same person. This conclusion is supported by the fact that the writer of the Advertisement exhibits a detailed knowledge of the tasks performed by the editor.

The determination of the nature and extent of the editor's role in the second edition is, however, a much more difficult task than the determination of his identity. The Advertisement states that Malthus inserted 'much new matter' in the second edition, but that the second edition was unfinished. The Advertisement states also that Malthus had completed the essential alterations, and that the editor found 'very little indeed has been required to put the work in a state fit for publication'. Nevertheless, the editor is said to have varied the text in some places, omitted some passages, and added some notes.[1]

The immediate reaction of a modern reader must be to note the apparent contradiction between the statement – 'very little indeed has been required to put the work in a state fit for publication' – and the cumulative extent of the alterations implicit in the other statements. The editor's concept of his editorial role must have been quite different from that of a modern editor. What he regarded as being 'slightly varied' might appear as a major alteration today.

The editorial contributions described as 'a few notes ... interspersed here and there' can be readily identified. They no doubt refer to the eight editorial footnotes added to the second edition of the *Principles* and identified as the editor's contributions by the letters '*Ed.*' placed at the end of each footnote.[2] These eight editorial footnotes reveal certain characteristics of the editor. He was familiar with some of the main theories under discussion in the economic literature of the time, and was able to discuss them with some competence.[3] In

---

[1] *Principles* 2.xi–xii. However, the statement that Malthus had inserted 'much new matter' appears to conflict with Empson's statement that when Malthus was reproached shortly before his death for his procrastination in publishing a second edition, he replied: 'My views are before the public. If I am to alter any thing, I can do little more than alter the language: And I don't know that I should alter it for the better.' (Empson, 'Life, Writing and Character', p. 472.)

[2] These eight editorial footnotes occurred on pp. 47, 125, 164, 291, 317–19, 321, 391, 405 of the second edition of the *Principles*. There is, of course, the possibility that the editor added additional footnotes *without* indicating his authorship. However this would not appear to be very probable, unless it occurred by an oversight. If the editor had taken care to indicate his authorship in eight cases, it is unlikely that he would have deliberately disguised his authorship in other cases.

[3] The footnotes covered such matters as the distinction between productive and unproductive labour (p. 47), the measure of value (p. 125), the reasons for the rise in the price of corn between 1793 and 1813 (p. 164), the determinants of the rate of profits (p. 291), the meaning of effectual demand (pp. 317–19), the remedy for gluts (p. 321), and the relationship between prices and the quantity of money (p. 391).

general he supported Malthus' ideas, but did not hesitate to supplement Malthus' presentation and even to criticise Malthus where he thought it necessary. The editorial footnotes thus suggest that the editor was an economist of some standing. It is obvious that he did not regard his editorship as merely a clerical task, but felt that he was able and indeed would be expected to make some contributions in his own right. This degree of competence in political economy is also a characteristic of the author of the Advertisement. It is apparent in his presentation in 2.viii–ix of the distinction between value understood as the general power of purchasing, and value understood as the sacrifice required to procure a commodity. The reference in 2.ix to N. W. Senior, *Three Lectures on the Cost of Obtaining Money*, 1830, is further evidence of familiarity with the current literature.

Despite the fact that the editor's contribution, as indicated in the Advertisement, must have been substantial by modern editorial standards, it is unlikely that he would have been responsible for all the alterations in the second edition that do not occur in the Manuscript Revisions. Such a radical alteration of Malthus' text would imply that the editor was virtually a joint author of the second edition.

The Manuscript Revisions in Malthus' hand are the major source of evidence for identifying the alterations in ed. 2 that were made by Malthus, not by the editor. Even when the MR entry is only an abbreviated phrase, it is reasonable to conclude that Malthus was responsible for the alteration in ed. 2 beginning with that phrase. There is less certainty of course about the MR entries that are omitted from ed. 2, or that are incorporated in ed. 2 with alterations. It does not necessarily follow that the editor was responsible for such omissions and alterations. As noted above, it is possible that the initial entries made by Malthus in MR were later altered or deleted by Malthus himself in documents that are now lost.

In some of the alterations, internal evidence indicates that they were made by Malthus, not by the editor. The use of the first person singular pronoun – I, me, myself – in a number of alterations is fairly conclusive proof that those alterations were made by Malthus. Even if an editor set out to rectify Malthus' ideas, it is unlikely that in doing so he would have deliberately pretended to be Malthus. On the contrary, the editor in his signed footnotes refers to Malthus in the third person (for example, 'the author') and in one instance specifically attributes an alteration to Malthus.

Some of the alterations can be attributed to Malthus on the basis of their similarity to ideas published by Malthus between 1820 and 1834, for example, in *The Measure of Value Stated and Illustrated*, 1823, and in *Definitions in Political Economy*, 1827. The most notable, and controversial, instance is probably his view expressed in *The Measure of Value* that the 'value of labour' must always remain constant. However, alterations that can be definitely attributed to Malthus on the basis of textual evidence represent only a small proportion of the total number of alterations. Unless further evidence becomes available, the question of the extent of the editor's role in the second edition must remain largely unanswered, and thus there must be some element of doubt in deciding which of the alterations can be attributed to Malthus, and which to the editor. There could even be some doubt about the authenticity of passages that occur in an unaltered form in ed. 2; it is conceivable that the editor either overlooked or deliberately omitted some alterations made by Malthus. The hermeneutical dilemma that confronts us is that, because abundant circumstantial evidence shows that Malthus made considerable changes in ed. 2, we cannot rely solely upon ed. 1 as the authoritative version of Malthus' final views, but at the same time, because of the unclear role of the editor, we cannot accept ed. 2 in its entirety as an authentic representation of Malthus' views. Although these difficulties of attribution might never be satisfactorily resolved, they should not be allowed to distract attention from an appreciation of the substantive content of the two editions of the *Principles*.

GENERAL DESCRIPTION OF THE ALTERATIONS

The alterations involved a very wide range of topics, covering virtually all the major subject areas of political economy; for example, wealth, value, demand, supply, land, rent, labour, wages, employment, capital, machinery, profits, expectations, consumption, saving, investment, Say's law, effective demand, distribution, money, population, foreign trade, taxation, *laissez-faire* and public works, the national debt, and the methodology of political economy – in particular, the 'doctrine of proportions', the rules for definitions, and the plurality and reciprocity of causes. It is difficult to give a quantitative estimate of the alterations. Some involved a change in only one word, while others involved a change extending over many pages of the text.[1] It is not very meaningful therefore merely to total the number of alterations, but for what it is worth the total number of entries recording the alterations in Volume II below is 2,399.

A considerable number of the alterations seem to be quite trivial and unnecessary. They appear to have no doctrinal significance, and were presumably included in the belief that they would improve the clarity or literary style of the text. Whether they achieve that improvement is in many instances doubtful. The occurrence of these trivial changes does however provide an interesting insight into Malthus' approach (assuming that Malthus, not the

---

[1] For example, Chapter II, Section VII in ed. 1 (pp. 126–33) was replaced by Chapter II, Sections VI and VII in ed. 2 (pp. 111–35). See 1.126a, 1.133a.

editor, was responsible for them). They indicate a punctilious, even pedantic, attention to detail, which some readers might not regard as a virtue, but which is probably preferable to its opposite. Amongst these trivial alterations are to be found many instances where an impersonal style of expression is substituted for a more personal one.[1] Such alterations tell us little or nothing about Malthus' economic doctrines, but they indicate that his approach to the second edition was characterised by a desire to give to his statements a greater degree of formality. Other trivial changes are characterised by the removal of superfluous and non-essential words, and by an apparent desire to achieve a more concise expression.[2]

Many of the alterations consist of a movement away from an extreme and universal statement towards a more guarded and moderate statement.[3] These alterations have important, substantive, and not merely stylistic, significance. They are in keeping with the methodological principle enunciated by Malthus that many propositions in political economy require limitations and exceptions.[4] However, along with this movement towards more moderate statements, there were some instances – fewer in number but still significant – of a movement in the opposite direction, i.e. towards stronger, more definite, and more extreme statements.[5]

The alterations in the second edition of the *Principles* are more frequent and more extensive in the earlier chapters than in the later ones. This is true also for the Manuscript Revisions. There are several possible explanations for this uneven distribution. One possibility is that Malthus undertook the revision of the early chapters with an enthusiastic attention to detail, but that his enthusiasm waned as the task progressed. Another possible explanation is that in making his alterations Malthus had intended to proceed systematically from beginning to end of the *Principles*, but did not have time to complete the alterations before his death. If this interpretation is correct it would mean that the views expressed in the later, less-corrected part of the *Principles* are not necessarily Malthus' final views. A third possibility which must not be overlooked is that the editor of the second edition might have left out some of the alterations made by Malthus, and added some of his own. But another possible explanation of the relatively small number of alterations in the later chapters of the *Principles*, and one that seems to be supported by the evidence of Malthus' post-1820 writings, is that Malthus' views on the subject matter of the earlier chapters (Wealth, Productive and Unproductive Labour, Rent, Wages, and

---

[1] See, for example, 1.37e where 'I do not mean to say' was altered to 'it is not meant to be said', and 1.373a where 'I believe' was altered to 'it will be found'.
[2] See for example 1.26e.   [3] See for example 1.21a.
[4] 'there is no truth of which I feel a stronger conviction than that there are many important propositions in political economy which absolutely require limitations and exceptions;' (1.8).
[5] See for example 1.37c.

Profits) proved to be less settled than his views on the subject matter of the later chapters (Progress of Wealth).

Any attempt to assess the substantive significance of the alterations necessarily involves a number of difficult hermeneutical problems.

(1) As noted above, there are uncertainties about the extent of the editor's interventions, and hence about the extent to which the alterations can be attributed to Malthus.

(2) It cannot be automatically assumed that the omission of certain views from ed. 2 means that Malthus no longer held the omitted views. The omission might have been due to any one of a number of reasons, or to a combination of reasons. For example, a passage might have been omitted because Malthus believed it was not clearly expressed, or because he thought it was not directly relevant to the context; or because he considered he had dealt adequately with the matter elsewhere.

(3) Problems of interpretation arise with the introduction of new material, either with or without the alteration or omission of existing material. It cannot be automatically assumed that new material represents a substantive alteration. It is conceivable that new material was introduced to improve the literary style, or to achieve greater clarity of expression, without any intention to change the basic doctrines.

(4) The alterations are not necessarily contradictories or contraries.[1] In many instances in ed. 2, alterations take the form of a change in emphasis, or a change in the degree of assent given to a proposition, or a change from a universal to a more moderate position.

(5) A single alteration may be sufficient evidence in some cases of a change of opinion; in other cases, a single alteration, taken in isolation may be too slight to warrant any inference, but the cumulative evidence of a number of similar alterations may indicate, with some degree of probability, a change of opinion. An example of this occurred on the question of the effects of the introduction of machinery. Malthus' attitude as expressed in ed. 1 was quite optimistic. The cumulative evidence of a number of apparently insignificant alterations in ed. 2 suggests an even more optimistic attitude in ed. 2.

(6) In attempting to assess the analytical significance of the alterations between the two editions of the *Principles*, we must distinguish two criteria of significance. On the one hand, there are the ideas that Malthus appeared to regard as

---

[1] There are only a few instances in Malthus' writings where he explicitly stated that he had changed his opinion; for example, on the measure of value (see Malthus, *The Measure of Value Stated and Illustrated*, 1823, p. 23), and on the demand for labour (see 1.261g). He believed that Torrens treated him unjustly in saying that 'it is a singular fact, and one which it is not improper to impress upon the public, that, in the leading questions of economical science, Mr. Malthus scarcely ever embraced a principle, which he did not subsequently abandon.' (*An Essay on the External Corn Trade*, op. cit. pp. vii–ix). Ricardo agreed that this statement by Torrens was unfair. See Ricardo, *Works*, Vol. VI, pp. 202, 205.

significant; on the other hand, there are the ideas that the subsequent history of economics has regarded as significant. The two criteria do not always produce the same result. An example of this occurred in the case of the distinction between intrinsic and extrinsic value, introduced by Malthus in ed. 2 of the *Principles* (see 1.60e). Malthus believed that there had been 'no more fruitful source of error in the very elements of political economy' (*Principles* 2.60) than the failure to distinguish between intrinsic and extrinsic value. This distinction has been largely ignored in the subsequent history of economics.

(7) Problems of interpretation also arise from the fact that in some cases the changes appear to be contradictory and inconclusive. For example, in a number of alterations Malthus seems to suggest that land is distinct from capital, and that rent is distinct from profits. But other alterations seem to suggest the opposite view. The most that we can conclude from the alterations is that Malthus' views on these subjects were complex and subject to considerable variation over the years, and that it is difficult to be certain where he finally stood. But even this rather unsatisfactory conclusion could be useful as an antidote to facile and simplistic interpretations of Malthus' political economy.

(8) Any assessment of the degree of significance of the alterations will obviously depend on the point of view of the assessor. For example, the historian of economic thought interested in the development of concepts could consider some of the alterations extremely important, but they might not impress the applied economist looking for quick answers to current problems.

(9) Before reaching any definite conclusions about the change in Malthus' views on a particular issue, it is necessary to relate each particular change in the *Principles* to the totality of his views on that issue as expressed in other parts of the *Principles*, and indeed in his other works and correspondence. This task is rendered difficult by the fact that Malthus' views on a given topic were not always collected together in the same part of the *Principles*. For example, some of his most important statements on rent in ed. 1 and hence some of the most interesting alterations on rent in ed. 2, are to be found not in Chapter III which deals specifically with rent, but in Chapter II, Section IV which deals with labour-employed as a measure of value. Also, perhaps his best known statement on saving and investment ('No political economist of the present day can by saving mean mere hoarding') occurs not in Chapter V ('Of the Profits of Capital'), nor in Chapter VII, Section III ('Of Accumulation, or the Saving from Revenue to add to Capital'), but in Chapter I, Section II, dealing with productive and unproductive labour. In order to obtain a total picture of the alterations in his views on any given topic, it is often necessary therefore to collate alterations from many parts of the *Principles*.

In referring to the alterations between the two editions of the *Principles*, the author of the Advertisement to the Second Edition speaks exclusively of the alterations in Malthus' views on the measure of value. While these comments in the Advertisement provide useful background information on the development of Malthus' views on the measure of value, they have inadvertently done a great disservice by omitting any reference to the many topics, other than the measure of value, on which alterations occurred. Readers of the Advertisement could be excused for believing that ed. 2 of the *Principles* differed from ed. 1 only or mainly on the question of value. But that is not the case. The alterations on value constitute the largest single consecutive alteration, but the number of alterations, taken collectively, on other topics is at least as significant. And in view of the fact that the question of the measure of value appears to have become (rightly or wrongly) an economic backwater, the alterations on other topics perhaps have a much greater analytical significance than the alterations on value.

The great number and variety of the alterations in MR and ed. 2 show that, in the fifteen years following ed. 1, Malthus was continually engaged in reworking the *Principles* – deleting, adding, transposing, and rewriting. They show that although when the occasion required it he could write and publish a tract quickly to meet an urgent need or to influence a current social issue – for example, the first edition of the *Essay* in 1798, the pamphlet on the *High Price of Provisions* in 1800, and his defences of the East India College in 1813 and 1817 – he could also undertake the long and painstaking task of scholarly revision and refinement.

CONCLUSION

William Empson attributed the long delay in the publication of the second edition to Malthus' deference to the opinions of his adversaries who would expect replies in his second edition.[1] The author of the Advertisement in the second edition of the *Principles* attributed the long delay to Malthus' preoccupation with the publication of *The Measure of Value*, 1823, and *Definitions in Political Economy*, 1827, and to his other pursuits and his personal circumstances.[2] Whatever the explanation of the delay, it is obvious that, given Malthus' frequent expressions of his eagerness to publish a second edition, and the very large number of alterations he made in preparing for it, his failure to achieve the desired second edition must have been a source of continuing personal frustration.

Francis Horner said in 1808 that Malthus' great defect was 'a want of precision in the statement of his principles, and distinct perspicuity in upholding the consequences which he traces from them'.[3] If Malthus was in fact guilty of the want of precision alleged by Horner, the many changes between the two

---

[1] 'The periodical press, in the meantime, showed that he had all along active adversaries in the field, who would expect from him, on his reappearance, additional matters of greater novelty than he had it in his power honestly or usefully to produce' (Empson, 'Life, Writing and Character', p. 472).
[2] 'The intervention of these minor publications and Mr. Malthus' other pursuits prevented him from sooner devoting himself to the second edition of his *Political Economy*.' (*Principles* 2.x).
[3] Letter of 27 October 1808 to J. A. Murray in *Memoirs and Correspondence of Francis Horner, M.P.*, Vol. I, pp. 463–64.

editions of the *Principles* and in the Manuscript Revisions testify to his persistent attempts to overcome that fault. They also indicate that he was attentive to the views of his contemporaries, and was willing to adjust his own views in response to their criticisms when he deemed them justified. His attempts to respond to his critics and his involvement in current debates indicate that he came to regard the second edition as much more than a mere refinement and re-ordering of the first. But the influence of his critics on the two editions of the *Principles* should not be exaggerated. They certainly played an important role, but the critic who seems to have had the greatest influence on the development of Malthus' thought was Malthus himself. We must remember that Malthus was a professor for thirty years and that he was constantly engaged in preparing and revising lectures for his students. Many of the alterations between the two editions were probably the result of his attempts to define his own thoughts more clearly, and to fashion them into an intellectually justifiable and satisfying synthesis. His *Definitions in Political Economy* is evidence of this internalist dialectical process. Many of the alterations in ed. 2 of the *Principles* would have occurred even if there had been no external critics. This raises the question of how much longer, if he had survived, he would have spent in the preparation of the second edition. Because of the nature of the undertaking he had apparently set himself, it was probably inevitable that the second edition would be posthumous.

PRINCIPLES

OF

POLITICAL ECONOMY

CONSIDERED

WITH A VIEW TO THEIR PRACTICAL

APPLICATION.

———◆———

By the Rev. T. R. MALTHUS, M.A. F.R.S.

PROFESSOR OF HISTORY AND POLITICAL ECONOMY IN THE
EAST INDIA COLLEGE, HERTFORDSHIRE.

a

══════════

LONDON:

JOHN MURRAY, ALBEMARLE-STREET.   b

———

1820.   c

London: Printed by C. Roworth,
Bell yard, Temple-bar.

a

CONTENTS.

a

PRINCIPLES

OF

POLITICAL ECONOMY.

INTRODUCTION.

It has been said, and perhaps with truth, that the conclusions of Political Economy partake more of the certainty of the stricter sciences than those of most of the other branches of human knowledge. Yet we should fall into a serious error if we were to suppose that any propositions, the practical results of which depend upon the agency of so variable a being as man, and the qualities of so variable a compound as the soil, can ever admit of the same kinds of proof, or lead to the same certain conclusions, as those which relate to figure and number. There are indeed in political economy great general principles, to which exceptions are of the most rare occurrence, and prominent land-marks which may almost always be depended upon as safe guides; but even these, when examined, will be found to resemble in most particulars the great general rules in morals and poli-

tics founded upon the known passions and propensities of human nature : and whether we advert
to the qualities of man, or of the earth he is destined to cultivate, we shall be compelled to acknowledge, that the science of political economy
bears a nearer resemblance to the science of morals
and politics than to that of mathematics.

This conclusion, which could hardly fail to be
formed merely from a view of the subjects about
which political economy is conversant, is further
strengthened by the differences of opinion which
have prevailed among those who have directed a
large share of talent and attention to this study.

During the prevalence of the mercantile system,
the interest which the subject excited was confined almost exclusively to those who were engaged in the details of commerce, or expected
immediate benefit from its results. The differences
which prevailed among merchants and statesmen,
which were differences rather in practice than
principle, were not calculated to attract much attention. But no sooner was the subject raised into
a science by the works of the Economists and of
Adam Smith, than a memorable schism divided,
for a considerable time, the students of this new
branch of knowledge, on the fundamental questions—What is wealth? and from what source or
sources is it derived?

Happily for the interests of the science and its
usefulness to society, the Economists and Adam
Smith entirely agreed on some of those great
general principles which lead to the most impor-

tant practical conclusions; such as the freedom of trade, and the leaving every person, while he adheres to the rules of justice, to pursue his own interest his own way, together with some others: and unquestionably their agreement on these principles affords the strongest presumption of their truth. Yet the differences of the Economists and Adam Smith were not mere differences in theory; they were not different interpretations of the same phenomena, which would have no influence on practice; but they involved such views of the nature and origin of wealth, as, if adopted, would lead, in almost every country, to great practical changes, particularly on the very important subject of taxation.

Since the æra of these distinguished writers, the subject has gradually attracted the attention of a greater number of persons, particularly during the last twenty or thirty years. All the main propositions of the science have been examined, and the events which have since occurred, tending either to illustrate or confute them, have been repeatedly discussed. The result of this examination and discussion seems to be, that on some very important points there are still great differences of opinion. Among these, perhaps, may be reckoned—The definitions of wealth and of productive labour—The nature and measures of value—The nature and extent of the principles of demand and supply—The origin and progress of rent—The causes which determine the wages of labour and the profits of stock—The causes which practically retard and limit the progress of wealth—

The level of the precious metals in different countries—The principles of taxation, &c. On all these points, and many others among the numerous subjects which belong to political economy, differences have prevailed among persons whose opinions are entitled to attention. Some of these questions are to a certain degree theoretical; and the solution of them, though obviously necessary to the improvement of the science, might not essentially affect its practical rules; but others are of such a nature, that the determination of them one way or the other will necessarily influence the conduct both of individuals and of governments; and their correct determination therefore must be a matter of the highest practical importance.

In a science such as that of political economy, it is not to be expected that an *universal* assent should be obtained to all its important propositions; but, in order to give them their proper weight and justify their being acted upon, it is extremely desirable, indeed almost necessary, that a considerable *majority* of those who, from their attention to the subject, are considered by the public as likely to be the most competent judges, should agree in the truth of them.

Among those writers who have treated the subject scientifically, there is not perhaps, at the present moment, so general an agreement as would be desirable to give effect to their conclusions; and the writers who peculiarly call themselves practical, either draw no general inferences, or are so much influenced by narrow, partial, and sometimes interested views, that no reliance can be placed on them for the establishment of general rules. The last twenty or thirty years have besides been marked by a train of events of a most extraordinary kind; and there has hardly yet been time so to arrange and examine them as to see to what extent they confirm or invalidate the received principles of the science to which they relate.

The present period, therefore, seems to be unpropitious to the publication of a new systematic treatise on political economy. The treatise which we already possess is still of the very highest value; and till a more general agreement shall be found to take place, both with respect to the controverted points of Adam Smith's work, and the nature and extent of the additions to it, which the more advanced stage of the science has rendered necessary, it is obviously more advisable that the different subjects which admit of doubt should be treated separately. When these discussions have been for some time before the public, and a sufficient opportunity has been given, by the collision of different opinions and an appeal to experience, to separate what is true from what is false, the different parts may then be combined into a consistent whole, and may be expected to carry with it such weight and authority as to produce the most useful practical results.

The principal cause of error, and of the differences which prevail at present among the scientific writers on political economy, appears to me to be

α

a precipitate attempt to simplify and generalize; and while their more practical opponents draw too hasty inferences from a frequent appeal to partial facts, these writers run into a contrary extreme, and do not sufficiently try their theories by a reference to that enlarged and comprehensive experience which, on so complicated a subject, can alone establish their truth and utility.

To minds of a certain cast there is nothing so captivating as simplification and generalization. It is indeed the desirable and legitimate object of genuine philosophy, whenever it can be effected consistently with truth; and for this very reason, the natural tendency towards it has, in almost every science with which we are acquainted, led to crude and premature theories.

In political economy the desire to simplify has occasioned an unwillingness to acknowledge the operation of more causes than one in the production of particular effects; and if one cause would account for a considerable portion of a certain class of phenomena, the whole has been ascribed to it without sufficient attention to the facts, which would not admit of being so solved. I have always thought that the late controversy on the bullion question presented a signal instance of this kind of error. Each party being possessed of a theory which would account for an unfavourable exchange, and an excess of the market price above the mint price of bullion, adhered to that single view of the question, which it had been accustomed to consider as correct; and scarcely one writer seemed willing to to admit of the operation of both theories, the combination of which, sometimes acting in conjunction and sometimes in opposition, could alone adequately account for the variable and complicated phenomena observable.*

It is certain that we cannot too highly respect and venerate that admirable rule of Newton, not to admit more causes than are necessary to the solution of the phenomena we are considering, but the rule itself implies, that those which really are necessary must be admitted. Before the shrine of truth, as discovered by facts and experience, the fairest theories and the most beautiful classifications must fall. The chemist of thirty years ago may be allowed to regret, that new discoveries in the science should disturb and confound his previous systems and arrangements; but he is not entitled to the name of philosopher, if he does not give them up without a struggle, as soon as the experiments which refute them are fully established.

The same tendency to simplify and generalize, produces a still greater disinclination to allow of modifications, limitations, and exceptions to any rule or proposition, than to admit the operation of more causes than one. Nothing indeed is so unsatisfactory, and gives so unscientific and unmas-

α

β

a

* It must be allowed, however, that the theory of the Bullionists, though too exclusive, accounted for much the largest proportion of the phenomena in question; and perhaps it may be said with truth that the Bullion Report itself was more free from the error I have adverted to than any other work that appeared.

γ

terly an air to a proposition as to be obliged to
make admissions of this kind; yet there is no truth
of which I feel a stronger conviction than that
there are many important propositions in political
economy which absolutely require limitations and
exceptions; and it may be confidently stated that
the frequent combination of complicated causes,
the action and reaction of cause and effect on each
other, and the necessity of limitations and exceptions in a considerable number of important propositions, form the main difficulties of the science, and
occasion those frequent mistakes which it must be
allowed are made in the prediction of results.

To explain myself by an instance. Adam Smith
has stated, that capitals are increased by parsimony, that every frugal man is a public benefactor,*
and that the increase of wealth depends upon the
balance of produce above consumption.† That
these propositions are true to a great extent is
perfectly unquestionable. No considerable and
continued increase of wealth could possibly take
place without that degree of frugality which occasions, annually, the conversion of some revenue
into capital, and creates a balance of produce above
consumption; but it is quite obvious that they are
not true to an indefinite extent, and that the principle
of saving, pushed to excess, would destroy the motive to production. If every person were satisfied
with the simplest food, the poorest clothing, and
the meanest houses, it is certain that no other sort

* Wealth of Nations, Book II. c. iii. pp. 15—18. 6th edit.
† Book IV. c. iii. p. 250.

of food, clothing, and lodging would be in existence; and as there would be no adequate motive to the proprietors of land to cultivate well, not only the wealth derived from conveniences and luxuries would be quite at an end, but if the same divisions of land continued, the production of food would be prematurely checked, and population would come to a stand long before the soil had been well cultivated. If consumption exceed production, the capital of the country must be diminished, and its wealth must be gradually destroyed from its want of power to produce; if production be in a great excess above consumption, the motive to accumulate and produce must cease from the want of will to consume. The two extremes are obvious; and it follows that there must be some intermediate point, though the resources of political economy may not be able to ascertain it, where, taking into consideration both the power to produce and the will to consume, the encouragement to the increase of wealth is the greatest.

The division of landed property presents another obvious instance of the same kind. No person has ever for a moment doubted that the division of such immense tracts of land as were formerly in possession of the great feudal proprietors must be favourable to industry and production. It is equally difficult to doubt that a division of landed property may be carried to such an extent as to destroy all the benefits to be derived from the accumulation of capital and the division of labour, and to occasion the most extended poverty. There is here

a

then a point as well as in the other instance, though we may not know how to place it, where the division of property is best suited to the actual circumstances of the society, and calculated to give the best stimulus to production and to the increase of wealth and population. It follows clearly that no general rule can be laid down respecting the advantage to be derived from saving, or the division of property, without limitations and exceptions; and it is particularly worthy of attention that in cases of this kind, where the extremes are obvious and striking, but the most advantageous mean cannot be marked, that in the progress of society effects may be produced by an unnoticed approximation to this middle point, which are attributed to other causes, and lead to false conclusions.

The tendency to premature generalization occasions also, in some of the principal writers on political economy, an unwillingness to bring their theories to the test of experience. I should be the last person to lay an undue stress upon isolated facts, or to think that a consistent theory, which would account for the great mass of phenomena observable, was immediately invalidated by a few discordant appearances, the reality and the bearings of which, there might not have been an opportunity of fully examining. But certainly no theory can have any pretension to be accepted as correct, which is inconsistent with general experience. Such inconsistency appears to me at once a full and sufficient reason for its rejection.

Under such circumstances it must be either radically false, or essentially incomplete; and in either case, it can neither be adopted as a satisfactory solution of existing phenomena, nor acted upon with any degree of safety for the future.

The first business of philosophy is to account for things as they are; and till our theories will do this, they ought not to be the ground of any practical conclusion. I should never have had that steady and unshaken confidence in the theory of population which I have invariably felt, if it had not appeared to me to be confirmed, in the most remarkable manner, by the state of society as it actually exists in every country with which we are acquainted. To this test I appealed in laying it down; and a frequent appeal to this sort of experience is pre-eminently necessary in most of the subjects of political economy, where various and complicated causes are often in operation, the presence of which can only be ascertained in this way. A theory may appear to be correct, and may really be correct under given premises; it may further *appear* that these premises are the same as those under which the theory is about to be applied; but a difference, which might before have been unobserved, may shew itself in the difference of the results from those which were expected; and the theory may justly be considered as failing, whether this failure arises from an original error in its formation, or from its general inapplicability, or specific misapplication, to actual circumstances.

Where unforeseen causes may possibly be in operation, and the causes that are foreseen are liable to great variations in their strength and efficacy, an accurate yet comprehensive attention to facts is necessary, both to prevent the multiplication of erroneous theories, and to confirm and sanction those that are just.

The science of political economy is essentially practical, and applicable to the common business of human life. There are few branches of human knowledge where false views may do more harm, or just views more good. I cannot agree, therefore, with a writer in one of our most popular α critical journals, who considers the subjects of population, bullion, and corn laws in the same light as the scholastic questions of the middle ages, and puts marks of admiration to them expressive of his utter astonishment that such perishable stuff should engage any portion of the public attention.*

In the very practical science of political economy perhaps it might be difficult to mention three subjects more practical than those unfortunately selected for a comparison with scholastic questions. But in fact, most of the subjects which belong to it are peculiarly applicable to the common concerns of mankind. What shall we say of all the questions relating to taxation, various and extensive as they are? It will hardly be denied that they come home to the business and bosoms of mankind. What shall we say of the laws which regulate exchangeable value, or every act of pur-

* Quarterly Review, No. xxix. Art. viii.

chase and exchange which takes place in our markets? What of the laws which regulate the profits of stock, the interest of money, the rent of land, the value of the precious metals in different countries, the rates of exchange, &c. &c. ?

The study of the laws of nature is, in all its branches, interesting. Even those physical laws by which the more distant parts of the universe are governed, and over which, of course, it is impossible for man to have the slightest influence, are yet noble and rational objects of curiosity; but the laws which regulate the movements of human society have an infinitely stronger claim to our attention, both because they relate to objects about which we are daily and hourly conversant, and because their effects are continually modified by human interference.

There are some eminent persons so strongly attached to the received general rules of political economy, that, though they are aware that in practice some exceptions to them may occasionally occur; yet they do not think it wise and politic to notice them, for fear of directing the public attention too much and too frequently to exceptions, and thus weakening the force and utility of the general rules.   a

It is, for instance, one of the most general rules   b in political economy, that governments should not interfere in the direction of capital and industry, but leave every person, so long as he obeys the laws of justice, to pursue his own interest in his own way, as the best security for the constant

and equable supply of the national wants. Though
to this rule they allow that exceptions may possibly occur; yet thinking that the danger from the
officious meddling of governments is so much greater
than any which could arise from the neglect of
such exceptions, they would be inclined to make
the rule universal.

ab   In this, however, I cannot agree. Though
I should most readily allow that altogether more
evil is likely to arise from governing too much,
than from a tendency to the other extreme;
c   yet, still, if the consequences of not attending to
these exceptions were of sufficient magnitude and
frequency to be conspicuous to the public, I should
be decidedly of opinion, that the cause of general
principles was much more likely to lose than to
d   gain by concealment. Nothing can tend so
strongly to bring theories and general principles
into discredit as the occurrence of consequences,
e   from particular measures, which have not been
foreseen. Though in reality such an event forms
no just objection to theory, in the general and
proper sense of the term; yet it forms a most
valid objection to the specific theory in question,
as proving it in some way or other wrong; and
with the mass of mankind this will pass for an
impeachment of general principles, and of the
knowledge or good faith of those who are in the
habit of inculcating them. It appears to me, I
confess, that the most perfect sincerity, together
with the greatest degree of accuracy attainable,
founded upon the most comprehensive view of all

the circumstances of the case, are necessary to give that credit and circulation to general principles which is so desirable. And no views of temporary advantage, nor, what is more likely to operate, the fear of destroying the simplicity of a general rule, should ever tempt us to deviate from the strict line of truth, or to conceal or overlook any circumstances that may interfere with the universality of the principle.

There is another class of persons who set a very high value upon the received general rules of political economy, as of the most extensive practical use. They have seen the errors of the mercantile system refuted and replaced by a more philosophical and correct view of the subject; and having made themselves masters of the question so far, they seem to be satisfied with what they have got, and do not look with a favorable eye on new and further inquiries, particularly if they do not see at once clearly and distinctly to what beneficial effects they lead.

This indisposition to innovation, even in science, may possibly have its use, by tending to check crude and premature theories; but it is obvious that, if carried too far, it strikes at the root of all improvement. It is impossible to observe the great events of the last twenty-five years in their relation to subjects belonging to political economy, and sit down satisfied with what has been already done in the science. But if the science be manifestly incomplete, and yet of the highest importance, it would surely be most unwise to

restrain inquiry, conducted upon just principles,
even where the immediate practical utility of it
was not visible. In mathematics, chemistry, and
every branch of natural philosophy, how many are
the inquiries necessary to their improvement and
completion, which, taken separately, do not appear
to lead to any specifically advantageous purpose!
How many useful inventions, and how much valuable and improving knowledge would have been
lost, if a rational curiosity and a mere love of information had not generally been allowed to be a
sufficient motive for the search after truth !

I should not, therefore, consider it as by any
means conclusive against further inquiries in political economy, if they would not always bear
the rigid application of the test of *cui bono ?*   But
such, in fact, is the nature of the science, so inti-
mately is it connected with the business of mankind, that I really believe more of its propositions
will bear this test than those of any other department of human knowledge.

α

To trace distinctly the operations of that circle
of causes and effects in political economy which are
acting and re-acting on each other, so as to foresee
their results, and lay down general rules accordingly, is, in many cases, a task of very great difficulty.
But there is scarcely a single inquiry belonging
to these subjects, however abstruse and remote it
may at first sight appear, which in some point or
other does not bear directly upon practice. It is
unquestionably desirable, therefore, both with a
view to the improvement and completion of the

science, and the practical advantages which may be expected from it, that such inquiries should be pursued; and no common difficulty or obscurity should be allowed to deter those who have leisure and ability for such researches.

In many cases, indeed, it may not be possible to predict results with certainty, on account of the complication of the causes in action, the different degrees of strength and efficacy with which they may operate, and the number of unforeseen circumstances which are likely to interfere; but it is surely knowledge of the highest importance to be able to draw a line, with tolerable precision, between those cases where the expected results are certain, and those where they are doubtful; and further to be able satisfactorily to explain, in the latter case, the reasons of such uncertainty.

To know what can be done, and how to do it, is, beyond a doubt, the most valuable species of information. The next to it is, to know what cannot be done, and why we cannot do it. The first enables us to attain a positive good, to increase our powers, and augment our happiness: the second saves us from the evil of fruitless attempts, and the loss and misery occasioned by perpetual failure.

But these inquiries demand more time and application than the practical statesman, whom of all others they most nearly concern, can give to them. In the public measures of every state all are, no doubt, interested; but a peculiar responsibility, as well as interest, must be felt by those

who are the principal advisers of them, and have
the greatest influence in their enactment; and if
they have not leisure for such researches themselves, they should not be unwilling, under the
guidance of a sound discretion, to make use of the
advantages which may' be afforded by the leisure
of others. They will not indeed be justified in
taking any decided steps, if they do not themselves
see, or at least think they see, the way they are
going; but they may be fairly expected to make
use of all the lights which are best calculated to
illumine their way, and enable them to reach the
object which they have in view.

It may perhaps be thought that, if the great
principle so ably maintained by Adam Smith be
true, namely, that the best way of advancing a
people towards wealth and prosperity is *not* to interfere with them, the business of government, in
matters relating to political economy, must be
most simple and easy.

But it is to be recollected, in the first place, that
there is a class of duties connected with these subjects, which, it is universally acknowledged, belongs
to the Sovereign; and though the line appears to
be drawn with tolerable precision, when it is considered generally; yet when we come to particulars, doubts may arise, and certainly in many instances have arisen, as to the subjects to be included in this classification. To what extent education and the support of the poor should be public
concerns? What share the Government should
take in the construction and maintenance of roads,

canals, public docks? What course it should adopt
with regard to colonization and emigration, and in
the support of forts and establishments in foreign
countries? On all these questions, and many
others, there may be differences of opinion; and
on all these questions the sovereign and his minis-
ters are called upon to decide.

Secondly, every actual government has to administer a body of laws relating to agriculture,
manufactures, and commerce, which was formed at
a period comparatively unenlightened, and many
of which, therefore, it must be desirable to repeal: a
but to see fully the amount of partial evil arising b
from present change, and the extent of general
good to be effected by it, so as to warrant active
interference, requires no inconsiderable share of
knowledge and judgment; while to remain inac-
tive under such circumstances, can only be justified by a conviction, founded on the best grounds,
that in any specific change contemplated, taken in
all its consequences, the balance of evil will preponderate. c

Thirdly, there is one cause in every state which
absolutely impels the government to action, and
puts an end to the possibility of letting things alone.
This is the necessity of taxation; and as taxes cannot, in the nature of things, be imposed without interfering with individual industry and wealth, it
becomes a matter of the very highest importance to
know how they may take place with the least possible prejudice to the prosperity of the state, and
the happiness of individuals.

With regard to this latter subject indeed, it bears on so many points, that the truth or falsehood of the theories on all the principal questions in political economy would occasion, or at least ought to occasion, a practical difference in the mode of raising some of the actual taxes. It is well known that, if the theory of the Economists were true, all taxes should be laid on the land; and it depends entirely upon the general laws which regulate the wages of labour, the profits of stock, the rent of land, exchangeable value, the currencies of different countries, the production and distribution of wealth, &c. &c. whether any existing system of taxation be the best, or whether it might be altered for the better.

It is obviously, therefore, impossible for a government strictly to let things take their natural course; and to recommend such a line of conduct, without limitations and exceptions, could not fail to bring disgrace upon general principles, as totally inapplicable to practice.

It may, however, safely be asserted, that a propensity to govern too much is a certain indication of ignorance and rashness. The ablest physicians are the most sparing in the use of medicine, and the most inclined to trust to the healing power of nature. The statesman, in like manner, who knows the most of his business, will be the most unwilling to interrupt the natural direction of industry and capital. But both are occasionally called upon to interfere, and the more science they respectively possess, the more judiciously will they do it ; nor will the acknowledged propriety of interfering but little supersede, in any degree, the use of the most extensive professional knowledge in both cases.

One of the specific objects of the present work is to prepare the general rules of political economy   a for practical application, by a frequent reference to experience, and by taking as comprehensive a   b view as I can of all the causes that concur in the production of particular phenomena.

I am sufficiently aware, that in this mode of con-   c ducting inquiry, there is a chance of falling into errors of an opposite kind to those which arise from a tendency to simplification. Certain appearances, which are merely co-existent and incidental, may be mistaken for causes ; and a theory formed upon this mistake will unite the double disadvantage of being both complex and incorrect. I   d am inclined to think that Adam Smith occasionally fell into this error, and drew inferences from actual appearances, not warranted by general principles. From the low price of wheat, for instance, during the first half of the last century, he seems to infer that wheat is generally cheaper in rich   e than in poor countries; and from the small quantity of corn actually imported during that period, even in the scarcest years, he infers generally, that   f the quantity imported can never be such as to interfere with the home growth. The actual state of things at a subsequent period, and particularly during the last twenty-five years, has sufficiently shewn that these appearances were merely inci-

dental; thāt a very rich country may have its corn extremely dear, as we should naturally expect; and that importation in England has amounted to
a   more than $\frac{1}{10}$ instead of $\frac{1}{371}$* part of the crop raised
b   in the country; and may, therefore, essentially interfere with the home growth.

Aware, however, of my liability to this error on the one side, and to the error of not referring sufficiently to experience on the other, my aim will be to pursue, as far as I am able, a just mean between the two extremes, and to approach, as near I can, to the great object of my research—the truth.

Many of the doctrines of Adam Smith, which had been considered as settled, have lately been called in question by writers entitled to great attention; but they have often failed, as it appears to me, to make good their objections; and in all such cases I have thought it desirable to examine anew, with reference to such objections, the grounds on which his doctrines are founded.

It has been my wish to avoid giving to my work a controversial air. Yet to free it entirely from controversy, while one of my professed objects is to discuss controverted opinions, and to try their truth by a reference to an enlarged experience, is obviously not possible. There is one modern work, in particular, of very high reputation, some of the fundamental principles of which have appeared to me, after the most mature deliberation, to be erroneous; and I should not have done jus-

* Wealth of Nations, B. IV. c. ii. p. 190. 6th edit.

tice to the ability with which it is written, to the high authority of the writer, and the interests of the science of which it treats, if it had not specifically engaged a considerable portion of my attention. I allude to Mr. Ricardo's work, " *On the Principles of Political Economy* and *Taxation.*"

I have so very high an opinion of Mr. Ricardo's talents as a political economist, and so entire a conviction of his perfect sincerity and love of truth, that I frankly own I have sometimes felt almost staggered by his authority, while I have remained unconvinced by his reasonings. I have thought that I must unaccountably have overlooked some essential points, either in my own view of the subject, or in his; and this kind of doubt has been the principal reason of my delay in publishing the present volume. But I shall hardly be suspected of not thinking for myself on these subjects, or of not feeling such a degree of confidence in my own conclusions, after having taken full time to form them, as to be afraid of submitting them to the decision of the public.

To those who are not acquainted with Mr. Ricardo's work, and do not properly appreciate the ingenuity and consistency of the system which it maintains and developes with so much ability, I am apprehensive that I shall appear to have dwelt too long upon some of the points on which we differ. But as they are, for the most part, of great importance both theoretically and practically, and as it appeared to me extremely desirable, with a view to the interests of the science, that they should, if possible, be settled, I did not feel myself justified in giving less time to the consideration of them.

I am far from saying that I may not be wrong in the conclusions at which I have arrived, in opposition to those of Mr. Ricardo. But I am conscious that I have taken all the means to be right, which patient investigation and a sincere desire to get at the truth can give to the actual powers of my understanding. And with this consciousness, both with respect to the opinions I have opposed, and those which I have attempted to establish, I feel no reluctance in committing the results to the decision of the public.

T. R. MALTHUS.

East India College,
   Dec. 1, 1819.

CHAPTER I.

ON THE DEFINITIONS OF WEALTH AND PRO-   a
DUCTIVE LABOUR.

SECTION I.

On the Definitions of Wealth.

Of the subjects which have given rise to differences of opinion among political economists, the
definition of wealth is not the least remarkable.
Such differences could hardly have taken place, if
the definition had been obvious and easy; but, in
reality, the more the subject is considered, the
more it will appear difficult, if not impossible, to
fix on one not liable to some objection. In a
work, however, on a science the great object of
which is, to inquire into the causes which influence
the progress of wealth, it seems natural to look   b
for some definition of those objects, the increase or
decrease of which we are about to estimate; and
if we cannot arrive at perfect accuracy, so as to
embrace all we wish and exclude all we wish in   c
some short description, it seems desirable to ap-   d
proach as near to such a description as we can.   e
It is known not to be very easy to draw a distinct
line between the animal, vegetable, and mineral
kingdoms; yet the advantage of such a classifica-   f
tion is universally acknowledged; and no one, on

a account of a difficulty in a few cases of little consequence, would refuse to make use of so convenient an arrangement.

It has sometimes been said that every writer is at liberty to define his terms as he pleases, provided he always uses them strictly in the sense proposed. Such a liberty, however, may be fairly b doubted ; at least it must be allowed that if a person chooses to give a very inadequate or unusual definition in reference to the subject on which he proposes to treat, he may at once render his inquiries completely futile. If, for instance, a writer, professing to treat of the wealth of nations, were d to define wealth to consist exclusively of broad cloth, it is obvious that, however consistent he might be in the use of his terms, or however valuable a treatise he might produce on this one article, e he would evidently have given but very little information to those who were looking for a treatise f on wealth, according to the common acceptation of the term.

So important, indeed, is an appropriate definition, that perhaps it is not going too far to say, that the g comparative merits of the systems of the Econoh mists and Adam Smith depend mainly upon their different definitions of wealth and of productive i labour. If the definitions which the Economists have given of wealth and of productive labour be j correct, *their* system has the advantage : if the definitions which Adam Smith has given of wealth and of productive labour be the most correct, *his* system is superior.

Of those writers who have either given a regular definition of wealth, or have left the sense in which they understand the term to be collected from their works, some appear to have confined it within too narrow limits, and others to have extended it greatly too far.   In the former class the Economists stand pre-eminent.   They have confined wealth, or riches, to the neat produce derived from the land; and in so doing they have greatly diminished the value of their inquiries, in reference to the most familiar and accustomed sense in which the term wealth is understood.

Among the definitions which have extended the meaning of the term wealth too far, Lord Lauderdale's may be taken as an example.   He defines wealth to be, " All that man desires as useful and delightful to him." *

This definition obviously includes every thing, whether material or intellectual, whether tangible or otherwise, which contributes to the advantage or pleasure of mankind, and, of course, includes the benefits and gratifications derived from religion, from morals, from political and civil liberty, from oratory, from instructive and agreeable conversation, from music, dancing, acting, and other similar sources.   But an inquiry into the nature and causes of these kinds of wealth would evidently extend beyond the bounds of any single science.   If we wish to attain any thing like precision in our inquiries, when we treat of wealth,

* Inquiry into the Nature and Origin of Public Wealth, c. ii. p. 57. 2d edit.

we must narrow the field of inquiry, and draw
some line, which will leave us only those objects,
the increase or decrease of which is capable of
being estimated with more accuracy.

The line, which it seems most natural to draw,
is that which separates material from immaterial
objects, or those which are capable of accumulation and definite valuation, from those which rarely
admit of these processes, and never in such a degree as to afford useful practical conclusions.

Adam Smith has no where given a very regular
and formal definition of wealth; but that the
meaning which he attaches to the term is confined
to material objects, is, throughout his work, sufficiently manifest.   His prevailing description of
wealth may be said to be, " the annual produce
a   of land and labour."   The objections to it, as a
definition, are, that it refers to the sources of
wealth before we are told what wealth is, and that
b   it is besides not sufficiently discriminate, as it
c   would include all the useless products of the earth,
as well as those which are appropriated and enjoyed by man.

To avoid these objections, and to keep at an
d   equal distance from a too confined or too indis-
e   criminate sense of the term, I should define wealth
to be, those *material* objects which are necessary,
f   useful, or agreeable to mankind.   And I am inclined to believe, that the definition, thus limited,
includes nearly all the objects which usually enter
into our conceptions when we speak of wealth or
riches; an advantage of considerable importance,

so long as we retain these terms both in common   a
use, and in the vocabulary of political economy.

It is obviously, indeed, rather a metaphorical   b
than a strict use of the word wealth, to apply it to
every benefit or gratification of which man is susceptible; and we should hardly be prepared to
acknowledge the truth of the proposition which
affirmed, that riches were the sole source of human
happiness.

It may fairly, therefore, I think, be said, that   c
the wealth spoken of, in the science of political
economy, is confined to material objects.

A country will therefore be rich or poor accord-   d
ing to the abundance or scarcity with which these
material objects are supplied, compared with the   e
extent of territory; and the people will be rich
or poor according to the abundance with which   f
they are supplied, compared with the population.

SECTION II.

On Productive and Unproductive Labour.   g

THE question of *productive* labour is closely con-   h
nected with the definition of wealth.   Both the
Economists and Adam Smith have uniformly ap-   i
plied the term *productive* to that species of labour   j
which produces what they call wealth, accord-   k
ing to their several views of its nature and origin.
The Economists, therefore, who confine wealth to   l
the products of the soil, mean by *productive* labour   m
that labour alone which is employed upon the land.

Adam Smith, who considers all the material objects
which are useful to man as wealth, means by productive labour, that labour which realizes itself
either in the production or increased value of such
material objects.

This mode of applying the term, productive la-
a   bour, to the labour which is productive of wealth,
b   however wealth may be defined, is obviously useful,
and, with a view to clearness and consistency in the
use of the terms of political economy, should always be adhered to. But as some writers have not
used the terms in this way, and as those who have
been disposed so to use them have not agreed in
their definitions of wealth, it was to be expected
that the term *productive* labour should give rise to
great differences of opinion.

c   The doctrine laid down by Adam Smith on this
subject has been controverted by two opposite
parties, one of which has imputed to him an incorrect and unphilosophical extension of the term
productive to objects which it ought not to in-
d   clude, and others have accused him of a similar
want of precision for attempting to establish a dis-
e   tinction between different sorts of labour where no
distinction is to be found.

In proceeding to give my reasons for adopting
f   the opinion of Adam Smith, I shall first endeavour
to shew that some such classification of the differ-
g   ent kinds of labour is really called for in an in-
h   quiry into the nature and causes of the wealth of
nations, and that a considerable degree of confusion
would be introduced into the science of political

economy by an attempt to proceed without it. We shall be less disposed to be disturbed by plausible cavils, or even by a few just exceptions to the complete accuracy of a definition, if we are convinced that the want of precision which is imputed to it, is beyond comparison less in amount and importance than the want of precision which would result from the rejection of it.

In the first place then, it will readily be granted that as capital, in whatever way it may be defined, is absolutely necessary to the division of labour and the use of machinery, its powerful influence on the progress of national wealth must be considered as incontrovertibly established. But in tracing the cause of the different effects of produce employed as capital, and of produce consumed as revenue, we shall find that it arises from the different kinds of labour maintained by each; and in speaking, therefore, and treating of capital, it seems quite necessary to have some term for the kind of labour which it generally employs, in contradistinction to the kind of labour generally employed by revenue, in order to explain its nature and operation, and the causes of its increase.

Secondly, it is stated by Adam Smith, and it must be allowed to be stated justly, that the produce which is annually saved is as regularly consumed as that which is annually spent, but that it is consumed by a different set of people. If this be the case, and if saving be allowed to be the immediate cause of the increase of capital, it must

a

b

c

d

e

f

g

h

i

j

a   be absolutely necessary, in all discussions relating to the progress of wealth, to distinguish by some particular title a set of people who appear to act so important a part in accelerating this progress. Almost all the lower classes of people of every society are employed in some way or other, and if there were no grounds of distinction in their employments, with reference to their effects on the national wealth, it is difficult to conceive what would be the use of saving from revenue to add to capital, as it would be merely employing one set

b   of people in preference to another, when, according to the hypothesis, there is no essential difference

c   between them.　How then are we to explain the nature of saving, and the different effects of parsimony and extravagance upon the national capital? No political economist of the present day can by saving mean mere hoarding; and beyond this contracted and inefficient proceeding, no use of the

d   term, in reference to national wealth, can well be imagined, but that which must arise from a different application of what is saved, founded upon a real distinction between the different kinds of la-

e   bour which may be maintained by it.

      If the labour of menial servants be as productive of wealth as the labour of manufacturers, why should not savings be employed in their maintenance, not only without being dissipated, but with

f   a constant increase of value? But menial servants, lawyers, or physicians, who save from their salaries,

g   are fully aware that their savings would be immediately dissipated again if they were advanced to

themselves instead of being employed in the main-   a
tenance of persons of a different description. To
consider the expenditure of the unproductive labourers of Adam Smith, as advances made to themselves, and of the same nature as the advances of
the master-manufacturer to his workmen, would
be at once to confound the very useful and just
distinction between those who live upon wages
and those who live upon profits, and would render
it quite impossible to explain the frequent and important operations of saving from revenue to add
to capital, so absolutely necessary to the continued
increase of wealth.*

It is not the question at present whether saving   b
may or may not be carried too far (a point which
will be considered in its proper place); but whether
we can talk intelligibly of saving and accumulation,
and discuss their effects on national wealth without
allowing some distinction in the different kinds
of labour.

Thirdly, it has been stated by Adam Smith, and   α
stated truly, that there is a balance very different   c
from the balance of trade, which, according as it   d
happens to be favourable or unfavourable, occa-
sions the prosperity or decay of every nation: this   e

                                                          f

* One of the most able impugners of the doctrine of Adam
Smith respecting productive labour is Mr. Ganilh, in his valuable
Work on the various Systems of Political Economy ; but he appears to me to fail entirely, when he attempts to shew that savings
are preserved instead of being destroyed, when consumed by the
idle classes. I cannot understand in what sense it can be said that
menial servants annually reproduce the capital by which they are
fed. Book III. c. ii.

a is the balance of the annual produce and consumption. If in given periods the produce of a country

b exceeds its consumption, the means of increasing

c its capital will be provided, its population will soon increase, or the actual numbers will be better accommodated, and probably both. If the consumption in such periods fully equals the produce, no means of increasing the capital will be afforded, and the society will be nearly at a stand. If the

d consumption exceeds the produce, every succeeding period will see the society worse supplied, and its prosperity and population will be evidently on the decline.

e But if this balance be so important, if upon it depends the progressive, stationary, or declining state of a society, surely it must be of importance to distinguish those who mainly contribute to render this balance favourable from those who chiefly

f contribute to make the other scale preponderate. Without some such distinction we shall not be able to trace the causes why one nation is thriving and

g another is declining; and the superior riches of those countries where merchants and manufacturers abound, compared with those in which the

h retainers of a court and an overgrown aristocracy predominate, will not admit of an intelligible ex-

i planation.

 If a taste for idle retainers and a profusion of menial servants had continued among the great landholders of Europe from the feudal times to the present, the wealth of its different kingdoms would

j have been very different from what it now is.

Adam Smith has justly stated that the growing
taste of our ancestors for material conveniences
and luxuries, instead of personal services, was the
main cause of the change. Personal services neither   a
require nor generate capital; and while they continue the predominant taste, must necessarily divide the great mass of society into two classes,
the proprietors of land and their servants, the rich
and the poor, one of which is in a state of abject
dependance upon the other. But a taste for material objects, however frivolous, almost always
requires for its gratification the accumulation of
capital, and the existence of manufacturers or mer-   b
chants, wholesale dealers and retail dealers. The   c
face of society is thus wholly changed. A middle
class of persons, living upon the profits of stock,
rises into wealth and consequence. And an in-   d
creasing accumulation of capital almost exclusively
derived from the mercantile and manufacturing   e
classes effects, to a considerable extent, the division and alienation of those immense landed properties, which, if the fashion of personal services
had continued, might have remained to this time
nearly in their former state, and prevented the in-   f
crease of wealth on the land as well as elsewhere.

I am hardly aware how the causes of the increas-   g
ing riches and prosperity of Europe since the feudal
times could be traced, if we were to consider personal services as equally productive of wealth with
the labours of merchants and manufacturers.

Surely then some distinction between the different kinds of labour, with reference to their dif-

                                                          h

ferent effects on national wealth, must be admitted
to be not only useful but necessary; and if so, the
a   next question is, what this distinction should be,
b   and where the line between productive and unproductive labour should be drawn.

The opinion that the term, productive labour,
should be exclusively confined to the labour em-
c   ployed upon the land has been maintained by the
d   Economists and their followers. As another
opportunity will occur of discussing the general
merits of their system, it will only be necessary to
observe here that, whatever advantages their defi-
e   nition may boast in point of precision and consis-
f   tency, yet for the practical and useful purposes of
comparing different countries together, with re-
g   gard to all those objects which usually enter into
h   our conceptions when we speak of wealth, it is
much too confined. Two countries of the same
territory and population might possess the same
number of agricultural labourers, and even direct
the same quantity of skill and capital to the culti-
i   vation of the soil; and yet, if a considerable portion
of the remaining population in one of them consisted of manufacturers and merchants, and in the
other of menial servants and soldiers, the former
might have all the indications of wealth, and the
j   latter all the symptoms of poverty. The number
of agricultural labourers, therefore, cannot alone
determine the national wealth. We evidently
want some definition of productiveness, which
k   shall refer to the effects of manufacturing and
mercantile capital and skill; and unless we con-

sider the labour which produces these most important results as productive of riches, we shall find it quite impossible to trace the causes of those different appearances in different nations, which all persons, whatever may be their theories, universally agree in attributing to different degrees of wealth. a b

The opinion which goes to the opposite extreme of the one here noticed, and calls all labour equally productive, has already been almost sufficiently considered in the endeavour to shew, that a distinction between the different kinds of labour is really wanted in an inquiry into the nature and causes of the wealth of nations. c

I shall only add here, that some such distinction must be considered as so clearly the corner-stone of Adam Smith's work, and the foundation on which the main body of his reasonings rests, that, if it be denied, the superstructure which he has raised upon it must fall to the ground. Of course I do not mean to say, that his reasonings should not fall if they are erroneous; but it appears to me in some degree inconsistent, in those who allow of no distinction in the different kinds of labour, to attribute any considerable value to an *Inquiry into the nature and causes of the Wealth of Nations,* in which the increase of the quantity and skill of what is called productive labour is the main hinge on which the progress of national opulence and prosperity is made to turn. d e f g h

There is, indeed, another way of considering the subject, which though different from that of i

Adam Smith, would not invalidate his reasonings, and would merely require a slight alteration in the terms used.

a   If we do not confine wealth to tangible and material objects, we might call all labour productive, but productive in different degrees; and the only change that would be required in Adam Smith's work, on account of this mode of considering the subject, would be, the substitution of the terms more productive and less productive, for those of productive and unproductive.

b   All labour, for instance, might be stated to be productive of value to the amount of the value paid for it, and in proportion to the degree in which the produce of the different kinds of labour, when sold at the price of free competition, exceeds in value the price of the labour employed upon them.

c   Upon this principle the labours of agriculture would, generally speaking, be the most productive; because the produce of nearly all the land actually in use is not only of sufficient exchangeable value to pay the labourers employed upon it, but the profits of the stock advanced by the farmers, and the rents of the land let by the proprietors. Next to the labours of agriculture, those labours would in general be most productive the operations of which were most assisted by capital or the results of previous labour, as in all those cases the exchangeable value produced would most exceed the value of the labour employed in the production, and would support, in the shape of profits, the greatest number of additional persons, and tend most to the accumulation of capital.

The labour least productive of wealth would be   a
that, the results of which were only equal in exchangeable value to the value paid for such labour,
which would support therefore no other classes of
society but the labourers actually employed, would
replace little or no capital, and tend the least directly and effectively towards that kind of accumulation which facilitates future production. In
this last division of productive labour would, of
course, be found all the unproductive labourers of
Adam Smith.

This mode of considering the subject has, per-   b
haps, some advantages in particular points over
that of Adam Smith. It would establish a useful
and tolerably accurate scale of productiveness, instead of dividing labour only into two kinds, and
drawing a hard line of distinction between them.
It would determine, in the very definition, the
natural pre-eminence of agriculture, which Adam
Smith is obliged to explain afterwards, and, at the
same time, shew the numerous cases where an increase of manufacturing and mercantile labour
would be more productive, both to the state and
to individuals, than an increase of agriculture; as
in all those where, from a greater demand for
manufactured and mercantile products, compared
with the produce of the land, the profits of manufacturing and mercantile capital were greater than
both the rent and profits combined of labour employed upon new and less fertile land.

It would answer sufficiently to all the reason-   c
ings of Adam Smith on the accumulation of capi-

tal, the distinction between capital and revenue, the nature and effects of saving, and the balance of produce and consumption, merely by using the terms more and less productive, for productive and unproductive; and would have the additional advantage of keeping more constantly in view the necessary union of capital and skill with the more productive kinds of labour; and thus shew the reason why all the labourers of a savage nation might, according to Adam Smith, be productive, and yet the nation increase very slowly in wealth and population, while a rapid increase of both might be taking place in an improved country under a proportion of productive labourers very much inferior.

a   With regard to the kinds of labour which Adam Smith has called unproductive, and for which classification his theory has been most objected to, their productiveness to the amount of their worth in the estimation of the society, varying, of course, according to the different degrees of skill acquired, and the different degrees of plenty or scarcity in which they are found, would be fully allowed, though they would still always be distinguished from those more productive kinds of labour which support other classes of the society besides the labourers themselves.

b   Agricultural labour would stand in the first rank, for this simple reason, that its gross produce is sufficient to maintain a portion of all the three great classes of society; those who live upon rent, those who live upon profits, and those who live

upon wages. Manufacturing and mercantile labour would stand in the next rank; because the
value of its produce will support a portion of two
of these orders of society. And the unproductive
labourers of Adam Smith would stand in the third
rank of productiveness; because their labours directly support no other classes but themselves.

This seems to be a simple and obvious classifica-   a
tion, and places the different kinds of labour in a
natural order with regard to productiveness, without interfering in any respect with their mutual
dependance on each other as stimulants to each
other's increase.

The great objection to this scale of productive-   b
ness is that, at its first setting out, it makes the
circumstance of the payment made for any particular kind of exertion, instead of the quality of
the produce, the criterion of its being productive.
According to Adam Smith, the exertion which
produces a pair of stockings is productive labour,
whether they are knit by a lady for her amusement, or made by a regular stocking-weaver; but,
according to the present theory, as no payment
has been made for them, they cannot be considered
as wealth. Upon the same principle the song of
a strolling actress, or the declamation of a speaker
at the Westminster Forum, would be the result of
productive labour, because paid for; while a very
superior song by a lady, or a speech in the House
of Commons from the first orator of the age,
abounding in eloquence and information, would be   c
unproductive.

a   And yet, if we once desert matter, and still
make no distinction of this kind, with reference to
payment, we are at once thrown upon a field so
wide, as utterly to confound all attempts to estimate the comparative quantity of productive labour in different countries.   If the exertion which
produces a song, whether paid for or not, be productive labour, why should the exertion which
produces the more valuable result of instructive
and agreeable conversation be excluded? why
should we exclude the efforts necessary to dis-
cipline our passions, and become obedient to all
the laws of God and man, the most valuable of all
labours? why, indeed, should we exclude any exertion, the object of which is to obtain happiness
or avoid pain, either present or future? and yet
under this description may be comprehended the
exertions of every human being during every moment of his existence.   It is quite clear, therefore,
that, with any view to the use which may be made
of the term, it must be more confined.

b   It may be said, indeed, with regard to the term
labour, that it seems to imply valuation and payment, and has nothing to do with unbought, voluntary exertions.   But the whole difficulty returns
in the definition of riches; and if we do not confine them to material objects, and yet wish to make
some practical use of the term in comparing different countries together, we must include in our
definition only those personal services which are
bought, and thus draw the line which separates
what ought to be called riches from what ought

not to be so denominated, between objects which
may in all respects be precisely the same, except
that one is the result of paid labour, and the other
of unbought exertions.

If, for instance, we were to define wealth to be
whatever has value in exchange, it is obvious that
acting, dancing, singing, and oratory would sometimes be wealth and sometimes not; and even
with regard to food and the most essential necessaries of life, excessive plenty or the custom of
producing without exchanging, would render the
definition nugatory.

   a

If, in denominating personal services wealth, we
do not look to the quality of what is produced,
but merely to the effect of the payment received
for it in stimulating other wealth, this is introducing a new and separate consideration, which
has no relation to the direct production of wealth.
In this view it will be seen that I attach very great
importance to the unproductive labourers of Adam
Smith; but this is evidently not as producers themselves, but as stimulating others to produce, by the
power which they possess of making a demand in
proportion to the payment they have received. In
this sense the mortgagee and public creditor are
productive labourers to the amount of what they
receive.   But though the division of property
occasioned by these classes of society may be useful, and tend indirectly to stimulate the production of wealth by increasing demand, it would be
confounding all natural distinctions to call them
productive labourers.   It would be equally incor-

   b

   c

   d

   e

rect to assert that the unproductive labourers of
Adam Smith necessarily create the wealth which
a   pays them. It is true that the desire to enjoy the
convenience or parade of personal attendance and
b   the benefit of medical advice has a strong tendency
c   to stimulate industry; but they are both purchased
in large quantities by persons who have no means
of increasing their incomes in consequence of this
expenditure, and sometimes they are bought by
the actual destruction of capital, and the positive
d   diminution of the power of production. Though
we allow, therefore, fully their tendency to act as
e   a stimulus to the production of wealth, yet they
f   can never be said necessarily to create it; and
even under the circumstances most favourable to
their influence, their operation is obviously indirect, and not immediate.

When we consider then the difficulties which present themselves on every supposition we can make,
it may fairly be doubted whether it is probable that
we shall be able to find a distinction more useful
for practical purposes, and, on the whole, less objectionable in point of precision, than that of Adam
Smith; which draws the line that distinguishes
riches from other kinds of value, between what is
g   matter and what is not matter, between what has
duration and what has no duration, between what
is susceptible of accumulation and definite valuation, and what is without either one or both of
these essential properties.

Some degree of duration, and a consequent sus-
ceptibility of accumulation, seems to be essential

to our usual conceptions of wealth, not only because produce of this kind seems to be alone capable of forming those accumulations which tend so
much to facilitate future production, but because
they alone contribute to increase that store reserved   a
for consumption, which is certainly one of the most   b
distinguishing marks of riches compared with poverty. The characteristic of poverty seems to be
to live from hand to mouth. The characteristic of   c
riches is to have a store to apply to for the commodities wanted for immediate consumption. But   d
in every case of productive labour, as explained by
Adam Smith, there is always a period, though in
some cases it may be very short, when either the
stock destined to replace a capital, or the stock reserved for immediate consumption is distinctly
augmented by it; and to this quality of adding to
the national stock, the term, enriching or productive of riches seems to be peculiarly appropriate.

But it is not enough that it should be susceptible of accumulation, and of adding to the national
stock, to entitle it to be called productive according to the general meaning of Adam Smith. In   e
order to make the term useful for practical purposes, the kind of labour to which it refers should   f
be susceptible of some sort of definite valuation.
The laws of the legislator, the precepts of the moralist, and the conclusions of the natural philosopher, may certainly be said to be susceptible of
accumulation and of receiving assistance from past
labour; but how is it possible to estimate them, or
to say to what amount the country has been en-

a riched by them? whereas the labour which is the necessary condition of the supply of material objects is estimated in the price at which they are sold, and may fairly be presumed to add to the wealth of the country an amount at least equal to
b the value paid for such labour. And probably,
c with few or no exceptions, it is only the kind of labour which is realized upon material products that is at once susceptible of accumulation and definite valuation.

d It has been observed by Monsieur Garnier in his valuable edition of the *Wealth of Nations,* that it seems very strange and inconsistent to denominate musical instruments riches, and the labour which produces them productive, while the music which they yield, and which is the sole object for which they are made, is not to be considered in the same light; and the performers, who can alone put them to their proper use, are called unproductive
α labourers.* But the difference between material products and those which are not matter sufficiently warrants the distinction in point of precision and consistency; and the utility of it is immediately obvious from the facility of giving a definite valuation to the instruments, and the absolute impossibility of giving such a valuation to all the tunes which may be played upon them.

It has also been observed by the same authority that it is still more inconsistent to denominate the clerk of a merchant a productive labourer, and a

* Vol. V. Note xx.

clerk employed by the government, who may in   a
some cases have precisely the same kind of business to do, an unproductive labourer.*   To this,   α
however, it may be replied, that in all business
conducted with a view to the profit of individuals,
it may fairly be presumed that there are no more   b
clerks or labourers of any kind employed, nor with
higher salaries, than necessary.   But the same pre-   c
sumption cannot be justly entertained with regard   d
to the business of government; and as the results
of the labours of its servants are not brought to
market, nor their salaries distributed with the same
rigid attention to the exchangeable value of their
services, no just criterion is afforded for determining this value.   e

At the same time it may be remarked, that if a
servant of government performs precisely the same   f
kind of labour in the preparation or superintendance of material products as the servant of a merchant, he ought to be considered as a productive
labourer, and one among the numerous instances   g
which are always occurring of productive labourers,
or labourers occasionally productive, to be found
among those classes of society which, with regard   h
to the great mass of their exertions, may with propriety be characterized as unproductive.   This kind
of exception must of course frequently happen,
not only among the servants of government, but
throughout the whole range of menial service, and
in every other situation in society.   Almost every

* Vol. V. Note xx.

person indeed must occasionally do some productive labour; and the line of separation which
Adam Smith has drawn between productive and
unproductive labour may be perfectly distinct, although the denomination which he has given to the
different classes of society, founded on their general character, must unavoidably be inaccurate with
regard to the exertions of some individuals.

a   It should also be recollected that Adam Smith
b   fully allows the value and importance of many
   sorts of labour which he calls unproductive. From
   the enumeration indeed which he has made of
c   these different sorts, he must be aware that some
d   of them produce a value with which the results of
   the labour employed in making ribbands and laces,
e   or indeed of any other labour but that which directly supplies our most pressing physical wants,
   cannot for a moment be compared. Indirectly indeed and remotely, there cannot be a doubt that
   even the supply of these physical wants is most
   powerfully promoted by the labours of the moralist,
   the legislator, and those who have exerted them-
f   selves to obtain a good government; but the main
   value of these labours evidently depends upon the
g   encouragement which they give to the full deve-
h   lopment of talents and industry, and their consequent invariable tendency to increase the quantity
i   of material wealth. So far, therefore, as they contribute to promote this supply, their general effect,
j   though not its precise amount, will be estimated in
k   the quantity of those material objects which the
   country can command; and so far as they contri-

bute to other sources of happiness besides those
which are derived from matter, it may be more   a
correct to consider them as belonging to a class of
objects, many of which cannot, without the greatest   b
confusion, be made to enter into the gross calcula-   c
tions which relate to national wealth. To estimate
the value of Newton's discoveries or the delight
communicated by Shakspeare and Milton by the
price at which their works have sold, would be but
a poor measure of the degree in which they have
elevated and enchanted their country ; nor would
it be less groveling and incongruous to estimate the
benefit which the country has derived from the
Revolution of 1688 by the pay of the soldiers, and
all other payments concerned in effecting it.

On the whole, therefore, allowing that the labours of the moralist and the manufacturer, the
legislator and the lacemaker, the agriculturist and
the vocal performer, have all for their object the
gratification of some want or wish of mankind, it
may still be the most natural, useful, and correct   d
classification which the subject will admit, first to
separate, under the name of wealth or riches, every
thing which gratifies the wants of man by means
of material objects, and then to denominate productive, every kind of labour which is directly productive of wealth, that is, so directly, as to be estimated in the value of the objects produced.   e

The reader will see that I have not introduced   f
this discussion with a view to the establishment of
any nice and subtle distinctions without a practical
object. My purpose is to shew that there is really   g

a   some difficulty in the definition of wealth, and of
productive labour; but that this difficulty should
not deter us from adopting any classifications which
b   are really useful in conducting inquiry; that in
treating of the nature and causes of the wealth of
nations a distinction between the different sources
of gratification and the different kinds of labour
c   seems to be not only highly useful, but almost absolutely necessary; and consequently that we should
be satisfied with the best classification which we
can get on these subjects, although it may not in
all its parts be unobjectionable.

CHAPTER II.

ON THE NATURE AND MEASURES OF VALUE.   a

SECTION I.

Of the different Sorts of Value.   b

Most writers in treating of the nature of value,   c
have considered it as having two different meanings, one, value in use, and the other, value in exchange. It may be questioned whether in fact we   d
are in the habit of using the term in the first of
these two senses. We do not often hear of the
value of air and water, although they are bodies in
the highest degree useful, and indeed essentially
necessary to the life and happiness of the human   e
race. It may be admitted, however, that the term,   f
taken perhaps in a metaphorical rather than a lite-   g
ral sense, may imply, and is sometimes used to imply, whatever is necessary or beneficial to us, and   h
in this sense may apply, without impropriety, to a   i
clear spring of water or to a fine air, although no
question could arise respecting their value in exchange.

As this meaning, therefore, of the word value
has already been admitted by many writers into
the vocabulary of political economy, and, although
not much sanctioned by custom, is justifiable in a   j
metaphorical if not in a literal sense, it may not be

worth while to reject it; and it need only be observed that as the application of the word value in
this way is very much less frequent than in the
other, it should never appear alone, but should always be marked by the addition, *in use.*

a   Value in exchange is founded, as the term seems
to imply, on the will and power to exchange one
commodity for another. It does not depend merely
upon the scarcity in which commodities exist, nor
upon the inequality of their distribution; but upon
the circumstance of their not being distributed according to the wills and powers of individuals, or
in such quantities to each, as the wills and powers
of individuals will enable them ultimately to effect
by means of exchanges.

b   If nature were to distribute, in the first instance,
all her goods precisely as they are ultimately distributed previous to consumption, there would be
no question of exchanges or exchangeable value,
and yet the mass of commodities would both exist
in a degree of scarcity and be very unequally divided.

c   In this distribution one man might have only
bread, and another venison and claret in addition to
bread. The man who had only bread might wish
to make an exchange, but would not have the
power, and the man who had venison and claret
besides bread would have the power to make an
exchange, but not the wish. Under these circumstances the commodities possessed by each would
not be brought into contact, and the relative value
of bread and venison would never be determined.

d   To determine this, it is necessary that the posses-

sors of venison should want bread, as well as that the
possessors of bread should want venison, and when
this was the case, venison and bread would soon be
brought into comparison with each other, and the
means afforded of ascertaining their relative values.

Every exchange, therefore, must imply, not   a
only the power and will to give some article in ex-   b
change for one more wanted, but a reciprocal de-   c
mand in the party possessing the article wanted,   d
for the article proposed to be exchanged for it.   e

When this reciprocal demand exists, the rate at   f
which the exchange is made, or the portion of one
commodity which is given for an assigned portion   g
of the other, will depend upon the relative estima-   h
tion in which they are held by the parties, founded
on the desire to possess, and the difficulty or faci-   i
lity of procuring possession.

Owing to the necessary difference of the desires   j
and powers of individuals, it is probable that the
contracts thus made were in the first instance very   k
different from each other.   Among some individuals it might be agreed to give six pounds of
bread for a pound of venison, and among others
only two.   But the man who was ready and willing to give six pounds of bread for a pound of
venison, if he heard of a person at a little distance
who would take two pounds for the same quantity,
would of course not continue to give six; and the
man who would consent to give a pound of venison for only two pounds of bread, if he could any
where else obtain six, would not continue to make
an exchange from which he derived only two.   l

After a certain time it might be expected that an average would be formed, founded upon all the offers of bread, compared with all the offers of venison. And thus, as is very happily described by Turgot, a current value of all commodities in frequent use would be established.*

It would be known, not only that a pound of venison was worth four pounds of bread, but that it was also worth perhaps a pound of cheese, a quarter of a peck of wheat, a quart of wine, a certain portion of leather, &c. &c. each of an average quality.

Each commodity would in this way measure the exchangeable value of all others, and would, in its turn, be measured by any one of them. Each commodity would also be a representative of value. The possessor of a quart of wine might consider himself in possession of a value equal to four pounds of bread, a pound of cheese, a certain portion of leather, &c. &c. and thus each commodity would, with more or less accuracy and convenience, possess two essential properties of money, that of being both a representative and measure of value.

But long before it is conceivable that this general valuation of commodities, with regard to each other, should have taken place to any considerable extent, or with any tolerable degree of accuracy, a great difficulty in the estimation of relative value would be constantly recurring, from the want of a reciprocal demand. The possessor of

* Formation et Distribution des Richesses, § xxxv.
† Id. § xli.

venison might want bread, but the possessor of
bread to whom he applies may not want venison,   a
or by no means that quantity which the owner   b
would wish to part with. This want of reciprocal
demand must occasion, in many instances, and in   c
places not very remote from each other, the most
unequal exchanges, and except in large fairs or
markets, where a great quantity and variety of
commodities were brought together, would seem
almost to preclude the possibility of any thing like
such a general average valuation of commodities as   d
has been just described.

Every man, therefore, in order to secure this reciprocal demand, would endeavour, as is justly
stated by Adam Smith,* so to carry on his business as to have by him, besides the produce of his
own particular trade, some commodity for which
there was so general and constant a demand, that
it would scarcely ever be refused in exchange for
what he wanted. In order that each individual
in a society should be furnished with that share of
its whole produce to which he is entitled by his   e
wants and powers, it is not only necessary that
there should be some measure of this share, but
some medium by which he can obtain it in the
quantity and at the time best suited to him.

The constantly recurring want of some such
medium occasioned the use of various commodities
for this purpose in the early periods of society.

Of these, cattle seem to have been the most
general. Among pastoral nations cattle are not   f

* Wealth of Nations, Book I. c. iv.   g

a   only kept without difficulty or loss by those who may receive them, but as they form the principal possessions and wealth of society in this stage of its progress, they must naturally have been the subject of frequent exchanges, and their exchangeable value, in consequence, compared with other commodities, would be pretty generally known.

It seems to be quite necessary indeed, that the commodity chosen for a medium of exchange should, in addition to the other qualities which may fit it for that purpose, be in such frequent b   use, as that its current value should be tolerably well established.

A curious and striking proof of this, is that, notwithstanding the peculiar aptitude of the precious metals to perform the functions of a medium of exchange, they had not been used for that purpose in Mexico at the period of its conquest by the Spaniards, although these metals were in some degree of plenty as ornaments, and although the want of some medium of exchange was clearly evinced by the use of the nuts of cacao for that purpose.*

It is probable that as the practice of smelting and refining the ores of the precious metals had not yet been resorted to, the supply of them was not sufficiently steady, nor was the use of them sufficiently c   general to fit them for the purpose required.

In Peru, where the precious metals were found by the Spaniards in much greater abundance, the practice of smelting and refining the richest ores had begun to prevail, although no shafts had been sunk

α   * Robertson's America, Vol. III. Book vii. p. 215.

to any depth in the earth.* But in Peru the state
of property was so peculiar, and so nearly ap-   a
proaching to a community of goods, that a medium
of exchange seems not to have been called for, at
least, there is no account of the use of either of the
precious metals or of any other commodity in the
capacity of money.

In the Old World, the art of smelting and refin-   b
ing the ores of gold, silver, and copper, seems to
have been known to some of the most improved
nations of which we have accounts, from the earliest ages; and as soon as the annual accumulations   c
of these metals and the means used to obtain them
had rendered their supply to a certain degree
steady, and they had been introduced into common use in the shape of ornaments, instruments,   d
and utensils, their other peculiar and appropriate
qualities, such as their durability, divisibility, uniformity of substance, and great value in a small
compass, would naturally point them out as the
best commodity that could be selected to answer
the purpose of a measure of value and medium of   e
exchange.

But when they were adopted as the general
measure of value, it would follow of course that
all commodities would be most frequently com-   f
pared with this measure. The precious metals   g
would be, on almost all occasions, the commodity
named, and might properly, therefore, be called the
nominal value of the commodities to the measure
of which they were applied.

* Robertson's America, Vol. III. Book vii. p. 252.

a   This sort of value has sometimes been exclusively designated by the name of price; and though it is not uncommon to speak of the price of a commodity in labour, or in other commodities, and the term when so used is sufficiently intelligible, yet it would certainly be better to confine it strictly to the value of commodities estimated in the precious metals, or in the currencies of different countries which profess to represent them; and, indeed, when used without the above additions, this is what the term is always understood to mean. Price then may be considered as a more confined term than value, and as representing one, and one only of the senses in which the more general term is used.

b   The introduction of a measure which determined the nominal and relative value of commodities,
c   and of a medium which would be accepted at all times in exchange for them, was a most important step in the progress of society, and tended to facilitate exchanges and stimulate production to an extent which, without such an instrument, would have been perfectly impossible.

It is very justly observed by Adam Smith, that it is the nominal value of goods, or their prices only, which enter into the consideration of the
d   merchant. It matters very little to him whether a hundred pounds, or the goods which he purchases
e   with this sum, will command more or less of the necessaries and conveniences of life in Bengal than in London. What he wants is an instrument by which he can obtain the commodities in which he

deals and estimate the relative values of his sales
and purchases.   His returns come to him wherever
he lives; and whether it be in London or Calcutta,   a
his gains will be in proportion to the excess of the   b
amount at which he sells his goods compared with
the amount which they cost him to bring to market, estimated in the precious metals.

But though the precious metals answer very   c
effectually the most important purposes of a measure of value, in the encouragement they give to
the distribution and production of wealth; yet it
is quite obvious that they fail as a measure of the
exchangeable value of objects in different countries, or at different periods in the same country.

If we are told that the wages of day-labour in   d
a particular country are, at the present time, four-
pence a day; or that the revenue of a particular
sovereign, 700 or 800 years ago, was 400,000*l.* a
year; these statements of nominal value convey no
sort of information respecting the condition of the
lower classes of people, in the one case, or the resources of the sovereign, in the other.   Without   e
further knowledge on the subject, we should be
quite at a loss to say, whether the labourers in the
country mentioned were starving, or living in great
plenty; whether the king in question might be
considered as having a very inadequate revenue,
or whether the sum mentioned was so great as to
be incredible.*

* Hume very reasonably doubts the possibility of William the   f
Conqueror's revenue being £400,000 a year, as represented by an
ancient historian, and adopted by subsequent writers.

a

b

    It is quite obvious that in cases of this kind, and they are of constant recurrence, the value of wages, incomes, or commodities estimated in the precious metals, will be of little use to us alone.

c

What we want further is some estimate of a kind which may be denominated real value in exchange, implying the quantity of the necessaries and conveniences of life which those wages, incomes, or commodities will enable the possessor of them to

d

command. Without this knowledge, the nominal values above mentioned may lead us to the most erroneous conclusions; and in contradistinction to such values, which often imply an increase or decrease of wealth merely in name, the term real value in exchange seems to be just and appropriate, as implying an increase or decrease in the power of commanding real wealth, or the most substantial goods of life.

e

    That a correct measure of real value in exchange would be very desirable cannot be doubted, as it would at once enable us to form a just estimate and comparison of wages, incomes, and commodities, in all countries and at all periods; but when we consider what a measure of real value in exchange implies, we shall feel doubtful whether any one commodity exists, or can easily be supposed to exist, with such properties, as would qualify it to become a standard measure of this kind. Whatever article, or even mass of articles, we refer to, must itself be subject to change; and all that we can hope for is an approximation to the measure which is the object of our search.

We are not however justified, on this account,   a
in giving a different definition of real value in exchange, if the definition already adopted be at
once the most usual and the most useful. We
have the power indeed arbitrarily to call the labour
which has been employed upon a commodity its
real value; but in so doing we use words in a different sense from that in which they are custom-
arily used; we confound at once the very important distinction between *cost* and *value*; and render
it almost impossible to explain, with clearness, the
main stimulus to the production of wealth, which,
in fact, depends upon this distinction.

The right of making definitions must evidently   b
be limited by their propriety, and their use in the
science to which they are applied. After we have
made a full allowance for the value of commodities
in use, or their intrinsic capacities for satisfying
the wants of mankind, every other interpretation
of the term value seems to refer to some power in
exchange; and if it do not refer to the power of
an article in exchange for some one commodity
named, such as money, it must refer to its power
in exchange for 3 or 4, 5 or 6, 8 or 10 together,
to the mass of commodities combined, or to its
power of commanding labour which most nearly
represents this mass.

There can be no question of the propriety and   c
usefulness of a distinction between the power of a
commodity in commanding the precious metals,
and its power of commanding the necessaries and
conveniences of life, including labour. It is a

distinction absolutely called for, whenever we are comparing the wealth of two nations together, or whenever we are estimating the value of the precious metals in different states and at different periods of time. And till it has been shewn that some other interpretation of the term real value in exchange, either agrees better with the sense in which the words are generally applied, or is decidedly more useful in an inquiry into the nature and causes of the wealth of nations, I shall continue to think, that the most proper definition of real value in exchange, in contradistinction to nominal value in exchange, is, the power of commanding the necessaries and conveniences of life, including labour, as distinguished from the power of commanding the precious metals.

a   If then we continue to apply the term value in the first sense mentioned, we shall have three sorts of value—

1. Value in use; which may be defined to be the intrinsic utility of an object.

b   2. Nominal value in exchange ; which may be defined to be the value of commodities in the precious metals.

c   3. Real value in exchange ; which may be defined to be the power of an object to command in exchange the necessaries and conveniences of life, including labour.

d   The distinctions here made between the different kinds of value are, in the main, those of Adam Smith ; though it must be acknowledged that he has not been sufficiently careful to keep them al-

ways separate. In speaking of the value of corn,
he has sometimes left us in doubt whether he
means value in use, or real value in exchange;*   α
and he sometimes, as I shall have occasion to notice further on, confounds the cost of a commodity   β
in labour with its value in commanding labour,
which are essentially different.†

These instances however may, perhaps, be fairly   a
considered in the light of inadvertences.   At the
end of the third chapter of his first book he has   γ
explained value in use in the same manner as it
has been explained here; and in part of the succeeding chapter, *on the real and nominal prices of*   σ
commodities, he has made exactly the same distinction between real and nominal value, the propriety of which, as it has been controverted, it has
been my endeavour to establish. To these distinctions he has, in the main, adhered; they properly belong to his system; and he has only devi-
ated from them when, from some cause or other,
he was not fully aware of the inconsistency of
such deviation.

SECTION II.

Of Demand and Supply, as they affect Exchangeable Value.

THE terms Demand and Supply are so familiar
to the ear of every reader, and their application in

* Wealth of Nations, Book IV. Chap. v. p. 278. 6th Edit.   b
† Id. Book I. Chap. v.   c

single instances so fully understood, that in the slight use which has hitherto been made of them, it has not been thought necessary to interrupt the

a   course of the reasoning by explanations and definitions. These terms, however, though in constant use, are by no means applied with precision. And before we proceed farther, it may be advisable to clear this part of the ground as much as possible, that we may be certain of the footing on which we stand. This will appear to be the more necessary, as it must be allowed, that of all the principles

b   in political economy, there is none which bears so large a share in the phenomena which come under its consideration as the principle of supply and demand.

c   It has been already stated, that all value in exchange depends upon the power and will to exchange one commodity for another; and when, by the introduction of a general measure of value and medium of exchange, society has been divided, in common language, into buyers and sellers, demand may be defined to be, the will combined with the power to purchase, and supply, the production of commodities combined with the intention to sell

de   them. In this state of things, the relative values of commodities in money, or their prices, are deter-

f   mined by the relative demand for them, compared

g   with the supply of them : and this law appears to be so general, that probably not a single instance of a change of price can be found which may not be satisfactorily traced to some previous change in

h   the causes which affect the demand or supply.

In examining the truth of this position we must constantly bear in mind the terms in which it is expressed; and recollect that, when prices are said to be determined by demand and supply, it is not meant that they are determined either by the demand alone or the supply alone, but by their relation to each other.

But how is this relation to be ascertained? It has been sometimes said that supply is always equal to demand, because no permanent supply of any commodity can take place for which there is not a demand so effective as to take off all that is offered. In one sense of the terms in which demand and supply have occasionally been used, this position may be granted. The actual *extent* of the demand, compared with the actual *extent* of the supply, are always on an average proportioned to each other. If the supply be ever so small, the extent of the effective demand cannot be greater; and if the supply be ever so great, the extent of the demand, or the consumption, will either increase in proportion, or a part of it will become useless and cease to be produced. It cannot, therefore, be in this sense that a change in the proportion of demand to supply affects prices; because in this sense demand and supply always bear the same relation to each other. And this uncertainty in the use of these terms renders it an absolutely necessary preliminary in the present inquiry clearly to ascertain what is the nature of that change in the mutual relation of demand and supply, on which the prices of commodities so entirely depend.

a   The demand for a commodity has been defined to be, the will combined with the power to purchase it.

b   The greater is the degree of this will and power with regard to any particular commodity, the greater

c or the more intense may be fairly said to be the demand for it. But however great this will and

de power may be among the purchasers of a commodity, none of them will be disposed to give a high price for it, if they can obtain it at a low one; and

f as long as the abilities and competition of the

g sellers induce them to bring the quantity wanted

h to market at a low price, the real intensity of the demand will not shew itself.

    If a given number of commodities, attainable by labour alone, were to become more difficult of acquisition, as they would evidently not be obtained unless by means of increased exertion, we might

i surely consider such increased exertion, if applied, as an evidence of a greater intensity of demand, or

j of a power and will to make a greater sacrifice in

k order to obtain them.

    In fact it may be said, that the giving a greater

lm price for a commodity absolutely and necessarily implies a greater intensity of demand; and that the real question is, what are the causes which

n either call forth or render unnecessary the expression of this intensity of demand?

    It has been justly stated, that the causes which tend to raise the price of any article estimated in some commodity named, and supposed for short

o periods not essentially to vary, are an increase in

the number or wants of its purchasers, or a deficiency   a
in its supply ; and the causes which lower the price   b
are a diminution in the number or wants of its pur-   c
chasers, or an increased abundance in its supply.

The first class of these causes is obviously cal-   d
culated to call forth the expression of a greater intensity of demand, and the other of a less.

If, for instance, a commodity which had been
habitually demanded and consumed by a thousand
purchasers were suddenly to be wanted by two
thousand, it is clear that before this increased extent of demand could be supplied, some must go   e
without what they wanted; and it is scarcely pos-   f
sible to suppose that the intensity of individual
demand would not increase among a sufficient   g
number of these two thousand purchasers, to take   hi
off all the commodity produced at an increased
price.   At the same time, if we could suppose it
possible that the wills and powers of the purcha-   j
sers, or the intensity of their demand, would not
admit of increase, it is quite certain that, however
the matter might be settled among the contending
competitors, no rise of price could take place.   k

In the same manner, if a commodity were to be
diminished one half in quantity, it is scarcely possible to suppose that a sufficient number of the
former purchasers would not be both willing and   l
able to take off the whole of the diminished quan-   m
tity at a higher price ; but if they really would not
or could not do this, the price could not rise.

On the other hand, if the permanent cost of producing the commodity were doubled, it is evident

a that only such a quantity could be permanently
b produced as would supply the wants of those who
c were able and willing to make a sacrifice for the
d attainment of their wishes equal to double the
amount of what they did before. The quantity of
the commodity which would be brought to market
under these circumstances might be extremely
different. It might be reduced to the supply of a
single individual, or might remain precisely the
same as before. If it were reduced to the supply
of a single individual, it would be a proof that only
one of all the former purchasers was both able and
e willing to make an effective demand for it at the
advanced price. If the supply remained the same,
it would be a proof that all the purchasers were in
this state, but that the expression of this intensity
f of demand had not before been rendered necessary.
g In the latter case, there would be the same quantity
h supplied and the same quantity demanded; but
there would be a much greater intensity of de-
i mand called forth; and this may be fairly said to
be a most important change in the relation be-
j tween the supply and the demand of these com-
k modities; because, without the increased intensity
of demand, which in this case takes place, the commodity would cease to be produced; that is, the
failure of the supply would be contingent upon
l the failure of the power or will to make a greater
m sacrifice for the object sought.
n   Upon the same principles, if a commodity
were to become much more abundant, compared
with the former number of purchasers, this in-

creased supply could not be all sold, unless the
price were lowered. Each seller wishing to dis-
pose of that part of the commodity which he possessed would go on lowering it till he had effected   a
his object; and though the wills and powers of the   b
old purchasers might remain undiminished, yet as
the commodity could be obtained without the expression of the same intensity of demand as before,
this demand would of course not then shew itself.

A similar effect would obviously take place from
the consumers of a commodity requiring a less
quantity of it.

If, instead of a temporary abundance of supply
compared with the demand, the cost of producing
any particular commodity were greatly diminished,
the fall of price would in the same manner be occasioned by an increased abundance of supply,
either actual or contingent. In almost all practical
cases it would be an actual and permanent increase,
because the competition of sellers would lower the   c
price; and it very rarely happens that a fall of price
does not occasion an increased consumption. On
the supposition, however, of the very rare case that
a definite quantity only of the commodity was re-   d
quired, whatever might be its price, it is obvious
that from the competition of the producers a greater
quantity would be brought to market than could
be consumed, till the price was reduced in proportion to the increased facility of production; and
this excess of supply would be always contingent   e
on the circumstance of the price being at any time   f
higher than the price which returns average profits.   g

In this case of a fall of prices, as in the other of a
rise of prices, the actual quantity of the commodity
supplied and consumed may possibly, after a short
struggle, be the same as before; yet it cannot be
said that the demand is the same. It may indeed
exist precisely in the same degree, and the actual
consumers of the commodity might be perfectly
ready to give what they gave before rather than go
without it; but such has been the alteration in
the means of supply compared with the demand,
that the competition of the producers renders the
same intensity of demand no longer necessary to
effect the supply required; and not being necessary, it is of course not called forth, and the price
falls.

It is evidently, therefore, not merely *extent* of
actual demand, nor even the extent of actual demand compared with the extent of actual supply,
which raises prices, but such a change in the relation between supply and demand as renders necessary the expression of a greater intensity of demand, in order either peaceably to divide any actual
produce, or prevent the future produce of the same
kind from failing.

And, in the same manner, it is not merely
extent of actual supply, nor the extent of the
actual supply compared with the actual demand,
that lowers prices, but such a change in the relation of the supply, compared with the demand, as
renders a fall of price necessary, in order to take
off a temporary abundance, or to prevent a constant excess of supply contingent upon a diminu-

tion in the cost of production, without a propor-   a
tionate diminution in the price of the produce.   b

If the terms demand and supply be understood
and used in the way here described, there is no
case of price, whether temporary or permanent,
which they will not determine; and in every instance
of bargain and sale it will be perfectly correct to
say that the price will depend upon the relation   c
of the demand to the supply.   d

I wish it particularly to be observed that in this   e
discussion I have not given any new meaning to
the terms, demand and supply.   In the use which
I have occasionally made of the words *intense* and   fg
intensity as applied to demand, my sole purpose   h
has been to explain the meaning which has hitherto
always been attached to the term demand when it   i
is said to raise prices.   Mr. Ricardo in his chapter
*On the influence of demand and supply on prices,**
observes, that " the demand for a commodity cannot be said to increase, if no additional quantity of
it be purchased or consumed."   But it is obvious,
as I have before remarked, that it is not in the
sense of mere extent of consumption that demand
raises prices, because it is almost always when the   j
prices are the lowest that the *extent* of consump-   k
tion is the greatest.   This, therefore, cannot be
the meaning hitherto attached to the term, demand,
when it is said to raise prices.   Mr. Ricardo, however, subsequently quotes Lord Lauderdale's statements respecting value,† and allows them to be true,

* Principles of Polit. Econ. chap. xxx. p. 493. 2d edit.   l
† Id. p. 495.   m

a as applied to monopolized commodities, and the market prices of all other commodities for a limited

b period. He would allow, therefore, that the deficiency of any article in a market would occasion a

c great demand for it, compared with the supply, and raise its price, although in this case less than usual of the article must be purchased by the consumers. Demand, in this sense, is obviously quite different from the sense in which Mr. Ricardo had

d before used the term. The one implies extent of consumption, the other intensity of demand, or the will and power to make a greater sacrifice in order to obtain the object wanted. It is in this latter

e sense alone that demand raises prices; and my sole object in this section is to shew that, whenever we

f talk of demand and supply as influencing prices,

g whether market or natural, the terms should always be understood in the sense in which Mr. Ricardo and every other person has hitherto understood them, when speaking of commodities bought

h and sold in a market.

SECTION III.

i *Of the Cost of Production as it affects Exchangeable Value.*

It may be said, perhaps, that even according to the view given of demand and supply in the pre-

j ceding section, the permanent prices of a great mass of commodities will be determined by the

kl cost of their production. This is true, if we in-

clude all the component parts of price stated by
Adam Smith, though not if we consider only those   a
stated by Mr. Ricardo. But, in reality, the two   b
systems, one of which accounts for the prices of
the great mass of commodities by the cost of their
production, and the other accounts for the prices
of all commodities, under all circumstances, permanent as well as temporary, by the relation of the
demand to the supply, though they touch each
other necessarily at a greater number of points,
have an essentially different origin, and require,
therefore, to be very carefully distinguished.

In all the transactions of bargain and sale there   c
is evidently a principle in constant operation, which   d
can determine, and does actually determine, the
prices of commodities, quite independently of any   e
considerations of cost, or of the quantity of labour   f
and capital employed upon their production. And
this is found to operate, not only permanently upon
that class of commodities which may be considered
as monopolies, but temporarily and immediately
upon all commodities, and strikingly and pre-eminently so upon all sorts of raw produce.

It has never been a matter of doubt that the
principle of supply and demand determines ex-   g
clusively, and very regularly and accurately, the
prices of monopolized commodities, without any   h
reference to the cost of their production ; and our   i
daily and uniform experience shews us that the
prices of raw products, particularly of those which   j
are most affected by the seasons, are at the moment
of their sale determined always by the higgling of

the market, and differ widely in different years
and at different times, while the labour and capital
employed upon them may have been very nearly
the same.   This is so obvious, that probably very
few would hesitate to believe what is certainly
true, that, if in the next year we could by any process exempt the farmers from all cost in the production of their corn and cattle, provided no
change were made in the quantity brought to
market, and the society had the same wants and
the same powers of purchasing, the prices of raw
products would be the same as if they had cost
the usual labour and expense to procure them.

With regard, therefore, to a class of commodities
of the greatest extent, it is acknowledged that the
existing market prices are, at the moment they are
fixed, determined upon a principle quite distinct
from the cost of production, and that these prices
are in reality almost always different from what
they would have been, if this cost had regulated
them.

There is indeed another class of commodities,
such as manufactures, particularly those in which
the raw material is cheap, where the existing market
prices much more frequently coincide with the
cost of production, and may appear, therefore, to
be exclusively determined by it.   Even here,
however, our familiar experience shews us that
any alteration in the demand and supply quite
overcomes for a time the influence of this cost;
and further, when we come to examine the subject
more closely, we find that the cost of production

itself only influences the prices of these commodities as the payment of this cost is the necessary condition of their continued supply.   a

But if this be true, it follows that the great principle of demand and supply is called into action to determine what Adam Smith calls natural prices as well as market prices.   b

c

It will be allowed without hesitation that no change can take place in the market prices of commodities without some previous change in the relation of demand and supply.   And the question is, whether the same position is true.in reference to natural prices?   This question must of course be determined by attending carefully to the nature of the change which an alteration in the cost of production occasions in the state of the demand and supply, and particularly to the specific and immediate cause by which the change of price that takes place is effected.   d

e

f

We all allow, that when the cost of production diminishes, a fall of price is generally the consequence; but what is it, specifically, which forces down the price of the commodity?   It has been shewn in the preceding section that it is an actual or contingent excess of supply.   g

We all allow that, when the cost of production increases, the prices of commodities generally rise.   But what is it which specifically forces up the price?   It has been shewn that it is a contingent failure of supply. Remove these contingencies, that is, let the extent of the supply remain exactly the same, without contingent failure or excess, whether the price of production rises or falls, and   h

i

j

k

l

m

there is not the slightest ground for supposing that any variation of price would take place.

a   If, for instance, all the commodities that are consumed in this country, whether agricultural or manufactured, could be produced, during the next

b   ten years, without labour, and yet could only be supplied exactly in the same quantities as they

c   would be in a natural state of things; then, sup-

d   posing the wills and the powers of the purchasers to remain the same, there cannot be a doubt that all prices would also remain the same. But, if this be allowed, it follows, that the relation of the sup-

e   ply to the demand, either actual or contingent, is the dominant principle in the determination of prices whether market or natural, and that the cost of production can do nothing but in subordination

f   to it, that is, merely as this cost affects actually or contingently the relation which the supply bears to the demand.

It is not however necessary to resort to imaginary cases in order to fortify this conclusion. Actual experience shews the principle in the clearest light.

In the well known instance, noticed by Adam Smith, of the insufficient pay of curates, notwithstanding all the efforts of the legislature to raise it,*

g   a striking proof is afforded that the *permanent* price of an article is determined by the demand and supply, and not by the cost of production.

h   The real cost of production would, in this case, be more likely to be increased than diminished by the

i   * Wealth of Nations, Book I. c. x. p. 202. 6th edit.

subscriptions of benefactors; but being paid by   a
others and not by the individuals themselves, it
does not regulate and limit the supply; and this
supply, on account of such encouragement, becoming and continuing abundant, the price is and   b
must always be low, whatever may be the real cost
of the education given.

The effects of the poor-rates in lowering the
wages of labour present another practical instance   c
of the same kind. It is not probable that public
money should be more economically managed than
the income of individuals. Consequently the cost
of rearing a family cannot be supposed to be diminished by parish assistance; but, a part of the   d
expense being borne by the public, a price of labour adequate to the maintenance of a certain
family is no longer a necessary condition of its
supply; and as, by means of parish rates, this supply can be obtained without such wages, the real
costs of supplying labour no longer regulate its   e
price.

In fact, in every kind of bounty upon production, the same effects must necessarily take place;
and just in proportion as such bounties tend to   f
lower prices, they shew that prices depend upon
the supply compared with the demand, and not
upon the costs of production.

But the most striking instance which can well
be conceived to shew that the cost of production
only influences the prices of commodities as it regu-   g
lates their supply, is continually before our eyes, in
the artificial value which is given to Bank notes, by   h

limiting their amount. Mr. Ricardo's admirable and
efficient plan for this purpose proceeds upon the just
principle, that, if you can limit the supply of notes,
so that they shall not exceed the quantity of gold
which would have circulated, if the currency had
been metallic, you will keep the notes always of
the same value as gold.   And I am confident he
would allow that if this limitation could be completely effected without the paper being exchangeable for gold, the value of the notes would not be
altered.   But, if an article which costs comparatively nothing in making, though it performs one
of the most important functions of gold, can be
kept to the value of gold by being supplied in the
same quantity, it is the clearest of all possible
proofs that the value of gold itself no further depends upon the cost of its production, than as this
cost influences its supply, and that if the cost were
to cease, provided the supply were not increased,
the value of gold in this country would still remain the same.

It does not, however, in any degree follow from
what has been said, that labour and the costs of
production have not a most powerful effect upon
prices.   But the true way of considering these
costs is, as the necessary condition of the supply
of the objects wanted.

Although, at the time of the actual exchange of
two commodities, no circumstance affects it but
the relation of the supply to the demand; yet, as
almost all the objects of human desire are obtained
by the instrumentality of human exertion, it is

clear that the supply of these objects must be
regulated—first, by the quantity and direction of   a
this exertion; secondly, by the assistance which
it may receive from the results of previous labour;   b
and thirdly, by the abundance or scarcity of the
materials on which it has to work, and of the food
of the labourer. It is of importance, therefore, to
consider the different conditions which must be
fulfilled, in order that any commodity should continue to be brought to market.   c

The first condition is, that the labour which has   d
been expended on it should be so remunerated in
the value of the objects given in exchange, as to   e
encourage the exertion of a sufficient quantity of
industry in the direction required, as without such
adequate remuneration the supply of the commodity must necessarily fail. If this labour should
be of a very severe kind, few comparatively would
be able or willing to engage in it; and, upon the   f
common principles of exchangeable value before
explained, it would rise in price. If the work
were of a nature to require an uncommon degree
of dexterity and ingenuity, a rise of price would
take place in a greater degree; but not certainly,   g
as stated by Adam Smith, on account of the esteem
which men have for such talents,* but on account
of their rarity, and the consequent rarity of the
effects produced by them. In all these cases the
remuneration will be regulated, not by the intrinsic
qualities of the commodities produced, but by the   h
state of the demand for them compared with the
supply, and of course by the demand and supply

* Wealth of Nations, Book I. c. vi. p. 71. 6th edit.   i

of the sort of labour which produced them. If
a the commodities have been obtained by the exertion of manual labour exclusively, aided at least
b only by the unappropriated bounties of nature, the
whole remuneration will, of course, belong to the
c labourer, and the usual value of this remuneration,
in the existing state of the society, would be the
usual price of the commodity.

The second condition to be fulfilled is, that the
assistance which may have been given to the la-
d bourer, from the previous accumulation of objects
which facilitate future production, should be so
remunerated as to continue the application of this
assistance to the production of the commodities
required. If by means of certain advances to the
labourer of machinery, food, and materials previously collected, he can execute eight or ten times
as much work as he could without such assistance,
the person furnishing them might appear, at first,
to be entitled to the difference between the powers
of unassisted labour and the powers of labour so
assisted. But the prices of commodities do not
depend upon their intrinsic utility, but upon the
e supply and the demand. The increased powers of
labour would naturally produce an increased supply of commodities; their prices would consequently
fall; and the remuneration for the capital advanced
would soon be reduced to what was necessary, in
f the existing state of the society, to bring the articles to the production of which they were applied
to market. With regard to the labourers employed, as neither their exertions nor their skill would

necessarily be much greater than if they had   a
worked unassisted, their remuneration would be   b
nearly the same as before, and would depend entirely upon the exchangeable value of the kind of   c
labour they had contributed, estimated in the
usual way by the demand and the supply. It is   d
not, therefore, quite correct to represent, as Adam   e
Smith does, the profits of capital as a deduction
from the produce of labour. They are only a fair
remuneration for that part of the production contributed by the capitalist, estimated exactly in the
same way as the contribution of the labourer.

The third condition to be fulfilled is, that the
price of commodities should be such as to effect   f
the continued supply of the food and raw materials used by the labourers and capitalists; and we
know that this price cannot be paid without yielding a rent to the landlord on almost all the land
actually in use. In speaking of the landlords,
Adam Smith's language is again exceptionable.
He represents them, rather invidiously, as loving
to reap where they have never sown, and as obliging   g
the labourer to pay for a licence to obtain those
natural products, which, when land was in common, cost only the trouble of collecting.* But he
would himself be the first to acknowledge that, if
land were not appropriated, its produce would
be, beyond comparison, less abundant, and conse-   h
quently dearer; and, if it be appropriated, some   i
persons or other must necessarily be the proprietors. It matters not to the society whether these

* Wealth of Nations, Book I. ch. vi. p. 74. 6th edit.   j

persons are the same or different from the actual labourers of the land. The price of the produce will be determined by the general supply compared with the general demand, and will be precisely the same, whether the labourer pays a rent, or uses the land without rent. The only difference is that, in the latter case, what remains of this price, after paying the labour and capital, will go to the same person that contributed the labour, which is almost equivalent to saying, that the labourer would be better off, if he were a possessor of land as well as labour—a fact not to be disputed, but which by no means implies that the labourer, who in the lottery of human life has not drawn a prize of land, suffers any hardship or injustice in being obliged to give something in exchange for the use of what belongs to another. The possessors of land, whoever they may be, conduct themselves, with regard to their possessions, exactly in the same way as the possessors of labour and of capital, and exchange what they have, for as many other commodities as the society is willing to give them for it.

The three conditions therefore above specified must, in every society, be necessarily fulfilled, in order to obtain the supply of by far the greater part of the commodities which it wants; and the compensation which fulfils these conditions, or the price of any exchangeable commodity, may be considered as consisting of three parts—that which pays the wages of the labourer employed in its production; that which pays the profits of capital

by which such production has been facilitated;
and that which pays the rent of land, or the re-   ab
muneration for the raw materials and food furnished by the landlord;—the price of each of these
component parts being determined exactly by the
same causes as those which determine the price of
the whole.

The price which fulfils these conditions is pre-   c
cisely what Adam Smith calls the natural price.
I should be rather more disposed to call it the ne-   d
cessary price, because the term necessary better
expresses a reference to the conditions of supply,
and is, on that account, susceptible of a more
simple definition.   To explain natural price, Adam
Smith is obliged to use a good deal of circumlocu-
tion; and though he makes it on the whole sufficiently clear, yet, as he calls to his assistance two
other terms, each of which might almost as well
have been used as the one adopted, the definition
is not quite satisfactory.*   If, however, we use
the term suggested, the definition of necessary
price will be very easy and simple.   It will be,
the price necessary, in the actual circumstances
of the society, to bring the commodity regularly
to the market.   This is only a shorter description
of what Adam Smith means by natural price, as
contradistinguished from market price, or the price
at which commodities actually sell in the market,
which, from the variations of the seasons or the
accidental miscalculations of the suppliers, are
sometimes sold higher and sometimes lower than

* Book I. chap. vii.   e

the price which is necessary to fulfil the conditions of a regular supply.

a   When a·commodity is sold at this its natural price, Adam Smith says, it is sold for precisely what it is worth. But here, I think, he has used

b   the term worth in an unusual sense. Commodities are continually said to be worth more than they have cost, ordinary profits included; and according to the customary and proper use of the term

cd   *worth*, we could never say, that a certain quantity of corn, or any other article, was not worth more

e   when it was scarce, although no more labour and

f   capital might have been employed about it. The *worth* of a commodity is its market price, not its natural or necessary price; it is its value in ex-

g   change, not its cost; and this is one of the instances in which Adam Smith has not been sufficiently

h   careful to keep them separate.*

i   But if it appear generally that the cost of pro-

j   duction only determines the prices of commodities,

k   as the payment of it is the necessary condition of their supply, and that the component parts of this cost are themselves determined by the same causes which determine the whole, it is obvious that we cannot get rid of the principle of demand and supply

l   by referring to the cost of production. Natural and necessary prices appear to be regulated by this principle, as well as market prices; and the only difference is, that the former are regulated by the

m   ordinary and average relation of the demand to the supply, and the latter, when they differ from the

n   * Book I. chap. vii.

former, depend upon the extraordinary and acci-   a
dental relations of the demand to the supply.   b

c

SECTION IV.

Of the Labour which a Commodity has Cost considered as a   d
Measure of Exchangeable Value.
e

Adam Smith, in his chapter on the real and nominal price of commodities,* in which he considers labour as an universal and accurate measure   f
of value, has introduced some confusion into his
inquiry by not adhering strictly to the same mode
of applying the labour which he proposes for a
measure.

Sometimes he speaks of the value of a commodity as being determined by the quantity of labour   g
which its production has cost, and sometimes by
the quantity of labour which it will command in
exchange.

These two measures are essentially different;   h
and, though certainly neither of them can come
under the description of a standard, one of them is
a very much more useful and accurate measure of
value than the other.

When we consider the degree in which labour   i
is fitted to be a measure of value in the first sense
used by Adam Smith, that is, in reference to the
quantity of labour which a commodity has cost in
its production, we shall find it radically defective,

* Book I. chap. v.

a   In the first place, a moment's consideration will shew us that it cannot be applied in a positive sense. It is indeed almost a contradiction in terms to say that the exchangeable value of a commodity is proportioned to the quantity of labour employed upon it. Exchangeable value, as the term implies, evidently means value in exchange for some other commodities; but if, when more labour is employed upon one commodity, more labour is also employed on the others for which it is exchanged, it is quite obvious that the exchangeable value of the first commodity cannot be proportioned to the labour employed upon it. If, for instance, at the same time that the labour of producing corn increases, the labour of producing money and many other commodities increases, there is at once an end of our being able to say with truth that all things become more or less valuable in proportion as more or less labour is employed in their production. In this case it is obvious that more labour has been employed upon corn, although a bushel of corn may still exchange for no more money nor labour than before. The exchangeable value of corn, therefore, has certainly not altered in proportion to the additional quantity of labour which it has cost in its production.

b   But, even if we take this measure always in a relative sense, that is, if we say that the exchangeable value of commodities is determined by the *comparative* quantity of labour expended upon each, there is no stage of society in which it will be found correct.

In the very earliest periods, when not only land
was in common, but scarcely any capital was used
to assist manual exertions, exchanges would be
constantly made with but little reference to the
quantity of labour which each commodity might
have cost. The greatest part of the objects exchanged would be raw products of various kinds,
such as game, fish, fruits, &c. with regard to which,
the effects of labour are always uncertain. One
man might have employed five days' labour in procuring an object which he would subsequently be
very happy to exchange for some other object
that might have cost a more fortunate labourer
only two, or perhaps one day's exertion. And this
disproportion between the exchangeable value of
objects and the labour which they had cost in production would be of perpetual recurrence.

I cannot, therefore, agree either with Adam
Smith or Mr. Ricardo in thinking that, " in that
rude state of society which precedes both the
accumulation of stock and the appropriation of
land, the proportion between the quantities of
labour necessary for acquiring different objects
seems to be the only circumstance which can afford
any rule for exchanging them for one another. "*
The rule, which would be acted upon in the exchange of commodities, is unquestionably that
which has been so happily described by Turgot,
and which I have stated in the first section of this
chapter. The results of this rule might or might
not agree, on an average, with those of the rule

* Principles of Polit. Econ. c. i. p. 4. 2d edit.

a   founded on the quantity of labour which each article had cost; but if they did not, or if commodities were found by accident, or the labour employed
upon them was utterly unknown when they were
brought to market, the society would never be at
a loss for a rule to determine their exchangeable
b   value; and it is probable that the exchanges actually made in this stage of society would be less
frequently proportioned to the labour which each
object had cost than in any other.

c   But in fact there is scarcely any stage of society,
however barbarous, where the cost of production
is confined exclusively to labour.   At a very early
d   period, profits will be found to form an important
part of this cost, and consequently to enter largely
into the question of exchangeable value as a neces-
e   sary condition of supply.   To make even a bow
and arrow, it is obviously necessary that the wood
and reed should be properly dried and seasoned;
f   and the time that these materials must necessarily
be kept by the workman before his work is completed, introduces at once a new element into the
gh   computation of cost.   We may estimate the labour
employed in any sort of capital just upon the same
principle as the labour employed in the immediate
i   production of the commodity.   But the varying
quickness of the returns is an entirely new element,
which has nothing to do with the quantity of labour employed upon the capital, and yet, in every
j   period of society, the earliest as well as the latest, is
of the utmost importance in the determination of
k   prices.

The fixed capital necessary to hollow out a canoe, may consist of little more than a few stone hatchets and shell chissels; and the labour necessary to make them might not add much to the labour subsequently employed in the work to which they were applied; but it is likewise necessary that the workman should previously cut down the timber, and employ a great quantity of labour in various parts of the process very long before there is   a
a possibility of his receiving the returns for his   b
exertions, either in the use of the canoe, or in the commodities which he might obtain in exchange for it; and during this time he must of course advance the whole of his subsistence. But the providence,   c
dence, foresight, and postponement of present enjoyment   d
joyment for the sake of future benefit and profit, which are necessary for this purpose, have always been considered as rare qualities in the savage; and it can scarcely admit of a doubt that the articles which were of a nature to require this long preparation would be comparatively very scarce, and would have a great exchangeable value in proportion to the quantity of labour which had been actually employed upon them, and on the capital necessary to their production. On this account, I should think it not improbable, that a canoe   e
might, in such a state of society, possess double the exchangeable value of a number of deer, to produce which successively in the market might have cost precisely the same number of days' labour, including the necessary fixed capital of the   f
bows and arrows, &c. used for killing them; and

a the great difference of price in this case would
arise from the circumstance that the returns for
the labour of killing each successive deer always
b came in within a few days after it was employed,
c while the returns for the labour expended on the
d canoe were delayed perhaps beyond a year. Whatever might be the rate of profits, the comparative
slowness of these returns must tell proportionally
on the price of the article; and, as there is reason
to think that among savages the advances necessary for a work of slow returns would be comparatively seldom made, the profits of capital would be
extremely high, and the difference of exchangeable
value in different commodities which had cost in
their production, and in the production of the necessary capital, the same quantity of labour, would
be very great.

e If to this cause of variation we add the exception
noticed by Mr. Ricardo, arising from the greater
or less proportion of fixed capital employed in different commodities, the effects of which would
shew themselves in a very early period of savage
life; it must be allowed that the rule which de-
clares " that commodities never vary in value unless a greater or less quantity of labour be bestowed on their production," cannot possibly, as
stated by Mr. Ricardo, be " of universal application
in the early stages of society."*

In countries advanced in civilization, it is ob-
f vious that the same causes of variation in the ex-

g * Principles of Polit. Econ. p. 31. 2d edit.

changeable value of commodities, independently   a
of the labour which they may have cost, must prevail, as in the early periods of society, and as might
be expected some others. Probably indeed the   b
profits of stock will not be so high, and consequently neither the varying proportions of the
fixed capitals, nor the slowness or quickness of the
returns will produce the same proportionate difference on prices; but to make up for this, the difference in the quantity of fixed capital employed is
prodigious, and scarcely the same in any two commodities; and the difference in the returns of capital varies sometimes from two or three days to   c
two or three years.   d

The proposition of Mr. Ricardo, which shews   ef
that a rise in the price of labour lowers the price
of a large class of commodities,* has undoubtedly a
very paradoxical air; but it is nevertheless true;
and the appearance of paradox would vanish if it
were stated more naturally.   g

Mr. Ricardo would certainly allow that the effect   hi
he contemplates is produced by a fall of profits, which
he thinks is synonimous with a rise of wages. It is
not necessary here to enter into the question how far
he is right in this respect; but undoubtedly no one
could have thought the proposition paradoxical, or
even in the slightest degree improbable, if he had
stated that a fall of profits would occasion a fall of
price in those commodities, where from the quantity   j
of fixed capital employed, the profits of that capital
had before formed the principal ingredient in the   k
cost of production. But this is what he has in

* Principles of Polit. Econ. pp. 34 and 41. 2d edit.   l

a   substance said. In the particular case which he has
b   taken to illustrate his proposition, he supposes no
      other labour employed than that which has been
      applied in the construction of the machine, or fixed
      capital used; and consequently the price of the year-
      ly produce of this machine would be formed merely
      of the ordinary profits of the £20,000 which it is
      supposed to have cost, together with a slight addi-
      tion to replace its wear and tear. Now it is quite
c   certain that if, from any cause whatever, the ordi-
      nary profits of stock should fall, the price of the com-
de   modity so produced would fall. This is sufficiently
      obvious. But the effects arising from an opposite
      supposition, equally consistent with facts, have not
      been sufficiently considered by Mr. Ricardo, and
      the general result has been totally overlooked.
f   The state of the case, in a general view of it, seems
g   to be this. There is a very large class of commodi
      ties, in the production of which, owing to the quan-
      tity of fixed capital used and the long time that
      elapses before the returns of the capital, whether
      fixed or circulating, come in, the proportion which
      the value of the capital bears to the value of the
      labour which it yearly employs is, in various degrees,
      very considerable. In all these cases it is natural to
h   suppose, that the fall of price arising from a fall of
      profits should, in various degrees, more than coun-
      terbalance the rise of price which would naturally
i   be occasioned by a rise in the price of labour ; and
      consequently on the supposition of a rise in the
j   money price of labour and a fall in the rate of pro-
      fits, all these commodities will, in various degrees,
      naturally fall in price.

On the other hand, there is a large class of com-   a
modities, where, from the absence of fixed capital
and the rapidity of the returns of the circulating
capital from a day to a year, the proportion which   b
the value of the capital bears to the quantity of   c
labour which it employs is very small.   A capital   d
of a hundred pounds, which was returned every
week, could employ as much labour annually as
2,600*l.* the returns of which came in only at the
end of the year; and if the capital were returned
nearly every day, as it is practically, in some few
cases, the advance of little more than the wages
of a man for a single day might pay above 300
days' labour in the course of a year.   Now it is
quite evident, that out of the profits of these trifling capitals it would not only be absolutely impossible to take a rise in the price of labour of
seven per cent., but it would be as impossible to   e
take a rise of ½ per cent.   On the first supposition, a rise of only ½ per cent. would, if the price
of the produce continued the same, absorb more
than all the profits of the 100*l.*; and in the other
case much more than all the capital advanced.   If,
therefore, the prices of commodities, where the
proportion of labour is very great compared with
the capital which employs it, do not rise upon an
advance in the price of labour, the production of
such commodities must at once be given up.   But
they certainly will not be given up.   Consequently   f
upon a rise in the price of labour and fall of   g
profits, there will be a large class of commodities
which will rise in price; and it cannot be correct   h

to say, "that no commodities whatever are raised
in exchangeable value merely because wages rise;
they are only so raised when more labour is bestowed on their production, when wages fall, or
when the medium in which they are estimated falls
in value."* It is quite certain that merely because wages rise and profits fall, all that class of
commodities (and it will be a large class) will rise
in price, where, from the smallness of the capital
employed, the fall of profits is in various degrees
more than overbalanced by the rise of wages.

ab
c
d
e

f

There will, however, undoubtedly be a class of
commodities which, from the effects of these opposite causes, will remain stationary in price. But
from the very nature of the proposition, this class
must theoretically form little more than a line;
and where, I would ask, is this line to be placed?
Mr. Ricardo, in order to illustrate his proposition,
has placed it, at a venture, among those commodities where the advances consist solely in the payment of labour, and the returns come in exactly
in the year.† But the cases are extremely rare
where the returns of a capital are delayed for a
year, and yet no part of this capital is employed
either in the purchase of materials or machinery;
and in fact there seems to be no justifiable ground
for pitching upon this peculiar case as precisely
the one where, under any variation in the price of
labour, the price of the commodity remains the

g
h

* Ricardo's Political Economy, p. 41. 2d edit.
† Polit. Econ. p. 33. 2d edit.

same, and a rise or fall of wages is exactly compensated by a fall or rise of profits.   At all events   a
it must be allowed, that wherever the line may be
placed, it can embrace but a very small class of   b
objects; and upon a rise in the price of labour, all   c
the rest will either fall or rise in price, although
exactly the same quantity of labour' continues to
be employed upon them.   d

What then becomes of the doctrine, that the   e
exchangeable value of commodities is proportioned
to the labour which has been employed upon
them?   Instead of their remaining of the same
value while the same quantity of labour is employed upon them, it appears that, from well known
causes of constant and universal operation, the   f
prices of all commodities vary when the *price* of
labour varies, with very few exceptions; and of
what description of commodities these few exceptions consist, it is scarcely possible to say before-
hand.

But the different proportions of fixed capital,   g
and the varying quickness of the returns of circulating capital, are not the only causes which, in improved countries, prevent the exchangeable value
of commodities from being proportioned to the
quantity of labour which has been employed upon
them.   Where commerce prevails to any extent,
foreign commodities, not regulated, it is acknowledged, by the quantity of labour and capital employed upon them, form the materials of many
manufactures.   In civilized states taxation is every
where making considerable changes in prices with-

out any reference to labour. And further, where
all the land is appropriated, the payment of rent is
another condition of the supply of most of the
commodities of home growth and manufacture.

It is unquestionably true, and it is a truth which
involves very important consequences, that the
cost of the main vegetable food of civilized and
improved countries, which requires in its production a considerable quantity of labour and capital,
is resolvable almost entirely into wages and profits,
as will be more fully explained in the next chapter.
But though it follows that the price of corn is thus
nearly independent of rent, yet as this price, so
determined, does actually pay rent on the great
mass of the lands of the country, it is evident that
the payment of rent, or, what comes to the same
thing, of such a price as will pay rent, is a necessary condition of the supply of the great mass of
commodities.

Adam Smith himself states, that rent "enters
into the composition of the price of commodities
in a different way from wages and profit." "High
or low wages or profit (he says) are the causes of
high or low price; high or low rent is the effect
of it. It is because high or low wages and profit
must be paid, in order to bring a particular commodity to market, that its price is high or low.
But it is because its price is high or low, a great
deal more, or very little more, or no more, than
what is sufficient to pay those wages and profits,
that it affords a high rent, or a low rent, or no rent
at all."* In this passage Adam Smith distinctly

a

b

c

d

e

* Wealth of Nations, Book I. c. xi. p. 226. 6th edit.

allows that rent is a consequence, not a cause of
price; but he evidently does not consider this admission as invalidating his general doctrine respecting the component parts of price. Nor in reality
is it invalidated by this admission. It is still true
that the cost of the great mass of commodities is   a
resolvable into wages, profits, and rent. Some of
them may cost a considerable quantity of rent, and
a small quantity of labour and capital; others a
great quantity of labour and capital, and a small
quantity of rent; and a very few may be nearly
resolvable into wages and profits, or even wages
alone. But, as it is known that the latter class is
confined to a very small proportion of a country's
products, it follows that the payment of rent is an
absolutely necessary condition of the supply of the
great mass of commodities, and may properly be
considered as a component part of price.

Allowing then that the price of the main vege-   bc
table food of an improving country is determined   d
by the quantity of labour and capital employed to
produce it under the most unfavourable circumstances, yet if we allow, at the same time, that an
equal value of produce is raised on rich land with
little labour and capital, we can hardly maintain,
with any propriety of language, the general proposition that the quantity of labour realized in different commodities regulates their exchangeable
value.* On account of the varieties of soil alone
constant exchanges are taking place, which directly

* Ricardo's Polit. Econ. c. i. p. 5.   e

contradict the terms in which the proposition is
expressed; and in whatever way rent may be regulated, it is obviously necessary to retain it as an ingredient in the costs of production in reference to
the great mass of commodities; nor will the propriety of thus retaining it be affected by the circumstance, that the rent paid on commodities of
the same description is variable, and in some few
cases little or none.

Under the full admission, therefore, just made,
that the price of the main vegetable food of an improving agricultural country is, in reference to the
whole quantity produced, a necessary price, and
coincides with what is required to repay the labour
and capital which is employed under the most unfavourable circumstances, and pays little or no
rent, we still do not seem justified in altering the
old language respecting the component parts of
price, or what I should be more disposed to call
the necessary conditions of supply.

But there are some parts of the land and of its
products which have much more the character of
a monopoly than the main food of an improving
country; and it is universally acknowledged that
the exchangeable value of commodities which are
subjected either to strict or partial monopolies cannot be determined by the labour employed upon
them. The exchangeable value of that vast mass
of property in this country which consists of the
houses in all its towns, is greatly affected by the
strict monopoly of ground rents; and the necessity
of paying these rents must affect the prices of al

most all the goods fabricated in towns. And though
with regard to the main food of the people it is true
that, if rents were given up, an equal quantity of
corn could not be produced at a less price; yet the
same cannot be said of the cattle of the country.
Of no portion of this species of food is the price
resolvable into labour and capital alone.

a
b

All cattle pay rent, and in proportion to their
value not very far from an equal rent. In this respect they are essentially different from corn. By
means of labour and dressing, a good crop of corn
may be obtained from a poor soil, and the rent paid
may be quite trifling compared with the value of
the crop; but in uncultivated land the rent must
be proportioned to the value of the crop, and,
whether great or small per acre, must be a main
ingredient in the price of the commodity produced.
It may require more than an hundred acres in the
highlands of Scotland to rear the same weight of
mutton as might have been reared on five acres of
good pasture; and something no doubt must be
allowed for the greater labour of attendance and
the greater risk on a poor soil and in an exposed
situation; but independently of this deduction,
which would probably be inconsiderable, the rent
paid for the same quantity of mutton would be
nearly the same. If this rent were greatly diminished, there cannot be a doubt that the same
quantity of cattle might be produced in the market
at much lower prices without any diminution of
the profits or wages of any of the persons concerned; and consequently it is impossible to esti-

mate the value of cattle by the quantity of labour
a   and capital, and still less by the mere quantity of
b   labour which has been expended upon them.

c   It may possibly be said that although rent is
unquestionably paid on all and every part of the
cattle produced in this country; yet that the rent
of uncultivated land is determined by the price of
cattle; that the price of cattle is determined by the
cost of production on such good natural pastures
or improved land as would yield a considerable
rent if employed in raising corn, because the poor
uncultivated lands of a populous country are never
sufficient to produce all the animal food required;
that the rents of the different qualities of land
which must thus be devoted to the rearing of
cattle depend upon the price of the main food of
the country; and that the price of the main food of
d   the country depends upon the labour and capital
necessary to produce it on the worst land actually
so employed. This is to be sure rather a circui-
tous method of proving the intimate connection
between cattle and labour, and certainly will not
justify us in saying that the relative value of sheep
and shirts is proportioned to the comparative quantity of labour expended upon each.

e   But in fact one of the links in this chain of dependance will not hold, and the connexion between cattle and labour is thus at once broken off.
Though the price of the main food of a country
f   depends upon the labour and capital necessary to
produce it on the worst land in use; yet the rent
of land, as will be shewn more fully in the next

chapter, is not regulated by the price of produce. Among the events of the most common occurrence in all nations, is an improvement in agriculture which leads to increased produce and increased population, and after a time to the cultivation of naturally poorer land, with the same price of produce, the same price of labour, and the same rate of profits. But in this case the rents of all the old lands in tillage must rise, and with them of course the rents of natural pastures and the price of cattle, without any change in the price of labour or any increased difficulty in producing the means of subsistence.

The statement just made applies to many other   a
important commodities, besides animal food. In   b
the first place, it includes wool and raw hides, the materials of two most important manufactures; and applies directly to timber and copse wood, both articles of great consequence. And secondly, there are some products, such as hops, for instance, which cannot be grown upon poor soils. Such products it is impossible to obtain without paying a rent; and if this rent varies, while the quantity of labour employed in the production of a given quantity of corn remains the same, there can be no ground whatever for asserting that the value of such products is regulated by labour.

If it be said that the doctrine which entirely re-   c
jects rent, and resolves the prices of all commodities into wages and profits, never refers to articles which have any connexion with monopoly, it may be answered, that this exception includes the great

d

mass of the articles with which we are acquainted.
The lands which afford the main supply of corn
α   are evidently as pecies of monopoly, though subject
to different laws and limits from common monopolies; and even the last land taken into cultivation for corn, if it has an owner, must pay the small
rent which it would yield in natural pasture. It
has just been shewn that monopoly must in the
most direct manner affect the price of cattle, the
other great branch of human food; and with regard to the materials of clothing and lodging, there
are very few that do not actually pay a rent, not
only on the great mass of each kind, but on those
a   which are grown on the poorest land actually employed for their production. To say that the
prices of wool, leather, flax, and timber are deter-
b   mined by the cost of their production on the land
which pays no rent, is to refer to a criterion which
it is impossible to find. I believe it may be safely
asserted that there is no portion of wool, leather,
flax, and timber produced in this country which
comes from land that can be so described.

c   We cannot, therefore, get rid of rent in reference to the great mass of commodities. In the
case where we come the nearest to it, namely, in
the production of the main food of the country,
the attempt to resolve the exchangeable value of
all the different portions of this food into labour
and profits alone, involves a contradiction in terms;
and as no error seems to arise from considering rent
as a component part of price, after we have properly explained its origin and progress, it appears

to me essential, both to correctness of language and
correctness of meaning, to say that the cost of pro-   a
ducing any commodity is made up of all the wages,
all the profits, and all the rent which in the actual
circumstances of the society are necessary to bring
that particular commodity to market in the quantity required; or, in other words, that the payment
of these expenses is the necessary condition of its
supply.

If we were determined to use only one term, it   b
would certainly be more correct to refer to capital   c
rather than to labour; because the advances which
are called capital generally include' the other two.
The natural or necessary prices of commodities depend upon the amount of capital which has been
employed upon them, together with the profits of
such capital at the ordinary rate during the time
that it has been employed.   But as the amount of
capital advanced consists of the amount of wages
paid from the first to the last, together with the
amount of rent paid either directly to the landlord
or in the price of raw materials, the use of the
three terms seems to be decidedly preferable, both
as more correct, (rent being, in many cases, not an
advance of capital,) and also as conveying more of
the information that is wanted.

But if rent enters into the raw materials of al-   d
most all manufactures, and of almost all capital,
both fixed and circulating, the advance necessary
to pay it will greatly affect the amount of capital
employed, and combined with the almost infinite
variety that must take place in the duration of

these advances, will most essentially affect that part of price which resolves itself into profits.

ab
c

Supposing, what is probably not true, that there is land in an improved and populous country which pays no rent whatever directly ; yet rent will be paid even by the cultivator of such land in the timber which he uses for his ploughs, carts, and buildings, in the leather which he requires for harness, in the meat which he consumes in his own family, and in the horses which he purchases for tillage. These advances, as far as rent alone is concerned, would at once prevent the price of the produce from being proportioned to the quantity of labour employed upon it; and when we add the profits of these advances according to their amount and the periods of their return, we must acknowledge that even in the production of corn, where no direct

d

rent is paid, its price must be affected by the rent involved in the fixed and circulating capital employed in cultivation.

e

Under all the variations, therefore, which arise from the different proportions of fixed capital employed, the different quickness of the returns of the circulating capital, the quantity of foreign commodities used in manufactures, the acknow-

f

ledged effects of taxation, and the almost universal prevalence of rent in the actual state of all im-

g

proved countries, we must I think allow that, however curious and desirable it may be to know the

h

exact quantity of labour which has been employed

i

in the production of each particular commodity,

j

it is certainly not this labour which determines

their relative values in exchange, at the same time   a
and at the same place.

But if, at the same place and at the same time, the
relative values of commodities are not determined   b
by the labour which they have cost, in production, it is clear that this measure cannot deter-   cd
mine their relative values at different places and
at different times. If, in London and at the pre-   e
sent moment, other causes besides labour concur
in regulating the average prices of the articles
bought and sold, it is quite obvious, that because a
commodity in India now, or in England 500 years
ago, cost in its production double the quantity of
labour which it does in London at present, we
could not infer that it was doubly valuable in ex-   f
change; nor, if we found from a comparison of
money prices, that its value in exchange were dou-   g
ble compared with the mass of commodities, could
we with any degree of safety infer that it had cost,
in its production, just double the quantity of labour.

If, for instance, it were to appear that a yard of   h
fine broad cloth in the time of Edward the Third
cost in its fabrication twenty days' common labour,
and in modern times only ten, it would follow of
course that by improvements of different kinds,
the facility of fabricating broad cloth had been
doubled; but to what extent this circumstance
would have affected its relative value in exchange,
it would not be possible to determine without an
appeal to facts. The alteration in its exchangeable
value generally, or in reference to the mass of com-

modities, would of course depend upon the proportionate facility or difficulty with which other commodities were fabricated, and in reference to particular articles, the labour of fabricating which had remained the same, or was accurately known, it would still depend upon all those circumstances which have already been stated, as preventing the labour which a commodity has cost in its produc-

a   tion, from being a correct measure of relative value, even at the same place and at the same time.

b   In order to shew that the quantity of labour which a commodity has cost is a better measure of value than the quantity which it will command, Mr. Ricardo makes the supposition, that a given quantity of corn might require only half the quantity of labour in its production at one time which it might require at another and subsequent period, and yet that the labourer might be paid in both periods with the same quantity of corn;* in which case, he says, we should have an instance of a commodity which had risen to double its former exchangeable value, according to what he conceives to be the just definition of value, although it would command no more labour in exchange than before.

c   This supposition, it must be allowed, is a most improbable one.   But, supposing such an event to take place, it would strikingly exemplify the incorrectness of his definition, and shew at once the marked distinction which must always exist between cost and value.   We have here a clear case

d   * Principles of Political Economy, chap. i. p. 8. 2d edit.

of increased cost in the quantity of labour to a
double amount; yet it is a part of the supposition
that the commodity, which has been thus greatly
increased in the cost of its production, will not purchase more of that article, which is, beyond comparison, the most extensive and the most important
of all the objects which are offered in exchange,
namely, labour. This instance shews at once that
the quantity of labour which a commodity has cost
in its production, is not a measure of its value in
exchange.

It will be most readily allowed that the labour   a
employed in the production of a commodity, including the labour employed in the production of
the necessary capital, is the principal ingredient
among the component parts of price, and, *other*   b
things being equal, will determine the relative
value of all the commodities in the same country,
or, more correctly speaking, in the same place.
But, in looking back to any past period, we should
ascertain the relative values of commodities at
once, and with much more accuracy, by collecting
their prices in the money of the time. For this
purpose, therefore, an inquiry into the quantity of
labour which each commodity had cost, would be
of no use. And if we were to infer that, because   c
a particular commodity 300 years ago had cost ten
days' labour and now costs twenty, its exchangeable value had doubled, we should certainly run
the risk of drawing a conclusion most extremely
wide of the truth.

It appears then, that the quantity of labour   d

which a commodity has cost in its production, is neither a correct measure of relative value at the same time and at the same place, nor a measure of real value in exchange, as before defined, in different countries and at different periods.

———————

a

SECT. V.

Of Money, when uniform in its cost, considered as a Measure of Value.

bc   Upon the principle, that the labour which a commodity has cost in its production, is at once a measure of real and relative value, it has been thought, that if there were any article to be found which would at all times cost the same quantity of labour d   in its production, it might be used as an accurate and standard measure of value.* It is acknowledged that the precious metals do not possess this quality. The world has been at different periods supplied from mines of different degrees of fertility. This difference of fertility necessarily implies that different quantities of labour are at different times required in the production of the same quantity of metal ; and the different degrees of skill applied at different periods in the working of mines, must be an additional source of variableness in the quantity

e   * Ricardo on the Principles of Political Economy and Taxation, ch. i. p. 24. 2d edit.

of labour which a given weight of coin has cost to bring it to market.

It may be curious however to consider how far the precious metals would be an accurate measure of the quantities of labour employed upon each commodity, even if these sources of variableness were removed, and if it were really true that given quantities of the metals always required in their production the same quantity of labour.   a

It is an acknowledged truth that the precious metals, as they are at present procured and distributed, are an accurate measure of exchangeable value, at the same time and in the same place; and it is certain that the supposition here made would not destroy, or in any respect impair, this quality which they now possess. But it was shewn in the last section that the exchangeable value of commodities is scarcely ever proportioned to the quantity of labour employed upon them. It follows therefore necessarily that the money prices of commodities could not, even on the supposition here made, represent the quantity of labour employed upon them.   b   c

There is indeed no supposition which we can make respecting the mode of procuring the precious metals, which can ever render the prices of commodities a correct measure of the quantity of labour which they have severally cost. These prices will always be found to differ at least as much from the quantity of labour employed upon each commodity, as the quantity of labour does from their exchangeable values. To shew this, let   d   e

a   us suppose; first, that the precious metals require
for their production at the mines which yield no
rent, a certain quantity of fixed and circulating
capital employed for a certain time. In this case,
it follows from the reasonings of the preceding sec-
b   tion and even from the admissions of Mr. Ricardo,
α   that none of the commodities which would ex-
for a given quantity of silver, would contain the
same quantity of labour as that silver, except those
c   which had been produced, not only by the same
quantity of labour, but by the same quantities of
d   the two kinds of capital employed for the same
time and in the same proportions: and, in the case
e   of a rise in the price of labour, all commodities
which still contained the same quantity of labour
would alter in price, except those very few which
were circumstanced exactly in the same manner
with regard to the capitals by which they were
produced as the precious metals.

f   Let us suppose, secondly, that the production of
the precious metals required no fixed capital, but
g   merely advances in the payment of manual labour
h   for a year. This case is so very unusual, that I
should almost doubt whether any commodities
could be found which would at once be of the
same exchangeable value, and contain the same
quantity of labour as a given portion of the precious metals; and of course upon a rise in the price
of labour, almost all commodities would rise or fall
in price.

i   Let us suppose, thirdly, that labour alone, without any advances above the food of a day, were suf-

ficient to obtain the precious metals, that is, that half an ounce of silver and $\frac{1}{15}$ of an ounce of gold could always, on an average, be found by a day's search on the sea-shore. In this case it is obvious that every commodity, which had required in its production any sort or quantity of capital beyond the advance of necessaries for a day, would differ in price from any portion of gold or silver which had cost the same quantity of labour. With regard to the effects of a rise in the price of labour, they cannot be the subject of our consideration, as it is evident that no rise in the price of labour could take place on the present supposition. A day's labour must always remain of the same money price, and corn could only rise as far as the diminution in the necessaries of the labourer would allow. Still, however, though the money price of the labourer could not rise, the rate of profits might fall; and on a fall in the rate of profits, every commodity would fall compared with money.

On either of the above suppositions, the operation of the causes mentioned in the last section would so modify the prices of commodities, that we should be as little able as we are at present, to infer from these relative prices the relative proportions of labour employed upon each commodity.

But independently of the causes here adverted to, the precious metals have other sources of variation peculiar to them. On account of their durability, they conform themselves slowly and with difficulty to the varieties in the qualities of other commodities, and the varying facilities which attend their production.

a

The market prices of gold and silver depend upon the quantity of them in the market compared with the demand; and this quantity has been in part produced by the accumulation of hundreds of years, and is but slowly affected by the annual supply from the mines.

b

It is justly stated by Mr. Ricardo* that the agreement of the market and natural prices of all commodities, depends at all times upon the facility with which the supply can be increased or diminished, and he particularly notices gold, or the precious metals, as among the commodities where this effect cannot be speedily produced. Consequently if by great and sudden improvements in machinery, both in manufactures and agriculture, the facility of production were generally increased, and the wants of the population were supplied with much less labour, the value of the precious metals compared with commodities ought greatly to rise; but, as they could not in a short time be adequately diminished in quantity, the prices of commodities would cease to represent the quantity of labour employed upon them.

c

Another source of variation peculiar to the precious metals would be the use that is made of them in foreign commerce; and unless this use were given up, and the exportation and importation of them were prohibited, it would unquestionably

d

* Principles of Political Economy and Taxation, ch. xiii. p. 255.

answer to some countries possessing peculiar advantages in their exportable commodities, to buy their gold and silver abroad rather than procure them at home. At this present moment, I believe it is unquestionably true that England purchases the precious metals with less labour than is applied to obtain them directly from the mines of Mexico. But if they could be imported by some countries from abroad with less labour than they could be obtained at home, it would answer to other countries to export them in exchange for commodities, which they either could not produce on their own soil, or could obtain cheaper elsewhere. And thus, in reference to the relative value of commodities both in different countries at the same period, and in the same country at different periods, it is obvious that the prices in money might be subject to considerable variations, without being accompanied by any proportionate variations in the quantities of labour which they had cost.

The objections hitherto considered in this and the preceding sections are some of those which present themselves upon the supposition that each nation possessed mines, or even could procure at home the precious metals at all times with the same quantity of labour without capital; but these, it must be allowed, are extravagant hypotheses. If however we were to assume the more natural one, of the mines, wherever they are, and in all ages, costing always the same quantity of labour and capital in the working, we should see immediately from the present distribution of the precious metals, how little comparatively they could be depended upon as measuring, in different countries and at different times, the quantities of labour which commodities have cost.

a   If indeed the fertility of the mines were always the same, we should certainly get rid of that source of variation which arises from the existing contrary quality, and of the effects of such a discovery as that of the American mines. But other great and obvious sources of variation would remain. The uniform fertility of the mines would not essentially alter the proportions in which the precious metals would be distributed to different countries; and the great differences, which are now known to take place in their value in different

b   places, when compared with corn and labour, would probably continue nearly the same.

c   According to all the accounts we have received of prices in Bengal, a given quantity of silver will there represent or command six or eight times more

d   labour and provisions than in England. In all parts of the world articles of equal money prices exchange for each other. It will consequently happen that, in the commerce carried on between the two countries, the product of a day's English labour must exchange for the product of five or six days of Indian labour, after making a sufficient allowance for the difference of profits.

e   Perhaps it will be said that the high comparative value of silver in India arises mainly from the effects of the discovery of the American mines not having yet been adequately communicated to this part of the world: but it must be recollected that the

discovery is now of long standing; and that the
difference in the relative value of gold and silver,
compared with their values in Europe, which most
clearly indicated an incomplete communication, is
now at an end.   I am disposed to think therefore,
that the high value of silver in India arises mainly
from other causes. But at all events the difference
is now so enormous as to allow of a great abate-
ment, and yet to leave it very considerable.

   It is not however necessary to go to India in order   a
to find similar differences in the value of the precious metals, though not perhaps so great.   Russia,
Poland, Germany, France, Flanders, and indeed almost all the countries in Europe, present instances
of great variations in the quantity of labour and
provisions which can be purchased by a given
quantity of silver.   Yet the relative values of the
precious metals in these countries must be very
nearly the same as they would be, if the American
mines had been at all times of a uniform fertility :
and consequently, by their present relative values,
we may judge how little dependence could be
placed on a coincidence in different countries between the money prices of commodities and the
quantities of labour which they had cost, even on
the supposition that money was always obtained
from the mines in America by the same quantity
of labour and capital.

   But if we are not fully satisfied with this kind   b
of reference to experience, it is obvious that the
same conclusion follows inevitably from theory.
In those countries where the precious metals are

necessarily purchased, no plausible reason can be assigned why the quantity of them should be in proportion to the difficulty of producing the articles with which they are purchased.

a   When the English and Indian muslins appear in the German markets, their relative prices will be

b   determined solely by their relative qualities, without the slightest reference to the very different quantities of human labour which they may have cost; and the circumstance that in the fabrication of the Indian muslins five or six times more labour has been employed than in the English, will not enable them to command greater returns of money to India.

c   In the ports of Europe no merchants are to be found who would be disposed to give more money for Swedish wheat, than Russian, Polish, or American, of the same quality, merely because more labour had been employed in the cultivation of it, on account of its being grown on a more barren soil. If India and Sweden therefore had no other means of buying silver in Europe than by the export of muslins and corn, it would be absolutely impossible for them to circulate their commodities at a money price, compared with other countries, proportioned to the relative difficulty with which they were produced, or the quantity of labour which had been employed upon them. It is indeed universally allowed, that the power of purchasing foreign commodities of all kinds depends upon the relative cheapness, not the relative dearness, of the articles that can be exported; and therefore, although the actual currency of an individual country, other circumstances being nearly equal, may be distributed among the different commodities bought and sold, according to the quantity of labour which they have severally cost, the supposition that the same sort of distribution would take place in different countries, involves a contradiction of the first principles of commercial intercourse.*

It appears then that no sort of regularity in the production of the precious metals, not even if all countries possessed mines of their own, and still less if the great majority were obliged to purchase their money from others, can possibly render the money prices of commodities a correct measure of the quantity of labour which has been employed upon them, either in the same or different countries, or at the same or different periods.

a

How far the precious metals so circumstanced, may be a good measure of the *exchangeable* value of commodities, though not of the labour which has been employed upon them, is quite another question. It has been repeatedly stated that the precious metals, in whatever way they may be obtained, are a correct measure of exchangeable value at the same time and place. And certainly the less subject to variation are the modes of procuring them, the more they will approach to a measure of exchangeable value at different times and in different places.

b

* Mr. Ricardo very justly states that, even on the supposition which he has made respecting the precious metals, the foreign interchange of commodities is not determined by the quantity of labour which they have relatively cost.

c

a   If, indeed, they were procured according to one of the suppositions made in this section, that is, if each nation could at all times obtain them by the same quantity of labour without any advances of capital, then, with the exception of the temporary disturbances occasioned by foreign commerce and the sudden invention of machinery, the

b   exchangeable value in money in reference to the labour which it would command, would be the same in all countries and at all times; and the specific reason why the precious metals would in this

c   case approach near to a correct measure of real value in exchange is, that it is the only supposition in which their cost in labour can ever be the same as their exchangeable value in labour. In the case supposed, money would certainly be of a uniform value. It would at all times both cost the same quantity of labour and command the same quantity; but we have seen that, in reference to those commodities where any sort of capital was used, their values, compared either with the precious metals or each other, could never be propor-

d   tioned to the labour which they had cost.

---

e   **SECT. VI.**

f   *Of the Labour which a Commodity will command, considered as a Measure of real Value in Exchange.*

When we consider labour as a measure of value in the sense in which it is most frequently applied

by Adam Smith, that is, when the value of an object is estimated by the quantity of labour of a given description (common day-labour, for instance)   a
which it can command, it will appear to be un-   b
questionably the best of any one commodity, and to unite, more nearly than any other, the qualities of a real and nominal measure of exchangeable value.

In the first place, in looking for any one object   c
as a measure of exchangeable value, our attention would naturally be directed to that which was most extensively the subject of exchange. Now of all objects it cannot be disputed, that by far the greatest mass of value is given in exchange for labour either productive or unproductive.

Secondly, the value of commodities, in ex-   d
change for labour, can alone express the degree in which they are suited to the wants and tastes of society, and the degree of abundance in which they are supplied, compared with the desires and numbers of those who are to consume them. By improvements in machinery, cloth, silks, cottons, hats, shoes, money, and even corn, for some years might all be very greatly increased in quantity at the same time. Yet while this remarkable alteration had taken place in these commodities, the value of any one of them in exchange for any other, or even compared with the mass of the others collectively, might remain exactly the same. It is obvious therefore that, in order to express the important effects arising from facility of production, we must take into our consideration either the quan-

tity of labour which commodities have cost, or the quantities of labour which they will command. But it was shewn in the last two sections, that the quantity of labour, which commodities have cost, never approaches to a correct measure of exchangeable value, even at the same time and place. Consequently, our attention is naturally directed to the labour which commodities will command.

a

Thirdly, the accumulation of capital, and its efficiency in the increase of wealth and population, depends almost entirely upon its power of setting labour to work ; or, in other words, upon its power of commanding labour. No plenty of commodities can occasion a real and permanent increase of capital if they are of such a nature, or have fallen so much in value that they will not command more labour than they have cost. When this happens from permanent causes, a final stop is put to accumulation ; when it happens for a time only, a temporary stop to accumulation takes place, and population is in both cases affected accordingly. As it appears then that the great stimulus to production depends mainly upon the power of commodities to command labour, and especially to command a greater quantity of labour than they have cost, we are naturally led to consider this power of commanding labour as of the utmost importance in an estimate of the exchangeable value of commodities.

b

These are some of the general considerations which, in a search for a measure of value, would direct our first attention to the labour which commodities will command; and a more particular consideration of the qualities of this measure will convince us that no one other object is equally adapted to the purpose.

It is universally allowed that, in the same place, and within moderately short periods of time, the precious metals are an unexceptionable measure of value; but whatever is true of the precious metals with respect to nominal prices, is true of labour applied in the way proposed.

It is obvious, for instance, that, in the same place and at the same time, the different quantities of day-labour which different commodities can command, will be exactly in proportion to their relative values in exchange; and, if any two of them will purchase the same quantity of labour of the same description, they will invariably exchange for each other.

The merchant might safely regulate his dealings, and estimate his commercial profits by the excess of the quantity of labour which his imports would command, compared with his exports. Whether the value of a commodity had arisen from a strict or partial monopoly; whether it was occasioned principally by the scarcity of the raw material, the peculiar sort of labour required in its construction, or unusually high profits; whether its value had been increased by an increased cost of production, or diminished by the application of machinery; whether its value at the moment depended chiefly upon permanent, or upon temporary causes;—in all cases, and under all circumstances, the quantity of labour which it will command, or, what comes

a

b
c

d

e

f

g

h

i

j

k

l

a to the same thing, the quantity of labour or la-
b bour's worth, which people will give to obtain it,
   will be a very exact measure of its exchangeable
   value. In short, this measure will, in the same place,
c and at the same time, exactly accord with the no-
d minal prices of commodities, with this great advantage in its favour, that it will serve to explain
   very accurately and usefully all variations of value,
   without reference to a circulating medium.
ef   It may be said, perhaps, that in the same place
   and at the same time exactly, almost every commodity may be considered as an accurate measure
g of the relative value of others, and that what has
   just been said of labour may be said of cloth, cot-
h ton, iron, or any other article. Any two commodities which at the same time and in the same place
i would purchase or command the same quantity of
jk cloth, cotton or iron, of a given quality, would
   have the same relative value, or would exchange
l for each other. This is no doubt true, if we take
   the same time precisely; but not, if a moderate
   latitude be allowed, such as may be allowed in the
   case of labour or of the precious metals. Cloth,
   cotton, iron and similar commodities, are much more
   exposed to sudden changes of value, both from the
   variations of demand, and the influence of machinery and other causes, than labour. Day-labour,
   taking the average of summer and winter, is the
   most steady of all exchangeable articles; and the
   merchant who, in a foreign venture, the returns of
   which were slow, was sure of gaining fifteen per cent.
   estimated in labour, would be much more secure

of finally gaining fifteen per cent. of real profits, than he, who could only be sure of gaining fifteen per cent. estimated in cloth, cotton, iron, or even money.

While labour thus constitutes an accurate mea-   a
sure of value in the same place, and within short periods of time, it approaches the nearest of any one commodity to such a measure, when applied to different places and distant periods of time.

Adam Smith has considered labour in the sense   b
here understood as so good a measure of corn, or, what comes to the same thing, he has considered corn as so good a measure of labour, that in his Digression on the value of silver during the four last centuries, he has actually substituted corn for labour, and drawn the same conclusions from his inquiry as if the one were always an accurate measure of the other.

In doing this I think he has fallen into an im-   c
portant error, and drawn inferences inconsistent with his own general principles. At the same time, we must allow that, from century to century, and in different and distant countries where the precious metals greatly vary in value, corn, as being the principal necessary of life, may fairly be considered as the best measure of the real exchangeable value of labour; and consequently the power of a commodity to command labour will, at distant times and in different countries, be the best criterion of its power of commanding the first necessary of life—corn.

With regard to the other necessaries and conve-   d

niences of life, they must in general be allowed to depend still more upon labour than corn, because in general more labour is employed upon them after they come from the soil. And as, *all other things being equal,* the quantity of labour which a commodity will command will be in proportion to the quantity which it has cost; we may fairly presume that the influence of the different quantities of labour which a commodity may have cost in its production, will be sufficiently taken into consideration in this estimate of value, together with the further consideration of all those circumstances, besides the labour actually employed on them in which they are not equal. The great pre-eminence of that measure of value, which consists in the quantity of labour which a commodity will command, over that which consists in the quantity of labour which has been actually employed about it, is, that while the latter involves merely one cause of exchangeable value, though in general the most considerable one; the former, in addition to this cause, involves all the different circumstances which influence the rates at which commodities are actually exchanged for each other.

a   It is evident that no commodity can be a good measure of real value in exchange in different places and at distant periods, which is not at the same time a good measure of nominal value in these places and at these distant periods; and in this respect it must be allowed, that the quantity of common labour that an article will command, which necessarily takes into account every cause that in-

fluences exchangeable value, is an unexceptionable measure.

It should be further remarked, that although in   a
different countries and at distant periods, the same
quantity of labour will command very different
quantities of corn—the first necessary of life; yet
in the progress of improvement and civilization it
generally happens, that when labour commands the
smallest quantity of food, it commands the greatest
quantity of other commodities, and when it commands the greatest quantity of food, it commands the smallest quantity of other necessaries
and conveniences; so that when, in two countries,
or in two periods differently advanced in improvement, two objects command the same quantity of
labour, they will often command nearly the same
quantity of the necessaries and conveniences of
life, although they may command different quantities of corn.

It must be allowed then that, of any one commo-   b
dity, the quantity of common day-labour which
any article will command, appears to approach the
nearest to a measure of real value in exchange.

But still, labour, like all other commodities, varies   c
from its plenty or scarcity compared with the demand for it, and, at different times and in different
countries, commands very different quantities of
the first necessary of life; and further, from the
different degrees of skill and of assistance from
machinery with which labour is applied, the products of labour are not in proportion to the quantity
exerted.   Consequently, labour, in any sense in

which the term can be applied, cannot be considered as an accurate and standard measure of real
value in exchange. And if the labour which a
commodity will command cannot be considered in
this light, there is certainly no other quarter in
which we can seek for such a measure with any
prospect of success.

a

SECTION VII.

Of a Mean between Corn and Labour considered as a
Measure of Real Value in Exchange.

b   No one commodity then, it appears, can justly be
considered as a standard measure of real value in
exchange; and such an estimate of the comparative prices of all commodities as would determine
the command of any one in particular over the
necessaries, conveniences, and amusements of life,
including labour, would not only be too difficult
and laborious for use, but generally quite imprac-
ticable. Two objects, however, might, in some
cases, be a better measure of real value in exchange
than one alone, and yet be sufficiently manageable
for practical application.

c   A certain quantity of corn of a given quality,
on account of its capacity of supporting a certain
number of human beings, has always a definite
and invariable value in use; but both its real and

nominal value in exchange is subject to considerable variations, not only from year to year, but
from century to century. It is found by experience that population and cultivation, notwithstanding their mutual dependence on each other,
do not always proceed with equal steps, but are
subject to marked alternations in the velocity of
their movements. Exclusive of annual variations,
it appears that corn sometimes remains dear, compared with labour and other commodities, for many
years together, and at other times remains cheap,
compared with the same objects, for similar periods. At these different periods, a bushel of corn
will command very different quantities of labour
and other commodities. In the reign of Henry
VII., at the end of the 15th and beginning of the
16th centuries, it appears, from the statute price
of labour and the average price of wheat, that half
a bushel of this grain would purchase but little
more than a day's common labour ; and, of course,
but a small quantity of those commodities in the
production of which much labour is necessary.
A century afterwards, in the latter part of the
reign of Elizabeth, half a bushel of wheat would
purchase three days' common labour, and, of
course, a considerable quantity comparatively of
those commodities on which labour is employed.
Consequently, from century to century as well as
from year to year, a given quantity of corn appears to measure very imperfectly the quantity of
the necessaries, conveniences, and amusements of

life, which any particular commodity will command in exchange.

a

The same observation will hold good if we take day-labour, the measure proposed by Adam Smith; and the same period in our history will illustrate the variation from century to century of this measure. In the reign of Henry VII. a day's labour, according to the former statement, would purchase nearly half a bushel of wheat, the chief necessary of life, and consequently the chief article in the general estimate of real value in exchange. A century afterwards, a day's labour would only purchase one-sixth of a bushel,—a most prodigious difference in this main article. And though it may be presumed that a day's labour in both periods would purchase much more nearly the same quantity of those articles where labour enters as a principal ingredient, than of corn, yet the variations in its command over the first necessary of life, at different periods, must alone disqualify it from being an accurate measure of real value in exchange from century to century.

b

Though neither of these two objects, however, taken singly, can be considered as a satisfactory measure of value, yet by combining the two, we may perhaps approach to greater accuracy.

c

When corn compared with labour is dear, labour compared with corn must necessarily be cheap. At the period that a given quantity of corn will command the greatest quantity of the necessaries, conveniences, and amusements of life, a given quantity of labour will always command the smallest quantity of such objects; and at the period when corn commands the smallest, labour will command the greatest quantity of them.

If, then, we take a mean between the two, we shall evidently have a measure corrected by the contemporary variations of each in opposite directions, and likely to represent more nearly than either the same quantity of the necessaries, conveniences, and amusements of life, at the most distant periods, and under all the varying circumstances to which the progress of population and cultivation is subject.   a

For this purpose, however, it is necessary that we should fix upon some measure of corn which may be considered, in respect of quantity, as an equivalent to a day's labour; and perhaps in this country, a peck of wheat, which is about the average daily earnings of a good labourer in good times, may be sufficiently accurate for the object proposed. Any commodity therefore which, at different periods, will purchase the same number of days' labour and of pecks of wheat, or parts of them, each taken in equal proportions, may be considered, upon this principle, as commanding pretty nearly the same quantity of the necessaries, conveniences, and amusements of life ; and, consequently, as preserving pretty nearly its real value in exchange at different periods. And any commodity which at different periods is found to purchase different quantities of corn and labour thus taken, will evidently have varied compared with a   b

measure subject to but little variation, and consequently may be presumed to have varied proportionably in its real value in exchange.

a   In estimating the real value in exchange of commodities in different countries, regard should be
had to the kind of food consumed by the labouring
classes ; and the general rule should be to compare
them in each country with a day's labour, and a
quantity of the prevailing sort of grain, equal to
the average daily earnings of a good labourer.
Thus, if the money price of a commodity in England would purchase five days' labour and five pecks
of corn, and the money price of a commodity in
Bengal would purchase five days' labour, and five
times the quantity of rice usually earned in a day
by a good labourer, according to an average of a
very considerable period, these commodities might
be considered in each country as of equal real value
in exchange ; and the difference in their money
values would express pretty nearly the different
values of silver in England and Bengal.

b   The principal defect of the measure here proposed arises from the effect of capital, machinery
and the division of labour in varying, in different
countries and at different periods, the results of day-
labour and the prices of manufactured commodities : but these varying results no approximation
hitherto suggested has ever pretended to estimate ;
and, in fact, they relate rather to riches than to exchangeable value, which, though nearly connected,
are not always the same ; and on this account, in
an estimate of value, the cheapness arising from

skill and machinery may without much error be neglected.

Mr. Ricardo asks " why should gold, or corn, or labour be the standard measure of value, more than coals or iron, more than cloth, soap, candles, and the other necessaries of the labourer? Why, in short, should any commodity, or all commodities together, be the standard, when such a standard is itself subject to fluctuations in value?"* I trust that the question here put has been satisfactorily answered in the course of this inquiry into the nature and measures of value. And I will only add here that some one, or more, or all commodities together, must of necessity be taken to express exchangeable value, because they include every thing that can be given in exchange. Yet a measure of exchangeable value thus formed, it is acknowledged, is imperfect; and we should certainly have been obliged to Mr. Ricardo if he had substituted a better. But what measure has he proposed to substitute? The sacrifice of toil and labour made in the production of a commodity; that is, its cost, or, more properly speaking, a portion of its cost, from which its value in exchange is practically found, under different circumstances, to vary in almost every degree. Cost and value are always essentially different. A commodity, the cost of which has doubled, may be worth in exchangeable value no more than before, if other commodities have likewise doubled. When the cost of commodities however is esti-

* Princ. of Polit. Econ. c. xx. p. 343. 2d edit.

α   mated upon the principles of Adam Smith, their
money cost and average money value will generally meet. But when cost is estimated upon the
principles of Mr. Ricardo, by the quantity of labour applied, the labour cost and labour value
scarcely ever agree. Wherever there are profits,
(and the cases are very rare indeed in which there
are none,) the value of a commodity in exchange
for labour is uniformly greater than the labour
which has been employed upon it.

a   We have therefore to choose between an imperfect measure of exchangeable value, and one that
is necessarily and fundamentally erroneous.

b   If Mr. Ricardo says that by value, when he uses
it alone, he does not mean exchangeable value,
then he has certainly led us into a great error in
many parts of his work; and has finally left us
without substituting any measure of exchangeable
value for the one to which he objects. There
never was any difficulty in finding a measure of
cost, or indeed of value, if we define it to be cost.
The difficulty is, to find a measure of real value in
exchange, in contradistinction to nominal value or
price. There is no question as to an accurate standard, which is justly considered as unattainable. But,
of all the articles given in exchange, labour is, beyond comparison, the largest and most important;
and next to it stands corn. The reason, why
corn should be preferred to coals or iron, is surely
very intelligible. The same reason combined with
others holds for preferring labour to corn. And
the reasons given in this section are, I trust, suffi-

cient for preferring, in some cases, a mean between corn and labour to either of them taken separately. Where corn is not one of the articles to be measured, as in the case of an estimate of the value of the precious metals, or any particular commodity, a mean between corn and labour is certainly to be preferred to labour alone; but where corn is one of the main articles to be measured, as in an estimate of the exchangeable value of the whole produce of a country, the command of such produce over domestic and foreign labour is still the best criterion to which we can refer.

a

CHAPTER III.

α

OF THE RENT OF LAND.

SECTION I.

Of the Nature and Causes of Rent.

THE rent of land may be defined to be that portion of the value of the whole produce which remains to the owner of the land, after all the outgoings belonging to its cultivation, of whatever kind, have been paid, including the profits of the capital employed, estimated according to the usual

a and ordinary rate of the profits of agricultural stock at the time being.

It sometimes happens that, from accidental and temporary circumstances, the farmer pays more, or less, than this; but this is the point towards which the actual rents paid are constantly gravitating, and which is therefore always referred to when the term is used in a general sense.

b Rent then being the excess of price above what is necessary to pay the wages of the labour and the profits of the capital employed in cultivation, the first object which presents itself for inquiry, is, the cause or causes of this excess of price.

After very careful and repeated revisions of the subject, I do not find myself able to agree entirely

in the view taken of it, either by Adam Smith, or
the Economists; and still less, by some more mo-   a
dern writers.

Almost all these writers appear to me to consider rent as too nearly resembling, in its nature, and
the laws by which it is governed, that excess of
price above the cost of production, which is the
characteristic of a common monopoly.

Adam Smith, though in some parts of the ele-
venth chapter of his first book he contemplates
rent quite in its true light,* and has interspersed
through his work more just observations on the
subject than any other writer, has not explained
the most essential cause of the high price of raw   b
produce with sufficient distinctness, though he
often touches on it; and by applying occasionally
the term monopoly to the rent of land, without   α
stopping to mark its more radical peculiarities, he
leaves the reader without a definite impression of
the real difference between the cause of the high   c
price of the necessaries of life, and of monopolized
commodities.

* I cannot, however, agree with him in thinking that all land   β
which yields food must *necessarily* yield rent. The land which is   d
successively taken into cultivation in improving countries, may   e
only pay profits and labour. A fair profit on the stock employed,   f
including, of course, the payment of labour, will always be a sufficient inducement to cultivate. But, practically, the cases are very
rare, where land is to be had by any body who chooses to take it:
and probably it is true, almost universally, that all appropriated   g
land which yields food in its natural state, always yields a rent,   h
whether cultivated or uncultivated.

a   Some of the views which the Economists have taken of the nature of rent appear to me also, to be quite just; but they have mixed them with so much error, and have drawn such unwarranted inferences from them, that what is true in their doctrines has produced little effect. Their great practical conclusion, namely, the propriety of taxing exclusively the neat rents of the landlords, evidently depends upon their considering these

b   rents as completely disposeable, like that excess of price above the cost of production, which distinguishes a common monopoly.

M. Say, in his valuable Treatise on Political Economy, in which he has explained with great clearness many points not sufficiently developed by Adam Smith, has not treated the subject of rent in a manner entirely satisfactory. In speaking of the different natural agents which, as well as the land, co-operate with the labours of man, he observes: "Heureusement personne n'a pu dire, le vent et le soleil m'appartiennent, et le service qu'ils rendent doit m'être payé."* And, though he acknowledges that, for obvious reasons, property in land is necessary, yet he evidently considers rent as almost exclusively owing to such appro-

c   priation, and to external demand.

In the excellent work of M. de Sismondi, *De la Richesse Commerciale*, he says, in a note on the

d   * Vol. II. p. 124. Of this work a new and much improved edition has lately been published, which is highly worthy the attention of all those who take an interest in these subjects.

subject of rent : " Cette partie de la rente foncière est celle que les Economistes ont décorée du nom du *produit net,* comme étant le seul fruit du travail qui ajoutât quelque chose à la richesse nationale. On pourroit, au contraire, soutenir contre eux, que c'est la seule partie du produit du travail, dont la valeur soit purement nominale, et n'ait rien de réelle : c'est en effet le résultat de l'augmentation de prix qu'obtient un vendeur en vertu de son privilège, sans que la chose vendue en vaille réellement davantage."*

The prevailing opinions among the more modern writers in our own country have appeared to me to incline towards a similar view of the subject; and, not to multiply citations, I shall only add, that in a very respectable edition of the *Wealth of Nations,* lately published by Mr. Buchanan, of Edinburgh, the idea of monopoly is pushed still farther. And, while former writers, though they considered rent as governed by the laws of monopoly, were still of opinion that this monopoly in the case of land was necessary and useful, Mr. Buchanan sometimes speaks of it even as prejudicial, and as depriving the consumer of what it gives to the landlord.

In treating of productive and unproductive labour in the last volume, he observes, that,† " The neat surplus by which the Economists estimate the utility of agriculture, plainly arises from the high price of its produce, which, however advantageous

* Vol. I. p. 49.   † Vol. IV. p. 134.

to the landlord who receives it, is surely no advantage to the consumer who pays it. Were the produce of agriculture to be sold for a lower price, the same neat surplus would not remain, after defraying the expenses of cultivation; but agriculture would be still equally productive to the general stock; and the only difference would be, that, as the landlord was formerly enriched by the high price, at the expense of the community, the community will now profit by the low price, at the expense of the landlord. The high price in which the rent or neat surplus originates, while it enriches the landlord who has the produce of agriculture to sell, diminishes, in the same proportion, the wealth of those who are its purchasers; and on this account it is quite inaccurate to consider the landlord's rent as a clear addition to the national wealth."

In other parts of this work he uses the same, or even stronger language, and in a note on the subject of taxes, he speaks of the high price of the produce of land as advantageous to those who receive it, but proportionably *injurious* to those who pay it. " In this view," he adds, " it can form no general addition to the stock of the community, as the neat surplus in question is nothing more than a revenue transferred from one class to another, and, from the mere circumstance of its thus changing hands, it is clear that no fund can arise out of which to pay taxes. The revenue which pays for the produce of land exists already in the hands of those who purchase that produce;

and, if the price of subsistence were lower, it would still remain in their hands, where it would be just as available for taxation, as when by a higher price it is transferred to the landed proprietor."*

That there are some circumstances connected with rent, which have a strong affinity to a natural monopoly, will be readily allowed. The extent of the earth itself is limited, and cannot be enlarged by human demand. The inequality of soils occasions, even at an early period of society,   a a comparative scarcity of the best lands ; and this scarcity is undoubtedly one of the causes of rent properly so called. On this account, perhaps the term *partial monopoly* may be fairly applicable to it. But the scarcity of land, thus implied, is by no means alone sufficient to produce the effects observed. And a more accurate investigation of the subject will shew us how different the high price   b of raw produce is, both in its nature and origin, and the laws by which it is governed, from the high price of a common monopoly.

The causes of the excess of the price of raw produce above the costs of production, may be stated   c d to be three.

First, and mainly, That quality of the earth, by   e which it can be made to yield a greater portion of   f the necessaries of life than is required for the maintenance of the persons employed on the land.

2dly, That quality peculiar to the necessaries of   g life of being able, when properly distributed, to   α

* Vol. III. p. 212.

create their own demand, or to raise up a number of demanders in proportion to the quantity of necessaries produced.

And, 3dly, The comparative scarcity of fertile land, either natural or artificial.

a   The quality of the soil here noticed as the primary cause of the high price of raw produce, is the gift of nature to man.   It is quite unconnected with monopoly, and yet is so absolutely essential to the existence of rent, that without it no degree of scarcity or monopoly could have occasioned an excess of the price of raw produce above what was necessary for the payment of wages and profits.

If, for instance, the soil of the earth had been such, that, however well directed might have been the industry of man, he could not have produced from it more than was barely sufficient to main-

b   tain those whose labour and attention were necessary to its products; though, in this case, food and raw materials would have been evidently scarcer than at present, and the land might have been in the same manner monopolized by particular owners; yet it is quite clear, that neither rent nor any essential surplus produce of the land in the form of high profits and high wages could have existed.

On the other hand, it will be allowed, that in whatever way the produce of a given portion of land may be actually divided, whether the whole is distributed to the labourers and capitalists, or a part is awarded to a landlord, the *power* of such land to yield rent is exactly proportioned to its

c   fertility, or to the general surplus which it can be

made to produce beyond what is strictly necessary
to support the labour and keep up the capital employed upon it. If this surplus be as 1, 2, 3, 4,
or 5, then its *power* of yielding a rent will be as
1, 2, 3, 4, or 5 ; and no degree of monopoly—no
possible increase of external demand can essentially
alter their different *powers*.   a

But if no rent can exist without this surplus,
and if the power of particular soils to pay rent be   b
proportioned to this surplus, it follows that this
surplus from the land, arising from its fertility,
must evidently be considered as the foundation or
main cause of all rent.

Still however, this surplus, necessary and important as it is, would not be sure of possessing a value
which would enable it to command a proportionate
quantity of labour and other commodities, if it had
not a power of raising up a population to consume
it, and, by the articles produced in return, of cre-
ating an effective demand for it.

It has been sometimes argued, that it is mistaking the principle of population to imagine, that
the increase of food or of raw produce alone can
occasion a proportionate increase of population.
This is no doubt true ; but it must be allowed, as
has been justly observed by Adam Smith, that
" when food is provided, it is comparatively easy
to find the necessary clothing and lodging " And   c
it should always be recollected, that land does not
produce one commodity alone, but, in addition to
that most indispensable of all commodities—food,   d

it produces the materials for clothing, lodging, and firing.*

It is therefore strictly true, that land produces the necessaries of life—produces the means by which, and by which alone, an increase of people may be brought into being and supported. In this respect it is fundamentally different from every other kind of machine known to man ; and it is natural to suppose that the use of it should be attended with some peculiar effects.

If an active and industrious family were possessed of a certain portion of land, which they could cultivate so as to make it yield food, and the materials of clothing, lodging, and firing, not only for themselves but for five other families, it follows, from the principle of population, that, if they properly distributed their surplus produce, they would soon be able to command the labour of five other families, and the value of their landed produce would soon be worth five times as much as the value of the labour which had been employed in raising it.   But if, instead of a portion of land

a
α

* It is however certain that, if either these materials be wanting, or the skill and capital necessary to work them up be prevented from forming, owing to the insecurity of property or any other cause, the cultivators will soon slacken in their exertions, and the motives to accumulate and to increase their produce will greatly diminish.   But in this case there will be a very slack demand for labour : and, whatever may be the nominal cheapness of provisions, the labourer will not really be able to command such a portion of the necessaries of life, including, of course, clothing, lodging, &c. as will occasion an increase of population.

b

which would yield all the necessaries of life, they
possessed only, in addition to the means of their
own support, a machine which would produce
hats or coats for fifty people besides themselves, no
efforts which they could make would enable them
to ensure a demand for these hats or coats, and
give them in return a command over a quantity of
labour considerably greater than their fabrication
had cost. For a long time, and by possibility for
ever, the machine might be of no more value than
that which would result from its making hats or
coats for the family. Its further powers might
be absolutely thrown away from the want of demand; and even when, from external causes totally independent of any efforts of their own, a
population had risen to demand the fifty hats, the   a
value of them in the command of labour and other
commodities might permanently exceed but very
little the value of the labour employed in making
them.

After the new cotton machinery had been introduced into this country, a hundred yards of muslin
of a certain quality would not probably command
more labour than twenty-five yards would before;   b
because the supply had increased faster than the   c
demand, and there was no longer a demand for
the whole quantity produced at the same price.
But after great improvements in agriculture have
been adopted upon a limited tract of land, a quarter of wheat will in a short time command just as
much labour as before; because the increased produce, occasioned by the improvements in cultiva-

a

tion, is found to create a demand proportioned to the supply, which must still be limited; and the value of corn is thus prevented from falling like the value of muslins.

Thus the fertility of the land gives the power of yielding a rent, by yielding a surplus quantity of necessaries beyond the wants of the cultivators; and the peculiar quality belonging to the necessaries of life, when properly distributed, tends strongly and constantly to give a value to this surplus by raising up a population to demand it.

These qualities of the soil and of its products have been, as might be expected, strongly insisted

b

upon by the Economists in different parts of their works; and they are evidently admitted as truths by Adam Smith, in those passages of the *Wealth of Nations*, in which he approaches the nearest to

c

the doctrines of the Economists. But modern writers have in general been disposed to overlook them, and to consider rent as regulated upon the principles of a common monopoly, although the distinction is. of great importance, and appears obvious and striking in almost any instance that we

d

can assume.

If the fertility of the mines of the precious metals all over the world were diminished one half, it will be allowed that, as population and wealth do not necessarily depend upon gold and silver, such an event might not only be consistent with an undiminished amount of population and

e

wealth, but even with a considerable increase of both. In this case however it is quite certain that the rents, profits, and wages paid at the different mines in the world might not only not be diminished, but might be considerably increased. But if the fertility of all the lands in the world were to be diminished one half;* inasmuch as population and wealth strictly depend upon the quantity of the necessaries of life which the soil affords, it is quite obvious that a great part of the population and wealth of the world would be destroyed, and with it a great part of the effective demand for necessaries. The largest portion of the lands in most countries would be thrown completely out of cultivation, and wages, profits, and rents, particularly the latter, would be greatly diminished on all the rest. I believe there is hardly any land in this country employed in producing corn, which yields a rent equal in value to the wages of the labour and the profits of the stock necessary to its cultivation. If this be so, then, in the case supposed,

* Mr. Ricardo has supposed a case (p. 505.) of a diminution of fertility of one-tenth, and he thinks that it would increase rents by pushing capital upon less fertile land. I think, on the contrary, that in any well cultivated country it could not fail to lower rents, by occasioning the withdrawing of capital from the poorest soils. If the last land before in use would do but little more than pay the necessary labour and a profit of 10 per cent. upon the capital employed, a diminution of a tenth part of the gross produce would certainly render many poor soils no longer worth cultivating. And, on Mr. Ricardo's supposition, where, I would ask, is the increased demand and increased price to come from, when, from the greater quantity of labour and capital necessary for the land, the means of obtaining the precious metals, or any other commodities, to exchange for corn, would be greatly reduced?

a

b the quantity of produce being only half of what
was before obtained by the same labour and capital,
it may be doubted whether any land in England

c could be kept in tillage. All effective demand for
corn of home growth would be at an end; and if a
supply could not be obtained from abroad, the
population of the country must be diminished to
perhaps one-fifth of its former amount.

The produce of certain vineyards in France,
which, from the peculiarity of their soil and situation, exclusively yield wine of a certain flavour, is
sold, of course, at a price very far exceeding the

d cost of production. And this is owing to the
greatness of the competition for such wine, compared with the scantiness of its supply, which con-
fines the use of it to so small a number of persons
that they are able, and, rather than go without it,
willing to give an excessively high price. But,
if the fertility of these lands were increased so
as very considerably to increase the produce, this
produce might so fall in value as to diminish most
essentially the excess of its price above the cost of
production. While, on the other hand, if the vineyards were to become less productive, this excess
might increase to almost any extent.*

e   * Mr. Ricardo says, (p. 505.) in answer to this passage, that,
"*given the high price,* rent must be high in proportion to abundance and not scarcity," whether in peculiar vineyards' or on
common corn lands. But this is begging the whole of the question. The price cannot be given. By the force of external demand
and diminished supply the produce of an acre of Champaigne
grapes might permanently command fifty times the labour that

f   had been employed in cultivating it; but no possible increase of

The obvious cause of these effects is, that, in all common monopolies, the demand is exterior to, and independent of, the production itself. The number of persons, who might have a taste for scarce wines, and would be desirous of entering into a competition for the purchase of them, might increase almost indefinitely, while the produce itself was decreasing; and its price, therefore, would have no other limit than the numbers, powers, and caprices of the competitors for it.

In the production of the necessaries of life, on the contrary, the demand is dependent on the produce itself, and the effects are therefore widely different. In this case it is physically impossible that   a the number of demanders should increase, while the quantity of produce diminishes, since the demanders can only exist by means of the produce.

In all common monopolies, an excess of the value of the produce above the value of the labour   b employed in obtaining it, may be created by external demand. In the partial monopoly of the   c land which produces necessaries, such an excess can only be created by the qualities of the soil.   de

In common monopolies, and all productions except necessaries, the laws of nature do very little towards proportioning their value in exchange to their value in use. The same quantity of grapes or cottons might, under different circumstances, be worth permanently three or three hundred days la-

external demand or diminution of supply could ever permanently enable the produce of an acre of corn to command more labour than it would support.

a   bour. In the production of necessaries alone, the
laws of nature are constantly at work to regulate
their exchangeable value according to their value in
use; and though from the great difference of external
circumstances, and particularly the greater plenty
b   or scarcity of land, this is seldom or ever fully effected ; yet the exchangeable value of a given
c   quantity of necessaries in commanding labour always tends to approximate towards the value of
d   the quantity of labour which it can maintain, or in
other words, to its value in use.

In all common monopolies, the price of the produce, and consequently the excess of price above
the cost of production, may increase without any
definite bounds. In the partial monopoly of the
e   land which produces necessaries, the price of the
produce cannot by any possibility exceed the value
f   of the labour which it can maintain; and the excess of its price above the cost of its production is
subjected to a limit as impassable. This limit is
the surplus of necessaries which the land can be
made to yield beyond the lowest wants of the cultivators, and is strictly dependent upon the natural
or acquired fertility of the soil. Increase this fer-
g   tility, the limit will be enlarged, and the land may
yield a high rent; diminish it, the limit will be
contracted, and a high rent will become impossible;
diminish it still further, the limit will coincide with
the cost of production, and all rent will disappear.

h   In short, in the one case, the power of the produce to exceed in price the cost of the production
i   depends mainly upon the degree of the monopoly;

in the other, it depends entirely upon the degree   a
of fertility. This is surely a broad and striking
distinction.*

Is it, then, possible to consider the price of the   b
necessaries of life as regulated upon the principle
of a common monopoly ? Is it possible, with M. de   c
Sismondi, to regard rent as the sole produce of labour, which has a value purely nominal, and the
mere result of that augmentation of price which a
seller obtains in consequence of a peculiar privi-
lege : or, with Mr. Buchanan, to consider it as no
addition to the national wealth, but merely as a
transfer of value, advantageous only to the landlords, and proportionably *injurious* to the consumers ?†

Is it not, on the contrary, a clear indication of a   d
most inestimable quality in the soil, which God
has bestowed on man—the quality of being able
to maintain more persons than are necessary to
work it ? Is it not a part, and we shall see farther
on that it is an absolutely necessary part, of that
surplus produce from the land, which has been   e
justly stated to be the source of all power and enjoyment ; and without which, in fact, there would

---

* Yet this distinction does not appear to Mr. Ricardo to be well   f
founded ! c. xxxi. p. 508. 2d edit.   g
† It is extraordinary that Mr. Ricardo (p. 501.) should have   hi
sanctioned these statements of M. Sismondi and Mr. Buchanan,
Strictly, according to his own theory, the price of corn is always a
natural or necessary price. In what sense then can he agree with   j
these writers in saying, that it is like that of a common monopoly,
or advantageous only to the landlords, and proportionably *injurious*
to the consumers ?

be no cities, no military or naval force, no arts, no learning, none of the finer manufactures, none of the conveniences and luxuries of foreign countries, and none of that cultivated and polished society, which not only elevates and dignifies individuals, but which extends its beneficial influence through a   the whole mass of the people?

SECTION II.

On the necessary Separation of the Rent of Land from the Profits of the Cultivator and the Wages of the Labourer.

bc   In the early periods of society, or more remark- ably perhaps, when the knowledge and capital of an old society are employed upon fresh and fertile land, the surplus produce of the soil shews d   itself chiefly in extraordinary high profits, and extraordinary high wages, and appears but little in the shape of rent. While fertile land is in abundance, and may be had by whoever asks for it, nobody of course will pay a rent to a land- lord. But it is not consistent with the laws of nature, and the limits and quality of the earth, that this state of things should continue. Diversities of soil and situation must necessarily exist in all coun- tries. All land cannot be the most fertile: all situations cannot be the nearest to navigable rivers and markets. But the accumulation of capital be- e   yond the means of employing it on land of the greatest natural fertility, and the most advantageously situated, must necessarily lower profits; while the tendency of population to increase beyond the means of subsistence must, after a certain time, lower the wages of labour. a

The expense of production will thus be diminished; but the value of the produce, that is, the quantity of labour, and of the other products of labour (besides corn) which it can command, instead of diminishing, will be increased. There will be an increasing number of people demanding subsistence, and ready to offer their services in any way in which they can be useful. The exchangeable value of food will therefore be in excess above the cost of production, on all the more fertile lands; and this excess is that portion of the general surplus derived from land which has been peculiarly denominated rent. b c d e f

The quality of the earth first mentioned, or its power to yield a greater portion of the necessaries of life than is required for the maintenance of the persons employed in cultivation, is obviously the foundation of this rent, and the limit to its possible increase. The second quality noticed, or the tendency of an abundance of food to increase population, is necessary both to give a value to the surplus of necessaries which the cultivators can obtain on the first land cultivated; and also to create a demand for more food than can be procured from the richest lands. And the third cause, or the comparative scarcity of fertile land, which is clearly the natural consequence of the second, is finally necessary to separate a portion of the ge- g h

neral surplus from the land, into the specific form
of rent to a landlord.*

a   Nor is it possible that rents should permanently
remain as parts of the profits of stock, or of the
b wages of labour. If profits and wages were not to
fall, then, without particular improvements in cultivation, none but the very richest lands could be
brought into use. The fall of profits and wages
which practically takes place, undoubtedly trans-
fers a portion of produce to the landlord, and forms
a part, though, as we shall see farther on, only a
c part of his rent. But if this transfer can be considered as injurious to the consumers, then every
d increase of capital and population must be considered as injurious; and a country which might
maintain well ten millions of inhabitants ought to
be kept down to a million. The transfer from pro-
e fits and wages, and such a price of produce as yields

f   * Mr. Ricardo has quite misunderstood me, when he represents
me as saying that rent immediately and necessarily rises or falls
g with the increased or diminished fertility of the land. (p. 507.)
How far my former words would bear this interpretation the
h reader must judge ; but I was not aware that they could be so
construed ; and having stated three causes as necessary to the production of rent, I could not possibly have meant to say that rent
would vary always and exactly in proportion to one of them. I
i distinctly stated, indeed, that in the early periods of society, the
surplus produce from the land, or its fertility, appears but little in
jk the shape of rent. Surely he has expressed himself most inadvertently while correcting me, by referring to the comparative scarcity
l of the most fertile land as the only cause of rent, (p. 506.) although
he has himself acknowledged, that without positive fertility, no
m rent can exist. (p. 507.) If the *most* fertile land of any country
no were still very poor, such country could yield but very little rent.

rent, which have been objected to as injurious, and as depriving the consumer of what it gives to the landlord, are absolutely necessary in order to obtain any considerable addition to the wealth and revenue of the first settlers in a new country;   a and are the natural and unavoidable consequences of that increase of capital and population for which nature has provided in the propensities of the human race.

When such an accumulation of capital takes   b place on the lands first chosen, as to render the returns of the additional stock employed less than   c could be obtained from inferior land,* it must evidently answer to cultivate such inferior land. But the cultivators of the richer land, after profits had   d fallen, if they paid no rent, would cease to be mere farmers, or persons living upon the profits of agricultural stock; they would evidently unite the characters of landlords and farmers—a union by no means uncommon, but which does not alter in any   e degree the nature of rent, or its essential separation from profits and wages.

If the profits of stock on the inferior land taken   f into cultivation were thirty per cent. and portions of the old land would yield forty per cent., ten per cent. of the forty would obviously be rent by whomsoever received. When capital had further accumulated,   gh

---

* The immediate motive for the cultivation of fresh land can only be the prospect of employing an increasing capital to greater advantage than on the old land. A rise in the market-price of   i corn could not alone furnish such a motive.

and labour fallen* on the more eligible lands of a country, other lands, less favourably circumstanced with respect to fertility or situation, might be occupied with advantage. The expenses of cultivation, including profits, having fallen, poorer land, or land more distant from rivers and markets, though yielding at first no rents, might fully repay these expenses, and fully answer to the cultivator. And again, when either the profits of stock, or the wages of labour, or both, have still further fallen, land still poorer or still less favourably situated, might be taken into cultivation. And at every step it is clear, that if the price of produce do not fall, the rent of land must rise. And the price of produce will not fall so long as the industry and ingenuity of the labouring classes, assisted by the capitals of those not employed upon the land, can find something to give in exchange to the cultivators and landlords, which will stimulate them to continue undiminished their agricultural exertions, and maintain their excess of produce.

* When a given portion of labour and capital yields smaller returns, whether on new land or old, the loss is generally divided between the labourers and capitalists, and wages and profits fall at the same time. This is quite contrary to Mr. Ricardo's language. But the wages we refer to are totally different. He speaks of the cost of producing the necessaries of the labourer; I speak of the necessaries themselves. In the same language Mr. Ricardo says, (p. 115.) that the rise of rent never falls upon the farmer. Yet does not the fall of profits go to rent? It is of very little consequence to the farmer and labourer, even on Mr. Ricardo's theory, that they continue to receive between them the same nominal sum of money, if that sum in exchange for necessaries is not worth half what it was before.

It may be laid down, therefore, as an incontrovertible truth, that as a nation reaches any considerable degree of wealth, and any considerable full-
ness of population, the separation of rents, as a
kind of fixture upon lands of a certain quality, is
a law as invariable as the action of the principle
of gravity; and that rents are neither a mere
nominal value, nor a value unnecessarily and in-
juriously transferred from one set of people to
another; but a most real and essential part of the   a
whole value of the national property, and placed   b
by the laws of nature where they are, on the land,   c
by whomsoever possessed, whether by few or many,
whether by the landlord, the crown, or the actual
cultivator.

This then is the mode in which rent would separate itself from profits and wages, in a natural
state of things, the least interrupted by bad government, or any kind of unnecessary monopoly;
but in the different states in which mankind have
lived, it is but too well known that bad government and unnecessary monopolies have been fre-   d
quent; and it is certain that they will essentially
modify this natural progress, and often occasion a
premature formation of rent.

In most of the great eastern monarchies, the sovereign has been considered in the light of the
owner of the soil.   This premature monopoly of
the land joined with the two properties of the soil,
and of its products first noticed, has enabled the
government to claim, at a very early period, a certain portion of the produce of all cultivated land;
and under whatever name this may be taken, it is

essentially rent. It is an excess both of the quantity, and of the exchangeable value of what is produced above the actual costs of cultivation.

But in most of these monarchies there was a great extent of fertile territory; the natural surplus of the soil was very considerable; and while the claims upon it were moderate, the remainder was sufficient to afford such ample profits and wages as could not be obtained in any other employment, and would allow of a rapid increase of population.

It is obvious, however, that it is in the power of a sovereign who is owner of the soil in a very rich territory to obtain, at an early stage of improvement, an excessive rent. He might, almost from the first, demand all that was not necessary to allow of a moderate increase of the cultivators, which, if their skill was not deficient, would afford him a larger *proportion* of the whole produce in the shape of a tax or rent, than could probably be obtained at any more advanced period of society; but then of course only the most fertile lands of the country could be cultivated; and profits, wages and population would come to a premature stop.

It is not to be expected that sovereigns should push their rights over the soil to such an extreme extent, as it would be equally contrary to their own interest, and to that of their subjects; but there is reason to believe that in parts of India, and many other eastern countries, and probably even in China, the progress of taxation on the land, founded upon the sovereign's right to the soil, together with other customary payments out of the raw produce, have

forcibly and prematurely lowered the profits of
stock, and the wages of labour on the land, and   a
have thrown great obstacles in the way of progressive cultivation and population in latter times,
while much good land has remained waste. This
will always be the case, when, owing to an unnecessary monopoly, a greater portion of the
surplus produce is taken in the shape of rent or
taxes, than would be separated by the natural fall   b
of profits and wages. But whatever may be the
nature of the monopoly of land, whether necessary
or artificial, it will be observed that the power of
paying a rent or taxes on the land, is completely
limited by its fertility; and those who are disposed
to underrate the importance of the two first causes
of rent which I have stated, should look at the
various distributions of the produce in kind which
take place in many parts of India, where, when
once the monopoly has enabled the sovereign to
claim the principal part of the rent of the soil,   c
every thing else obviously depends upon the sur-   d
plus of necessaries which the land yields, and the
power of these necessaries to command labour.

It may be thought, perhaps, that rent could not
be forcibly and prematurely separated from profits
and wages so as unnaturally to reduce the latter,   e
because capital and labour would quit the land if
more could be made of them elsewhere; but it
should be recollected, that the actual cultivators of
the soil in these countries are generally in a very
low and degraded condition; that very little capital
is employed by them, and scarcely any which they

can remove and employ in another business; that the surplus produce possessed by the government soon raises up a population to be employed by it, so as to keep down the price of labour in other departments to the level of the price in agriculture; and that the small demand for the products of manufacturing and commercial industry, owing to the poverty of the great mass of society, affords no room for the employment of a large capital, with high profits in manufactures and commerce. On account of these causes which tend to lower profits, and the difficulty of collecting money, and the risk of lending it which tend to raise interest, I have long been of opinion, that though the rate of interest in different countries is almost the only criterion from which a judgment can be formed of the rate of profits; yet that in such countries as India and China, and indeed in most of the eastern and southern regions of the globe, it is a criterion subject to the greatest uncertainty. In China, the legal interest of money is three per cent. per month.* But it is impossible to suppose, when we consider the state of China, so far as it is known to us, that capital employed on land can yield profits to this amount; or, indeed, that capital can be employed in any steady and well-known trade with such a return.

In the same way extraordinary accounts have been given of the high rate of interest in India;

* Penal Code, Staunton, p. 158. The market-rate of interest at Canton is said, however, to be only from twelve to eighteen per cent. Id. note XVII.

but the state of the actual cultivators completely
contradicts the supposition, that, independently of
their labour, the profits upon their stock is so considerable; and the late reduction of the government paper to six per cent. fully proves that, in
common and peaceable times, the returns of capital, which can be depended upon in other sorts
of business, are by no means so great as to warrant
the borrowing at a very high rate of interest.

It is probable that, with the exception of occasional speculations, the money that is borrowed at   a
the high rates of interest noticed in China and India,
is borrowed in both countries, rather with a view   b
to expenditure or the payment of debts, than with
a view to profit.

Some of the causes, which have been noticed as
tending prematurely and irregularly to raise rents
and lower profits in the countries of the east, operated without doubt to a certain extent in the early
stages of society in Europe. At one period most
of the land was cultivated by slaves, and in the   c
metayer systems which succeeded, the division of
the crop was so arranged as to allow the cultivator
but little more than a scanty subsistence. In this
state of things the rate of profits on the land could
have but little to do with the general rate of profits. The peasant could not, without the greatest
difficulty, realize money and change his profession;
and it is quite certain that no one who had accumulated a capital in manufactures and commerce,
would employ it in cultivating the lands of others
as a *metayer*. There would thus be little or no

interchange of capital between trade and agricul-
a   ture, and their profits might in consequence be very
unequal.

It is probable however, as in the case of China
and India above mentioned, that profits would not
be excessively high. This would depend indeed
mainly upon the supply of capital in manufactures
and commerce; if capital were scarce, compared
with the demand for the products of these kinds
of industry, profits would certainly be high; and
all that can be said safely is, that we cannot
infer that they were very high, from the very high
rates of interest occasionally mentioned.

Rent then has been traced to the same common
nature with that general surplus from the land,
which is the result of certain qualities of the soil
and its produce; and it has been found to commence its separation from profits and wages, as
soon as they begin to fall from the scarcity of fertile land whether occasioned by the natural progress of a country towards wealth and population,
or by any premature and unnecessary monopoly
of the soil.

SECTION III.

Of the Causes which tend to raise Rents in the ordinary
b   *Progress of Society.*

In tracing more particularly the laws which govern the rise and fall of rents, the main causes

which diminish the expenses of cultivation, or re-   a
duce the costs of the instruments of production,
compared with the price of produce, require to be
more specifically enumerated. The principal of
these seem to be four :—1st, Such an accumulation of capital as will lower the profits of stock ;   b
2dly, such an increase of population as will lower
the wages of labour; 3dly, such agricultural im-   c
provements, or such increase of exertions as will
diminish the number of labourers necessary to produce a given effect; and 4thly, such an increase   d
in the price of agricultural produce, from increased
demand, as, without nominally lowering the ex-   e
pense of production, will increase the difference
between this expense and the price of produce.

If capital increases so as to become redundant in   f
those departments where it has been usually employed with a certain rate of profits, it will not
remain idle, but will seek employment either in the
same or other departments of industry, although   g
with inferior returns, and this will tend to push it
upon less fertile soils.

In the same manner, if population increases
faster than the demand for it, the labourers   h
must content themselves with a smaller quantity of necessaries ; and, the expense of labour in   i
kind being thus diminished, land may be cultivated
which could not have been cultivated before.

The two first causes, however, here mentioned   j
sometimes act so as to counterbalance one another.
An increase of capital raises the wages of labour,   kl
and a fall of wages raises the profits of stock ; but   m

these are only temporary effects. In the natural and regular progress of a country towards the accumulation of stock and the increase of population, the rate of profits and the real wages of labour permanently fall together. This may be effected by a permanent rise in the money price of corn, accompanied by a rise, but not a proportionate rise, in the money wages of labour. The rise in the money price of corn is counterbalanced to the cultivator by the diminished quantity of produce obtained by the same capital; and his profits, as well as those of all other capitalists, are diminished, by having to pay out of the same money returns higher money wages; while the command of the labourer over the necessaries of life is of course contracted by the inadequate rise of the price of labour compared with the price of corn.

But this exact and regular rise in the money price of corn and labour is not necessary to the fall of profits; indeed it will only take place in the regular way here described, when money, under all the changes to which a country is subjected, remains of the same value, according to the supposition of Mr. Ricardo,* a case which may be said never to happen. Profits may undoubtedly fall, and rent be separated, under any variations of the value of money. All that is necessary to the most regular and permanent fall of profits (and in this Mr. Ricardo would agree with me) is, that an increased proportion of the value of the whole produce obtained by a given quantity of capital, should be absorbed by labour. On the land, this

* Princ. of Polit. Econ. ch. i. p. 24. 2d ed.

is effected by a diminution of the produce, obtained
by the same capital without a proportionate diminution of the part absorbed by labour, which leaves
less for profits, at the same time that the real
wages of the labourer are diminished. But it is
obvious that if a smaller quantity of the necessaries of life derived from a given capital employed
on the land, be sufficient to supply both the capitalist and the labourer,* the expenses of cultivation
will be diminished, poorer land may be cultivated
under the new rates of wages and profits, and rent
will rise on that which was before in cultivation.

The third cause enumerated as tending to raise
rents by lowering the expenses of cultivation compared with the price of the produce is, such agricultural improvements or such increase of exertions,
as will diminish the number of labourers necessary
to produce a given effect.

In improving and industrious countries, not deficient in stimulants, this is a cause of great efficacy. If the improvements introduced were of such
a nature as considerably to diminish the costs of

* Mr. Ricardo has observed (p. 516.) in reference to the second
cause which I have here stated, as tending to raise rents, " that no
fall of wages can raise rents; for it will neither diminish the portion, nor the value of the portion of the produce which will be allot-
ted to the farmer and labourer together." But where, I would ask,
will the high real wages of America finally go? to profits? or to
rent? If labourers were permanently to receive the value of a
bushel of wheat a day, none but the richest lands could pay the
expense of working them. An increase of population and a fall
of such wages would be absolutely necessary to the cultivation of
poor land. How then can it be said that a fall of wages is not one
of the causes of a rise of rents?

production, without increasing in any degree the quantity of produce, then, as it is quite certain that no alteration would take place in the price of corn, the extravagant profits of the farmers would soon be reduced by the competition of capitals from manufactures and commerce; and as the whole *arena* for the employment of capital would rather have been diminished than increased, profits on land as well as elsewhere would soon be at their former level, and the increased surplus from the diminished expenses of cultivation would go to increase the rents of the landlords.

But if these improvements, as must always be the case, would facilitate the cultivation of new land, and the better cultivation of the old with the same capital, more corn would certainly be brought to market. This would lower its price; but the fall would be of short duration. The operation of that important cause noticed in the early part of this chapter, which distinguishes the surplus produce of the land from all others, namely, the power of the necessaries of life, when properly distributed, to create their own demand, or in other words the tendency of population to press against the means of subsistence, would soon raise the prices of corn and labour, and reduce the profits of stock to their former level, while in the mean time every step in the cultivation of poorer lands facilitated by these improvements, and their application to all the lands of a better quality before cultivated, would universally have raised rents : and thus, under an improving system of cultivation, rents might continue rising without any rise in the exchangeable

value of corn, or any fall in the real wages of la-   a
bour, or the general rate of profits.   b

The very great improvements in agriculture which
have taken place in this country are clearly demon-
strated by the profits of stock being as high now   c
as they were nearly a hundred years ago, when the
land supported but little more than half of its pre-   d
sent population. And the power of the necessaries
of life, when properly distributed, to create their
own demand is fully proved by the palpable fact,
that the exchangeable value of corn in the command of labour and other commodities is, to say   e
the least, undiminished, notwithstanding the many
and great improvements which have been succes-   f
sively introduced in cultivation, both by the intro-   gh
duction of better implements, and by an improved   i
system of managing the land. In fact, these im-   j
provements have gone wholly to the increase of
rents and the payment of taxes.

It may be added that, when improvements are   k
introduced in particular districts, which tend to
diminish the costs of production, the advantages
derived from them go immediately, upon the renewal of leases, to landlords, as the profits of stock   l
must necessarily be regulated by competition, according to the general average of the whole country. Thus the very great agricultural improvements which have taken place in some parts of
Scotland, the north of England, and Norfolk, have
raised, in a very extraordinary manner, the rents of
those districts, and left profits where they were.

It must be allowed then, that facility of production in necessaries,* unlike facility of production in all other commodities, is never attended with a permanent fall of price. They are the only commodities of which it can be said that their permanent value in the command of labour is nearly proportioned to their quantity. And consequently, in the actual state of things, all savings in the cost of producing them will permanently increase the surplus which goes to rent.

The fourth cause which tends to raise rents, is such an increase in the price of agricultural produce from whatever source arising, as will increase the difference between the price of produce, and the costs of production.

We have already adverted to a rise in the price of raw produce, which may take place in consequence of a regular increase of capital and population while money remains nearly of the same value. But this sort of rise is confined within narrow limits, and has little share in those great variations in the price of corn, which are most frequently the subject of observation. The kind of increased price, the effects of which I wish now more particularly to consider, is a rise of price from increased demand, terminating in an alteration in the value of the precious metals.

---

* Properly speaking, facility of production in necessaries can only be temporary, where there are gradations of land as far as barrenness, except when capital is prevented from increasing by the want of will to save. It may then be permanent. But though corn will, in that case, cost but little labour, its exchangeable value will be high, that is, it will command a great deal.

If a great and continued demand should arise among- surrounding nations for the raw produce of a particular country, the price of this produce would of course rise considerably ; and the expenses of cultivation rising only slowly and gradually to the same proportion, the price of produce might for a long time keep so much a head as to give a   α prodigious stimulus to improvement, and encourage the employment of much capital in bringing fresh land under cultivation, and rendering the old much more productive. If however the demand continued, the price of labour would ultimately rise to its former level, compared with corn; a decided fall in the value of money supported by the abundant exportation of raw produce might generally take place; labour would become extremely   a productive in the purchase of all foreign commodities; and rents might rise without a fall of profits or wages.

The state of money prices, and the rapid progress of cultivation in North America, tend strongly   b to illustrate the case here supposed. The price of wheat in the eastern states is nearly as high as in   c France and Flanders; and owing to the continued demand for hands, the money price of day-labour is nearly double what it is in England. But this   de high price of corn and labour has given great facilities to the farmers and labourers in the purchase   f of clothing and all sorts of foreign necessaries and conveniences. And it is certain that if the money prices of corn and labour had been both lower, yet had maintained the same proportion to each other,

a   land of the same quality could not have been cultivated, nor could equal rents have been obtained
b   with the same rate of profits and the same real
wages of labour.

Effects of a similar kind took place in our own
country from a similar demand for corn during the
twenty years from 1793 to the end of 1813, though
the demand was not occasioned in the same way.
For some time before the war, which commenced
in 1793, we had been in the habit of importing a
certain quantity of foreign grain to supply our
habitual consumption.   The war naturally increased the expense of this supply by increasing
the expense of freight, insurance, &c. ; and, joined
to some bad seasons and the subsequent decrees of
the French government, raised the price, at which
wheat could be imported, in the quantity wanted
to supply the demand, in a very extraordinary
c   manner.

This great rise in the price of imported corn,
although the import bore but a small proportion
to what was grown at home, necessarily raised in
the same proportion the whole mass, and gave the
same sort of stimulus to domestic agriculture as
would have taken place from a great demand for
our corn in foreign countries.   In the mean time,
the scarcity of hands, occasioned by an extending
war, an increasing commerce, and the necessity of
raising more food, joined to the ever ready invention of an ingenious people when strongly stimulated, introduced so much saving of manual labour
into every department of industry, that the new

and inferior land taken into cultivation to supply
the pressing wants of the society, was worked at a
less expense of labour than richer soils some years   a
before. Yet still the price of grain necessarily
kept up as long as the most trifling quantity of
foreign grain, which could only be obtained at a
very high price, was wanted in order to supply
the existing demand. With this high price, which
at one time rose to nearly treble in paper and above
double in bullion, compared with the prices before
the war, it was quite impossible that labour should   b
not rise nearly in proportion, and with it, of course,
as profits had not fallen, all the commodities into
which labour had entered.

We had thus a general rise in the prices of   c
commodities, or fall in the value of the precious
metals, compared with other countries, which our
increasing foreign commerce and abundance of
exportable commodities enabled us to sustain.   d
That the last land taken into cultivation in 1813
did not require more labour to work it than the
last land improved in the year 1790, is incontro-   e
vertibly proved by the acknowledged fact, that
the rate of interest and profits was higher in the
later period than the earlier. But still the pro-   f
fits were not so much higher as not to have rendered the interval most extremely favourable to   g
the rise of rents. This rise, during the interval in
question, was the theme of universal remark ; and
though a severe and calamitous check, from a com-   h
bination of unfortunate circumstances, has since   i
occurred ; yet the great drainings and permanent

improvements, which were the effects of so powerful an encouragement to agriculture, have acted
like the creation of fresh land, and have increased
the real wealth and population of the country,
without increasing the labour and difficulty of
raising a given quantity of grain.

It is obvious then that a fall in the value of the
precious metals, commencing with a rise in the
price of corn, has a strong tendency, while it lasts,
to encourage the cultivation of fresh land and the
formation of increased rents.

A similar effect would be produced in a country
which continued to feed its own people, by a great
and increasing demand for its manufactures. These
manufactures, if from such a demand the value of
their amount in foreign countries was greatly to
increase, would bring back a great increase of
value in return, which increase of value could not
fail to increase the value of the raw produce. The
demand for agricultural as well as manufactured
produce would be augmented; and a considerable
stimulus, though not perhaps to the same extent
as in the last case, would be given to every kind
of improvement on the land.

Nor would the result be very different from the
introduction of new machinery, and a more judicious division of labour in manufactures. It almost always happens in this case, not only that
the quantity of manufactures is very greatly increased, but that the value of the whole mass is
augmented, from the great extension of the demand
for them both abroad and at home, occasioned by

their cheapness. We see, in consequence, that in all rich manufacturing and commercial countries, the value of manufactured and commercial products bears a very high proportion to the raw products ;* whereas, in comparatively poor countries, without much internal trade and foreign commerce, the value of their raw produce constitutes almost the whole of their wealth.

In those cases where the stimulus to agriculture originates in a prosperous state of commerce and manufactures, it sometimes happens that the first step towards a rise of prices is an advance in the wages of commercial and manufacturing labour. This will naturally have an immediate effect upon the price of corn, and an advance of agricultural labour will follow. It is not, however, necessary, even in those cases, that labour should rise first. If, for instance, the population were increasing as fast as the mercantile and manufacturing capital, the only effect might be an increasing number of workmen employed at the same wages, which would occasion a rise in the price of corn before any rise had taken place in the wages of labour.

We are supposing, however, now, that labour does ultimately rise nearly to its former level compared with corn, that both are considerably higher,

* According to the calculations of Mr. Colquhoun, the value of our trade, foreign and domestic, and of our manufactures, exclusive of raw materials, is nearly equal to the gross value derived from the land. In no other large country probably is this the case.—Treatise on the Wealth, Power, and Resources of the British Empire, p. 96.

and that money has suffered a decided change of
value. Yet in the progress of this change, the
other outgoings, besides labour, in which capital is
expended, can never all rise at the same time, or
even finally in the same proportion. A period of
some continuance can scarcely fail to occur when
the difference between the price of produce and
the cost of production is so increased as to give a
great stimulus to agriculture; and as the increased
capital, which is employed in consequence of the
opportunity of making great temporary profits, can
seldom or ever be entirely removed from the land,
a part of the advantage so derived is permanent;
together with the whole of that which is occasioned
by a greater rise in the price of corn than in some
of the materials of the farmer's capital.

Mr. Ricardo acknowledges that, in a fall of the
value of money, taxed commodities will not rise in
the same proportion with others ; and, on the supposition of the fall in the value of money being
peculiar to a particular country, the same must
unquestionably be said of all the various commodities which are either wholly or in part imported
from abroad, many of which enter into the capital
of the farmer. He would, therefore, derive an increased power from the increased money price of
corn compared with those articles. A fall in the
value of money cannot indeed be peculiar to one
country without the possession of peculiar advantages in exportation; but with these advantages,
which we know are very frequently possessed, and
are very frequently increased by stimulants, a fall

in the value of money can scarcely fail permanently
to increase the power of cultivating poorer lands,
and of advancing rents.   a

Whenever then, by the operation of the four
causes above mentioned, the difference between
the price of produce and the cost of the instruments of production increases, the rents of land
will rise.

It is, however, not necessary that all these four
causes should operate at the same time ; it is only
necessary that the difference here mentioned should
increase. If, for instance, the price of produce
were to rise, while the wages of labour and the   b
price of the other branches of capital did not rise
in proportion, and at the same time improved modes   c
of agriculture were coming into general use, it is
evident that this difference might be increased,
although the profits of agricultural stock were not
only · undiminished, but were to rise decidedly
higher.

Of the great additional quantity of capital employed upon the land in this country during the   d
last twenty years, by far the greater part is supposed to have been generated on the soil, and not
to have been brought from commerce or manufactures. And it was unquestionably the high profits
of agricultural stock, occasioned by improvements
in the modes of agriculture, and by the constant
rise of prices, followed only slowly by a proportionate rise in the materials of the farmer's capital,
that afforded the means of so rapid and so advantageous an accumulation.

a   In this case cultivation has been extended, and rents have risen, although one of the instruments of production, capital, has been dearer.

b   In the same manner a fall of profits, and improvements in agriculture, or even one of them separately, might raise rents, notwithstanding a

c   rise of wages.

It is further evident, that no fresh land can be taken into cultivation till rents have risen, or would allow of a rise upon what is already cultivated.

d   Land of an inferior quality requires a great quantity of capital to make it yield a given produce; and if the actual price of this produce be not such as fully to compensate the cost of production, including profits, the land must remain uncultivated. It matters not whether this compensation is effected by an increase in the money price of raw produce, without a proportionate increase in the money price of the instruments of production; or by a decrease in the price of the instruments of production, without a proportionate decrease in the price of produce. What is absolutely necessary is, a greater *relative* cheapness of the instruments of production, to make up for the quantity of them required to obtain a given produce from poor land.

But whenever, by the operation of one or more of the causes before mentioned, the instruments of

e   production become cheaper, and the difference between the price of produce and the expenses of cultivation increases, rents naturally rise. It fol-

lows therefore as a direct and necessary consequence, that it can never answer to take fresh land
of a poorer quality into cultivation till rents have
risen, or would allow of a rise, on what is already
cultivated.

It is equally true, that without the same tendency to a rise of rents,* it cannot answer to lay
out fresh capital in the improvement of old land;
at least upon the supposition, that each farm is
already furnished with as much capital as can be
laid out to advantage, according to the actual rate
of profits.

It is only necessary to state this proposition to
make its truth appear. It certainly may happen,
(and I fear it happens very frequently) that farmers
are not provided with all the capital which could
be employed upon their farms at the actual rate of
agricultural profits. But supposing they are so
provided, it implies distinctly, that more could not
be applied without loss, till, by the operation of
one or more of the causes above enumerated, rents
had tended to rise.

It appears then, that the power of extending
cultivation and increasing produce, both by the
cultivation of fresh land and the improvement of
the old, depends entirely upon the existence of
such prices, compared with the expense of pro-

---

* Rents may be said to have a tendency to rise, when more
capital is ready to be laid out upon the old land, but cannot be
laid out without diminished returns. When profits fall in manufactures and commerce from the diminished price of goods, capitalists will be ready to give higher rents for the old farms.

a

duction, as would raise rents in the actual state of cultivation.

But though cultivation cannot be extended and the produce of a country increased, except in such a state of things as would allow of a rise of rents; yet it is of importance to remark, that this rise of rents will be by no means in proportion to the extension of cultivation or the increase of produce. Every relative fall in the price of the instruments of production may allow of the employment of a considerable quantity of additional capital; and when either new land is taken into cultivation or the old improved, the increase of produce may be considerable, though the increase of rents be trifling. We see, in consequence, that in the progress of a country towards a high state of cultivation, the quantity of capital employed upon the land and the quantity of produce yielded by it bear a constantly increasing proportion to the amount of rents, unless counterbalanced by extraordinary improvements in the modes of cultivation.*

* To the honour of Scotch cultivators it should be observed, that they have applied their capitals so very skilfully and economically, that at the same time that they have prodigiously increased the produce, they have increased the landlord's proportion of it. The difference between the landlord's share of the produce in Scotland and in England is quite extraordinary— much greater than can be accounted for, either by the natural soil or the absence of tithes and poors-rates.—See Sir John Sinclair's valuable Account of the Husbandry of Scotland; and the General Report not long since published—works replete with the most useful and interesting information on agricultural subjects.

According to the returns lately made to the
Board of Agriculture, the average proportion which
rent bears to the value of the whole produce seems
not to exceed one-fifth ;* whereas formerly, when
there was less capital employed and less value produced, the proportion amounted to one-fourth, one-
third, or even two-fifths.　Still, however, the nu-
merical difference between the price of produce
and the expenses of cultivation increases with the
progress of improvement ; and though the landlord has a less *share* of the whole produce, yet this
less share, from the very great increase of the produce, yields a larger quantity, and gives him a
greater command of corn and labour.　If the produce of land be represented by the number six,
and the landlord has one-fourth of it, his share
will be represented by one and a half.　If the produce of land be as ten, and the landlord has one-
fifth of it, his share will be represented by two,
In the latter case, therefore, though the proportion of the landlord's share to the whole produce
is greatly diminished, his real rent, independently
of nominal price, will be increased in the proportion of from three to four.　And, in general, in all
cases of increasing produce, if the landlord's share
of this produce do not diminish in the same proportion, which, though it often happens during the
currency of leases, rarely or never happens on the
renewal of them, the real rents of land must rise.

* See Evidence before the House of Lords, given by Arthur
Young, p. 66.

We see then that a progressive rise of rents seems to be necessarily connected with the progressive cultivation of new land, and the progressive improvement of the old : and that this rise is the natural and necessary consequence of the operation of four causes, which are the most certain indications of increasing prosperity and wealth—namely, the accumulation of capital, the increase of population, improvements in agriculture, and the high market price of raw produce, occasioned either by a great demand for it in foreign countries, or by the extension of commerce and manufactures.

SECTION IV.

Of the Causes which tend to lower Rents.

The causes which lead to a fall of rents are, as may be expected, exactly of an opposite description to those which lead to a rise : namely, diminished capital, diminished population, a bad system of cultivation, and the low market price of raw produce. They are all indications of poverty and decline, and are necessarily connected with the throwing of inferior land out of cultivation, and the continued deterioration of the land of a superior quality.*

The necessary effects of a diminished capital and diminished population in lowering rents, are too

* The effects of importing foreign corn will be considered more particularly in the next section, and a subsequent part of this chapter.

obvious to require explanation; nor is it less clear that an operose and bad system of cultivation might prevent the formation of rents, even on fertile land, by checking the progress of population and demand beyond what could be supplied from the very richest qualities of soil. I will only therefore advert to the fourth cause here noticed.

We have seen that a rise in the price of corn, terminating in an alteration in the value of the precious metals, would give a considerable stimulus to cultivation for a certain time, and some facilities permanently, and might occasion a considerable and permanent rise of rents. And this case was exemplified by what had happened in this country during the period from 1794 to 1814.

It may be stated in like manner, that a fall in the price of corn terminating in a rise in the value of money, must, upon the same principles, tend to throw land out of cultivation and lower rents. And this may be exemplified by what happened in this country at the conclusion of the war. The fall in the price of corn at that period necessarily disabled the cultivators from employing the same quantity of labour at the same price. Many labourers, therefore, were unavoidably thrown out of employment; and, as the land could not be cultivated in the same way, without the same number of hands, the worst soils were no longer worked, much agricultural capital was destroyed, and rents universally fell; while this great failure in the power of purchasing, among all those who either rented or possessed land, naturally occasioned a a general stagnation in all other trades. In the mean time, the fall in the price of labour from the competition of the labourers joined to the poverty of the cultivators, and the fall of rents both from the want of power and the want of will to pay the former rents, restored by degrees the prices of commodities, the wages of labour, and the rents of land, nearly to their former proportions, though all lower than they were before. The land which

b had been thrown out of tillage might then again be cultivated with advantage; but in the progress from the lower to the higher value of money, a

c period would have elapsed of diminished produce, diminished capital, and diminished rents. The country would recommence a progressive movement from an impoverished state; and, owing to a

d fall in the value of corn greater than in taxed commodities, foreign commodities, and others which form a part of the capital of the farmer and of the necessaries and conveniences of the labourer, the permanent difficulties of cultivation would be great compared with the natural fertility of the

e worst soil then actually in tillage.

f It appeared that, in the progress of cultivation

g and of increasing rents, it was not necessary that

h all the instruments of production should fall in price at the same time; and that the difference between the price of produce and the expense of cultivation might increase, although either the profits of stock or the wages of labour might be higher, instead of lower.

In the same manner, when the produce of a

country is declining, and rents are falling, it is not   a
necessary that all the instruments of production   b
should be dearer.   In the natural progress of de-   c
cline, the profits of stock are necessarily low; be-   d
cause it is specifically the want of adequate returns
which occasions this decline. After stock has been   e
destroyed, profits may become high and wages low;   f
but the low price of raw produce joined to the   g
high profits of a scanty capital may more than
counterbalance the low wages of labour, and render   hi
it impossible to cultivate land where much-capital
is required.   j

It has appeared also, that in the progress of
cultivation, and of increasing rents, rent, though   k
greater in positive amount, bears a less and less   l
proportion to the quantity of capital employed
upon the land, and the quantity of produce derived
from it. According to the same principle, when
produce diminishes and rents fall, though the
amount of rent will always be less, the proportion   m
which it bears to capital and produce will be   n
greater.   And as, in the former case, the diminished
proportion of rent was owing to the necessity of
yearly taking fresh land of an inferior quality into   o
cultivation, and proceeding in the improvement of
old land, when it would return only the common
profits of stock, with little or no rent; so, in the
latter case, the high proportion of rent is owing   p
to the discouragement of a great expenditure in
agriculture, and the necessity of employing the reduced capital of the country in the exclusive cultivation of the richest lands, and leaving the re-

mainder to yield what rent can be got for them in natural pasture, which, though small, will bear a large *proportion* to the labour and capital employed. In proportion, therefore, as the relative state of prices is such as to occasion a progressive fall of rents, more and more lands will be gradually thrown out of cultivation, the remainder will be worse cultivated, and the diminution of produce will proceed still faster than the diminution of rents.

If the doctrine here laid down respecting the laws which govern the rise and fall of rents, be near the truth, the doctrine which maintains that, if the produce of agriculture were sold at such a price as to yield less neat surplus, agriculture would be equally productive to the general stock, must be very far from the truth. With regard to my own conviction, indeed, I feel no sort of doubt that if, under the impression that the high price of raw produce, which occasions rent, is as injurious to the consumer as it is advantageous to the land-lord, a rich and improved nation were determined by law to lower the price of produce, till no surplus in the shape of rent any where remained, it would inevitably throw not only all the poor land, but all except the very best land, out of cultivation, and probably reduce its produce and population to less than one-tenth of their former amount.

SECTION V.

On the Dependance of the actual Quantity of Produce ob-
tained from the Land, upon the existing Rents and the   a
existing Prices.

From the preceding account of the progress of rent,
it follows that the actual state of the natural rent   b
of land is necessary to the actual produce; and
that the price of corn, in every progressive country,
must be just about equal to the cost of production
on land of the poorest quality actually in use, with
the addition of the rent it would yield in its natural state; or to the cost of raising additional produce on old land, which additional produce yields
only the usual returns of agricultural stock with   c
little or no rent.   d
    It is quite obvious that the price cannot be less;   ef
or such land would not be cultivated, nor such capital employed. Nor can it ever much exceed this
price, because it will always answer to the landlord to continue letting poorer and poorer lands,
as long as he can get any thing more than they
will pay in their natural state; and because it will
always answer to any farmer who can command
capital, to lay it out on his land, if the additional produce resulting from it will fully repay
the profits of his stock, although it yields nothing   g
to his landlord.
    It follows then, that the price of corn, in reference   h

to the *whole quantity* raised, is sold at the natural
or necessary price, that is, at the price necessary to
obtain the actual amount of produce, although by
far the largest part is sold at a price very much
above that which is necessary to its production,
owing to this part being produced at less expense,
while its exchangeable value remains undiminished.

The difference between the price of corn and the
price of manufactures, with regard to natural or
necessary price, is this; that if the price of any manufacture were essentially depressed, the whole
manufacture would be entirely destroyed; whereas,
if the price of corn were essentially depressed, the
quantity of it only would be diminished. There
would be some machinery in the country still
capable of sending the commodity to market at the
reduced price.

The earth has been sometimes compared to a
vast machine, presented by nature to man for the
production of food and raw materials; but, to make
the resemblance more just, as far as they admit of
comparison, we should consider the soil as a present
to man of a great number of machines, all susceptible of continued improvement by the application of capital to them, but yet of very different
original qualities and powers.

This great inequality in the powers of the machinery employed in producing raw produce, forms
one of the most remarkable features which distinguishes the machinery of the land from the machinery employed in manufactures.

When a machine in manufactures is invented,

which will produce more finished work with less
labour and capital than before, if there be no pa-   a
tent, or as soon as the patent has expired, a sufficient number of such machines may be made to
supply the whole demand, and to supersede entirely
the use of all the old machinery. The natural consequence is, that the price is reduced to the price
of production from the best machinery, and if
the price were to be depressed lower, the whole
of the commodity would be withdrawn from the
market.

The machines which produce corn and raw materials, on the contrary, are the gifts of nature, not
the works of man; and we find, by experience,
that these gifts have very different qualities and
powers. The most fertile lands of a country, those   b
which, like the best machinery in manufactures,
yield the greatest products with the least labour   c
and capital, are never found sufficient, owing to
the second main cause of rent before stated, to
supply the effective demand of an increasing po-   d
pulation. The price of raw produce, therefore,
naturally rises till it becomes sufficiently high to   e
pay the cost of raising it with inferior machines,
and by a more expensive process; and, as there
cannot be two prices for corn of the same quality,
all the other machines, the working of which requires less capital compared with the produce, must   f
yield rents in proportion to their goodness.

Every extensive country may thus be considered
as possessing a gradation of machines for the production of corn and raw materials, including in this

gradation not only all the various qualities of poor land, of which every large territory has generally an abundance, but the inferior machinery which may be said to be employed when good land is further and further forced for additional produce. As the price of raw produce continues to rise, these inferior machines are successively called into action; and as the price of raw produce continues to fall, they are successively thrown out of action. The illustration here used serves to shew at once the necessity of the actual price of corn to the actual produce, in the existing state of most of the countries with which we are acquainted, and the different effect which would attend a great reduction in the price of any particular manufacture, and a great reduction in the price of raw produce.

We must not however draw too large inferences from this gradation of machinery on the land. It is what actually exists in almost all countries, and accounts very clearly for the origin and progress of rent, while land still remains in considerable plenty. But such a gradation is not strictly necessary, either to the original formation, or the subsequent regular rise of rents. All that is necessary to produce these effects, is, the existence of the two first causes of rent formerly mentioned, with the addition of limited territory, or a scarcity of fertile land.

Whatever may be the qualities of any commodity, it is well known that it can have no exchangeable value, if it exists in a great excess above the wants of those who are to use it. But

such are the qualities of the necessaries of life that, in a limited territory, and under ordinary circumstances, they cannot be permanently in excess;   a
and if all the land of such a country were precisely   b
equal in quality, and all very rich, there cannot   c
be the slightest doubt, that after the whole of the land had been taken into cultivation, both the profits of stock, and the real wages of labour, would go on diminishing till profits had been reduced to what were necessary to keep up the actual capital,   d
and the wages to what were necessary to keep up   e
the actual population, while the rents would be   f
high, just in proportion to the fertility of the soil.

Nor would the effect be essentially different, if the quantity of stock which could be employed   g
with advantage upon such fertile soil were extremely limited, so that no further capital were   h
required for it than what was wanted for ploughing and sowing. Still there can be no doubt that capital and population might go on increasing in other employments, till they both came to a stand,   i
and rents had reached the limits prescribed by the powers of the soil, and the habits of the people.

In these cases it is obvious that the rents are not regulated by the gradations of the soil, or the different products of capital on the same land;   j
and that it is too large an inference from the theory   k
of rent to conclude with Mr. Ricardo, that " It is only because land is of different qualities with respect to its productive powers, and because in the progress of population, land of an inferior quality,

or less advantageously situated, is called into cultivation, that rent is ever paid for the use of it."*

There is another inference which has been drawn from the theory of rent, which involves an error of much greater importance, and should therefore be very carefully guarded against.

a   In the progress of cultivation, as poorer and poorer land is taken into tillage, the rate of *profits* must be limited in amount by the powers of the soil last cultivated, as will be shewn more fully in a subsequent chapter. It has been inferred from this, that when land is successively thrown out of cultivation, the rate of profits will be high in proportion to the superior natural fertility of the land which will then be the least fertile in cultivation.

b   If land yielded no rent whatever in its natural state, whether it were poor or fertile, and if the relative prices of capital and produce remained the
c   same, then the whole produce being divided be-
de   tween profits and wages, the inference might be just. But the premises are not such as are here
f   supposed. In a civilized country uncultivated land always yields a rent in proportion to its natural power of feeding cattle or growing wood; and of course, when land has been thrown out of tillage, particularly if this has been occasioned by the importation of cheaper corn from other countries, and consequently without a diminution of population,

g   * Principles of Political Economy, ch. ii. p. 54. This passage was copied from the first edition. It is slightly altered in the second, p. 51. but not so as materially to vary the sense.

the last land so thrown out may yield a moderate
rent in pasture, though considerably less than before. As was said in the preceding section, rent
will diminish, but not so much in proportion either   a
as the capital employed on the land, or the produce
derived from it. No landlord will allow his land
to be cultivated by a tillage farmer paying little
or no rent, when by laying it down to pasture,
and saving the yearly expenditure of capital upon   b
it, he can obtain a much greater rent. Conse-   c
quently, as the produce of the worst lands actually
cultivated can never be wholly divided between
profits and wages, and in the case above supposed,   d
not nearly so, the state of such land or its degree
of fertility cannot possibly regulate the rate of   e
profits upon it.   f
   If to this circumstance we add the effect arising   g
from a rise in the value of money, and the probable
fall of corn more than of working cattle, it is obvious that permanent difficulties will be thrown in   h
the way of cultivation, and that richer land may
not yield superior profits. The higher rent paid
for the last land employed in tillage, together with
the greater expense of the materials of capital com-   i
pared with the price of produce, may fully counterbalance, or even more than counterbalance, the
difference of natural fertility.
   With regard to the capital which the tenant may
lay out on his farm in obtaining more produce
without paying additional rent for it, the rate of
its returns must obviously conform itself to the
general rate of profits. If the prices of manufac-   jk

tured and mercantile commodities were to remain
the same notwithstanding the fall of labour, profits would certainly be raised ; but they would not
remain the same, as was shewn in the preceding
chapter. The new prices of commodities and the
new profits of stock would be determined upon
principles of competition ; and whatever the rate
was, as so determined, capital would be taken from
the land till this rate was attained. The profits of
capital employed in the way just described must
always follow, and can never lead or regulate.

It should be added, that in the regular progress
of a country towards general cultivation and improvement, and in a natural state of things, it may
fairly be presumed, that if the last land taken into
cultivation be rich, capital is scarce, and profits
will then certainly be high ; but if land be thrown
out of cultivation on account of means being found
of obtaining corn cheaper elsewhere, no such inference is justifiable. On the contrary, capital
may be abundant, compared with the demand for
corn and commodities, in which case and during
the time that such abundance lasts, whatever may
be the state of the land, profits must be low.

a   This is a distinction of the greatest practical importance, which it appears to me has been quite
overlooked by Mr. Ricardo.

It will be observed, that the rents paid for what
the land will produce in its natural state, though
b   they make a most essential difference in the questions relating to profits and the component parts
c   of price, in no respect invalidate the important doc-

trine that, in progressive countries in their usual　a
state with gradations of soil, corn is sold at its na-　b
tural or necessary price, that is, at the price necessary to bring the actual quantity to market. This
price must on an average be at the least equal to
the costs of its production on the worst land actually cultivated, together with the rent of such
land in its natural state : because, if it falls in any
degree below this, the cultivator of such land will
not be able to pay the landlord so high a rent as
he could obtain from the land without cultivation,
and consequently the land will be left uncultivated, and the produce will be diminished. The　c
rent of land in its natural state is therefore obviously so necessary a part of the price of all cultivated products, that, if it be not paid they will not
come to market, and the real price actually paid
for corn is, on an average, absolutely necessary to　d
the production of the same quantity, or, in the
words before stated, corn, in reference to the whole
quantity produced, is sold at its necessary price.

I hope to be excused for presenting to the
reader in various forms the doctrine, that corn, in
reference to the quantity actually produced, is
sold at its necessary price, like manufactures; be-　e
cause I consider it as a truth of high importance,
which has been entirely overlooked by the Economists, by Adam Smith, and all those writers who　f
have represented raw produce as selling always at
a monopoly price.

SECTION VI.

Of the Connexion between great comparative Wealth, and a high comparative Price of raw Produce.

Adam Smith has very clearly explained in what manner the progress of wealth and improvement tends to raise the price of cattle, poultry, the materials of clothing and lodging, the most useful minerals, &c. compared with corn; but he has not entered into the explanation of the natural causes which tend to determine the price of corn. He has left the reader indeed to conclude, that he considers the price of corn as determined only by the state of the mines, which at the time supply the

a   circulating medium of the commercial world. But this is a cause, which, though it may account for

b   the high or low price of corn positively, cannot

c   account for the relative differences in its price,

d   in different countries, or compared with certain classes of commodities in the same country.

I entirely agree with Adam Smith, that it is of great use to inquire into the causes of high price, as from the result of such inquiries it may turn out, that the very circumstance of which we complain, may be the necessary consequence and the most certain sign of increasing wealth and prosperity. But of all inquiries of this kind, none surely can be so important, or so generally interesting, as an inquiry into the causes which affect the price of corn, and occasion the differences in this price so observable in different countries.

These causes, in reference to the main effects observed, seem to be two:

1. A difference in the value of the precious metals, in different countries under different circumstances.

2. A difference in the quantity of labour and capital necessary to produce corn.

The first cause undoubtedly occasions the greatest portion of that inequality in the price of corn, which is the most striking and prominent, particularly in countries at a considerable distance from each other.   More than three-fourths of the prodigious difference between the price of corn in Bengal and England is probably occasioned by the difference in the value of money in the two countries ; and far the greater part of the high price of corn in this country, compared with most of the states in Europe, is occasioned in the same way. The main causes which affect the precious metals in different countries, are the greater or smaller demand for corn and labour, and the abundance or deficiency of exportable commodities.   With great facility of production in particular branches of industry, or, in other words, an abundance of exportable commodities, corn and labour may be maintained at a very high comparative price ; and in fact it is this high price specifically, which prevents the natural advantage attached to facility of production from being in a great degree lost by domestic competition, and practically ren-

ders the industry of all those nations, where corn
and labour are high, peculiarly productive in the
a   purchase of foreign commodities. But this subject shall be more fully discussed on another occasion. Our principal business at present is with the
second of the two causes before stated.

b   The second cause of the high comparative price
c   of corn is the high comparative cost of production.
d   If we could suppose the value of money to be the
same in all countries, then the cause of the higher
money price of corn in one country compared with
e   another, would be the greater quantity of capital
and labour, which must be employed to produce
f   it: and the reason why the price of corn would
be higher, and continually rising in countries already rich, and still advancing in prosperity and
αg   population, would be to be found in the necessity
of resorting constantly to poorer land—to machines which would require a greater expenditure
to work them—and which would consequently occasion each fresh addition to the raw produce of the
country to be purchased at a greater cost—in short,
it would be found in the important truth that corn,
h   in a *progressive country*, is sold at the price necessary to yield the actual supply; and that, as this
i   supply becomes more and more difficult, the price
j   must rise in proportion.
k   The price of corn, as determined by this cause,
will of course be greatly modified by other circumstances; by direct and indirect taxation; by improvements in the modes of cultivation; by the
saving of labour on the land; and particularly by
the importations of foreign corn. The latter cause,

indeed, may do away, in a considerable degree, the usual effects of great wealth on the price of corn; and this wealth will then shew itself in a different form.

Let us suppose seven or eight large countries not very distant from each other, and not very differently situated with regard to the mines. Let us suppose further, that neither their soils nor their skill in agriculture are essentially unlike; that their currencies are in a natural state; their taxes nothing; and that every trade is free, except the trade in corn. Let us now suppose one of them very greatly to increase in capital and manufacturing skill above the rest, and to become in consequence much more rich and populous. I should say, that this comparative increase of riches could not possibly take place, without a comparative advance in the price of raw produce; and that such advance of price would, under the circumstances supposed, be the natural sign and absolutely necessary consequence, of the increased wealth and population of the country in question.

Let us now suppose the same countries to have the most perfect freedom of intercourse in corn, and the expenses of freight, &c. to be quite inconsiderable: And let us still suppose one of them to increase very greatly above the rest, in manufacturing capital and skill, in wealth and population: I should then say, that as the importation of corn would prevent any great difference in the price of raw produce, it would prevent any great difference in the quantity of capital laid out upon the land,

a

b

c

d
e

f

g

h

i

and the quantity of corn obtained from it; that consequently, the great increase of wealth could not take place without a great dependence on the other nations for corn; and that this dependence, under the circumstances supposed, would be the natural sign and necessary consequence of the increased wealth and population of the country in question.

These I consider as the two alternatives necessarily belonging to a great comparative increase of wealth; and the supposition here made will, with proper allowances, apply to the state of Europe.

In Europe, the expenses attending the carriage of corn are often considerable. They form a natural barrier to importation; and even the country, which habitually depends upon foreign corn, must have the price of its raw produce considerably higher than the general level. Practically, also, the prices of raw produce in the different countries of Europe will be variously modified by very different soils, very different degrees of taxation, and very different degrees of improvement in the science of agriculture. Heavy taxation, and a poor soil, may occasion a high comparative price of raw produce, or a considerable dependence on other countries, without great wealth and population; while great improvements in agriculture and a good soil may keep the price of produce low, and the country independent of foreign corn, in spite of considerable wealth. But the principles laid down are the general principles on the subject; and in applying them to any particular case, the particular circumstances of such case must always be taken into the consideration.

With regard to improvements in agriculture, which in similar soils is the great cause which retards the advance of price compared with the advance of produce; although they are sometimes most powerful, and of very considerable duration, they cannot finally be sufficient to balance the necessity of applying to poorer land, or inferior machines. In this respect, raw produce is essentially different from manufactures.

The cost of manufactures, or the quantity of labour and capital necessary to produce a given quantity of them, has a constant tendency to diminish; while the quantity of labour and capital necessary to procure the last addition which has been made to the raw produce of a rich and advancing country, has a constant tendency to increase.

We see in consequence, from the combined operation of the two causes, which have been stated in this section, that in spite of continued improvements in agriculture, the money price of corn is generally the highest in the richest countries; while in spite of this high price of corn and consequent high price of labour, the money price of manufactures still continues lower than in poorer countries.

I cannot then agree with Adam Smith, in thinking that the low value of gold and silver is no proof of the wealth and flourishing state of the country where it takes place. Nothing of course can be inferred from it, taken absolutely, except the abundance of the mines ; but taken relatively, or in comparison with the state of other countries, much may inferred from it. If we are to measure the value of the precious metals in different countries, and at different periods in the same country, by the price of corn, as proposed by himself, it appears to me that whether we consider the first or second cause which has been referred to in this section, there are few more certain signs of wealth than the high average price of raw produce. With the value of money uniform in respect to cost, then, independently of importation and improvements in agriculture, the wealth and population of a country would be proportioned to the high price of its corn. And in the actual state of things, with great differences in the value of money, it may generally be presumed that those countries, which have the greatest abundance of exportable commodities, are either rich, or in the way rapidly to become rich.*

* This conclusion may appear to contradict the doctrine of the *level* of the precious metals. And so it does, if by *level* be meant level of value estimated in the usual way. I consider that doctrine, indeed, as quite unsupported by facts. The precious metals are always tending to a state of rest, or such a state of things as to make their movement unnecessary. But when this state of rest has been nearly attained, and the exchanges of all countries are nearly at par, the value of the precious metals in different countries, estimated in corn and labour, or the mass of commodities, is very far indeed from being the same. To be convinced of this, it is only necessary to look at England, France, Poland, Russia, and India, when the exchanges are at par. That Adam Smith, who proposes labour as the true measure of value at all times and in all places, could look around him, and yet say that the precious me-

It is of importance to ascertain this point; that   a
we may not complain of one of the most certain
proofs of the prosperous condition of a country.

SECTION VII.

*On the Causes which may mislead the Landlord in letting
his Lands, to the Injury both of himself and the
Country.*

In the progress of a country towards a high state
of improvement, the positive wealth of the landlord ought, upon the principles which have been
laid down, gradually to increase; although his relative condition and influence in society will probably rather diminish, owing to the increasing
number and wealth of those who live upon a still   b
more important surplus*—the profits of stock.

The progressive fall, with few exceptions, in   c
the value of the precious metals throughout Europe; the still greater fall, which has occurred in
the richest countries, together with the increase
of produce which has been obtained from the soil,

tals were always the highest in value in the richest countries, has
always appeared to me most unlike his usual attention to found his
theories on facts.

* I have hinted before, that profits may, without impropriety,   d
be called a surplus. But, whether surplus or not, they are the
most important source of wealth, as they are, beyond all question,
the main source of accumulation.

must all conduce to make the landlord expect
an increase of rents on the renewal of his leases.
But, in re-letting his farms, he is liable to fall
into two errors, which are almost equally prejudicial to his own interests, and to those of his
country.

In the first place, he may be induced, by the
immediate prospect of an exorbitant rent, offered
by farmers bidding against each other, to let his
land to a tenant without sufficient capital to cultivate it in the best way, and make the necessary
improvements upon it. This is undoubtedly a most
short-sighted policy, the bad effects of which have
been strongly noticed by the most intelligent land-
surveyors in the evidence lately brought before
Parliament; and have been particularly remarkable in Ireland, where the imprudence of the landlords in this respect, combined perhaps with some
real difficulty of finding substantial tenants, has
aggravated the discontents of the country, and
thrown the most serious obstacles in the way of
an improved system of cultivation. The consequence of this error is the certain loss of all that
future source of rent to the landlord, and wealth
to the country, which arises from increase of
produce.

The second error to which the landlord is liable,
is that of mistaking a mere temporary rise of prices,
for a rise of sufficient duration to warrant an increase of rents. It frequently happens that a
scarcity of one or two years, or an unusual demand
arising from any other cause, may raise the price

of raw produce to a height at which it cannot be maintained. And the farmers, who take land under the influence of such prices, will, on the return of a more natural state of things, probably fail, and leave their farms in a ruined and exhausted state. These short periods of high price are of great importance in generating capital upon the land, if the farmers are allowed to have the advantage of them; but if they are grasped at prematurely by the landlord, capital is destroyed instead of being accumulated; and both the landlord and the country incur a loss, instead of gaining a benefit.

A similar caution is necessary in raising rents,   a
even when the rise of prices seems as if it would be permanent. In the progress of prices and rents, rent ought always to be a little behind; not only to afford the means of ascertaining whether the rise be temporary or permanent, but even in the latter case, to give a little time for the accumulation of capital on the land, of which the landholder is sure to feel the full benefit in the end.

There is no just reason to believe, that if the   b
landlords were to give the whole of their rents to their tenants, corn would be more plentiful and   c
cheaper. If the view of the subject, taken in the preceding inquiry, be correct, the last additions made to our home produce are sold at nearly the   d
cost of production, and the same quantity could   e
not be produced from our own soil at a less price,   f
even without rent. The effect of transferring all rents to tenants, would be merely the turning them

a   into gentlemen, and tempting them to cultivate
their farms under the superintendence of careless
and uninterested bailiffs, instead of the vigilant eye
of a master, who is deterred from carelessness by
the fear of ruin, and stimulated to exertion by the
hope of a competence. The most numerous instances of successful industry, and well-directed
knowledge, have been found among those who
have paid a fair rent for their lands; who have
embarked the whole of their capital in their undertaking; and who feel it their duty to watch
b   over it with unceasing case, and add to it whenever
it is possible.

But when this laudable spirit prevails among a
tenantry, it is of the very utmost importance to
the progress of riches, and the permanent increase
c   of rents, that it should have the power as well as
the will to accumulate; and an interval of advancing prices, not immediately followed by a proportionate rise of rents, furnishes the most effective
d   powers of this kind. These intervals of advancing
prices, when not succeeded by retrograde move-
e   ments, most powerfully contribute to the progress
of national wealth. And practically I should say,
that when once a character of industry and economy has been established, temporary high profits
are a more frequent and powerful source of accu-
f   mulation than either an increased spirit of saving,
or any other cause that can be named.*   It is the

α   * Adam Smith notices the bad effects of high profits on the habits of the capitalist. They may perhaps sometimes occasion ex-

only cause which seems capable of accounting for the prodigious accumulation among individuals, which must have taken place in this country during the last war, and which left us with a greatly increased capital, notwithstanding the vast annual destruction of stock, for so long a period.

a

Among the temporary causes of high price, which may sometimes mislead the landlord, it is necessary to notice irregularities in the currency. b When they are likely to be of short duration, they must be treated by the landlord in the same manner as years of unusual demand. But when they continue so long as they have done in this country, c it is impossible for the landlord to do otherwise than regulate his rent accordingly, and take the chance of being obliged to lessen it again, on the return of the currency to its natural state.

With the cautions here noticed in letting farms, the landlord may fairly look forward to a gradual and permanent increase of rents; and, in general, not only to an increase proportioned to the rise in the *price* of produce, but to a still further in- d crease, arising from an increase in the *quantity* of produce.

If in taking rents, which are equally fair for the landlord and tenant, it is found that in successive e lettings, they do not rise rather more than in pro- f portion to the price of produce, it will generally be owing to heavy taxation.

travagance; but generally, I should say, that extravagant habits were a more frequent cause of a scarcity of capital and high profits, than high profits of extravagant habits.

Though it is by no means true, as stated by the Economists, that all taxes fall on the neat rents of the landlords, yet it is certainly true that they have little power of relieving themselves. It is also true that they possess a fund more disposable, and better adapted for taxation than any other. They are in consequence more frequently taxed, both directly and indirectly. And if they pay, as they certainly do, many of the taxes which fall on the capital of the farmer and the wages of the labourer, as well as those directly imposed on themselves, they must necessarily feel it in the diminution of that portion of the whole produce, which under other circumstances would have fallen to their share.

α

SECTION VIII.

a
On the strict and necessary Connexion of the Interests of the Landlord and of the State in a Country which supports its own Population.

b
It has been stated by Adam Smith, that the interest of the landholder is closely connected with that of the state;* and that the prosperity or adversity of the one involves the prosperity or adversity of the other. The theory of rent, as laid down in the present chapter, seems strongly to confirm

* Wealth of Nations, Book I. c. xi. p. 394. 6th edit.

this statement. If under any given natural resources in land, the main causes which conduce to
the interest of the landholder are increase of capital, increase of population, improvements in agriculture, and an increasing demand for raw produce
occasioned by the prosperity of commerce, it seems
scarcely possible to consider the interests of the
landlord as separated from those of the state and
people.

Yet it has been said by Mr. Ricardo that, " the
interest of the landlord is always opposed to that
of the consumer and the manufacturer,"* that is,
to all the other orders in the state. To this opinion
he has been led, very consistently, by the peculiar
view he has taken of rent, which makes him state,
that it is for the interest of the landlord that the
cost attending the production of corn should be increased,† and that improvements in agriculture
tend rather to lower than to raise rents.

If this view of the theory of rent were just, and
it were really true, that the income of the landlord
is increased by increasing the difficulty, and diminished by diminishing the facility, of production,
the opinion would unquestionably be well founded.
But if, on the contrary, the landlord's income is
practically found to depend upon natural fertility
of soil, improvements in agriculture, and inventions to save labour, we may still think, with Adam
Smith, that the landlord's interest is not opposed to
that of the country.

* Princ. of Polit. Econ. c. xxiv. p. 423. 2d edit.   † Ibid.

a

It is so obviously true, as to be hardly worth stating, that if land of the greatest fertility were in such excessive plenty compared with the population, that every man might help himself to as much as he wanted, there would be no rents or landlords properly so called. It will also be readily allowed, that if in this or any other country you could suppose the soil suddenly to be made so fertile, that a tenth part of the surface, and a tenth part of the labour now employed upon it, could more than support the present population, you would for some time considerably lower rents.

But it is of no sort of use to *dwell upon*, and draw general inferences from suppositions which never can take place.

What we want to know is, whether, living as we do in a limited world, and in countries and districts still more limited, and under such physical laws relating to the produce of the soil and the increase of population as are found by experience to prevail, the interests of the landlord are generally opposed to those of the society. And in this view of the subject, the question may be settled by an appeal to the most incontrovertible principles confirmed by the most glaring facts.

Whatever fanciful suppositions we may make about sudden improvements in fertility, nothing of this kind which we have ever seen or heard of in practice, approaches to what we know of the power of population to increase up to the additional means of subsistence.

Improvements in agriculture, however consi-

derable they may finally prove, are always found
to be partial and gradual. And as, where they
prevail to any extent, there is always an effective   ab
demand for labour, the increase of population occasioned by the increased facility of procuring food,
soon overtakes the additional produce. Instead
of land being thrown out of employment, more   c
land is cultivated, owing to the cheapness of the
instruments of cultivation, and under these circum-   d
stances rents must rise instead of fall. These re-   e
sults appear to me to be so completely confirmed
by experience, that I doubt, if a single instance in
the history of Europe, or any other part of the
world, can be produced, where improvements in
agriculture have been practically found to lower   f
rents.

I should further say, that not only have improvements in agriculture never lowered rents, but
that they have been hitherto, and may be expected
to be in future, the *main* source of the increase of
rents, in almost all the countries with which we
are acquainted.   g

It is a fundamental part of the theory which has
been explained in this chapter, that, as most countries consist of a gradation of soils, rents rise as
cultivation is pushed to poorer lands ; but still the   h
connexion between rent and fertility subsists in
undiminished force. The rich lands are those
which yield the rents, not the poor ones. The   ij
poor lands are only cultivated, because the increasing population is calling forth all the resources of

the country, and if there were no poor soils, these
resources would still be called forth ; a limited territory, however fertile, would soon be peopled ; and
without any increase of difficulty in the production of food, rents would rise.

It is evident then, that difficulty of production
has no kind of connexion with increase of rent, except as, in the actual state of most countries, it is
the natural consequence of an increase of capital
and population, and a fall of profits and wages ;
or, in other words, of an increase of wealth.

But after all, the increase of rents which results
from an increase of price occasioned solely by the
greater quantity of labour and capital necessary to
produce a given quantity of corn on fresh land, is
very much more limited than has been supposed ;
and by a reference to most of the countries with
which we are acquainted, it will be seen that, practically, improvements in agriculture and the saving
of labour on the land, both have been, and may be
expected in future to be, a much more powerful
source of increasing rents.

It has already been shewn, that for the very
great increase of rents which have taken place in
this country during nearly the last hundred years,
we are mainly indebted to improvements in agriculture, as profits have rather risen than fallen, and
little or nothing has been taken from the wages of
families, if we include parish allowances, and the
earnings of women and children. Consequently
these rents must have been a creation from the

skill and capital employed upon the land, and not a transfer from profits and wages, as they existed nearly a hundred years ago.

The peculiar increase of rents, which has taken place in the Highlands of Scotland during the last half century, is well known to have been occasioned in a great degree by the saving of labour on the land.

In Ireland, neither the wages of labour, nor the profits of stock on the land seem as if they could admit of any considerable reduction; but there can be no doubt that a great augmentation of rents might be effected by an improved system of agriculture, and a prosperous commerce, which, at the same time that it would sweep into flourishing cities the idlers which are now only half employed upon the land, would occasion an increasing demand for the products of agriculture, while the rates of profits and wages might remain as high as before.

Similar observations may be made with regard to Poland, and indeed almost all the countries of Europe. There is not one, in which the real wages of labour are high, and scarcely one in which the profits of agricultural stock are known to be considerable. If no improvements whatever in agriculture were to take place in these countries, and the future increase of their rents were to depend upon an increase of price occasioned solely by the increased quantity of labour necessary to produce food, I am inclined to think that the progress of their rents would be very soon stopped. The present rates of profits and wages are not such as would admit of much diminution ; and without increased skill in cultivation, and especially the saving of labour on the land, it is probable that no soils *much* poorer than those which are at present in use, would pay the expense of cultivation.

Even the rich countries of India and South America are not very differently circumstanced. From all the accounts we have received of these countries, I cannot believe that *agricultural* profits are high, and it is certain that the real wages of labour are in general low. And though profits and wages are not together so low as to prevent an increase of rents from an increase of cultivation without improvements in agriculture ; yet I conceive that their possible increase in this way would be quite trifling, compared with what it might be under an improved system of cultivation, and a prosperous commerce, even without any transfer from the labourer or cultivator.

The United States of America seem to be almost the only country with which we are acquainted, where the present wages of labour and the profits of agricultural stock are sufficiently high to admit of a considerable transfer to rents without improvements in agriculture. And probably it is only when the skill and capital of an old and industrious country are employed upon a new, rich, and extensive territory, under a free government, and in a favourable situation for the export of raw produce, that this state of things can take place.

. In old states, experience tells us that wages may be extremely low, and the profits of the cultivator

not high, while vast tracts of good land remain
uncultivated.   It is obvious indeed, that an operose'
and ignorant system of cultivation, combined with
such a faulty distribution of property as to check
the progress of demand, might keep the profits of
cultivation low, even in countries of the richest
soil.   And there is little doubt, from the very
large proportion of people employed in agriculture
in most unimproved territories, that this is a case
which not unfrequently occurs.   But in all instances of this kind, it must be allowed, that the
great source of the future increase of rents will be
improvements in agriculture and the demand occasioned by a prosperous external and internal commerce, and not the increase of price occasioned by
the additional quantity of labour required to produce a given quantity of corn.

If, however, in a country which continues to
grow nearly its own consumption of corn, or the
same proportion of that consumption, it appears
that every sort of improvement which has ever been
known to take place in agriculture, manufactures
or commerce, by which a country has been in-   a
riched, tends to increase rents, and every thing by
which it is impoverished, tends to lower them, it
must be allowed that the interests of the landlord,
and those of the state are, under the circumstances
supposed, absolutely inseparable.   b

Mr. Ricardo, as I have before intimated, takes   c
only one simple and confined view of the progress
of rent. He considers it as occasioned solely by
the increase of price, arising from the increased

difficulty of production.*   But if rents in many
countries may be doubled or trebled by improvements in agriculture, while in few countries they
could be raised a fourth or a fifth, and in some not
a tenth, by the increase of price arising from the
increased difficulty of production, must it not be
acknowledged, that such a view of rent embraces
only a very small part of the subject, and consequently that any general inferences from it must
be utterly inapplicable to practice?

It should be further observed, in reference to improvements in agriculture, that the mode in which
Mr. Ricardo estimates the increase or decrease of
rents is quite peculiar; and this peculiarity in the
use of his terms tends to separate his conclusions
still farther from truth as enunciated in the accustomed language of political economy.

In speaking of the division of the whole produce of the land and labour of the country between the three classes of landlords, labourers, and
capitalists, he has the following passage.

" It is not by the absolute quantity of produce
obtained by either class, that we can correctly judge
of the rate of profit, rent, and wages, but by the
quantity of labour required to obtain that produce.

---

* Mr. Ricardo always seems to assume, that increased difficulties thrown in the way of production will be overcome by increased price, and that the same quantity will be produced.   But
this is an unwarranted assumption.   Where is the increased price
to come from?   An increase of difficulty in the actual state of a
country's resources will always tend to diminish produce.

By improvements in machinery and agriculture the whole produce may be doubled; but if wages, rent and profits be also doubled, they will bear the same proportions to one another as before. But if wages partook not of the whole of this increase; if they, instead of being doubled, were only increased one half; if rent, instead of being doubled, were only increased three-fourths, and the remaining increase went to profit, it would, I apprehend, be correct for me to say, that rent and wages had fallen while profits had risen. For if we had an invariable standard by which to measure the value of this produce, we should find that a less value had fallen to the class of labourers and landlords, and a greater to the class of capitalists than had been given before."*

A little farther on, having stated some specific proportions, he observes, " In that case I should say, that wages and rent had fallen and profits risen, though, in consequence of the abundance of commodities, the *quantity* paid to the labourer and landlord would have increased in the proportion of 25 to 44."†

In reference to this statement, I should observe, that if the application of Mr. Ricardo's invariable standard of value naturally leads to the use of such language, the sooner the standard is got rid of, the better, as in an inquiry into the nature and causes of the wealth of nations, it must necessarily occasion perpetual confusion and error. For what does

a

* Princ. of Polit. Econ. chap. i. p. 43. 2d edit.   † Id. p. 44.   bc

it require us to say? We must say that the rents of the landlord have fallen and his interests have suffered, when he obtains as rent above three-fourths more of raw produce than before, and with that produce will shortly be able, according to Mr. Ricardo's own doctrines, to command three-fourths' more labour. In applying this language to our own country, we must say that rents have fallen considerably during the last forty years, because, though rents have greatly increased in exchangeable value,—in the command of money, corn, labour and manufactures, it appears, by the returns

α   to the Board of Agriculture, that they are now only a fifth of the gross produce,* whereas they were formerly a fourth or a third.

ab   In reference to labour, we must say that it is low in America, although we have been hitherto

c   in the habit of considering it as very high, both in money value and in the command of the necessaries and conveniences of life. And we must call it high in Sweden; because, although the labourer

d   only earns low money wages, and with these low wages can obtain but few of the necessaries and conveniences of life; yet, in the division of the whole produce of a laborious cultivation on a poor soil, a larger proportion may go to labour.†

e   * Reports from the Lords on the Corn Laws, p. 66.
f   † It is specifically this unusual application of common terms which has rendered Mr. Ricardo's work so difficult to be understood by many people. It requires indeed a constant and laborious effort of the mind to recollect at all times what is meant by high and low rents, and high or low wages. In other respects, it

Into this unusual language Mr. Ricardo has been   a
betrayed by the fundamental error of confounding
cost and value, and the further error of considering
raw produce in the same light as manufactures. It
might be true, that if, by improvements in machinery, the produce of muslins were doubled, the increased quantity would not command in exchange
a greater quantity of labour and of necessaries than
before, and would have little or no effect therefore on population.   But Mr. Ricardo has himself said, that " if improvements extended to all
the objects of the labourer's consumption, we
should find him probably, at the end of a very few
years, in possession of only a small, if any addition
to his enjoyments."*   Consequently, according to
Mr. Ricardo, population will increase in proportion
to the increase of the main articles consumed by
the labourer.

But if population increases according to the   b
necessaries which the labourer can command, the
increased quantity of raw produce which falls to
the share of the landlord must increase the exchangeable value of his rents estimated in labour,
corn and commodities.   And it is certainly by real
value in exchange, and not by an imaginary
standard, which is to measure *proportions* or cost
in labour, that the rents and interests of landlords

has always appeared to me that the style in which the work is
written, is perfectly clear. It is never obscure, but when either the
view itself is erroneous, or terms are used in an unusual sense.

* Princ. of Polit. Econ. ch. i. p. 9.   c

will be estimated.   It would often happen, that
after improvements had been taking place, rents
would rise according to the accustomed and natural meaning attached to the term, while they might
fall according to the new mode of estimating them
adopted by Mr. Ricardo.

a   I need hardly say, that, in speaking of the interests of the landlord, I mean always to refer to
what I should call his real rents and his real interests ; that is, his power of commanding labour,
and the necessaries and conveniences of life, whatever proportion these rents may form of the whole
produce, or whatever quantity of labour they may
have cost in producing.* But in fact, improvements
in agriculture tend, in a moderate time, even according to the concessions of Mr. Ricardo, to increase the *proportion* of the whole produce which
falls to the landlord's share; so that in any way
we can view the subject, we must allow that, in-

b
α   * This interpretation of the term rent is, I conceive, strictly consistent with my first definition of it.   I call it that *portion* (not *proportion)* of the value of the produce which goes to the landlord ;
and if the value of the whole produce of any given quantity of
land increases, the *portion* of value which goes to the landlord
may increase considerably, although the *proportion* which it bears
to the whole may diminish.   Mr. Ricardo has himself expressly
β   stated, p. 503. that whatever sum the produce of land sells for
above the costs of cultivating it, is money rent.   But if it continually happens that money rent rises, and is at the same time of
greater real value in exchange, although it bears a less *proportion*
to the value of the whole produce from the land in question, it
is quite obvious that neither money rent nor real rent is regulated
by this proportion.

dependently of the question of importations, the interest of the landlord is strictly and necessarily connected with that of the state.

SECTION IX.

On the Connexion of the Interests of the Landlord and of the State, in Countries which import Corn.

The only conceivable doubt which can arise respecting the strictest union between the interest of the landlord and that of the state, is in the question of importation. And here it is evident, that at all events the landlord cannot be placed in a worse situation than others, and by some of the warmest friends of the freedom of trade, he has justly been considered as placed in a much better. No person has ever doubted that the individual interests of the manufacturers of woollen, silk, or linen goods, might be injured by foreign competition ; and few would deny that the importation of a large body of labourers would tend to lower wages. Under the most unfavourable view, therefore, that we can take of the subject, the case of the landlord with regard to importation is not separated from that of the other classes of society.

But it has been stated by no less an authority than that of Adam Smith, that the freest importation of corn and raw produce cannot injure the farmers and landlords;* and it is almost universally allowed, that from the bulky nature of raw pro-

* Wealth of Nations, Book IV. ch. ii. p. 189. 6th edit.

duce, it must necessarily be more protected from foreign competition than almost any other commodity.

ab   The statement of Adam Smith is unquestionably too strong. The other is strictly true. Yet still it must be acknowledged, that the individual interests of landlords may suffer from importation, though not nearly so much as the interests of some of the

c   other classes of society. My reasons for thinking that, in some cases which are likely to occur, the diminution of rents which would be sustained in this way, would not be counterbalanced by proportionate advantages to the state, I have given at some length in the fifth edition of my Essay on the Principle of Population,* and to them I refer the reader.

d   But I will add a remark, which, if just, is certainly very important; namely, that the employment of capital upon the land in the way in which it is not unfrequently employed, appears to me the only considerable case where practically, and as the business is really conducted, the interest of the individual and of the state are not proportioned to each other.

e   If land were always considered as a merchantable instrument, bought and sold merely with a view to the profit which might be made of it, and worked exclusively by the proprietors, every increase of value and power which the instrument might acquire from being used and improved, would naturally enter into the computation in deciding

f   * Vol. ii. Book III. chap. xii.

whether a capital might be more profitably employed on land, or in commerce and manufactures;
and the advantage to the state, from the employment of such capital, would in general be proportioned in both cases to the advantage gained by
individuals. But, practically, this state of things
rarely exists. A very large portion of the lands of
most European countries is kept out of the market
by the right of primogeniture, the practice of entails, and the desire of maintaining a landed influence; and that part which is purchased by the
mercantile classes, and others who have acquired
moveable property, is generally purchased rather
with a view to secure a revenue from the wealth
already gained, and a share in the influence of the
old landholders, than to the means of making or
increasing their fortunes. The natural consequence
of these habits and feelings in the great body of
landholders is, that the cultivation of the country
must be chiefly carried on by tenants. And indeed
it is allowed, that not only the common routine of
farming is principally conducted by persons who
are not proprietors, but that even a very large part
of the great permanent improvements in agriculture, and in the instruments and modes of cultivation which have so peculiarly distinguished the last
thirty years, has been effected by the capitals of
the same class of people.

But if it be true, as I fully believe it is, that a
very large part of the improvements which have
taken place on the soil, has been derived from the
capital, skill and industry of tenants, no truth can

be more distinct and incontrovertible than that the advantage which such individuals have derived from a capital employed in agriculture, compared with a capital employed in commerce and manufactures, cannot have been proportioned to the advantages derived by the country ; or, in other words, that the interests of individuals in the employment of capital, have not in this case been identified with the interest of the state.

a   This position will be made perfectly clear, if we examine attentively what would be the relative effect to the individual and the state of the employment of a capital of 10,000*l*. in agriculture, or in manufactures under the circumstances described.

b   Let us suppose that a capital of 10,000*l*. might be employed in commerce or manufactures for twenty years, at a profit of about twelve per cent., and that the capitalist might retire, at the end of that term, with his fortune doubled. It is obvious that, to give the same encouragement to the employment of such a capital in agriculture, the same or nearly the same advantages must be offered to the individual. But in order to enable a person who employs his capital on rented land to convert his 10,000*l*. in the course of twenty years into 20,000*l*. it is certain that he must make annually higher profits, in order to enable him to recover that part of his capital which he has actually sunk upon the land, and cannot withdraw at the end of the term; and then, if he has been an essential improver, he must necessarily leave the land to his landlord, at the end of the lease, worth a considerably higher rent, independently of any change in the value of the circulating medium, than at the commencement of it. But these higher annual returns, which are necessary to the farmer with a temporary tenure to give him the common profits of stock, are continued, in part at least, in the shape of rent at the end of the lease, and must be so much gained by the state.

In the case of the capital employed in commerce and manufactures, the profit to the state is proportioned to the profit derived by the individual; in the case of the capital employed in agriculture it is much greater; and this would be true, whether the produce were estimated in money, or in corn and labour. In either way, under circumstances which in all probability have actually occurred, the profits to the state derived from the capital employed in agriculture might be estimated perhaps at fourteen or fifteen per cent., while the profits to the individuals, in both cases, may have been only twelve per cent.

Sir John Sinclair, in his Husbandry of Scotland, has given the particulars of a farm in East Lothian, in which the rent is nearly half the produce; and the rent and profits together yield a return of fifty-six per cent. on the capital employed. But the rent and profits together are the real measure of the wealth derived by the country from the capital so employed; and as the farm described is one where the convertible husbandry is practised, a system in which the greatest improvements have been made of late years, there is little doubt that a considerable part of this increase of wealth had been derived from the capital of the tenant who held the farm previous to the renewal of the lease, although such increase of wealth to the state could not have operated as a motive of interest to the individual so employing his stock.

a

If then during the war no obstacles had occurred to the importation of foreign corn, and the profits of agriculture had in consequence been only ten per cent. while the profits of commerce and manufactures were twelve, the capital of the country would of course have flowed towards commerce and manufactures; and measuring the interest of the state, as usual, by the interest of individuals, this would have been a more advantageous direction of it, in the proportion of twelve to ten. But, if the view of the subject just taken be correct, instead of a beneficial direction of it to a profit of twelve per cent. from a profit of ten per cent. as measured by the interests of the individuals concerned, it might have been a disadvantageous direction of it to a profit of only twelve per cent. from a profit of fourteen per cent. as measured by the interest of the state.

b

It is obvious therefore that the natural* restrictions upon the importation of foreign corn during the war, by forcibly raising the profits of domestic

c

* It is of great importance always to recollect that the high price of corn from 1798 to 1814 was occasioned by the war and the seasons,—not by corn-laws; and that a country with open ports may be subjected to very great alternations of price in war and in peace.

cultivation, may have directed the capital of the
country into a channel more advantageous than
that into which it would otherwise have flowed,
and instead of impeding the progress of wealth and
population, as at first one should certainly have
expected, may have decidedly and essentially promoted it.

And this, in fact, such restrictions not only may,
but must do, whenever the demand for corn grown
at home is such, that the profits of capitals employed on the new lands taken into cultivation,
joined to the rents which they generate, form together greater returns in proportion to the stock
employed, than the returns of the capitals engaged
in commerce and manufactures; because, in this
case, though foreign corn might be purchased,
without these restrictions, at a cheaper money price
than that at which it could be raised at home, it
would not be purchased at so small an expense of
capital and labour,* which is the true proof of the
advantageous employment of stock.

But if the progress of wealth has been rather accelerated than retarded by such restrictions upon

* If restrictions upon importation necessarily increased the
quantity of labour and capital required to obtain corn, they could
not of course be defended for a moment, with a view to wealth
and productive power. But if by directing capital to the land
they occasion permanent improvements, the whole question is
changed. Permanent improvements in agriculture are like the
acquisition of additional land. Even however, if they had no effect of this kind, they might be desirable on other grounds yet
more important. Late events must make us contemplate with no
small alarm a great increase in the *proportion* of our manufacturing population, both with reference to the happiness and to the
liberty of our country.

the importation of foreign corn, on account of the
greater quantity of raw produce that has been purchased by a given quantity of capital and labour
at home, than could have been purchased by the
same quantity of capital and labour from abroad,
it is quite obvious that the population must have
been accelerated rather than retarded; and certainly the unusually rapid increase of population
which is known to have taken place during the
last ten or fifteen years of the war so much beyond
the average of the century, tends strongly to confirm this conclusion.

a   The position here laid down may appear to be
rather startling; but the reader will see how it is
limited. It depends for its general effects upon
permanent improvements being made by a capital
which has only a temporary interest in the fruits of
such improvements; and, in reference to restrictions
upon importation, it depends upon the circumstance
that these restrictions by the increased demand
for the products of domestic agriculture which
they create, should have the effect of occasioning improvements which would otherwise not have
taken place. But neither of these usual concomi-
tants are absolutely necessary.

b   Considerable quantities of capital might be employed upon the land, and a temporary increase of
demand for domestic produce might take place,
without permanent improvements in agriculture.
All that is meant to be said is, that when, under
such circumstances, permanent improvements in
agriculture are really made, and rent is created, it
is impossible to resist the conclusion, that to such

extent the interest of the state in the exchangeable value created by such capital,* is decidedly greater than the interest of the individual.

This consideration, combined with those before adverted to, may make it at least a matter of doubt, whether even in the case of restrictions upon the importation of foreign corn, the interest of the state may not sometimes be the same as that of the landlords. But no such doubt exists respecting a restriction upon the importation of other commodities. And when we add, that in a state of perfectly free intercourse, it is eminently the interest of those who live upon the rents of land, that capital and population should increase, while to those who live upon the profits of stock and the wages of labour, an increase of capital and population is, to say the least of it, a much more doubtful benefit; it may be most safely asserted, that the interest of no other class in the state is so nearly and necessarily connected with its wealth and power, as the interest of the landlord.

* I refer to exchangeable value and rate of profits, not to abundance of conveniences and luxuries. In almost all improvements in machinery, the state is ultimately more benefited than the producers, but not in reference to rate of profits and real value in exchange.

a

SECTION X.

General Remarks on the Surplus Produce of the Land.

It seems rather extraordinary that the very great benefit which society derives from that surplus produce of the land which, in the progress of society, falls mainly to the landlord in the shape of rent, should not yet be fully understood and acknowledged. I have called this surplus a bountiful gift of Providence, and am most decidedly of opinion, that it fully deserves the appellation. But Mr. Ricardo has the following passage :—

" Nothing is more common than to hear of the advantages which the land possesses over every other source of useful produce, on account of the surplus which it yields in the form of rent. Yet when land is most abundant, when most productive and most fertile, it yields no rent; and it is only, when its powers decay, and less is yielded in return for labour, that a share of the original produce of the more fertile portions is set apart for rent. It is singular that this quality in the land, which should have been noticed as an imperfection, compared with the natural agents by which manufactures are assisted, should have been pointed out as constituting its peculiar pre-eminence. If air, water, the elasticity of steam, and the pressure of the atmosphere were of various qualities, if they could be appropriated, and each quality existed only in moderate abundance, they, as well as the land, would afford a rent, as the successive qualities were brought into use. With every worse quality employed, the value of the commodities in the manufacture of which they were used would rise, because equal quantities of labour would be less productive. Man would do more by the sweat of his brow, and nature perform less, and the land would be no longer pre-eminent for its limited powers."

" If the surplus produce which the land affords in the form of rent be an advantage, it is desirable that every year the machinery newly constructed should be less efficient than the old, as that would undoubtedly give a greater exchangeable value to the goods manufactured, not only by that machinery, but by all the other machinery in the kingdom; and a rent would be paid to all those who possessed the most productive machinery."*

Now, in referring to a gift of Providence, we   a
should surely speak of its value in relation to the laws and constitution of our nature, and of the world in which we live. But, if any person will take the trouble to make the calculation, he will see that if the necessaries of life could be obtained   b
without limit, and the number of people could be doubled every twenty-five years, the population which might have been produced from a single pair since the Christian æra, would have been sufficient, not only to fill the earth quite full of people, so that

* Princ. of Polit. Econ. ch. ii. p. 59.   c

four should stand in every square yard, but to fill all
the planets of our solar system in the same way, and
not only them, but all the planets revolving round
the stars which are visible to the naked eye, supposing each of them to be a sun, and to have as many
planets belonging to it as our sun has.   Under this
law of population, which, excessive as it may appear
when stated in this way, is, I firmly believe, best
suited to the nature and situation of man, it is quite
obvious that some limit to the production of food,
or some other of the necessaries of life, must exist.
Without a total change in the constitution of human nature, and the situation of man on earth, the
whole of the necessaries of life could not be furnished in the same plenty as air, water, the elasticity of steam, and the pressure of the atmosphere.
It is not easy to conceive a more disastrous present—one more likely to plunge the human race
in irrecoverable misery, than an unlimited facility
of producing food in a limited space. A benevo-
lent Creator then, knowing the wants and neces-
sities of his creatures, under the laws to which he
had subjected them, could not, in mercy, have furnished the whole of the necessaries of life in the
same plenty as air and water. This shews at once
the reason why the former are limited in quantity,
and the latter poured out in profusion. But if it
be granted, as it must be, that a limitation in the
power of producing food is obviously necessary to
man confined to a limited space, then the value of
the actual quantity of land which he has received,
depends upon the small quantity of labour neces-

sary to work it, compared with the number of persons which it will support; or, in other words,
upon that specific surplus so much under-rated by
Mr. Ricardo, which by the laws of nature termi-
nates in rent.

If manufactured commodities, by the gradations
of machinery supposed by Mr. Ricardo, were to
yield a rent, man, as he observes, would do more   α
by the sweat of his brow ;* and supposing him still
to obtain the same quantity of commodities, (which,
however, he would not,) the increase of his labour
would be in proportion to the greatness of the rent
so created. But the surplus, which a given quantity
of land yields in the shape of rent, is totally different. Instead of being a measure of the increase
of labour, which is necessary altogether to produce
the quantity of corn which the land can yield, it
is finally an exact measure of the *relief* from labour
in the production of food granted to him by a kind
Providence. If this final surplus be small, the labour of a large portion of the society must be
constantly employed in procuring, by the sweat of
their brows, the mere necessaries of life, and so-

---

* That is, supposing the gradations were towards worse machinery, some of which it was necessary to use, but not otherwise.   a
The reason why manufactures and necessaries will not admit of
comparison with regard to rents is, that necessaries, in a limited   b
territory, are always tending to the same exchangeable value,
whether they have cost little or much labour ; but manufactures,
if not subjected to an artificial monopoly, must fall with the facility   c
of producing them. We cannot therefore suppose the price to be
given ; but if we could, facility of production would, in both cases,
be equally a measure of relief from labour.

a ciety must be most scantily provided with convenient luxuries and leisure; while if this surplus be large, manufactures, foreign luxuries, arts, letters and leisure may abound.

It is a little singular, that Mr. Ricardo, who has, in general, kept his attention so steadily fixed on permanent and final results, as even to define the *natural* price of labour to be that price which would maintain a stationary population, although such a price cannot generally occur under moderately good governments, and in an ordinary state of things, for hundreds of years, has always, in treating of rent, adopted an opposite course, and referred almost entirely to temporary effects.

It is obviously with this sort of reference, that he has objected to Adam Smith for saying that, in rice countries a greater share of the produce would belong to the landlord than in corn countries, and that rents in this country would rise, if potatoes were to become the favourite vegetable food of the common people, instead of corn.* Mr. Ricardo could not but allow, indeed he has allowed,† that rents would be finally higher in both cases. But he immediately supposes that this change is put in execution at once, and refers to the temporary result of land being thrown out of cultivation. Even on this supposition however, all the lands which had been thrown up, would be cultivated again in a very much less time, than it would take to reduce the price of labour, in a natural state of things, to

b * Wealth of Nations, vol. i. Book I. c. xi. pp. 248—250. 6th edit.
c † Princ. of Polit. Econ. ch. xxiv. p. 423.

the maintenance only of a stationary population.
And therefore, with a view to permanent and final
results, which are the results which Mr. Ricardo
has mainly considered throughout his work, he   a
ought to have allowed the truth of Adam Smith's
statements.

But, in point of fact, there is every probability that
not even a temporary fall of rent would take place.
No nation ever has changed or ever will change
the nature of its food all at once. The process, both
in reference to the new system of cultivation to be
adopted, and the new tastes to be generated, must
necessarily be very slow.   In the greater portion
of Europe, it is probable, that a change from corn
to rice could never take place; and where it could,
it would require such great preparations for irrigation, as to give ample time for an increase of
population fully equal to the increased quantity
of food produced.   In those countries where rice
is actually grown, the rents are known to be very
high. Dr. Buchanan, in his valuable travels through   α
the Mysore, says, that in the watered lands below
the Ghâts, the government was in the habit of
taking two-thirds of the crop.*   This is an amount
of rent which probably no lands cultivated in corn
can ever yield ; and in those parts of India and
other countries, where an actual change has taken
place from the cultivation of corn to the cultivation of rice, I have little doubt that rents have
not only finally risen very considerably, but have
risen even during the progress of the change.

* Vol. ii. p. 212.

With regard to potatoes, we have very near to us an opportunity of studying the effects of their becoming the vegetable food of the great mass of a people. The population of Ireland has increased faster, during the last hundred years, than that of any other country in Europe; and under its actual government, this fact cannot be rationally accounted for, but from the introduction and gradual extension of the use of the potatoe. I am persuaded, that had it not been for the potatoe, the population of Ireland would not have more than doubled, instead of quadrupled, during the last century. This increase of population has prevented lands from being thrown out of cultivation, or given greater value to natural pasture, at the same time that it has occasioned a great fall in the comparative money wages of labour. This fall, experience tells us, has not been accompanied by a proportionate rise of profits, and the consequence is a considerable rise of rents. The wheat, oats and cattle of Ireland are sold to England and bear English money prices, while they are cultivated and tended by labour paid at half the money price; a state of things which must greatly increase either the revenue derived from profits, or the revenue derived from rents; and practical information assures us, that it is the latter which has derived the greatest benefit from it.

I think, therefore, that though it must lead to great errors, not to distinguish very decidedly the temporary rates of wages from their final rates, it would lead to no such error to consider the tempo-

rary effects of the changes of food which have been
referred to, as of the same kind with their final effects, that is, as tending always to raise rents. And
I am convinced, that if we make our comparisons
with any tolerable fairness, that is, if we compare
countries under similar circumstances, with respect
to extent, and the quantity of capital employed
upon the soil, which is obviously the only fair
mode of comparing them, we shall find that rent
will be in proportion to the natural and acquired
fertility of the land.

If the natural fertility of this island had been
double what it is, and the people had been equally
industrious and enterprising, the country would, according to all just theory, have been at this time
doubly rich and populous, and the rents of land
much more than double what they are now. On
the other hand, if the soil of the island had possessed only half its present fertility, a small portion
of it only, as I stated on a former occasion, would
have admitted of corn cultivation, the wealth and
population of the country would have been quite inconsiderable, and rents not nearly one half of what
they are now. But if, under similar circumstances,
rent and fertility go together, it is no just argument against their natural connexion to say that
rent is higher in England, where a great mass of
capital has been employed upon the land, than in
the more fertile country of South America, where,
on the same extent of territory, not a twentieth part
has been employed, and the population is extremely scanty.

The fertility of the land, either natural or acquired, may be said to be the only source of permanently high returns for capital. If a country
were exclusively manufacturing and commercial,
and were to purchase all its corn at the market
prices of Europe, it is absolutely impossible that the
returns for its capital should for any great length
of time be high.   In the earlier periods of history,
indeed, when large masses of capital were extremely
rare, and were confined to a very few towns, the
sort of monopoly which they gave to particular
kinds of commerce and manufactures tended to
keep up profits for a much longer time ; and great
and brilliant effects were undoubtedly produced by
some states which were almost exclusively commercial. But in modern Europe, the general abundance
of capital, the easy intercourse between different
nations, and the laws of domestic and foreign competition prevent the possibility of large permanent
returns being received for any other capitals than
those employed on the land.   No great commercial and manufacturing state in modern times,
whatever may have been its skill, has yet been
known permanently to make higher profits than
the average of the rest of Europe. But the capitals successfully employed on moderately good
land, may permanently and without fear of interruption or check, sometimes yield twenty per cent.,
sometimes thirty or forty, and sometimes even
fifty or sixty per cent.

A striking illustration of the effects of capitals employed on land compared with others, appeared in

the returns of the property-tax in this country. The
taxable income derived from the capitals employed
on land, was such as to yield to the property-tax
nearly 6½ millions, while the income derived from
the capitals employed in commerce and manufactures was only such as to yield two millions.*   It
is probably true, that a larger proportion of the incomes derived from the capitals employed in trade
and manufactures, escaped the tax, partly from
their subdivision, and partly from other causes; but
the deficiency so occasioned could in no respect
make up for the extraordinary productiveness of
the capitals employed in agriculture.†   And indeed
it is quite obvious that, in comparing two countries together with the *same* capitals and the *same*
rate of profits, one of which has land on which to
grow its corn, and the other is obliged to purchase
it, that which has the land, particularly if it be fertile, must be much richer, more populous, and have
a larger disposable income for taxation.

Another most desirable benefit belonging to a fertile soil is, that states so endowed are not obliged to
pay much attention to that most distressing and dis-
heartening of all cries to every man of humanity—
the cry of the master manufacturers and merchants
for low wages, to enable them to find a market for

* The Schedule D. included every species of professions.   The
whole amounted to three millions, of which the professions were
considered to be above a million.

† It must always be recollected, that the national profits on land
must be considered as including rents as well as the common agricultural profits.

their exports. If a country can only be rich by running a successful race for low wages, I should be disposed to say at once, perish such riches! But, though a nation which purchases the main part of its food from foreigners, is condemned to this hard alternative, it is not so with the possessors of fertile land.

a   The peculiar products of a country, though never probably sufficient to enable it to import a large proportion of its food* as well as of its conveniences and luxuries, will generally be sufficient to give full spirit and energy to all its commercial dealings, both at home and abroad; while a small sacrifice

b   of produce, that is, the not pushing cultivation too far, would, with prudential habits among the poor,† enable it to maintain the whole of a large po-

c   pulation in wealth and plenty. Prudential habits, among the labouring classes of a country mainly depending upon manufactures and commerce,

d   might ruin it. In a country of fertile land, such

e   * Cottons are no more a peculiar product of this country than silks: and woe will, I fear, befal us, greater than ever we have yet experienced, if the prosperity of our cotton trade should become necessary to purchase the food of any considerable body of our people!

f   † Under similar circumstances, with respect to capital, skill, &c., it is obvious that land of the same degree of barrenness could not be cultivated, if by the prevalence of prudential habits the la-

g   bourers were well paid; but to forego the small increase of produce and population arising from the cultivation of such land, would, in a large and fertile territory, be a slight and imperceptible sacrifice, while the happiness which would result from it to the great mass of the population, would be beyond all price.

habits would be the greatest of all conceivable
blessings.

Among the inestimable advantages which belong to that quality in the land, which enables it
to yield a considerable rent, it is not one of the
least, that in the progress of society it affords the
main security to man that nearly his whole time,
or the time of nearly the whole society, shall not
be employed in procuring mere necessaries. Ac-   a
cording to Mr. Ricardo, not only will each individual capital in the progress of society yield a
continually diminishing revenue, but the whole
amount of the revenue derived from profits will be
diminished; and there is no doubt that the labou-   b
rer will be obliged to employ a greater quantity of
labour to procure that portion of his wages which
must be spent in necessaries. Both these great
classes of society, therefore, may be expected to
have less power of giving leisure to themselves, or
of commanding the labour of those who administer to the enjoyments of society, as contradistin-   c
guished from those who administer to its necessary
wants. But, fortunately for mankind, the neat
rents of the land, under a system of private property, can never be diminished by the progress of
cultivation. Whatever proportion they may bear
to the whole produce, the actual amount must
always go on increasing, and will always afford a
fund for the enjoyments and leisure of the society,
sufficient to leaven and animate the whole mass.

If the only condition on which we could obtain
lands yielding rent were, that they should remain

with the immediate descendants of the first possessors, though the benefits to be derived from the
present would no doubt be very greatly diminished, yet from its general and unavoidable effects on society, it would be most unwise to refuse
it as of little or no value. But, happily, the benefit
is attached to the soil, not to any particular proprietors. Rents are the reward of present valour
a   and wisdom, as well as of past strength and cun-
ning. Every day lands are purchased with the
fruits of industry and talents.* They afford the
great prize, the *" otium cum dignitate"* to every
species of laudable exertion; and, in the progress of
society, there is every reason to believe, that, as
they become more valuable from the increase of capital and population, and the improvements in
agriculture, the benefits which they yield may be
divided among a much greater number of persons.

b   * Mr. Ricardo himself is an instance of what I am stating. He
c   is now become, by his talents and industry, a considerable landholder; and a more honourable and excellent man, a man who for
d   the qualities of his head and heart more entirely deserves what he
ef   has earned, or employs it better, I could not point out in the
whole circle of landholders.
     It is somewhat singular that Mr. Ricardo, a considerable recei-
ver of rents, should have so much underrated their national importance; while I, who never received, nor expect to receive any,
gh   shall probably be accused of overrating their importance. Our
different situations and opinions may serve at least to shew our
mutual sincerity, and afford a strong presumption, that to whatever bias our minds may have been subjected in the doctrines we
have laid down, it has not been that, against which perhaps it is
most difficult to guard, the insensible bias of situation and interest.

In every point of view, then, in which the subject can be considered, that quality of land which, by the laws of our being, must terminate in rent, appears to be a boon most important to the happiness of mankind; and I am persuaded, that its value can only be underrated by those who still labour under some mistake, as to its nature, and its effects on society.

CHAPTER IV.

OF THE WAGES OF LABOUR.

SECTION I.

a   *Of the Dependance of the Wages of Labour upon Supply and Demand.*

b   THE wages of labour are the remuneration to the labourer for his personal exertions.

c   They may be divided, like the prices of commodities, into real and nominal.

d   The real wages of labour consist of their value, estimated in the necessaries, conveniences, and luxuries of life.

e   The nominal wages of labour consist in their value, estimated in money.

f   As the value of labour, as well as of commodities, is most frequently compared with money, it will be advisable in general to adopt this mode of comparison, with a frequent reference, however, where it is necessary, to the money's worth, or the real wages of labour.

g   The money wages of labour are determined by the demand and supply of money, compared with the demand and supply of labour : and, during periods when money may be supposed to maintain nearly the same value, the variations in the wages of labour, may be said to be regulated by the variations in the demand compared with the supply of labour.

The principle of demand and supply is the paramount regulator of the prices of labour as well as of commodities, not only temporarily but permanently; and the costs of production affect these prices only as they are the necessary condition of the permanent supply of labour, or of commodities.   a

It is as the condition of the supply, that the prices of the necessaries of life have so important an influence on the price of labour.   A certain portion of these necessaries is required to enable the labourer to maintain a stationary population, a greater portion to maintain an increasing one; and consequently, whatever may be the prices of the necessaries of life, the money wages of the labourer must be such as to enable him to purchase these portions, or the supply cannot possibly take place in the quantity required.   b

To shew that what may be called the cost of producing labour only influences wages as it regulates the supply of labour, it is sufficient to turn our attention to those cases, where, under temporary circumstances, the cost of production does not regulate the supply; and here we shall always find that this cost immediately ceases to regulate prices.   c

When, from a course of abundant seasons, or any cause which does not impair the capitals of the farmers, the price of corn falls for some time to-   d

gether, the cost of producing labour may be said
to be diminished, but it is not found that the
wages of labour fall;* and for this obvious reason,
that the reduced cost of production cannot, under
sixteen or eighteen years, materially influence the
supply of labour in the market.   On the other hand,
when the prices of corn rise from a succession of
indifferent seasons, or any cause which leaves the
demand for labour nearly the same as before, wages
will not rise: because the same number of labourers remain in the market; and though the price of
production has risen, the supply is not for some
time affected by it.   So entirely, indeed, does the
effect of the cost of production on price depend
upon the manner in which it regulates supply, that
if in this, or any other country during the last
twenty years, the production of labour had cost absolutely nothing, but had still been supplied in
exactly the same proportion to the demand, the
wages of labour would have been in no respect different. Of the truth of this position, we may be quite
assured, by the instance alluded to in a former
α   chapter, of a paper currency so limited in quantity
as not to exceed the metallic money, which would
otherwise have circulated, in which case, though
the cost of the paper is comparatively nothing, yet,
as it performs the same function, and is supplied

a   * The fall in the price of labour which took place in 1815 and
1816 was occasioned solely by the diminution of demand, arising
from the losses of the farmers, and in no respect by the diminished
cost of production.

only in the same quantity as the money, it acquires the same value in exchange.

Adam Smith is practically quite correct, when he says, that, " the money price of labour is necessarily regulated by two circumstances; the demand for labour; and the price of the necessaries and conveniences of life."* But it is of great importance to a thorough understanding of the subject, to keep constantly under our view the precise   a mode in which the costs of production operate on the price of labour, and to see clearly and distinctly the constant and predominant action of the principle of supply and demand.   b

In all those cases which Adam Smith has so happily explained and illustrated, where an apparent irregularity takes place in the pay of different kinds   c of labour, it will be found, universally, that the causes to which he justly attributes them, are causes of a nature to influence the supply of labour in the particular departments in question. The   d five principal circumstances, which, according to him, make up for a small pecuniary gain in some employments, and counterbalance a great one in others, namely; 1. The agreeableness or disagreeableness of the employments themselves. 2. The easiness and cheapness, or the difficulty and expense of learning them. 3. The constancy or inconstancy of employment in them; 4. the small or great trust which must be reposed in those who exercise them; and 5. the probability or improba-

* Wealth of Nations, Book, i. ch. viii. p. 130. 6th edit.   α

a

bility of success in them,* are all obviously of this
description ; and in many of the instances, it would
not be easy to account for their effects on the price
of the different kinds of labour, upon any other
principle. One hardly sees, for instance, why the
cost of producing a poacher should be less than
that of a common labourer, or the cost of producing
a coal-heaver much greater ; yet they are paid very
differently. It is not easier to resolve the effects
on wages of the small or great trust which must be
reposed in a workman, or, the probability or impro-
bability of success in his trade, into the quantity of

b

labour which has been employed to bring him into
the market. Adam Smith satisfactorily shews,
that the whole body of lawyers is not remunerated
sufficiently to pay the expenses which the education of the whole body has cost ;† and it is obvious
that particular skill, both in trades and professions,
is paid high, with but little reference to the labour
employed in acquiring it, which, owing to superior talent, is often less than that which is frequently applied to the acquisition of inferior pro-
ficiency. But all these cases are accounted for in
the easiest and most natural manner, upon the
principle of supply and demand. Superior artists
are paid high on account of the scanty supply of
such skill, whether occasioned by unusual labour
or uncommon genius, or both. Lawyers as a body,
are not well remunerated, because the prevalence

α
β

* Wealth of Nations, B. i. ch. x. part i. p. 152. 6th edit.
† Id. p. 161.

of other motives, besides mere gain, crowds the
profession with candidates, and the supply is not
regulated by the cost of the education ; and in all
those instances, where disadvantages or difficulties
of any kind accompany particular employments, it
is obvious that they must be paid comparatively
high, because if the additional remuneration were
not sufficient to balance such disadvantages, the
supply of labour in these departments would be
deficient, as, *cæteris paribus*, every person would
choose to engage in the most agreeable, the least
difficult, and the least uncertain occupations.
The deficiency so occasioned, whenever it occurs,
will naturally raise the price of labour ; and the
advance of price, after some little oscillation, will
rest at the point where it is just sufficient to effect
the supply required.   a

Adam Smith has in general referred to the principle of supply and demand in cases of this kind,
but he has occasionally forgotten it :—" If one
species of labour," he says, " requires an uncommon degree of dexterity and ingenuity, the *esteem*
which men have for such talents will give a value
to their produce, superior to what would be due to
the time employed about it."*   And in another
place, speaking of China, he remarks, " That if in
such a country, (that is, a country with stationary
resources,) wages had ever been more than sufficient to maintain the labourer, and enable him to
bring up a family ; the competition of the labourers

* Wealth of Nations, Book I. ch. vi. p. 71. 6th edit.   α

and the interest of the masters, would soon reduce them to the lowest rate which is consistent with *common humanity*."* The reader will be aware, from what has been already said, that in the first case here noticed, it is not the esteem for the dexterity and ingenuity referred to, which raises the price of the commodity, but their scarcity, and the consequent scarcity of the articles produced by them, compared with the demand. And in the latter case, it is not common humanity which interferes to prevent the price of labour from falling still lower. If humanity could have successfully interfered, it ought to have interfered long before, and prevented any premature mortality from being occasioned by bad or insufficient food. But unfortunately, common humanity cannot alter the resources of a country. While these are stationary, and the habits of the lower classes prompt them to supply a stationary population cheaply, the wages of labour will be scanty ; but still they cannot fall below what is necessary, under the actual habits of the people, to keep up a stationary population ; because, by the supposition, the resources of the country are stationary, not increasing or declining, and consequently the principle of demand and supply would always interfere to prevent such wages as would either occasion an increase or diminution of people.

* Wealth of Nations, Book I. chap. vii. p. 108.

SECTION II.

Of the Causes which principally affect the Habits of the Labouring Classes.

Mr. Ricardo has defined the natural price of labour   a
to be " that price which is necessary to enable the
labourers one with another to subsist, and to perpetuate their race, without either increase or diminution."* This price I should really be disposed
to call a most unnatural price; because in a natural
state of things, that is, without great impediments   b
to the progress of wealth and population, such a   c
price could not generally occur for hundreds of   d
years. But if this price be really rare, and, in
an ordinary state of things, at so great a distance   e
in point of time, it must evidently lead to great
errors to consider the market-prices of labour
as only temporary deviations above and below
that fixed price to which they will very soon return.

The natural or necessary price of labour in any   f
country I should define to be, " that price which, in   g
the actual circumstances of the society, is necessary
to occasion an average supply of labourers, sufficient to meet the average demand." And the market   hi
price I should define to be, the actual price in the
market, which from temporary causes is sometimes

* Polit. Econ. c. v. p. 85. 2d edit.   j

above, and sometimes below, what is necessary to
supply this average demand.

The condition of the labouring classes of society
must evidently depend, partly upon the rate at
which the resources of the country and the demand
for labour are increasing; and partly, on the habits
of the people in respect to their food, clothing and
lodging.

If the habits of the people were to remain fixed,
the power of marrying early, and of supporting a
large family, would depend upon the rate at which
the resources of the country and the demand for
labour were increasing. And if the resources of
the country were to remain fixed, the comforts of
the lower classes of society would depend upon
their habits, or the amount of those necessaries and
conveniences, without which they would not consent to keep up their numbers.

It rarely happens, however, that either of them
remain fixed for any great length of time together.
The rate at which the resources of a country increase is, we well know, liable, under varying circumstances, to great variation; and the habits of
a people though not so liable, or so necessarily
subject to change, can scarcely ever be considered
as permanent. In general, their tendency is to
change together. When the resources of a country
are rapidly increasing, and the labourer commands
a large portion of necessaries, it is to be expected
that if he has the opportunity of exchanging his
superfluous food for conveniences and comforts, he
will acquire a taste for these conveniences, and

his habits will be formed accordingly. On the other hand, it generally happens that, when the resources of a country become nearly stationary, such habits, if they ever have existed, are found to give way; and, before the population comes to a stop, the standard of comfort is essentially lowered.

Still, however, partly from physical, and partly from moral causes, the standard of comfort differs essentially in different countries, under the same rate of increase in their resources. Adam Smith, in speaking of the inferior food of the people of Scotland, compared with their neighbours of the same rank in England, observes, " This difference in the mode of their subsistence is not the cause, but the effect, of the difference in their wages, though, by a strange misapprehension, I have frequently heard it represented as the cause."* It must be allowed, however, that this correction of a common opinion is only partially just. The effect, in this case as in many others, certainly becomes in its turn a cause; and there is no doubt, that if the continuance of low wages for some time, should produce among the labourers of any country habits of marrying with the prospect only of a mere subsistence, such habits, by supplying the quantity of labour required at a low rate, would become a constantly operating cause of low wages.

It would be very desirable to ascertain what are the principal causes which determine the different

* Book I. chap. viii. p. 114. 6th edit.

modes of subsistence among the lower classes of people of different countries ; but the question involves so many considerations, that a satisfactory solution of it is hardly to be expected. Much must certainly depend upon the physical causes of climate and soil ; but still more perhaps on moral causes, the formation and action of which are owing to a variety of circumstances.

a   From high wages, or the power of commanding a large portion of the necessaries of life, two very different results may follow ; one, that of a rapid increase of population, in which case the high wages are chiefly spent in the maintenance of large and frequent families : and the other, that of a decided improvement in the modes of subsistence, and the conveniences and comforts enjoyed, without a proportionate acceleration in the rate of increase.

In looking to these different results, the causes of them will evidently appear to be the different habits existing among the people of different countries, and at different times. In an inquiry into the causes of these different habits, we shall

b   generally be able to trace those which produce the first result to all the circumstances which contribute to depress the lower classes of the people, which make them unable or unwilling to reason from the past to the future and ready to acquiesce, for the sake of present gratification, in a very low standard of comfort and respectability ; and those which produce the second result, to all the circumstances which tend to elevate the character of the

c   lower classes of society, which make them approach

the nearest to beings who " look before and after,"   α
and who consequently cannot acquiesce patiently
in the thought of depriving themselves and their
children of the means of being respectable, virtuous
and happy.

Among the circumstances which contribute to
the character first described, the most efficient will
be found to be despotism, oppression, and ignorance:
among those which contribute to the latter character, civil and political liberty, and education.

Of all the causes which tend to generate prudential habits among the lower classes of society,
the most essential is unquestionably civil liberty.
No people can be much accustomed to form plans
for the future, who do not feel assured that their
industrious exertions, while fair and honourable,
will be allowed to have free scope ; and that the
property which they either possess, or may acquire,
will be secured to them by a known code of just
laws impartially administered.   But it has been
found by experience, that civil liberty cannot be
permanently secured without political liberty. Consequently, political liberty becomes almost equally
essential ; and in addition to its being necessary in
this point of view, its obvious tendency to teach
the lower classes of society to respect themselves
by obliging the higher classes to respect them,
must contribute greatly to aid all the good effects
of civil liberty.

With regard to education, it might certainly be
made general under a bad form of government,
and might be very deficient under one in other

respects good : but it must be allowed, that the chances, both with regard to its quality and its prevalence, are greatly in favour of the latter. Education alone could do little against insecurity of property ; but it would powerfully assist all the favourable consequences to be expected from civil and political liberty, which could not indeed be considered as complete without it.

According as the habits of the people had been determined by such unfavourable or favourable circumstances, high wages, or a rapid increase of the funds for the maintenance of labour, would be attended with the first or second results before described ; or at least by results which would approach to the one or the other, according to the proportions in which all the causes which influence habits of improvidence or prudence had been efficient.

Ireland, during the course of the last century, may be produced perhaps as the most marked instance of the first result. On the introduction of the potatoe into that country, the lower classes of society were in such a state of oppression and ignorance, were so little respected by others, and had consequently so little respect for themselves, that as long as they could get food, and that of the cheapest kind, they were content to marry under the prospect of every other privation. The abundant funds for the support of labour, occasioned by the cultivation of the potatoe in a favourable soil, which often gave the labourer the command of a quantity of subsistence quite un-

usual in the other parts of Europe, were spent almost exclusively in the maintenance of large and
frequent families ; and the result was, a most rapid
increase of population, with little or no melioration
in the general condition and modes of subsistence
of the labouring poor.

An instance somewhat approaching to the second
may be found in England, in the first half of the
last century.   It is well known, that during this
period the price of corn fell considerably, while the
wages of labour are stated to have risen.   During
the last forty years of the 17th century, and the
first twenty of the 18th, the average price of corn
was such as, compared with the wages of labour,
would enable the labourer to purchase, with a day's
earnings, two-thirds of a peck of wheat.   From
1720 to 1750 the price of wheat had so fallen, while
wages had risen, that instead of two thirds the labourer could purchase the whole of a peck of wheat
with a day's labour.*

This great increase of command over the necessaries of life did not, however, produce a proportionate increase of population.   It found the people
of this country living under an excellent government, and enjoying all the advantages of civil and
political liberty in an unusual degree.   The lower
classes of people had been in the habit of being
respected, both by the laws and the higher orders
of their fellow citizens, and had learned in consequence to respect themselves.   And the result was,

* See Sect. IV. of this chapter.

that, instead of an increase of population exclusively, a considerable portion of their increased real wages was expended in a marked improvement of the quality of the food consumed, and a decided elevation in the standard of their comforts and conveniences.

a   During the same period, the resources of Scotland do not appear to have increased so fast as those
b   of England ; but since the middle of the century, the former country has perhaps made a more rapid progress than the latter ; and the consequence has been, that, from the same causes, these increased
c   resources have not produced, exclusively, increase of population, but a great alteration for the better in the food, dress, and houses of the lower classes
d   of society.

The general change from bread of a very inferior quality to the best wheaten bread, seems to have been peculiar to the southern and midland counties of England, and may perhaps have been aided by adventitious circumstances.

e   The state of the foreign markets as opened by the bounty, together with the improving cultivation of the country, appears to have diminished, in some districts, the usual difference in the prices of the different kinds of grain. Though barley was largely grown and largely exported, it did not fall in price so much as wheat. On an average of the twenty years ending with 1705, compared with an average of twenty years ending with 1745, the quarter of wheat fell from 1l. 16s. 3d. to 1l. 9s. 10d. but malt during the same period remained at the

same price, or, if any thing, rather rose ;* and as
barley is supposed to be not a cheaper food than
wheat, unless it can be purchased at $\frac{2}{3}$ of the
price,† such a relative difference would have a
strong tendency to promote the change.

From the small quantity of rye exported, compared with wheat and barley, it may be inferred
that it did not find a ready vent in foreign markets ; and this circumstance, together with the
improving state of the land, diminished its cultivation and use.

With regard to oats, the prohibitory laws and
the bounty were not so favourable to them as to
the other grains, and more were imported than exported. This would naturally tend to check their
cultivation in the districts which were capable of
growing the sort of grain most certain of a market;
while the Act of Charles II. respecting the buying   α
up of corn to sell again, threw greater obstacles in
the way of the distribution of oats than of any
other grain.

By this Act, wheat might be bought up and
stored for future sale when the price did not exceed 48s. ; barley, when the price did not exceed
28s.; and oats, when the price did not exceed
13s. 4d. The limited rates of wheat and barley   a
were considerably above their ordinary and average
rates at that period, and therefore did not often in-

* Eden's State of the Poor. Table, Vol. III. p. 79.   In this   β
table, a deduction is made of $\frac{2}{5}$ for the quarter of middling wheat of   b
eight bushels, which is too much.

† Tracts on the Corn Trade, Supp. p. 199.   γ

terfere with their proper distribution; but the ordinary price of oats was supposed to be about 12s. the quarter, and consequently the limit of 13s. 4d. would be very frequently exceeded,* and obstacles would be continually thrown in the way of their transport from the districts of their growth to the districts where they might be wanted. But if, from the causes here described, the labouring classes of the South of England were partly induced, and partly obliged, to adopt wheat as their main food, instead of the cheaper kinds of grain, the rise of wages would at once be accounted for, consistently with the fall in the price of wheat; an event which, under an apparently slack demand for labour at the time, has been considered as so improbable by some writers, that the accuracy of the accounts has been doubted. It is evidently, however, possible, either on supposition of a voluntary determination on the part of the labouring classes to adopt a superior description of food, or a sort of obligation to do it, on account of the introduction of a new system of cultivation adapted to a more improved soil : and, in either case, the effects observable from 1720 to 1750 would appear; namely, an increased power of commanding the necessaries of life, without a proportionate increase of population. It is probable that both causes contributed their share to the change in question. When once the fashion of eating wheaten bread had become general in some countries, it would be likely to

* Tracts on the Corn Trade, p. 50.

spread into others, even at the expense of comforts
of a different description, and in all cases where
particular modes of subsistence, from whatever
causes arising, have been for any time established,
though such modes always remain susceptible of
change, the change must be a work of time and
difficulty. A country, which for many years had
principally supported its peasantry on one sort of
grain, must alter its whole system of agriculture
before it can produce another sort in sufficient
abundance; and the obstinacy with which habits
are adhered to by all classes of people, as in some
countries it would prevent high wages from improving the quality of the food, so in others it
would prevent low wages from suddenly deterio-
rating it; and such high or low wages would be
felt almost exclusively in the great stimulus or
the great check which they would give to population.

SECTION III.

*Of the Causes which principally influence the Demand for
Labour, and the Increase of the Population.*

There is another cause, besides a change in the
habits of the people, which prevents the population
of a country from keeping pace with the apparent   a
command of the labourer over the means of subsistence. It sometimes happens that wages are for   b

a time rather higher than they ought to be, in proportion to the demand for labour. This is the
most likely to take place when the price of raw
produce has fallen in value, so as to diminish the
power of the cultivators to employ the same or an
increasing number of labourers at the same price.
If the fall be considerable, and not made up in
value by increase of quantity, so many labourers
will be thrown out of work that wages, after a
period of great distress, will generally be lowered
in proportion. But if the fall be gradual, and
partly made up in exchangeable value by increase
of quantity, the money wages of labour will not
necessarily sink; and the result will be merely a
slack demand for labour, not sufficient perhaps to
throw the actual labourers out of work, but such
as to prevent or diminish task-work, to check the
employment of women and children, and to give
but little encouragement to the rising generation
of labourers. In this case the quantity of the necessaries of life actually earned by the labourer and
his family, may be really less than when, owing to
a rise of prices, the daily pay of the labourer will
command a smaller quantity of corn. The command of the labouring classes over the necessaries
of life, though apparently greater, is really less in
the former than in the latter case, and, upon all general principles, ought to produce less effect on the
increase of population.

This disagreement between apparent wages and
the progress of population will be further aggravated in those countries where poor laws are estab-

lished; and it has become customary to pay a portion of the labourers' wages out of the parish rates.
If, when corn rises, the farmers and landholders of
a parish keep the wages of labour down, and make
a regular allowance for children, it is obvious that
there is no longer any necessary connexion between the apparent wages of day labour and the
real means which the labouring classes possess of
maintaining a family.   When once the people are
reconciled to such a system, the progress of population might be very rapid, at a time when the
wages of labour, independently of parish assistance,
were only sufficient to support a wife and one
child, or even a single man without either wife or
child, because there might still be both encouragement to marriage, and the means of supporting
children.*

When the population of a country increases
faster than usual, the labouring classes must have
the command of a greater quantity of food than
they had before possessed, or at least applied to
the maintenance of their families.   This may be
obtained in various ways—by higher real wages,

---

* It is most fortunate for the country and the labouring classes
of society, that the bill which passed the House of Commons last
session, for taking from their parents the children of those who
asked for relief, and supporting them on public funds, did not pass
the House of Lords.   Such a law would have been the commencement of a new system of poor laws beyond all comparison worse
than the old : and it is difficult to conceive how it could have been
recommended by persons who agreed to publish the opinions which
appear in the greater part of the Report on the Poor Laws.

by saving in conveniences, by adopting a cheaper kind of food, by more task-work and the more general employment of the women and children, or by parish allowances.   But the actual application

a   of the greater quantity of food is, I conceive, necessary to the increase of population; and wherever such increase has taken place, some of these causes, by which a greater quantity of food is procured, will always be in action, and may generally be traced.

b   The high wages, both real and nominal of America, occasioned by the rapid accumulation of capital, and the power of selling produce, obtained by

c   a comparative small quantity of labour, at European prices, are unquestionably the cause of the

d   very rapid progress of the American population.

The peculiar increase of the population of Ireland, compared with other European countries, has obviously been owing to the adoption of a cheaper food, which might be produced in large quantities, and which, aided by the Cottar system of cultivation, has allowed the increase of people

e   to precede the demand for labour.

f   And the great increase of population of late years in England and Scotland has been owing to the power of the labouring classes to obtain a greater quantity of food, partly by temporary high wages in manufactures, partly by the increased use of potatoes, partly by increased task-work and the increased employment of women and children, partly by in-

g   creased parish allowances to families, and partly perhaps, (though I think but little taking the country throughout) by a saving in conveniences and luxuries.

In general, perhaps, more of these causes will be called into action by a rise of prices, which sometimes lowers the command of a day's labour over the necessaries of life, than by a fall of prices which sometimes raises it.

What is mainly necessary to a rapid increase of population, is a great and continued demand for labour; and this is occasioned by, and proportioned to, the rate at which the whole value of the capital and revenue of the country increases annually; because, the faster the value of the annual produce increases, the greater will be the power of purchasing fresh labour, and the more will be wanted every year.

It has been sometimes thought, that the demand for labour can only be in proportion to the increase of the circulating, not the fixed capital; and this is no doubt true in individual cases :* but it is not necessary to make the distinction in reference to a whole nation; because where the substitution of fixed capital saves a great quantity of labour, which cannot be employed elsewhere, it diminishes the value of the annual produce, and retards the increase of the capital and revenue taken together.

If, for instance, a capitalist who had employed £20,000 in productive labour, and had been in the habit of selling his goods for £22,000, making a

* See an ingenious pamphlet on the condition of the labouring classes by Mr. Barton.

a profit of 10 per cent., were to employ the same quantity of labour in the construction of a machine worth £20,000, which would enable him to carry on his business without labour in future, except as his machine might require repair, it is obvious that, during the first year, the same value of the annual produce and the same demand for labour would exist; but in the next year, as it would only be necessary for the capitalist, in order to obtain the same rate of profits as before, to sell his goods for a little more than £2,000 instead of £22,000, the value of the annual produce would fall, the capital would not be increased, and the revenue would be decidedly diminished; and upon the principle that the demand for labour depends upon the rate at which the value of the general produce, or of the capital and revenue taken together, increases, the slackness of the demand for labour under such circumstances would be adequately accounted for.

In general, however, the use of fixed capital is extremely favourable to the abundance of circulating capital; and if the market for the products can be proportionally extended, the whole value of the capital and revenue of a state is greatly increased by it, and a great demand for labour created.

The increase in the whole value of cotton products, since the introduction of the improved machinery, is known to be prodigious; and it cannot for a moment be doubted that the demand for labour in the cotton business has very greatly increased during the last forty years. This is indeed sufficiently proved by the greatly increased population of Manchester, Glasgow, and the other towns where the cotton manufactures have most flourished.

A similar increase of value, though not to the same extent, has taken place in our hardware, woollen, and other manufactures, and has been accompanied by an increasing demand for labour, notwithstanding the increasing use of fixed capital.

Even in our agriculture, if the fixed capital of horses, which, from the quantity of produce they consume, is the most disadvantageous description of fixed capital, were disused, it is probable, that a great part of the land which now bears corn would be thrown out of cultivation. Land of a poor quality would never yield sufficient to pay the labour of cultivating with the spade, of bringing manure to distant fields in barrows, and of carrying the products of the earth to distant markets by the same sort of conveyance. Under these circumstances, as there would be a great diminution in the quantity of corn produced, there would be a great diminution in the whole value of the produce; and the demand for labour and the amount of the population would be greatly diminished.*

* It has lately been stated, that spade cultivation will yield both a greater gross produce and a greater neat produce. I am always ready to bow to well established experience; but if such experience applies in the present case, one cannot sufficiently wonder at the continued use of plough and horses in agriculture. Even

On the other hand, if, by the gradual introduction of a greater quantity of fixed capital, we could cultivate and dress our soil and carry the produce to market at a much less expense, we might increase our produce very greatly by the cultivation and improvement of all our waste lands; and if the substitution of this fixed capital were to take place in the only way in which we can suppose it practically to take place, that is, gradually, there is no reason to doubt that the value of raw produce would keep up nearly to its former level; and its greatly increased quantity, combined with the greater proportion of the people which might be employed in manufactures and commerce, would unquestionably occasion a very great increase in the exchangeable value of the general produce, and thus cause a great demand for labour and a great addition to the population.

In general, therefore, there is little to fear that the introduction of fixed capital, as it is likely to take place in practice, will diminish the effective demand for labour; indeed it is to this source that we are to look for the main cause of its future in-

supposing however that the use of the spade might, on some soils, so improve the land, as to make the crop more than pay the additional expense of the labour, taken separately; yet, as horses must be kept to carry out dressing to a distance and to convey the produce of the soil to market, it could hardly answer to the cultivator to employ men in digging his fields, while his horses were standing idle in his stables. As far as experience has yet gone, I should certainly say, that it is commerce, price and skill, which will cultivate the wastes of large and poor territories—not the spade.

crease.   At the same time, it is certainly true, as
will be more fully stated in a subsequent part of
this volume, that if the substitution of fixed capi-   a
tal were to take place very rapidly, and before an   b
adequate market could be found for the more abundant supplies derived from it and for the new
products of the labour that had been thrown out
of employment, a slack demand for labour and
great distress among the labouring classes of so-   c
ciety would be universally felt.   But in this case,
the general produce, or the capital and revenue of   d
the country taken together, would certainly fall in
value, owing to a temporary excess of supply compared with the demand, and would shew that the   e
variations in this value, compared with the previous value paid in wages, are the main regulators
of the power and will to employ labour.

In the formation of the value of the whole pro-   f
duce of a country, a part depends upon price, and
a part upon quantity.   That part which depends
merely upon price is in its nature less durable and
less effective than that which depends upon quantity.   An increase of price, with little or no increase of quantity, must be followed very soon by   g
a nearly proportionate increase of wages; while   h
the command of these increased money wages
over the necessaries of life going on diminishing,
the population must come to a stop, and no further
rise of prices can occasion an effective demand for
labour.

On the other hand, if the quantity of produce
be increased so fast that the value of the whole

diminishes from excessive supply, it may not
command so much labour this year as it did in
the last, and for a time there will be no demand
for workmen.

These are the two extremes, one arising from
increased value without increased quantity ; and
the other from increased quantity without increased value.

It is obvious that the object which it is most desirable to attain is the union of the two.   There is
somewhere a happy medium, where, under the
actual resources of a country, the increase of
wealth and the demand for labour are a maximum;
but this point cannot be ascertained.   An increase
of quantity with steady prices, or even slightly
falling, is consistent with a considerable increase
of the general value of produce, and may occasion
a considerable demand for labour ; but in the actual state of things, and in the way in which the
precious metals are actually distributed, some increase of prices generally accompanies the most
effective demand for produce and population.   It
is this increase both of quantity and price which
most surely creates the greatest demand for labour,
excites the greatest quantity of industry, and generally occasions the greatest increase of population.

SECTION IV.

Of the Effect of a Fall in the Value of Money on the   a
Demand for Labour and the Condition of the Labourer.

Some writers of great ability have been of opinion
that rising prices, or a falling value of money, are   b
very unfavourable to the lower classes of society ;   c
and certainly there are some periods of our history
which seem strongly to countenance this opinion :
but I am inclined to think, that if these periods,
and the circumstances connected with them, be
examined with more attention, the conclusion
which has been drawn from them will not appear
so certain as has been generally imagined.   It will
be found that, in the instances in question, other
causes were in operation to which the effect referred to might more justly be attributed; and we   d
shall hardly have good reason to conclude, that
where an effective demand for labour accompanies
a fall in the value of money and no positive obstacles are thrown in the way of its rising, it will not,
in a moderately short time, follow the price of the
main food of the labourer.

   The period of our history universally noticed is   e
the 16th century, from the end of the reign of Henry
VII. to the end of the reign of Elizabeth.   During
this period it is an unquestionable fact that the real   f
wages of labour fell in an extraordinary manner,   g

and towards the latter end of the century they would not command much above one-third of the quantity of wheat which they did at the beginning of it.

α   Sir F. M. Eden has noticed the price of wheat in nineteen out of the twenty-four years of Henry VII.'s reign, and in some of the years two or three times. * Reducing the several notices in the same year first to an average, and then taking the average of the nineteen prices, it comes to 6s. 3¼d. the quarter, rather less than 9½d. the bushel, and 2⅗d. the peck.

β   By a statute passed in 1495 to regulate wages, the price of common day labour seems to have been 4d. or 4½d. without diet. All labourers and artificers, not specifically mentioned, are put down at 4d.; but in another part of the statute, even a woman labourer (I suppose in hay time) is set down at 4½d. and a carter at 5d. †

At the price of wheat just stated, if the wages of the labourer were 4d. he would be able to purchase, by a day's labour, a peck and three quarters of wheat, within half a farthing; if his wages were 4½d. he would be able to purchase half a bushel, within a farthing.

The notices of the price of day labour in the subsequent years are extremely scanty. There are none in the reigns of Henry VIII., Edward, and Mary. The first that occurs is in 1575, and

a   the price is mentioned at 8d. ‡ Taking an average

---

* State of the Poor, vol. iii. p. xli.
† Id. vol. iii. p. lxxxix.   ‡ Id. vol. iii. p. lx.

of the five preceding years in which the prices of wheat are noticed, including 1575, having previously averaged the several prices in the same year, as before, it appears that the price of the quarter of wheat was 1*l.* 2*s.* 2d. which is 2*s.* 9½*d.* the bushel, and 8¼*d.* the peck. At this price, a day's labour would purchase a peck of corn, within a farthing, or $\frac{16}{17}$ of a peck.

This is a diminution of nearly a half in the corn wages of labour; but at the end of the century, the diminution was still greater.

The next notice of the price of labour, with the exception of the regulations of the justices in some of the more northern counties, which can hardly be taken as a fair criterion for the south, is in 1601, when it is mentioned as 10*d.* Taking an average from the Windsor table of five years, which includes, however, one excessively dear year, and subtracting $\frac{1}{9}$ to reduce it to Winchester measure, it appears that the price of the quarter was 2*l.* 2*s.* 0*d.* which is 5*s.* 3*d.* the bushel, and 1*s.* 3½*d*, the peck. A day's labour would at this price purchase less than $\frac{2}{3}$ of a peck.*

This is unquestionably a prodigious fall in the

* The year 1597 seems to have been an extraordinary dear one, and ought not to be included in so short an average. If an average was taken of the five years beginning with 1598, the labourer would appear to earn about $\frac{4}{7}$ of a peck; and, on an average of ten years, from the same period, he would earn about $\frac{4}{5}$ of a peck. During the five years from 1594 to 1598 inclusive, the price of wheat seems to have been unusually high from unfavourable seasons.

ab

real wages of labour.   But it is of great importance to inquire whether the prices from which they fell are not as extraordinary as the prices to which they sunk ; and here I think we shall find that the prices the most difficult to be accounted for are the high prices of the 15th century, rather than the low prices of the 16th.

α

If we revert to the middle of the 14th century, at the time when the first general statute was passed to regulate wages, the condition of the labourer will appear to be very inferior to what it was during the greatest part of the 15th century. This fact may be established on unexceptionable evidence.   Statutes or regulations to fix the price of labour, though they do not always succeed in their immediate object, (which is generally the unjust

c

one, of preventing labour from rising,) may be considered as undeniable testimonies of what the prices of labour had been not long previous to the time of their passing.   No legislature in the most ignorant age could ever be so rash as arbitrarily to fix the prices of labour without reference to some past experience.   Consequently, though the prices in such statutes cannot be depended upon with regard to the future, they appear to be quite conclusive with regard to the past.   In the present case, indeed, it is expressly observed, that servants should be contented with such liveries and wages as they

β

received in the 20th year of the King's reign, and two or three years before. *

* Eden's State of the Poor, vol. i. p. 32.

From this statute, which was enacted in 1350,
the 25th of the King, for the most unjust and impolitic purpose of preventing the price of labour
from rising after the great pestilence, we may
infer that the price of day labour had been about
1½d. or 2d.   Common agricultural labour, indeed,
is not specifically mentioned; but the servants of
artificers are appointed to take 1½d., common car-
penters 2d., and a reaper, the first week in August,
also 2d., all without diet; from which we may conclude that the wages of common day labour must
have been as often 1½d. as 2d.*

Sir F. M. Eden has collected notices of the prices
of wheat in sixteen out of the twenty-five years
of Edward III. previous to the time of the passing
of the statute.   Taking an average as before, the
price of wheat appears to have been about 5s. 4d.
the quarter, which is 8d. the bushel, and 2d. the
peck.

At this price of wheat, if the labourer earned
1½d. a day, he could only purchase by a day's labour ¾ of a peck of wheat; if he earned 2d. he
could purchase just a peck.   In the former case, he
would earn less than half of the corn earned by
the labourer of Henry VII.; and in the latter case,
very little more than half.

But in the subsequent period of Edward
III.'s reign, the labourer appears to have been
much worse off.   The statute of labourers was renewed, and, it is said, enforced very rigidly, not-

* Eden's State of the Poor, vol. i. p. 33.

withstanding a considerable rise in the price of
α corn. *   On an average of the thirteen years out
of twenty-six, in which the prices of wheat are
noticed, the quarter is about 11s. 9d. which is
a about 1s. 5½d. the bushel, and 4¼d. the peck.

b   At this price, if the wages of labour had not
c risen, the condition of the labourer would be very
d miserable.   He would not be able to purchase so
much as half-a-peck of wheat by a day's labour,
about a fourth part of what he could subsequently
command in the reign of Henry VII.   It is
scarcely possible, however, to conceive that the
e wages of labour should not have risen in some
degree, notwithstanding the statute and its renewal; but even if they rose one half, they would
not have nearly kept pace with the price of corn,
which more than doubled; and during the last
twenty-five years of the reign of Edward III. the
earnings of the labourer in corn were probably
quite as low as during the last twenty-five years of
Elizabeth.

   In the reigns of Richard II. and Henry IV. the
price of wheat seems to have fallen nearly to what
it was in the first half of the reign of Edward
β III.   From 1377 to 1398 inclusive, it was about
5s. 7d. the quarter; and from 1399 to 1411, about
6s. 1d.†   It is difficult to ascertain how much the
f wages of labour had advanced; but if they had
risen so as to enable the labourer to support him-

---

* Eden's State of the Poor, vol. i. p. 36. 42.
† Id. vol. iii. p. xxv. et seq.

self, through the last twenty-six years of the reign of Edward III. and had not sunk again, in consequence of the subsequent fall, which is probable, the labourer, during these reigns, must have been well paid.

During the reign of Henry V. and the first part of Henry VI. to the passing of the statutes in 1444, the price of the quarter of wheat was about 8s. 8d.* This would be 1s. 1d. the bushel, and 3¼d. the peck. For the greater part of these thirty-two years, the wages of day labour seem to have been about 3d. They did not probably rise to what they were appointed to be in 1444, that is 4d. or 4½d., till the ten dear years preceding the statute, during which, the average price of the quarter was 10s. 8d. On an average of the whole period of thirty-two years, the wages of day labour appear to have purchased about a peck of corn, rather less perhaps, than more, in reference to the greater portion of the period.

From 1444 to the end of the century, the average money price of wheat was about 6s. while the wages of day labour continued at 4d. or 4½d. † At the latter of these prices of labour, wages would purchase exactly two pecks of wheat, or half a bushel, and at the former price ⅔ of half a bushel.

From the passing of the first statute of labourers

α

* Eden's State of the Poor, Table of Prices, vol. iii.

† Mr. Hallam, in his valuable Work on the Middle Ages, has overlooked the distinction between the reigns of Edward III. and Henry IV. with regard to the state of the labouring classes. The two periods appear to have been essentially different in this respect.

β

a

in 1350 to the end of the 15th century, a period
of 150 years, successive changes had been taking
place in the quantity of metal contained in the
same nominal sum; so that the pound of silver,
which in the middle of the reign of Edward III.
was coined into 1*l.* 2*s.* 6*d.* was, in the reign of
Hen. VII., coined into 1*l.* 17*s.* 6*d.*

One should naturally have expected, that this
depreciation of the coin would have shewn itself
first, and most conspicuously, in some exportable
commodity, such as corn, rather than labour; and
so it probably would, as it did afterwards in
the reign of Elizabeth, if wheat had not at the
same time been cheap in the rest of Europe, particularly in France. In fact, however, this great
fall in the intrinsic value of the coin was in no
respect made up by the slight rise of nominal price
which occurred in the course of that period. This
rise was only from about 5*s.* 4*d.* to 6*s.* or 6*s.* 3*d.*
Consequently a very considerable fall had really
taken place in the bullion price of wheat.

But the nominal price of labour, instead of rising
in the same slight degree as wheat, rose from 1½*d.*
or 2*d.* to 4*d.* or 4½*d.*, a rise much more than sufficient to cover the deterioration of the coin; so that
the bullion price of labour rose considerably, during
the time that the bullion price of wheat fell. It
is singular, that Adam Smith, in his Digression
concerning the value of silver during the four last
centuries, should not have noticed this circumstance. If he had been aware of this rise in the
bullion price of labour, his principles, which led

him to consider corn as a good measure of value
merely because it is the best measure of labour,
should have led him to a very different conclusion
from that which he has stated.   If we were to take   a
a mean between corn and labour, the value of silver
during these 150 years, instead of rising to double
what it was, would appear to have continued
nearly stationary.

It was during the favourable part of this period
that Sir John Fortescue wrote his work on *Absolute*   b
and Limited Monarchy, and contrasted the prosperous
and happy condition of the peasantry of England
with the miserable state of the peasantry of France.   c

But it is not sufficient to shew that the condition
of the lower classes of people in England during
the last half of the 15th century, was much superior to what it was either in the preceding century,
or subsequently during the depreciation of money
occasioned by the discovery of the American mines.
To prove that it was peculiar, we must compare it
with the condition of the people after the depreciation had ceased.

According to Adam Smith, the effects of the   α
discovery of the American mines seemed to be at
an end about 1638 or 40.   In 1651 the wages of   β
day-labour, as established by the justices in Essex
at the Chelmsford quarter-sessions, were for the
summer half year, harvest excepted, 1*s*. 2*d*.   This
is a considerable rise in the money price of labour
from the time of Elizabeth; but we shall find that
it is hardly proportionate to the rise of the price of

wheat. If we take an average of the five years preceding 1651,* the period to which the regulation would probably for the most part refer; it appears that the price of the quarter of wheat in the

α Windsor market, deducting $\frac{1}{9}$ to reduce it to Winchester measure, was $3l.$ $4s.$ $7d.$† the quarter, which would be about $8s.$ the bushel, and $2s.$ the peck. At this price of wheat, with wages at $14d.$ the la-

β bourer would only earn $\frac{7}{12}$ of a peck, half a peck, and $\frac{1}{12}$.

γ In 1661, soon after the accession of Charles II., wages were again regulated by the justices in Essex, at the Easter Sessions, and the price of common day-labour during the summer half year, with the exception of harvest time, was continued at $14d.$

If we take an average of the price of wheat for the five years preceding 1661, as before, it appears that the quarter was $2l.$ $9s.$ $3d.$ This is $6s.$ $2d.$ the bushel and $18\frac{1}{2}d.$ the peck. At this rate the labourer would earn about $\frac{3}{4}$ of a peck. It is true that the averages of the prices of corn here taken refer to dear times; but the wages were appointed just at these times: and in the regulations of 1651 it is expressly stated, that they are appointed, " having a special regard and consideration to the prices at this time of all kinds of victuals and apparel, both linen and woollen, and all other neces-

---

* As the regulation passed in April, the year 1651 is not included in the average.

σ † Encyclopædia Brit. Supp. Artic. Corn Laws, where a table is given with the $\frac{1}{9}$ deducted.

sary charges wherewith artificers, labourers and
servants have been more grievously charged with
than in times past."*

If we take an average of the twenty years from
1646 to 1665 inclusive, we shall find that the price
of wheat was rather above than below that of the
five years preceding 1661. The average price of
the quarter of wheat during these twenty years
was 2l. 10s. 0½d.† which is 6s. 3d. the bushel, and
nearly 19d. the peck. At this price, with wages
at 14d. the labourer for these twenty years would
hardly be able to earn so much as ¼ of a peck.

After 1665 the price of corn fell, but wages seem   a
to have fallen at the same time.

In 1682 wages at Bury in Suffolk were appointed to be 6d. in summer, and 5d. in winter
with diet, and double without. This makes the
summer wages 1s.; and according to the price of
wheat in the preceding five years, the labourer who   α
earned a shilling a day, could hardly command so
much as ¼ of a peck of wheat.

The average price of the quarter of wheat from
1665 to 1700 was about 2l. 2s. 6d. If we suppose
the wages of labour during this period to have
been about 1s. the earnings of the labourer would
be about ¼ of a peck of wheat. But there is reason
to think that the average wages were not so high   b
as 1s.

In the regulations of the justices at Warwick in

---

* Eden's State of the Poor, vol. iii. p. 98.   β
† Windsor Table, deducting ½.

1685,* common labourers were allowed to take only
8*d.* a day for the summer half year. Sir George
Shuckburgh puts down only 7½*d.* for the period
from 1675 to 1720 ;† and Arthur Young estimates
the average price of labour during the whole of
the 17th century at 10¼*d.*‡ If on these grounds we
were to estimate the wages of labour from 1665 to
the end of the century at 10½*d.* it would appear
that the earnings of the labourer, in the 17th century, after the depreciation of money had ceased,
were only sufficient to purchase ⅔ of a peck of
wheat. Taking however the more favourable supposition of 1*s.* a day as the earnings of the labourer,
they would purchase, as before stated, about ¾ of
a peck.

During the first twenty years of the 18th century, the price of corn fell, but not much ; and it
may be doubted whether the price of labour rose.

In 1725, a few years later than the period alluded
to, the wages of labour were settled by the justices
at Manchester. The best husbandry labourer, from
the middle of March till the middle of September,
was not to take more than 1*s.* a day without meat
and drink; but common labourers, and hedgers,
ditchers, palers, thrashers, or other task-work, only
10*d.* Mr. Howlett, as quoted by Sir F. Eden,§
states the price of day-labour, so late as 1737, at
only 10*d.* a day; and Sir F. Eden, writing in 1796,

* Eden's State of the Poor, vol. iii. p. 104.
† Philosoph. Trans. for 1798. Part i. p. 176.
‡ Annals of Agriculture, No. 270. p. 88.
§ Vol. I. p. 385.

observes, that from various information he had collected in different parts of England, he had reason
to think that the wages of labour had doubled*
during the last sixty years, which could hardly be
true, unless wages in the early part of the century
had been lower than 1s.

The average price of wheat for the first twenty
years of the century was rather less than 2l.; and
if the wages of labour were only 10d. or 10½d., the
labourer would earn considerably less than ¾ of a
peck. If the wages were 1s he would earn ⅘ of a
peck.

From 1720 to 1755 corn fell and continued low,
while the wages of labour seem to have been about
1s. During these thirty-five years the price of
wheat was about 33s. the quarter, or a little above
1s. the peck, and the labourer therefore, on an
average of thirty-five years together, would be able
to earn about a peck of wheat.

From this time corn began gradually to rise,
while wages do not appear to have risen in the
same proportion. The first authentic accounts that
we have of the price of labour, after corn had begun to rise, is in the extensive Agricultural Tours
of Arthur Young, which took place in 1767, 1768
and 1770. The general result of the price of labour from these tours, on the mean rate of the
whole year, was 7s. 4¼d. a week.† Taking an average
of the five years, from 1766 to 1770 inclusive, the

a

* Vol. I. p. 385.
† Annals of Agriculture, No. 271. p. 215.

α

price of the quarter of wheat was 2*l.* 7*s.* 8*d.* or nearly 48*s.** which would be 6*s.* the bushel, and 1*s.* 6*d.* the peck. At these prices of labour and wheat, the labourer would earn very nearly $\frac{5}{6}$ of a peck.

In 1810 and 1811, accounts from thirty-seven counties, which, according to Arthur Young, were quite satisfactory, make the wages of day-labour for the mean rate of the year 14*s.* 6*d.*† a week, or nearly 2*s.* 6*d.* a day. The price of wheat for five years ending with 1810 was 92*s.*—ending with 1811, 96*s.*‡ The prices both of labour and wheat appear to have doubled; and the labourer, in 1810 and 1811, could earn just about the same quantity of wheat as he could about forty years before, that is $\frac{5}{6}$ of a peck. The intermediate periods must necessarily have been subject to slight variations, owing to the uncertainty of the seasons, and an occasional advance in the price of corn, not immediately followed by an increased price of labour; but, in general, the average must have been nearly the same, and seldom probably for many years
a together differed much from $\frac{5}{6}$ of a peck.

* Deducting $\frac{1}{9}$ from the prices in the Windsor Table. Arthur Young deducts another 9th for the quality; but this is certainly too much, in reference to the general average of the kingdom to which the latest tables apply. I have therefore preferred adhering all along to the Windsor prices; and the reader will make what allowances he thinks fit for the quality, which, according to Mr.
α Rose, is not much above the average.

β † Annals of Agriculture, No. 271. p. 215 and 216.

γ ‡ Windsor Table, Supp. to Encyclopædia Brit. Art. Corn Laws.

SECTION V.

On the Conclusions to be drawn from the preceding Review. a
—Of the Prices of Corn and Labour during the five last
Centuries.

From this review of the prices of corn and labour,
during nearly the five last centuries, we may draw
some important inferences.

In the first place, I think it appears that the
great fall in the real wages of labour which took   b
place in the 16th century, must have been occasioned mainly by the great and unusual elevation
which they had previously attained, and not by the
discovery of the American mines and the consequent fall in the value of money. When we compare the wages of labour during the last half of the   c
15th century, with what they were both before
and subsequently, it appears that whatever may
have been the cause of these high wages, they
were evidently peculiar, and could not therefore be
permanent. This indeed is evident, not only by
comparing them with previous and subsequent periods, but by considering their positive amount.
Earnings of the value of nearly two pecks or half
a bushel of wheat a day would allow of the earliest
marriages, and the maintenance of the largest families. They are nearly the same as the earnings of
the American labourer. In such a country as   d
England was, even at that time, such wages could
only be occasioned by temporary causes. Among
these we must reckon, a general improvement in

the system of cultivation after the abolition of villanage, which increased the plenty of corn; and the comparatively rapid progress of commerce and manufactures, which occasioned a great demand for labour; while, owing to the wars in France, the civil wars between the Houses of York and Lancaster, and above all perhaps the slow change of habits among a people lately emancipated, this increase of produce and demand had not yet been followed by a proportionate effect on the population.

Certain it is that corn was very cheap both in France* and England; and labour in this country could not possibly have risen and kept high for so long a period as between sixty and seventy years, unless some peculiar cause or causes had restrained the supply of population, compared with the supply of corn and the demand for labour.

It is with the fact however of the very high wages of labour in the 15th century rather than

* It is a very curious fact, that the bullion price of corn continued unusually low in France from 1444 to 1510. *(Garnier's Richesse des Nations*, vol. ii. p. 184.) just during the same period that it was low in England. Adam Smith is inclined to attribute this fall and low price to a deficiency in the supply of the mines, compared with the demand; (B. i. ch. xi.) but this solution in no respect accounts for the rise of the bullion price of labour in England, at the time that the bullion price of corn was falling. Nothing can account for this fact, but a relative plenty of corn compared with labour—a state of things which has little to do with the mines. The low prices in France were probably connected with the abolition of villanage, and an extended cultivation in the reign of Charles VII. and his immediate successors, after the ravages of the English were at an end.

with the causes of it, that we are mainly concerned   a
at present, and of the fact there can be no doubt ;
but if the fact be allowed, it follows, that such
wages must have very greatly fallen during the
course of the following century, if the mines of
America had not been discovered.

What effect the depreciation of money might
have had in aggravating that increasing poverty of
the lower classes of society, which, with or with-   b
out such a depreciation, would inevitably have
fallen upon them, it is not easy to say. But from
the still lower wages which prevailed in the 17th
century after the depreciation had ceased, and from
what has happened of late years (which shall be
more fully noticed presently) I should not be disposed to consider a general rise in the price of corn,
occasioned by an alteration in the value of money,
and not by bad seasons, as likely to affect the labouring classes prejudicially for more than a very
few years. Still, however, it is quite certain that
the condition of the labouring classes of society   c
was growing much worse during the time that the
depreciation of money from the discovery of the
American mines was taking place; and whatever
may have been the cause, as the people would
always be comparing their situation with what it
had been, in their own recollection and that of
their fathers, it would inevitably excite great com-
plaints; and, after it had grown comparatively very
bad, as in the latter end of the reign of Elizabeth,
it was likely to lead to those measures relating to
the poor, which marked this period of our history.   d

Another inference which we may draw from the review is, that during the course of nearly 500 years, the earnings of a day's labour in this country have probably been more frequently below than above a peck of wheat; that a peck of wheat may be considered as something like a middle point, or rather above the middle point, about which the market wages of labour, varying according to the demand and supply, have oscillated; and that the population of a country may increase with some rapidity, while the wages of labour are even under this point.

The wages of day labour in France during the two last centuries, are said to have been pretty uniformly about the 20th part of a *septier* of wheat,* which would be a little above $\frac{4}{5}$ of a peck; but just before the revolution, at the time of Arthur Young's tour in France, they were only about $\frac{3}{4}$ of a peck. Since the revolution, they appear to have risen so as to command more than a peck.

A third inference which we may draw from this review is, that the seasons have a very considerable influence on the price of corn, not only for two or three years occasionally, but for fifteen or twenty years together. These periods of unfavourable seasons seem to supersede all the other causes which may be supposed to have the greatest influence upon prices. An instance of this occurs after the great pestilence in the time of Edward III. One should naturally have thought that the

* Wealth of Nations, b. i. c. xi. p. 313.

quantity of good land being abundant, compared with the population, corn would have been very cheap.   It was however, on the contrary, dear during the twenty-five subsequent years,—a fact which cannot be accounted for but from unfavourable seasons.

Another instance of the same kind had occurred in the reign of Edward II., during the whole of which, the average price of wheat was more than double what it had been during the greatest part of the reign of Edward I., and the first half of the reign of Edward III.—evidently owing to unfavourable seasons.

A third instance occurs during the civil wars of the 17th century.   So far from thinking that civil wars have a necessary tendency to make corn dear, I am disposed to agree with Sir F. Eden, in attributing a part of the high price of labour and the cheapness of corn in the 15th century, to the circumstance of a greater destruction of men than of cultivation having been occasioned in the civil wars of the Houses of York and Lancaster.   But in the civil wars of the 17th century no such cheapness of corn took place.   On the contrary, in the period from 1646 to 1665 the price of corn was higher both in France and England than it had ever been known for twenty years together, either before or since, exclusive of the prices of the last twenty-five years in this country.   For shorter periods, these unfavourable seasons are of frequent recurrence, and must essentially affect the condition of the labourer during ten or five years.   It de-

a

pends upon their continuance and other concomi-
a   tant circumstances, whether they raise the money
wages, or leave them as they were.

b   The periods of the lowest wages, or of the
greatest falls in real wages have been, when a considerable rise in the price of corn has taken place
under circumstances not favourable to a propor-
c   tionate rise in the price of labour.   This is the most
d   likely to happen in unfavourable seasons, when the
power of commanding labour at the old price
would by no means be increased in proportion to
the price of corn.   It may also happen when a
fall is taking place in the value of money, if any
previous causes have given an extraordinary stimulus to the progress of population.   In this case,
e   though the resources of the country may be increasing fast, the population may be increasing faster,
f   and the wages of labour will not rise in proportion
g   to the fall in the value of money.   To this cause I
am strongly disposed to attribute the inadequate
rise of the money wages of labour during the reigns
of Henry VIII., Mary, Edward VI., and Elizabeth.
The state of things in the early part of the 16th
century must have given a powerful stimulus to
population; and considering the extraordinary high
corn wages at this period, and that they could only
fall very gradually, the stimulus must have continued to operate with considerable force during
the greatest part of the century.   In fact, depopula-
tion was loudly complained of at the end of the 15th
and beginning of the 16th centuries, and a redundancy of population was acknowledged at the end

of the 16th.   And it was this change in the state
of the population, and not the discovery of the American mines, which occasioned so marked a fall in
the corn wages of labour.

If the discovery of the American mines had
found the labouring classes of the people earning
only the same wages which they appear to have
earned in the latter half of the reign of Edward III.,
and if the same increase of capital and resources   a
had taken place during the 16th century, as really
did take place, I feel not the slightest doubt, that   b
the money wages of labour would have increased
as fast as the money price of corn.   Indeed when   c
a fall in the value of money is accompanied, as it   d
frequently is, by a rapid increase of capital, there
is one reason, why, in the natural state of things,
the price of labour should feel it more than other
commodities.   The encouragement given to population by such increase of resources, could not appear with any effect in the market under sixteen   e
or eighteen years; and in the mean time the de-   fg
mand compared with the supply of labour would   h
be greater than the demand compared with the
supply of most other commodities.

It is on this account, that in the fall in the value
of money which took place from 1793 to 1814,
and which was unquestionably accompanied by a
great increase of capital, and a great demand for
labour, I am strongly of opinion, that if the price   i
of labour had not been kept down by artificial
means, it would have risen higher in proportion
than the average price of corn; and this opinion   j

a   is, I think, fairly borne out by facts. If according
to the last authentic accounts which had been ob-
b   tained of the price of labour, previous to 1814, it
appears that on an average of the returns of thirty-
seven counties in 1810 and 1811, the weekly wages
of day labour were 14s. 6d.,—a price, which, compared with the wages of 1767, 1768 and 1770,* is
equal to the rise in the price of wheat during the
c   same period, while it is known that in many counties and districts in the southern parts of England,
wages in 1810 and 1811 were unnaturally kept
down to 12s., 10s., 9s. and even 7s.6d. by the bane-
ful system of regularly maintaining the children
d   of the poor out of the rates, it may fairly be concluded that if this system had not prevailed over
e   a large part of England, the wages of labour would
have risen higher than in proportion to the price
of wheat.

f   And this conclusion is still further confirmed by
g   what has happened in Scotland and some parts of
the north of England. In these districts, all ac-
h   counts agree that the rise of wages was in fact
greater than the rise of corn, and that the condition
of the labourer till 1814 was decidedly improved,
even in spite of the taxes, many of which certainly
bore heavily on the conveniences and comforts of
the labourer, though they affected but little his
command over strict necessaries.

       In considering the corn wages of labour in the
i   course of this review, it has not been possible to

α   * Annals of Agriculture, No. 271. pp. 215 and 216.

make any distinction between the effects of a fall
in the price of corn and a rise in the price of labour.   a
In merely comparing the two objects with each
.other, the result is precisely similar; but their effects in the encouargement of population are some-   b
times very dissimilar, as I have before intimated.   c
There is no doubt that a great encouragement   d
to an increase of population is consistent with
a fall in the price of raw produce, because, notwithstanding this fall, the exchangeable value   e
of the whole produce of the country may still
be increasing compared with labour; but it
may sometimes happen that a fall in the price   f
of raw produce is accompanied by a diminished   g
power and will to employ labour; and in this case
the demand for labour and the encouragement to
population will not be in proportion to the apparent   h
corn wages of labour.

If a labourer commands a peck instead of $\frac{3}{4}$ of a   i
peck of wheat a day in consequence of a rise of
wages occasioned by a demand for labour, it is certain that all labourers may be employed who are
willing and able to work, and probably also their
wives and children; but if he is able to command
this additional quantity of wheat on account of a   j
fall in the price of corn which diminishes the ca-   k
pital of the farmer, the advantage may be more   l
apparent than real, and though labour for some   m
time may not nominally fall, yet as the demand for
labour may be stationary, if not retrograde, its current price will not be a certain criterion of what   n
might be earned by the united labours of a large

a   family, or the increased exertions of the head of it
       in task-work.

b   It is obvious, therefore, that the same current
       corn wages will, under different circumstances, have
c   a different effect in the encouragement of popula-
       tion.

d   It should also be observed, that in estimating
       the corn wages of labour I have uniformly
       taken wheat, the dearest grain. I have taken
       one grain to the exclusion of other necessaries,
e   because I wish to avoid complicating the subject;
       and have chosen wheat because it is the main
       food of the greatest part of the population in
       England.   But it is evident that at those pe-
       riods, or in those countries, in which the main
       food of the people does not consist of wheat, the
f   wheat wages that can be earned by a family will
       not form a just criterion of the encouragement
       given to population.   Although the wheat wages
       might be very unequal at two different periods or
       in two different countries, yet if in one case an in-
       ferior grain were habitually consumed, the en-
       couragement to the population might be the same.
       The Irish labourer cannot command the support
g   of so large a family upon wheat as the English,
       but he can command in general the support of a
h   much larger family upon the food on which he is
       accustomed to live; and consequently, population
       has increased much faster during the last century
       in Ireland than in England.

i   It appears then that, making a proper allowance
       for the varying value of other parts of the wages

of labour besides food, the quantity of the customary grain which a labouring family can actually
earn, is at once a measure of the encouragement
to population and of the condition of the labourer;
while the money price of such wages is the best
measure of the value of money as far as one commodity can go.   But it is of the utmost importance   a
always to bear in mind that a great command over
the necessaries of life may be effected in two ways,   b
either by rapidly increasing resources, or by the   c
prudential habits of the labouring classes; and that
as rapidly increasing resources are neither in the   d
power of the poor to effect, nor can in the nature
of things be permanent, the great resource of the
labouring classes for their happiness must be in
those prudential habits which, if properly exercised,
are capable of securing to the labourer a fair pro-   e
portion of the necessaries and conveniences of life,
from the earliest stage of society to the latest.

I have said nothing of the value of labour as   f
measured by the criterion assumed by Mr. Ricardo, that is, by the labour which has been expended in procuring the earnings of the labourer,
or the cost in labour of the labourer's wages; because it appears to me, that what I have called the
real and nominal wages of labour include every
thing which relates to the condition of the labourer, the encouragement to population, and the
value of money, the three great points which
chiefly demand our attention.   According to Mr.
Ricardo's view of the subject, nothing can be inferred on these points either from high or from low

wages. Such high or low wages serve only to determine the rate of profits, and their influence in this respect will be fully considered in the next chapter.

CHAPTER V.

OF THE PROFITS OF CAPITAL.

SECTION I.

Of Profits as affected by the increasing Difficulty of pro- a
curing the Means of Subsistence.

It has been usual, in speaking of that portion of
the national revenue which goes to the capitalist
in return for the employment of his capital, to call
it by the name of the profits of stock. But stock
is not so appropriate an expression in this case, as
capital. Stock is a general term, and may be de- b
fined to be all the material possessions of a country,
or all its actual wealth, whatever may be its destination; while capital is that particular portion of c
these possessions, or of this accumulated wealth,
which is destined to be employed with a view to d
profit. They are often, however, used indiscrimi-
nately; and perhaps no great error may arise from
it; but it may be useful to recollect that all stock
is not properly speaking capital, though all capital
is stock. e

The profits of capital consist of the difference between the value of the advances necessary to pro- f
duce a commodity, and the value of the commodity
when produced; and these advances are generally g

composed of accumulations which have previously cost in their production a certain quantity of wages, profit and rent, exclusive of the rent which, in the case of landed products, is paid directly.

a   The *rate* of profits is the proportion which
b   the difference between the value of the advances and the value of the commodity produced bears to
c   the value of the advances, and it varies with the variations of the value of the advances compared with
d   the value of the product. When the value of the advances is great compared with the value of the product, the remainder being small, the rate of profits will be low. When the value of the advances is inconsiderable the remainder being great, the rate of profits will be high.

e   The varying rate of profits, therefore, obviously depends upon the causes which alter the propor-
f   tion between the value of the advances and the
g   value of the produce; and this proportion may be altered either by circumstances which affect the value of the advances, or the value of the product.

hi   Of the advances necessary to production, the means of supporting labour are generally the greatest and most important. These means, therefore, will have the greatest influence on the value of the advances.

j   The two main causes which influence the means of supporting labour, are

k   1st. The difficulty or facility of production on the land, by which a greater or less proportion of the value of the whole produce is capable of supporting the labourers employed.

And 2dly, The varying relation of the quantity   a
of capital to the quantity of labour employed by
it, by which more or less of the necessaries of life
may go to each individual labourer.

Each of these causes is alone sufficient to occa-   b
sion all the variations of which profits are susceptible. If one of them only acted, its operation
would be simple. It is the combination of the
two, and of others in addition to them, sometimes
acting in conjunction and sometimes in opposition,
which occasions in the progress of society those
varied phenomena which it is not always easy to
explain.

If the first cause operated singly, and the wages   c
of the individual labourer were always the same,
then supposing that the skill in agriculture were
to remain unchanged, and that there were no
means of obtaining corn from foreign countries,
 he rate of profits must regularly and without any   de
interruption fall, as the society advanced, and as it
became necessary to resort to inferior machines
which required more labour to put in action.

It would signify little, in this case, whether the
last land taken into cultivation for food had
yielded a rent in its uncultivated state. It is certain that the landlord would not allow it to be cultivated, unless he could, at the least, obtain the
same rent for it as before. This must be considered as an absolute condition on the worst lands
taken into cultivation in an improved country.
After this payment was made, the remainder of

a
b the produce would be divided chiefly* between the
capitalist and the labourers, and it is evident that
if the number of labourers necessary to obtain a
given produce were continually increasing, and
c the wages of each labourer remained the same, the
portion destined to the payment of labour would
be continually encroaching upon the portion destined to the payment of profits; and the rate of
profits would of course continue regularly diminishing till, from the want of power or will to save,
the progress of accumulation had ceased.

In this case, and supposing an equal demand for
all the parts of the same produce,† it is obvious
that the profits of capital in agriculture would be
in proportion to the fertility of the last land taken
into cultivation, or to the amount of the produce
obtained by a given quantity of labour. And as
profits in the same country tend to an equality,
the general rate of profits would follow the same
course.

d
e   * I say *chiefly*, because, in fact, some rent, though it may be
trifling, is almost always paid in the materials of the farmer's
capital.

    † It is necessary to qualify the position in this way, because,
with regard to the main products of agriculture, it might easily
happen that all the parts were not of the same value. If a farmer
cultivated his lands by means of domestics living in his house
whom he found in food and clothing, his advances might always
be nearly the same in quantity and of the same high value in use;
but in the case of a glut from the shutting up of an accustomed
f   market, or a season of unusual abundance, a part of the crop might
be of no value either in use or exchange, and his profits could by
no means be determined, by the excess of the *quantity* produced,
g   above the advances necessary to produce it.

But a moment's consideration will shew us, that the supposition here made of a constant uniformity in the real wages of labour is not only contrary to the actual state of things, but involves a contradiction.

The progress of population is almost exclusively regulated by the quantity of the necessaries of life actually awarded to the labourer; and if from the first he had no more than sufficient to keep up the actual population, the labouring classes could not increase, nor would there be any occasion for the progressive cultivation of poorer land. On the other hand, if the real wages of labour were such as to admit of and encourage an increase of population, and yet were always to remain the same, it would involve the contradiction of a continued increase of population after the accumulation of capital, and the means of supporting such an increase had entirely ceased.

We cannot then make the supposition of a *natural* and *constant* price of labour, at least if we mean by such a price, an unvarying quantity of the necessaries of life. And if we cannot fix the real price of labour, it must evidently vary with the progress of capital and revenue, and the demand for labour compared with the supply.

We may however, if we please, suppose a uniform progress of capital and population, by which is not meant in the present case the same *rate* of progress permanently, which is impossible; but a uniform progress towards the greatest practicable amount, without temporary accelerations or retardations.

And before we proceed to the actual state of things, it may be curious to consider in what manner profits would be affected under these circumstances.

At the commencement of the cultivation of a fertile country by civilized colonists, and while rich land was in great plenty, a small portion only of the value of the produce would be paid in the form of rent. Nearly the whole would be divided between profits and wages; and the proportion which each would take, as far as it was influenced by the share of each individual labourer, must be determined by the demand and supply of capital compared with the demand and supply of labour.

As the society continued to proceed, if the territory were limited, or the soil of different qualities, it is quite obvious that the productive powers of labour as applied to the cultivation of land must gradually diminish; and as a given quantity of capital and of labour would yield a smaller and smaller return, there would evidently be a less and less produce to be divided between labour and profits.

If, as the powers of labour diminished, the physical wants of the labourer were also to diminish in the same proportion, then the same share of the whole produce might be left to the capitalist, and the *rate* of profits would not necessarily fall. But the physical wants of the labourer remain always the same; and though in the progress of society, from the increasing scarcity of provisions compared with labour, these wants are in general less fully supplied, and the real wages of labour gradually fall; yet it is clear that there is a limit, and probably at no great distance, which cannot be passed. The command of a certain quantity of food is absolutely necessary to the labourer in order to support himself, and such a family as will maintain merely a stationary population. Consequently, if poorer lands which required more labour were successively taken into cultivation, it would not be possible for the corn wages of each individual labourer to be diminished in proportion to the diminished produce; a greater proportion of the whole would necessarily go to labour; and the rate of profits would continue regularly falling till the accumulation of capital had ceased.

a
b

Such would be the necessary course of profits and wages in the progressive accumulation of capital, as applied to the progressive cultivation of new and less fertile land, or the further improvement of what had before been cultivated ; and on the supposition here made, the rates both of profits and of real wages would be highest at first, and would regularly and gradually diminish together, till they both came to a stand at the same period, and the demand for an increase of produce ceased to be effective.

c

In the mean time, it will be asked, what becomes of the profits of capital employed in manufactures and commerce, a species of industry not like that employed upon the land, where the productive powers of labour necessarily diminish ; but where these powers not only do not necessarily diminish, but very often greatly increase ?

In the cultivation of land, the immediate and main cause of the necessary diminution of profits appeared to be the increased quantity of labour necessary to obtain the same produce. In manufactures and commerce, it is the fall in the exchangeable value of the products of industry in these departments, compared with corn and labour.

The cost of producing corn and labour continually increases from inevitable physical causes, while the cost of producing manufactures and articles of commerce sometimes diminishes, sometimes remains stationary, and at all events increases much slower than the cost of producing corn and labour. Upon every principle therefore of demand and supply, the exchangeable value of these latter objects must fall, compared with the value of labour. But if the exchangeable value of labour continues to rise, while the exchangeable value of manufactures either falls, remains the same, or rises in a much less degree, profits must continue to fall; and thus it appears that in the progress of improvement, as poorer and poorer land is taken into cultivation, the rate of profits must be limited by the powers of the soil last cultivated. If the last land taken into cultivation can only be made to yield a certain excess of value above the value of the labour necessary to produce it, it is obvious that, upon the principles of competition, profits, generally, cannot possibly be higher than this excess will allow. In the ascending scale, this is a barrier which cannot be passed. But limitation is essentially different from regulation. In the de

scending scale, profits may be lower in any degree.   a
There is here no controlling necessity which determines the rate of profits ; and below the highest
limit which the actual state of the land will allow, ample scope is left for the operation of other   b
causes.

SECTION II.   c

*Of Profits as affected by the Proportion which Capital bears
to Labour.*

The second main cause which, by increasing the   d
amount of advances, influences profits, is the proportion which capital bears to labour.*

  This is obviously a cause which alone is capable   e
of producing the very greatest effects ; and on the
supposition of adequate variations taking place between the supplies of capital and the supplies of
labour, all the same effects might be produced on
profits as by the operation of the first cause, and in
a much shorter time.

  When capital is really abundant compared with   f
labour, nothing can prevent low profits ; and the

  * I have stated in a former chapter, that the demand for labour   g
does not depend upon capital alone, but upon capital and revenue
together, or the value of the whole produce ; but to illustrate the
present *supposition*, it is only necessary to consider capital and
labour. We may allow that no difficulty will occur with respect
to demand.

greatest facility of production is incapable of producing high profits, unless capital is scarce compared with labour.

a   But in order to see more clearly the powerful
effects of the second cause on profits, let us consider it for a moment as operating alone; and sup-
b   pose, that while the capital of a country continued
increasing, its population were checked and kept
short of the demand for it, by some miraculous
c   influence. Under these circumstances, every sort
of gradation might take place in the proportion
d   which capital would bear to labour, and we should
e   see in consequence every sort of gradation take
place in the rate of profits.

fg   If, in an early period of improvement, capital
were scarce compared with labour, the wages of labour being on this account low, while the productive powers of labour, from the fertility of the
land, were great, the proportion left for profits
would necessarily be very considerable, and the
rate of profits would be very high.

hi   In general, however, though capital may be
said to be scarce in the early periods of cultivation,
yet that particular portion of capital, which resolves itself into food, is often plentiful compared
with the population, and high profits and high real
wages are found together. In the most natural
state of things this is generally the case, though
it is not so when capital is prematurely checked by
extravagance, or other causes. But whether we
set out from low or high corn wages, the diminu-
j   tion in the rates of profits, from the gradual in-

crease of capital compared with labour, will remain undisturbed.

As capital at any time increases faster than la-   a
bour, the profits of capital will fall, and if a pro-   b
gressive increase of capital were to take place,   c
while the population, by some hidden cause, were
prevented from keeping pace with it, notwithstanding the fertility of the soil and the plenty of
food, then profits would be gradually reduced,
until, by successive reductions, the power and will
to accumulate had ceased to operate.   d

Profits in this case would experience exactly the   e
same kind of progressive diminution as they
would by the progressive accumulation of capital
in the present state of things; but rent and wages
would be very differently affected. From what
has before been stated on the subject of rent, the
amount of it in such a country could not be great.
According to the supposition, the progress of the
population is retarded, and the number of labourers
is limited, while land of considerable fertility remains uncultivated. The demand for fertile land
therefore, compared with the supply, would be comparatively inconsiderable; and in reference to the
whole of the national produce, the portion which
would consist of rent would depend mainly upon
the gradations of more fertile land that had been   f
cultivated before the population had come to a
stop, and upon the value of the produce to be
derived from the land that was not cultivated.

With regard to wages they would continue pro-   g
gressively to rise, and would give the labourer a

greater command not only of manufactures and
of the products of foreign commerce (as is generally the case in the present state of things) but
of corn and all other necessaries, so as to place him
in a condition continually and in all respects improving, as long as capital continued to increase.

In short, of the three great portions into which
the mass of produce is divided, rent, profits, and
wages, the two first would be low, because both the
supply of land and the supply of capital would be
abundant compared with the demand; while the
wages of labour would be very high, because the
supply of labourers would be comparatively
scanty; and thus the value of each would be
regulated by the great principle of demand and
supply.

If, instead of supposing the population to be
checked by some peculiar influence, we make the
more natural supposition of a limited territory,
with all the land of nearly equal quality, and of
such great fertility as to admit of very little capital being laid out upon it, the effects upon the
profits of capital would be just the same as in the
last instance, though they would be very different
on rents and wages. After all the land had been
cultivated, and no more capital could be employed
on it, there cannot be a doubt that rents would
be extremely high and profits and wages very
low. The competition of increasing capital in
manufactures and commerce would reduce the
rate of profits, while the principle of population
would continue to augment the number of the

labouring classes, till their corn wages were so low
as to check their further increase. It is probable
that, owing to the facility of production on the   a
land and the great proportion of persons em-   b
ployed in manufactures and commerce, the exports
would be great and the value of money very low.
The money price of corn and money wages would
perhaps be as high as when their cost in labour   c
had been double or treble; rents would rise to an   d
extraordinary pitch without any assistance from   e
poor lands, and the gradations of soil; and profits
might fall to the point only just sufficient to keep
up the actual capital without any additional labour
being necessary to procure the food of the labourer.

The effects which would obviously result from
the two suppositions just made, clearly shew
that the increasing quantity of labour required for
the successive cultivation of poorer land is not
theoretically necessary to a fall of profits from the
highest rate to the lowest.

The former of these two suppositions further
shews the extraordinary power possessed by the   f
labouring classes of society, if they chose to exercise it. The comparative check to population,
which was considered as occasioned by some miraculous influence, might in reality be effected by
the prudence of the poor; and it would unquestionably be followed by the result described. It
may naturally appear hard to the labouring classes
that, of the vast mass of productions obtained
from the land, the capital, and the labour of the

a
b

cd

e

f

g
hi
j
k

country, so small a portion should individually fall
to their share. But the division is at present determined, and must always in future be determined,
by the inevitable laws of supply and demand. If
the market were comparatively understocked with
labour, the landlords and capitalists would be
obliged to give a larger share of the produce to
each workman. But with an abundant supply of labour, such a share, for a permanence, is an absolute
impossibility. The rich have neither the power,
nor can it be expected that they should all have the
will, to keep the market understocked with labour.
Yet every effort to ameliorate the lot of the poor
generally, that has not this tendency, is perfectly
futile and childish. It is quite obvious therefore,
that the knowledge and prudence of the poor
themselves, are absolutely the *only* means by which
any general improvement in their condition can be
effected. They are really the arbiters of their own
destiny; and what others can do for them, is like
the dust of the balance compared with what they
can do for themselves. These truths are so important to the happiness of the great mass of society, that every opportunity should be taken of
repeating them.

But, independently of any particular efforts of
prudence on the part of the poor, it is certain that
the supplies of labour and the supplies of capital
do not always keep pace with each other. They
are often separated at some distance, and for a
considerable period; and sometimes population in-

creases faster than capital, and at other times capi-   ab
tal increases faster than population.

It is obvious, for instance, that from the very
nature of population, and the time required to
bring full-grown labourers into the market, a sudden increase of capital cannot effect a propor-   c
tionate supply of labour in less than sixteen or
eighteen years; and, on the other hand, when capi-   def
tal is stationary from the want of will to accumulate, it is well known that population in general
continues to increase faster than capital, till the   gh
wages of labour, are reduced to that standard
which, with the actual habits of the country, are
no more than sufficient to maintain a stationary
population.

These periods, in which capital and population   i
do not keep pace with each other, are evidently of
sufficient extent to produce the most important   j
results on the rate of profits, and to affect in the   kl
most essential manner the progress of national
wealth.

The value of the government long annuities has a
natural and inevitable tendency to diminish as they   m
approach nearer and nearer to the end of the   n
term for which they were granted.   This is a pro-   o
position which I conceive no person is inclined to
doubt; but under the fullest acknowledgment of
its truth, it would be a most erroneous calculation
to estimate the value of this kind of stock solely
by the number of years which it would have to
run.   It is well known that out of the compara-   p
tively short term of ninety years, so large a propor-

tion as twenty has sometimes elapsed, not only
without any diminution, but with an actual in-
ab   crease of value.

c   In the same manner, the natural and necessary
tendency of profits to fall in the progress of society, owing to the increasing difficulty of procuring food, is a proposition which few will be
d   disposed to controvert; but to attempt to estimate
the rate of profits in any country by a reference
to this cause alone, for ten, twenty, or even fifty
years together, that is for periods of sufficient
length to produce the most important effects on
national prosperity, would inevitably lead to the
greatest practical errors.

e   Yet notwithstanding the utter inadequacy of
this single cause to account for existing phenomena, Mr. Ricardo, in his very ingenious chapter
on profits, has dwelt on no other.

f   If the premises were all such as he has supposed
them to be, that is, if no other cause operated on
profits than the increasing difficulty of procuring
the food of the labourer, and no other cause affected the exchangeable and money value of commodities than the quantity of labour which they
had cost in production, the conclusions which he
has drawn would be just, and the rate of profits
would certainly be regulated in the way which he
has described. But, since in the actual state of things
the premises are most essentially different from
those which he has supposed; since another most
powerful cause operates upon profits, as I have endeavoured to shew in the present section; and since

the exchangeable value of commodities is not determined by the labour they have cost, as I endeavoured to shew in a former chapter, the conclusion   α
drawn by Mr. Ricardo must necessarily contradict experience; not slightly, and for short periods, as the market prices of some articles occasionally differ from the natural or necessary price, properly explained; but obviously and broadly, and for periods of such extent, that to overlook them, would not be merely like overlooking the resistance of the air in a falling body, but like overlooking the change of direction given to a ball by a second impulse acting at a different angle from the first.

It is impossible then to agree in the conclusion   a
at which Mr. Ricardo arrives in his chapter on profits, " that in all countries, and at all times, profits depend upon the quantity of labour required to provide necessaries for the labourer on that land, or with that capital which yields no rent."*

If by the necessaries of the labourer be meant,   b
such wages as will just keep up the population, or what Mr. Ricardo calls the natural wages of labour,   β
it is the same as saying that land of equal fertility will always yield the same profits—a proposition which must necessarily be untrue.

If, for instance, in one country, with the last   c
land taken into cultivation of a given fertility, capital were stationary, not from want of demand,

* Princ. of Polit. Econ. c. vi. p. 133. 2d edit.   d

but from great expenditure and the want of saving habits, it is certain that labour, after a time, would be paid very low, and profits would be very high.

a   If, in another country with similar land in cultivation, such a spirit of saving should prevail as to occasion the accumulation of capital to be more rapid than the progress of population, it is as certain that profits would be very low.

b   So understood therefore, the proposition cannot for a moment be maintained.

c   If, on the other hand, by necessaries be meant the actual earnings of the labourer, whatever they may be, the proposition is essentially incomplete. Even allowing that the exchangeable value of commodities is regulated by the quantity of labour that has been employed in their production, (which it has been shewn is not so,) little is done towards determining the rate of profits. It is merely a truism to say that if the value of commodities be divided between labour and profits, the greater is the share taken by one, the less will be left for the other; or in other words, that profits fall as labour rises, or rise as labour falls. We can know little of the laws which determine profits, unless, in addition to the causes which increase the price of necessaries, we explain the causes which award a larger or a smaller share of these necessaries to each labourer. And here it is obvious that we must have recourse to the great principles of demand and supply, or to that very principle of competition brought for-

ward by Adam Smith, which Mr. Ricardo ex-   α
pressly rejects, or at least considers as of so temporary a nature as not to require attention in a
general theory of profits.*

And yet in fact there is no other cause of per-   a
manently high profits than a deficiency in the
supply of capital; and under such a deficiency,
occasioned by extravagant expenditure, the profits
of a particular country might for hundreds of years
together continue very high, compared with others,
owing solely to the different proportions of capital
to labour.

In Poland, and some other parts of Europe, pro-   b
fits are said to be higher than in America; yet it
is probable that the last land taken into cultivation
in America is richer than the last land taken into   c
cultivation in Poland. But in America the labourer
earns perhaps the value of sixteen or eighteen quar-   d
ters of wheat in the year; in Poland only the value
of eight or nine quarters of rye. This difference in
the division of the same or nearly the same pro-   e
duce, must make an extraordinary difference in   f
the rate of profits; yet the causes which determine
this division can hardly be said to form any part of   g
Mr. Ricardo's theory of profits, although, far from
being of so temporary a nature that they may be
safely overlooked, they might contribute to operate   h
most powerfully for almost any length of time. Such
is the extent of America, that the price of its labour   i
may not essentially fall for hundreds of years; and   j

* Princ. of Polit. Econ. chap. vi. p. 132. and ch. xxi. 2d edit.   k

the effects of a scanty but stationary capital on an overflowing but stationary population might last for ever.

In dwelling thus upon the powerful effects which must inevitably be produced by the proportion which capital bears to labour, and upon the necessity of giving adequate weight to the principle of demand and supply or competition in every explanation of the circumstances which determine profits, it is not meant to underrate the importance of that cause which has been almost exclusively considered by Mr. Ricardo. It is indeed of such a nature as finally to overwhelm every other. To recur to the illustration already used—as the Long Annuities approach nearer and nearer to the term at which they expire, their value must necessarily so diminish, on this account alone, that no demand arising from plenty of money could possibly keep up their value. In the same manner, when cultivation is pushed to its extreme practical limits, that is, when the labour of a man upon the last land taken into cultivation will scarcely do more than support such a family as is necessary to maintain a stationary population, it is evident that no other cause or causes can prevent profits from sinking to the lowest rate required to maintain the actual capital.

But though the principle here considered is finally of the very greatest power, yet its progress is extremely slow and gradual; and while it is proceeding with scarcely perceptible steps to its final destination, the second cause, particularly when combined with others which will be noticed

in the next section, is producing effects which entirely overcome it, and often for twenty or thirty,
or even 100 years together, make the rate of profits
take a course absolutely different from what it
ought to be according to the first cause.

SECTION III.

Of Profits as affected by the Causes practically in operation.

We come now to the consideration of the causes
which influence profits in the actual state of things.
And here it is evident that we shall have in operation not only both the causes already stated, but
others which will variously modify them.

In the progressive cultivation of poorer land for
instance, as capital and population increase, profits,
according to the first cause, will regularly fall; but if
at the same time improvements in agriculture are
taking place, they may certainly be such as, for a
considerable period, not only to prevent profits from
falling, but to allow of a considerable rise. To
what extent, and for what length of time, this circumstance might interrupt the progress of profits
arising from the first cause, it is not easy to say;
but, as it is certain that in an extensive territory,
consisting of soils not very different in their natural
powers of production, the fall of profits arising

a

from this cause would be extremely slow, it is probable that for a considerable extent of time agricultural improvements, including of course the improved implements and machinery used in cultivation, as well as an improved system of cropping and managing the land, might more than balance it.

A second circumstance which would contribute to the same effect is, an increase of personal exertion among the labouring classes. This exertion is extremely different in different countries, and at

α

different times in the same country. A day's labour of a Hindoo, or a South-American Indian, will not admit of a comparison with that of an Englishman; and it has even been said, that though the money price of day-labour in Ireland is little more than the half of what it is in England, yet that Irish labour is not really cheaper than English, although it is well known that Irish labourers when in this country, with good examples and adequate wages to stimulate them, will work as hard as their English companions.

This latter circumstance alone clearly shews how different may be the personal exertions of the labouring classes in the same country at different times; and how different therefore may be the products of a given number of days labour, as the society proceeds from the indolence of the savage to the activity of the civilized state. This activity indeed, within certain limits, appears almost always to come forward when it is most called for, that is, when there is much work to be done without a full supply of persons to do it. The personal exertions of the South American Indian, the Hindoo, the Polish boor, and the Irish agricultural labourer, may be very different indeed 500 years hence.

The two preceding circumstances tend to diminish the expenses of production, or to reduce the relative amount of the advances necessary to obtain a certain value of produce. But it was stated at the beginning of this chapter, that profits depend upon the prices of products compared with the expenses of production, and must vary therefore with any causes which affect prices without proportionally affecting costs, as well as with any causes which affect costs without proportionally affecting prices.

A considerable effect on profits may therefore be occasioned by a third circumstance which not unfrequently occurs, namely, the unequal rise of some parts of capital, when the price of corn is raised by an increased demand. I was obliged to allude to this cause, and indeed to the two preceding ones, in the chapter on rents. I will only therefore add here, that when the prices of corn and labour rise and terminate in an altered value of money, the prices of many home commodities will be very considerably modified for some time, by the unequal pressure of taxation, and by the different quantities of fixed capital employed in their production ; and the prices of foreign commodities and of the commodities worked up at home from foreign materials, will permanently remain comparatively low. The rise of corn and labour at home will not proportionally raise the price of such products;

a   and as far as these products form any portion of the farmer's capital this capital will be rendered more productive; but leather, iron, timber, soap, candles, cottons, woollens, &c. &c. all enter more or less into the capitals of the farmer, or the wages of the labourer, and are all influenced in their

b   prices more or less by importation. While the value of the farmer's produce rises, these articles will not rise in proportion, and consequently a given value of capital will yield a greater value of

c   produce.

d   All these three circumstances, it is obvious, have a very strong tendency to counteract the effects arising from the necessity of taking poorer land into cultivation; and it will be observed that, as they are of a nature to increase in efficiency with the natural progress of population and improvement, it is not easy to say how long and to what extent they may balance or overcome them.

e   The reader will be aware that the reason why, in treating of profits, I dwell so much on agricultural profits is, that the whole stress of the question rests upon this point. The argument against the usual view which has been taken of profits, as depending principally upon the competition of capital, is founded upon the physical necessity of a fall of profits in agriculture, arising from the increasing quantity of labour required to procure the same food; and it is certain that if the profits on land permanently fall from this or any other cause, profits in manufactures and commerce must fall too, as it is an acknowledged truth that in an improved and civilized country the profits of stock, with few and temporary exceptions which may be easily accounted for, must be nearly on a level in all the different branches of industry to which capital is applied.

Now I am fully disposed to allow the truth of   a
this argument, as applied to agricultural profits, and also its natural consequences on all profits. This truth is indeed necessarily involved both in the *Principle of Population* and in the theory of   α
rent which I published separately in 1815. But I wish to shew, theoretically as well as practically, that powerful and certain as this cause is, in its final operation, so much so as to overwhelm every other; yet in the actual state of the world, its natural progress is not only extremely slow, but is so frequently counteracted and overcome by other causes as to leave very great play to the principle of the competition of capital; so that at any one period of some length in the last or following hundred years, it might most safely be asserted that profits had depended or would depend very much more upon the causes which had occasioned a comparatively scanty or abundant supply of capital than upon the natural fertility of the land last taken into cultivation.

The facts which support this position are obvious   b

and incontrovertible. Some of them have been stated in the preceding section, and their number might easily be increased. I will only add however one more, which is so strong an instance as to be alone almost decisive of the question, and having happened in our own country, it is completely open to the most minute examination.

From the accession of George II. in 1727 to the commencement of the war in 1739, the interest of money was little more than 3 per cent. The public securities which had been reduced to 4 per cent. rose considerably after the reduction. According to Chalmers, the *natural* rate of interest ran steadily at 3 per cent.;* and it appears by a speech of Sir John Barnard's that the 3 per cent. stocks sold at a premium upon Change. In 1750, after the termination of the war, the 4 per cent. stocks were reduced to 3½, for seven years, and from that time to 3 per cent. permanently.†

Excluding then the interval of war, we have here a period of twenty-two years, during which the general rate of interest was between 3½ and 3 per cent.

The temporary variations in the value of government securities will not certainly at all times be a correct criterion of the rate of profits or even of the rate of interest; but when they remain nearly steady for some time together, they must be considered as a fair approximation to a correct mea-

* Estimate of the Strength of Great Britain, c. vii. p. 115.
† Id. ch. vii. p. 120.

sure of interest; and when the public creditors of
a government consent to a great fall in the interest
which they had before received, rather than be
paid off, it is a most decisive proof of a great difficulty in the means of employing capital profitably,
and consequently a most decisive proof of a low
rate of profits.

After an interval of nearly seventy years from
the commencement of the period here noticed, and
forty years from the end of it, during which a
great accumulation of capital had taken place, and
an unusual quantity of new land had been brought
into cultivation, we find a period of twenty years
succeed in which the average market rate of interest was rather above than below 5 per cent.;
and we have certainly every reason to think, from
the extraordinary rapidity with which capital was
recovered, after it had been destroyed, that the rate
of profits in general was quite in proportion to this
high rate of interest.

The difficulty of borrowing on mortgage during
a considerable part of the time is perfectly well
known; and though the pressure of the public
debt might naturally be supposed to create some
alarm and incline the owners of disposable funds
to give a preference to landed security; yet it appears from the surveys of Arthur Young, that the
number of years purchase given for land was in
1811, 29¼, and forty years before, 32 or 32½,*—the

* Annals of Agriculture, No. 270. pp. 96. and 97. and No. 271.
p. 215. Mr. Young expresses considerable surprize at these results, and does not seem sufficiently aware, that the number of

most decisive proof that can well be imagined of an increase in the profits of capital employed upon land.

a The different rates of interest and profits in the two periods here noticed are diametrically opposed to the theory of profits founded on the natural quality of the last land taken into cultivation. The facts, which are incontrovertible, not only cannot be accounted for upon this theory, but in reference to it, either exclusively or mainly, they ought to be directly the reverse of what they are found to be in reality.

The nature of these facts, and the state of things under which they took place, (in the one case, in a

b state of peace with a slack demand for agricultural products, and in the other, a state of war with an

c unusual demand for these products,) obviously and

d clearly point to the *relative* redundancy or deficiency of capital, as, according to every probability, connected with them. And the question which now remains to be considered, is, whether the circumstances which have been stated in this section are sufficient to account theoretically for such a free operation of this principle, notwithstanding the progressive accumulation of capital, and the progressive cultivation of fresh land, as to allow of low profits at an earlier period of this

e progress and high profits at a later period. At all events, the facts must be accounted for, as they are

f years purchase given for land has nothing to do with prices, but mainly expresses the abundance or scarcity of movable capital compared with the means of employing it.

so broad and glaring, and others of the same kind
are in reality of such frequent recurrence, that I
cannot but consider them as at once decisive
against any theory of profits which is inconsistent
with them.

a

In the first period of the two which have been
noticed, it is known that the price of corn had
fallen, but that the wages of labour had not only
not fallen in proportion, but had been considered
by some authorities as having risen. Adam Smith
states the fall of corn and the rise of labour during
the first sixty-four years of the last century as a
sort of established fact;* but Arthur Young, in his
very useful inquiries into the prices of corn and
labour published in his Annals of Agriculture,
seems to think with some reason, that the fact is
not well authenticated, and is besides a little inconsistent with the apparently slack demand for
labour and produce and comparatively slow progress of population, which took place during the
period in question.† Allowing, however, even a
stationary price of labour, with a falling price of
corn, and the fall of agricultural profits is at once
accounted for. Such a state of prices might alone
be much more than sufficient to counteract the
effects arising from the circumstance of pretty
good land being yet uncultivated. When we add,
that the other outgoings belonging to the farmers'
capital, such as leather, iron, timber, &c. &c., are

b

c
d

e

* Wealth of Nations, Book I. ch. xi. p. 309. 313. 6th edit.
† Annals of Agriculture, No. 270. p. 89.

α

a   supposed to have risen while his main produce was
falling, we can be at no loss to account for a low
rate of agricultural profits, notwithstanding the
unexhausted state of the country.   And as to the
low rate of mercantile and manufacturing profits,
b   that would be accounted for at once by the proportion of capital to labour.

In the subsequent period, from 1793 to 1813, it
is probable that all the circumstances noticed in
this section concurred to give room for the opera-
c   tion of that principle which depends upon the proportion of capital to labour.

In the first place, there can be no doubt of the
improvements in agriculture which were going
forwards during these twenty years, both in reference to the general management of the land
and the instruments which are connected with
cultivation, or which in any way tend to facilitate
the bringing of raw produce to market.   2dly, the
increasing practice of task-work during these
twenty years, together with the increasing employment of women and children, unquestionably
occasioned a great increase of personal exertion;
and more work was done by the same number of
persons and families than before.

d   These two causes of productiveness in the powers
of labour were evidently encouraged and in a manner called into action by the circumstances of the
e   times, that is, by the high price of corn, which encouraged the employment of more capital upon
the land with the most effective modes of applying it, and by the increasing demand for labour,

owing to the number of men wanted in the army and navy at the same time that more than ever were wanted in agriculture and manufactures.

The third cause, which had a very considerable effect, much more indeed than is generally attributed to it, was a rise in the money price of corn without a proportionate rise in mercantile and manufacturing produce. This state of things always allows of some diminution in the corn wages of labour without a proportionate diminution of the comforts of the labourer; and if the money price of the farmer's produce increases without a proportionate increase in the price of labour and of the materials of which his capital consists, this capital becomes more productive and his profits must necessarily rise.

In a country in which labour had been well paid, it is obvious that an alteration in the proportion between labour and capital might occasion a rise in the rate of profits without supposing any increase in the productive powers of labour. But all the causes just noticed are of a nature to increase the productive powers both of labour and capital; and if in any case they are of sufficient force to overcome the effect of taking poorer land into cultivation, the rate of profits may rise consistently even with an increase in the real wages of labour.

In the case in question, though it is generally supposed that the money wages of labour did not rise in proportion to the rise in the price of provisions; yet I cannot help thinking, both from the acknowledged demand for labour and the rapid increase of population, that, partly owing to parish assistance and the more extended use of potatoes, and partly to task-work and the increased employment of women and children, the labouring classes had on an average an increased command over the necessaries of life. I am inclined to think, therefore, that the increased rate of profits from 1793 to 1813 did not arise so much from the diminished quantity of agricultural produce given to the labourer's family, as from the increase in the amount of agricultural produce obtained by the same number of families. As a matter of fact, I have no doubt that, as I stated in the chapter on rent, the capital employed upon the last land taken into cultivation in 1813 was more productive than the capital employed upon the last land taken into cultivation in 1727; and it appears to me that the causes which have been mentioned are sufficient to account for it theoretically, and to make such an event appear not only possible, but probable, and likely to be of frequent recurrence.

a   It will be said, perhaps, that some of the causes which have been noticed are in part accidental; and that in contemplating a future period, we cannot lay our account to improvements in agriculture, and an increase of personal exertions in the labouring classes. This is in some degree true. At the same time it must be allowed that a great demand for corn of home growth must tend greatly to encourage improvements in agriculture, and a great demand for labour must stimulate the actual population to do more work; and when to these two

circumstances we add the necessary effect of a
rising price of corn owing to an increase of wealth,
without a proportionate rise of other commodities,
the probabilities of an increase in the productive
powers of labour sufficient to counterbalance the
effect of taking additional land into cultivation
are so strong, that, in the actual state of most countries in the world, or in their probable state for some
centuries to come, we may fairly lay our account
to their operation when the occasion calls for them.

I should feel no doubt, for instance, of an increase
in the rate of profits in this country for twenty
years together, at the beginning of the twentieth
century, compared with the twenty years which
are now coming on; provided this near period
were a period of profound tranquillity and peace
and abundant capital, and the future period were
a period in which capital was scanty in proportion
to the demand for it owing to a war, attended by
the circumstances of an increasing trade and an
increasing demand for agricultural produce similar
to those which were experienced from 1793 to
1813.

But if this be so, it follows, that in the actual   a
state of things in most countries of the world, and
within limited periods of moderate extent, the
rate of profits will practically depend more upon
the causes which affect the relative abundance or
scarcity of capital, than on the natural powers of   bc
the last land taken into cultivation.   And consequently, to dwell on this latter point as the sole,
or even the main cause which determines profits,

must lead to the most erroneous conclusions. Adam Smith, in stating the cause of the fall of profits, has omitted this point, and in so doing has omitted a most important consideration; but in dwelling solely upon the abundance and competition of capital, he is practically much nearer the truth,* than those who dwell almost exclusively on the quality of the last land taken into cultivation.

a

b

SECTION IV.

Remarks on Mr. Ricardo's Theory of Profits.

c

According to Mr. Ricardo, profits are regulated by wages, and wages by the quality of the last land taken into cultivation. This theory of profits depends entirely upon the circumstance of the mass of commodities remaining at the same price, while money continues of the same value, whatever may be the variations in the price of labour. This uniformity in the value of wages and profits taken together is indeed assumed by Mr. Ricardo in all his calculations, from one end of his work to the other; and if it were true,

d

* Perhaps it ought to be allowed that Adam Smith, in speaking of the effects of accumulation and competition on profits, naturally means to refer to a limited territory, a limited population, and a limited demand; but accumulation of capital under these circumstances involves every cause that can affect profits.

we should certainly have an accurate rule which would determine the rate of profits upon any given rise or fall of money wages. But if it be not true, the whole theory falls to the ground. We can infer nothing respecting the rate of profits from a rise of money wages, if commodities, instead of remaining of the same price, are very variously affected, some rising, some falling, and a very small number indeed remaining stationary. But it was shewn in a former chapter * that this must necessarily take place upon a rise in the price of labour. Consequently the money wages of labour cannot regulate the rate of profits.

This conclusion will appear still more strikingly true, if we adopt that supposition respecting the mode of procuring the precious metals which would certainly maintain them most strictly of the same value, that is, if we suppose them to be procured by a uniform quantity of unassisted labour without any advances in the shape of capital beyond the necessaries of a single day. That the precious metals would in this case retain, more completely than in any other, the same value, cannot be denied, as they would both cost and command the same quantity of labour. But in this case, as was before stated, the money price of labour could never permanently rise. We cannot however for a moment imagine that this impossibility of a rise or fall in the money price of labour could in any respect impede or interrupt the

* Chap. ii. sects. 4 and 5.

natural career of profits. The continued accumulation of capital and increasing difficulty of procuring subsistence would unquestionably lower profits. All commodities, in the production of which the same quantity of labour continued to be employed, but with the assistance of capitals of various kinds and amount, would fall in price, and just in proportion to the degree in which the price of the commodity had before been affected by profits; and with regard to corn, in the production of which more labour would be necessary,

a   this article would rise in money price, notwithstanding the capital used to produce it, just to

b   that point which would so reduce corn wages as to render the population stationary; and thus all the effects upon profits, attributed by Mr. Ricardo to a rise of money wages, would take place while money wages and the value of money remained

c   precisely the same. This supposition serves further to shew how very erroneous it must be to consider the fall of profits as synonimous with a rise of money wages, or to make the money price of labour the great regulator of the rate of profits. It is obvious that, in this case, profits can only be regulated by the principle of competition, or of demand and supply, which would determine the degree in which the prices of commodities would fall; and their prices, compared with the uniform

d   price of labour, would mainly regulate the rate of profits.

e   But Mr. Ricardo never contemplates the fall of prices as occasioning a fall of profits, although prac-

tically in many cases, as well as on the preceding
supposition, a fall of profits must be produced in
this way.

Let us suppose a prosperous commercial city,   a
greatly excelling in some manufactures, and purchasing all its corn abroad.   At first, and perhaps
for a considerable time, the prices of its manufactures in foreign markets might be such as, compared with the price of its imported corn, to yield
high profits; but, as capital continued to be accumulated and employed in larger quantities on the
exportable manufactures, such manufactures, upon
the principles of demand and supply, would in all
probability fall in price.   A larger portion of them
must then be exchanged for a given portion of
corn, and profits would necessarily fall.   It is true
that, under these circumstances, the labouring manufacturer must do more work for his support, and
Mr. Ricardo would say that this is the legitimate
cause of the fall of profits.   In this I am quite
willing to agree with him; but surely the specific
cause, in this case, of more work being necessary to
earn the same quantity of corn is the fall in the
prices of the exportable manufactures with which
it is purchased, and not a rise in the price of corn,
which may remain exactly the same.   The fall in
these manufactures is the natural consequence of
an increase of supply arising from an accumulation
of capital more rapid than the extension of demand
for its products; and that the fall of profits so
occasioned depends entirely upon the principles of
demand and supply will be acknowledged, if we

acknowledge, as we certainly must do, that the opening a new market for the manufactures in question would at once put an end to the fall of profits.

a   Upon the same principle, of considering the prices of commodities as constant, Mr. Ricardo is of opinion, that if the prices of our corn and labour were to fall, the profits of our foreign trade would rise in proportion. But what is it, I would ask, that is to fix the prices of commodities in foreign markets?—not merely the quantity of labour which has been employed upon them, because, as was no-

α   ticed in a former chapter, commodities will be found selling at the same price in foreign markets, which have cost very different quantities of labour. But if they are determined, as they certainly are, both on an average and at the moment, by supply and demand, what is to prevent a much larger supply, occasioned by the competition of capital thrown out of employment, from rapidly lowering prices, and with them reducing the rate of profits?

b   If the price of corn during the last twenty-five years could have been kept at about fifty shillings the quarter, and the increasing capital of the country had chiefly been applied to the working up of exportable commodities for the purchase of foreign corn, I am strongly disposed to believe that the profits of stock would have been lower instead of higher. The millions which have been employed in permanent agricultural improvements* have had

c   * The millions of capital which have been expended in drainings, and in the roads and canals for the conveyance of agricul-

no tendency whatever to lower profits; but if, in conjunction with a large portion of the common capital employed in domestic agriculture, they had .been added to the already large capitals applied to the working up of exportable commodities, I can scarcely feel a doubt that the foreign markets would have been more than fully supplied; that the prices of commodities would have been such as to make the profits of stock quite low;* and that there would have been both a greater mass of moveable capitals at a loss for employment, and a greater disposition in those capitals to emigrate than has actually taken place.

Mr. Ricardo has never laid any *stress* upon the influence of permanent improvements in agriculture on the profits of stock, although it is one of the most important considerations in the whole compass of Political Economy, as such improvements unquestionably open the largest *arena* for the employment of capital without a diminution of profits.   He observes, that " however extensive a country may be, where the land is of a poor quality, and where the importation of food is prohibited, the most moderate accumulations of capital

tural products, have tended rather to raise than lower profits; and millions and millions may yet be employed with the same advantageous effect.

* Our present body of manufacturers, when they call for imported corn, think chiefly of the additional demand for their goods occasioned by the increased imports, and seem quite to forget the prodigious increase of supply which must be occasioned by the competition of so many more capitals and workmen in the same line of business.

332 OF THE PROFITS OF CAPITAL. [CH. V.

will be attended with great reductions in the rate of profits, and a rapid rise in rent; and on the contrary, a small but fertile country, particularly if it freely permits the importation of food, may accumulate a large stock of capital, without any great diminution in the rate of profits, or any great increase in the rent of land."*

a   Adverting to the known effects of permanent improvements on the land, I should have drawn an inference from these two cases precisely the reverse of that which Mr. Ricardo has drawn. A very extensive territory, with the soil of a poor quality, yet all, or nearly all capable of cultivation, might, by continued improvements in agriculture, admit of the employment of a vast mass of capital for hundreds of years, with little or with no fall of profits; while the small but fertile territory, being very soon filled with all the capital it could employ on the land, would be obliged to employ its further accumulations in the purchase of corn with falling manufactures; a state of things which might easily reduce profits to their lowest rate before one-third of the capital had been accumulated that had been accumulated in the former case.

b   A country, which accumulates faster than its neighbours, might for hundreds of years still keep up its rate of profits, if it were successful in making permanent improvements on the land; but, if with the same rapidity of accumulation it were to depend chiefly on imported corn, its profits could

c   * Princ. of Pol. Econ. ch. vi. p. 135. 2d edit.

scarcely fail to fall; and the fall would probably
be occasioned, not by a rise in the bullion price of
corn in the ports of Europe, but by a fall in the bullion price of the exports with which the corn was
purchased by the country in question.

These statements appear to me to accord with   a
the most correct theory of profits, and they certainly seem to be confirmed by experience. I have
already adverted to the unquestionable fact of the
profits on land being higher in 1813 than they
were above eighty years before, although in the
interval millions and millions of accumulated capital had been employed on the soil. And the
effect of falling prices in reducing profits is but
too evident at the present moment. In the largest
article of our exports, the wages of labour are now
lower than they probably would be in an ordinary
state of things if corn were at fifty shillings a quarter.
If, according to the new theory of profits, the prices
of our exports had remained the same, the master
manufacturers would have been in a state of the
most extraordinary prosperity, and the rapid accumulation of their capitals would soon have employed all the workmen that could have been found.
But, instead of this, we hear of glutted markets,
falling prices, and cotton goods selling at Kam-
schatka lower than the costs of production.

It may be said, perhaps, that the cotton trade   b
happens to be glutted; and it is a tenet of the new
doctrine on profits and demand, that if one trade
be overstocked with capital, it is a certain sign
that some other trade is understocked. But where,

I would ask, is there any considerable trade that is
confessedly understocked, and where high profits
have been long pleading in vain for additional
capital? The war has now been at an end above
four years; and though the removal of capital generally occasions some partial loss, yet it is seldom
long in taking place, if it be tempted to remove by
great demand and high profits; but if it be only dis-
couraged from proceeding in its accustomed course
by falling profits, while the profits in all other
trades, owing to general low prices, are falling at
the same time, though not perhaps precisely in the
same degree, it is highly probable that its motions
will be slow and hesitating.

a   It must be allowed then, that in contemplating
the altered relation between labour and the produce obtained by it which occasions a fall of
profits, we only take a view of half the question
if we advert exclusively to a rise in the wages of
labour without referring to a fall in the prices of
commodities. Their effects on profits may be precisely the same; but the latter case, where there
is no question respecting the state of the land,
shews at once how much profits depend upon the
prices of commodities, and upon the cause which
determines these prices, namely the supply compared with the demand.

b   At all times indeed, and on every supposition,
the great limiting principle which depends upon
the increasing difficulty of procuring food from
the soil, or on the still more general cause, a limitation of the population, in whatever way it may

be occasioned, is ready to act; and, if not overcome
by countervailing facilities, will necessarily lower
the rate of profits on the land, and from the land   a
this fall will extend to all other departments of
industry. But even this great principle operates   b
according to the laws of demand and supply and
competition.

The specific reason why profits must fall as
the land becomes more and more exhausted is,
that from the intrinsic nature of necessaries, and
of the soil from which they are procured, the
demand for them and the price of them cannot   c
possibly go on increasing in proportion to the
expense of producing them. The cost in labour of   d
producing capital increases faster than the value
of such capital when produced, or its efficiency in
setting fresh labourers to work. The boundary to
the further value of and demand for corn, lies clear   e
and distinct before us. Putting importation out of
the question, it is precisely when the produce of
the last land taken into cultivation will but just
replace the capital and support the population employed in cultivating it. Profits must then be at
their lowest theoretical limit. In their progress
towards this point, the continued accumulation of
capital will always have a *tendency* to lower them;
and at no one period can they ever be higher than
the state of the land, under all the circumstances,
will admit.

They may be lower, however, as was before   f
stated, in any degree, from an abundant supply of
capital compared with the demand for produce;   g

a and practically they are very rarely so high as the actual state of the land combined with the smallest possible quantity of food awarded to the labourer

bc would admit of. But what would be the effects upon the profits of stock of any given increase of capital, or even of any given increase of the labour necessary to produce a certain quantity of corn, it

d would be quite impossible to say before hand.

e In the case of a mere increase of capital, however large, it has appeared that circumstances might occur to prevent any fall of profits for a great length of time. And, even in the case of an increase in the quantity of labour necessary to produce corn, it would depend entirely upon the principles of demand and supply and competition, whether the increase in the price of corn

f would be such as to throw almost the whole of the increased difficulty of production upon labour, or such as to throw almost the whole of it upon profits, or finally such as to divide the loss more equally in various proportions between them.

No theory of profits therefore can approach towards correctness, which attempts to get rid of the principle of demand and supply and competition.

CHAPTER VI.

OF THE DISTINCTION BETWEEN WEALTH AND VALUE.

It has been justly stated by Adam Smith that a man is rich or poor according to the degree in which he can afford to enjoy the necessaries, conveniences, and amusements of human life. And it follows from this definition that, if the bounty of nature furnished all the necessaries, conveniences and amusements of life to every inhabitant of a country in the fullest measure of proportion to his wishes, such a country would be in the highest degree wealthy, without possessing any thing which would have exchangeable value, or could command a single hour's labour.

In this state of things, undoubtedly, wealth has nothing to do with exchangeable value. But as this is not the actual state of things, nor likely to be so at any future time; as the bounty of nature furnishes but few of the necessaries, conveniences and amusements of life to man without the aid of his own exertions; and as the great stimulus to exertion is the desire to possess what can only be possessed by means of some labour or sacrifice, it will be found that, in the real state in which man is placed on earth, wealth and exchangeable value,

a   though still by no means the same, are much more
nearly connected than they have sometimes been
supposed to be.

In considering the different quantities of the
same commodity which, under different circumstances, have the same exchangeable value, the distinction is indeed perfectly obvious.   Stockings
do not lose half their power of contributing to the
comfort and convenience of the wearer, because
by improved machinery they can be made at half
the price, or their exchangeable value be reduced
one half.   It will be readily allowed that the man
who has two pairs of stockings of the same quality
instead of one pair, possesses, as far as stockings
are concerned, a double portion of the conveniences
of life.

b   Yet even in this case he is not in all respects
doubly rich. If, indeed, he means to use them
c   himself, he really has twice as much wealth, but
if he means to exchange them for other commo-
d   dities, he has not; as one pair of stockings, under
certain circumstances, may command more labour
e   and other commodities than even two or even three
pairs after very great improvements have been made
in the machinery used in producing them.   In all
cases however of this description, the nature of the
difference between wealth and value is sufficiently
marked.

But when we come to compare objects of different kinds, there is no other way of estimating
the degree of wealth which the possession and enjoyment of them confer on the owner, than by the

relative estimation in which they are respectively   a
held, evinced by their relative exchangeable values.   b
If one man has a certain quantity of tobacco, and
another a certain quantity of muslin, we can only
determine which of the two is the richer by ascertaining their relative command of wealth in the   c
market.   And even if one country exports corn,
and imports lace and cambrics, notwithstanding
that corn has a more marked and definite value in
use than any other commodity, the estimate must
be formed exactly in the same way.   Luxuries are
a part of wealth as well as necessaries.   The country would not have received lace and cambrics in
exchange for its corn unless its wealth, or its necessaries, conveniences and luxuries taken together,
had been increased by such exchange; and this
increase of wealth cannot possibly be measured in
any other way than by the increase of value so
occasioned, founded upon the circumstance that
the commodities received are more wanted and
held in higher estimation than those which were
sent away.

Wealth, however, it will be allowed, does not   d
always increase in proportion to the increase of
value; because an increase of value may sometimes
take place under an actual diminution of the ne-   e
cessaries, conveniences and luxuries of life; but
neither does it increase in proportion to the mere
quantity of what comes under the denomination
of wealth, because the various articles of which
this quantity is composed may not be so propor-

tioned to the wants and powers of the society as
to give them their proper value. The most useful
commodity, in respect of its qualities, if it be absolutely in excess, not only loses its exchangeable
value, but its power of supplying the wants of the
society to the extent of its quantity, and part of it
therefore loses its quality of wealth. If the roads
and canals of England were suddenly broken up
and destroyed, so as to prevent all passage and
interchange of goods, there would at first be no
diminution of commodities, but there would be
immediately a most alarming diminution both of
value and wealth. A great quantity of goods
would at once lose their value by becoming utterly
useless; and though others would rise in particular
a   places, yet from the general want of power to purchase, the rise would by no means compensate for
the fall. The whole exchangeable value of the
b   produce estimated in labour, corn, or money, would
be greatly diminished; and it is quite obvious that
the wealth of the society would be most essentially
impaired; that is, its wants would not be in any
degree so well supplied as before.

It appears then that the wealth of a country depends partly upon the quantity of produce obtained
by its labour, and partly upon such an adaptation
c   of it to the wants and powers of the existing popu-
d   lation as is calculated to give it value.

But where wealth and value are perhaps the
e   most nearly connected, is in the constant necessity
of the latter to the production of the former. In

the actual state of things, no considerable quantity of wealth can be obtained except by considerable exertions; and unless the value which an individual or the society places on the object when obtained fully compensates the sacrifice which has been made to obtain it, such wealth will not be produced in future. If labour alone be concerned in its production, as in shrimping, in the collection of hirts and wild strawberries, and some other exertions of mere manual labour, it is obvious that this wealth will not be collected, will not be used to supply any of the wants of the society, unless its value when collected will, at the least, command as much labour as the collection of it cost.

If the nature of the object to be obtained requires advances in the shape of capital, as in the vast majority of instances, then by whomsoever this capital is furnished, whether by the labourers themselves or by others, the commodity will not be produced, unless the estimation in which it is held by the society or its value in exchange be such, as not only to replace all the advances of labour and other articles which have been made for its attainment, but to pay the usual profits of capital.

It is obviously therefore the value of commodities, or the sacrifice of labour and of other articles which people are willing to make in order to obtain them, that in the actual state of things may be said to be the sole cause of the existence of wealth; and this value is founded on the wants of

mankind, and the adaptation of particular commodities to supply these wants, independently of the
actual quantity of labour which these commodities

a   may cost in their collection or production. It is
this value which is not only the great stimulus to
the production of all kinds of wealth, but the
great regulator of the forms and relative quantities in which it shall exist. No species of wealth
can be brought to market for a continuance, unless
some part of the society sets a value upon it equal to
its natural or necessary price, and is both able and
willing to make a sacrifice to this extent in order
to obtain it. A tax will entirely put an end to the
production of a commodity, if no one of the society is disposed to value it at a price equal to the
new conditions of its supply. And on the other
hand, commodities will be continually increased

b   in quantity so long as the numbers of those, who
are able and willing to give a value for them equal
to this price, continue to increase.

In short, the market prices of commodities are
the immediate causes of all the great movements

c   of society in the production of wealth, and these
market prices always express clearly and unequi-
vocally the exchangeable value of commodities at
the time and place in which they are exchanged,

d   and differ only from natural and necessary prices

e   as the actual state of the demand and supply, with
regard to any particular article, may differ from the

f   ordinary and average state.

g   The reader of course will observe that in using

the term value, or value in exchange, I always mean it to be understood in that enlarged and, as I conceive, accustomed and correct sense, according to which I endeavoured to explain and define it in the Second Chapter of this work, and never in the confined sense in which it has been lately applied by Mr. Ricardo, as depending exclusively upon the actual quantity of labour employed in production.* Understood in this latter sense, value, certainly, has not so intimate a connection with wealth. In comparing two countries together of different degrees of fertility, or in comparing an agricultural with a manufacturing and commercial country, their relative wealth would be very different from the proportion of labour employed by each in production; and certainly the increasing quantity of labour necessary to produce any commodity would be very far indeed from being a stimulus to its increase. In this sense therefore wealth and value are very different.

But if value be understood in the sense in which it is most generally used, and according to which

a

---

* Mr. Ricardo says, (ch. xx. p. 343.) "That commodity is alone invariable, which at all times requires the same sacrifice of toil and labour to produce it." What does the term "invariable" mean here? It cannot mean *invariable* in its exchangeable value; because Mr. Ricardo has himself allowed that commodities which have cost the same sacrifice of toil and labour will very frequently not exchange for each other. As a measure of value in exchange this standard is much more variable than those which he has rejected; and in what other sense it is to be understood, it is not easy to say.

b

I have defined it, wealth and value, though certainly not always the same, will appear to be very nearly connected; and in making an estimate of wealth, it must be allowed to be as grave an error to consider quantity without reference to value, as to consider value without reference to quantity.

———————

a

CHAPTER VII.

b

ON THE IMMEDIATE CAUSES OF THE PROGRESS
OF WEALTH.

SECTION I.

Statement of the particular Object of Inquiry.

THERE is scarcely any inquiry more curious, or,
from its importance, more worthy of attention,
than that which traces the causes which practically
check the progress of wealth in different countries,
and stop it, or make it proceed very slowly, while
the power of production remains comparatively
undiminished, or at least would furnish the means
of a great and abundant increase of produce and
population.

In a former work * I endeavoured to trace the
causes which practically keep down the population
of a country to the level of its actual supplies.
It is now my object to shew what are the causes
which chiefly influence these supplies, or call the
powers of production forth into the shape of increasing wealth.

Among the primary and most important causes
which influence the wealth of nations, must un-

* Essay on the Principle of Population.

questionably be placed, those which come under the head of politics and morals. Security of property, without a certain degree of which, there can be no encouragement to individual industry, depends mainly upon the political constitution of a country, the excellence of its laws and the manner in which they are administered. And those habits which are the most favourable to regular exertions as well as to general rectitude of character, and are consequently most favourable to the production and maintenance of wealth, depend chiefly upon the same causes, combined with moral and religious instruction. It is not however my intention at present to enter fully into these causes, important and effective as they are; but to confine myself chiefly to the more immediate and proximate causes of increasing wealth, whether they may have their origin in these political and moral sources, or in any others more specifically and directly within the province of political economy.

It is obviously true that there are many countries, not essentially different either in the degree of security which they afford to property, or in the moral and religious instruction received by the people, which yet, with nearly equal natural capabilities, make a very different progress in wealth. It is the principal object of the present inquiry to explain this; and to furnish some solution of certain phenomena frequently obtruded upon our attention, whenever we take a view of the different states of Europe, or of the world; namely, countries with great powers of production comparatively poor, and countries with small powers of production comparatively rich.

If the actual riches of a country not subject to repeated violences and a frequent destruction of produce, be not after a certain period in some degree proportioned to its power of producing riches, this deficiency must have arisen from the want of an adequate stimulus to continued production. The practical question then for our consideration is, what are the most immediate and effective stimulants to the continued creation and progress of wealth.

SECTION II.

Of the Increase of Population considered as a Stimulus to the continued Increase of Wealth.

Many writers have been of opinion that an increase of population is the sole stimulus necessary to the increase of wealth, because population, being the great source of consumption, must in their opinion necessarily keep up the demand for an increase of produce, which will naturally be followed by a continued increase of supply.

That a permanent increase of population is a powerful and necessary element of increasing demand, will be most readily allowed; but that the increase of population alone, or, more properly

a

speaking, the pressure of the population hard against the limits of subsistence, does not furnish an effective stimulus to the continued increase of wealth, is not only evident in theory, but is confirmed by universal experience. If want alone, or the desire of the labouring classes to possess the necessaries and conveniences of life, were a sufficient stimulus to production, there is no state in Europe, or in the world, that would have found any other practical limit to its wealth than its power to produce; and the earth would probably before this period have contained, at the very least, ten times as many inhabitants as are supported on its surface at present.

But those who are acquainted with the nature of effective demand, will be fully aware that, where the right of private property is established, and the wants of society are supplied by industry and barter, the desire of any individual to possess the necessary conveniences and luxuries of life, however intense, will avail nothing towards their production, if there be no where a reciprocal demand for something which he possesses. A man whose only possession is his labour has, or has not, an effective demand for produce according as his labour is, or is not, in demand by those who have the disposal of produce. And no productive labour will ever be in demand unless the produce when obtained is of greater value than the labour which obtained it. No fresh hands can be employed in any sort of industry merely in consequence of the demand for its produce occa-

sioned by the persons employed. No farmer will
take the trouble of superintending the labour of
ten additional men merely because his whole produce will then sell in the market at an advanced
price just equal to what he had paid his additional
labourers. There must be something in the previous state of the demand and supply of the commodity in question, or in its price, antecedent to
and independently of the demand occasioned by   a
the new labourers, in order to warrant the employment of an additional number of people in its
production.

It will be said perhaps that the increase of
population will lower wages, and, by thus diminishing the costs of production, will increase the profits of the capitalists and the encouragement to
produce. Some temporary effect of this kind may
no doubt take place, but it is evidently very strictly
limited. The fall of wages cannot go on beyond   b
a certain point without not only stopping the progress of the population but making it even retrograde; and before this point is reached, it will pro-   c
bably happen that the increase of produce occasioned by the labour of the additional number of
persons will have so lowered its value, as more   d
than to counterbalance the fall of wages, and thus
to diminish instead of increase the profits of the
capitalists and the power and will to employ more
labour.

It is obvious then in theory that an increase of
population, when an additional quantity of labour
is not wanted, will soon be checked by want of   e

employment, and the scanty support of those employed, and will not furnish the required stimulus
to an increase of wealth proportioned to the power
of production.

But, if any doubts should remain with respect to
the *theory* on the subject, they will surely be dissipated by a reference to *experience*. It is scarcely
possible to cast our eyes on any nation of the
world without seeing a striking confirmation of
what has been advanced. Almost universally, the
actual wealth of all the states with which we are
acquainted is very far short of their powers of production; and almost universally among those
states, the slowest progress in wealth is made where
the stimulus arising from population alone is the
greatest, that is, where the population presses the
hardest against the limits of subsistence. It is
quite evident that the only fair way, indeed the
only way, by which we can judge of the practical effect of population alone as a stimulus to
wealth, is to refer to those countries where, from
the excess of population above the funds applied
to the maintenance of labour, the stimulus of
want is the greatest. And if in these countries,
which still have great powers of production, the
progress of wealth is very slow, we have certainly
all the evidence which experience can possibly
give us, that population alone cannot create an
effective demand for wealth.

To suppose an actual and permanent increase of
population is to beg the question. We may as
well suppose at once an increase of wealth; be-

cause an actual and permanent increase of popu-   a
lation cannot take place without a proportionate
or nearly proportionate increase of wealth. The
question really is, whether encouragements to
population, or even the natural tendency of population to increase beyond the funds for its main-   b
tenance, so as to press hard against the limits of   c
subsistence, will, or will not, alone furnish an adequate stimulus to the increase of wealth. And
this question, Spain, Portugal, Poland, Hungary,
Turkey, and many other countries in Europe, together with nearly the whole of Asia and Africa,
and the greatest part of America, distinctly answer
in the negative.

SECTION III.

*Of Accumulation, or the Saving from Revenue to add to
Capital, considered as a Stimulus to the Increase of
Wealth.*

Those who reject mere population as an adequate
stimulus to the increase of wealth, are generally
disposed to make every thing depend upon accumulation. It is certainly true that no permanent and
continued increase of wealth can take place without a continued increase of capital; and I cannot
agree with Lord Lauderdale in thinking that this
increase can be effected in any other way than by

saving from the stock which might have been destined for immediate consumption, and adding it
to that which is to yield a profit; or in other
words, by the conversion of revenue into capital.*

But we have yet to inquire what is the state of
things which generally disposes a nation to accumulate; and further, what is the state of things
which tends to make that accumulation the most
effective, and lead to a further and continued
increase of capital and wealth.

It is undoubtedly possible by parsimony to devote at once a much larger share than usual of the
produce of any country to the maintenance of
a   productive labour; and it is quite true that the
labourers so employed are consumers as well as
bc   unproductive labourers; and as far as the labourers
are concerned, there would be no diminution of
consumption or demand.   But it has already been
shewn that the consumption and demand occa-
d   sioned by the persons employed in productive la-
e   bour can never alone furnish a motive to the
accumulation and employment of capital; and
with regard to the capitalists themselves, together
with the landlords and other rich persons, they
have, by the supposition, agreed to be parsimonious, and by depriving themselves of their usual

* See Lord Lauderdale's Chapter on Parsimony, in his Inquiry
into the Nature and Origin of Public Wealth, ch. iv. p. 198. 2d.
edit.   Lord Lauderdale appears to have gone as much too far in
deprecating accumulation, as some other writers in recommending
f   it.   This tendency to extremes is exactly what I consider as
the great source of error in political economy.

conveniences and luxuries to save from their revenue and add to their capital. Under these circumstances, I would ask, how it is possible to suppose that the increased quantity of commodities,
obtained by the increased number of productive
labourers, should find purchasers, without such a
fall of price as would probably sink their value
below the costs of production, or, at least, very
greatly diminish both the power and the will to
save.

It has been thought by some very able writers,
that although there may easily be a glut of particular commodities, there cannot possibly be a glut
of commodities in general ; because, according to
their view of the subject, commodities being always exchanged for commodities, one half will
furnish a market for the other half, and production
being thus the sole source of demand, an excess in
the supply of one article merely proves a deficiency
in the supply of some other, and a general excess is
impossible.   M. Say, in his distinguished work on
political economy, has indeed gone so far as to
state that the consumption of a commodity by
taking it out of the market diminishes demand,
and the production of a commodity proportionably
increases it.

This doctrine, however, to the extent in which
it has been applied, appears to me to be utterly
unfounded, and completely to contradict the
great principles which regulate supply and demand.

It is by no means true, as a matter of fact,

that commodities are always exchanged for commodities. The great mass of commodities is exchanged directly for labour, either productive or unproductive; and it is quite obvious that this mass of commodities, compared with the labour with which it is to be exchanged, may fall in value from a glut just as any one commodity falls in value from an excess of supply, compared either with labour or money.

In the case supposed there would evidently be an unusual quantity of commodities of all kinds in the market, owing to the unproductive labourers of the country having been converted, by the accumulation of capital, into productive labourers; while the number of labourers altogether being the same, and the power and will to purchase for consumption among landlords and capitalists being by supposition diminished, commodities would necessarily fall in value, compared with labour, so as to lower profits almost to nothing, and to check for a time further production. But this is precisely what is meant by the term glut, which, in this case, is evidently general not partial.

M. Say, Mr. Mill,* and Mr. Ricardo, the prin-

* Mr. Mill, in a reply to Mr. Spence, published in 1808, has laid down very broadly the doctrine that commodities are only purchased by commodities, and that one half of them must always furnish a market for the other half. The same doctrine appears to be adopted in its fullest extent by the author of an able and useful article on the Corn Laws, in the Supplement to the Encyclopædia Britannica, which has been referred to in a previous chapter.

cipal authors of the new doctrines on profits, appear to me to have fallen into some fundamental errors in the view which they have taken of this subject.

In the first place, they have considered commodities as if they were so many mathematical figures, or arithmetical characters, the relations of which were to be compared, instead of articles of consumption, which must of course be referred to the numbers and wants of the consumers.

If commodities were only to be compared and exchanged with each other, then indeed it would be true that, if they were all increased in their proper proportions to any extent, they would continue to bear among themselves the same relative value; but, if we compare them, as we certainly ought to do, with the numbers and wants of the consumers, then a great increase of produce with comparatively stationary numbers and with wants diminished by parsimony, must necessarily occasion a great fall of value estimated in labour, so that the same produce, though it might have *cost* the same quantity of labour as before, would no longer *command* the same quantity; and both the power of accumulation and the motive to accumulate would be strongly checked.

It is asserted that effectual demand is nothing more than the offering of one commodity in exchange for another. But is this all that is necessary to effectual demand? Though each commodity may have cost the same quantity of labour and capital in its production, and they may be

a
exactly equivalent to each other in exchange, yet
why may not both be so plentiful as not to command more labour, or but very little more than
they have cost; and in this case, would the demand
for them be effectual? Would it be such as to encourage their continued production? Unquestionably not. Their relation to each other may not
have changed; but their relation to the wants of
b
the society, their relation to bullion, and their relation to domestic and foreign labour, may have
c
experienced a most important change.

It will be readily allowed that a new commodity
thrown into the market, which, in proportion to
the labour employed upon it, is of higher exchangeable value than usual, is precisely calculated to
increase demand; because it implies, not a mere
d
increase of quantity, but a better adaptation of the
produce to the tastes, wants and consumption of
the society. But to fabricate or procure commodities of this kind is the grand difficulty; and they
certainly do not naturally and necessarily follow
an accumulation of capital and increase of commodities, most particularly when such accumulation
and increase have been occasioned by economy of
consumption, or a discouragement to the indulgence of those tastes and wants, which are the
e
very elements of demand.

Mr. Ricardo, though he maintains as a general
position that capital cannot be redundant, is obliged
to make the following concession. He says,
" There is only one case, and that will be temporary, in which the accumulation of capital with a

low price of food may be attended with a fall of
profits; and that is, when the funds for the maintenance of labour increase much more rapidly than
population;—wages will then be high and profits
low. If every man were to forego the use of
luxuries and be intent only on accumulation, a
quantity of necessaries might be produced for
which there could not be any immediate consumption. Of commodities so limited in number, there
might undoubtedly be an universal glut; and consequently there might neither be demand for an
additional quantity of such commodities, nor profits on the employment of more capital. If men
ceased to consume, they would cease to produce."
Mr. Ricardo then adds, " This admission does not
impugn the general principle."*   In this remark I   a
cannot quite agree with him. As, from the nature   b
of population, an increase of labourers cannot be
brought into the market, in consequence of a particular demand, till after the lapse of sixteen or
eighteen years, and the conversion of revenue into   c
capital may take place much more rapidly; a
country is always liable to an increase of the funds   d
for the maintenance of labour faster than the increase of population. But if, whenever this occurs,
there may be a universal glut of commodities, how   e
can it be maintained, as a general position, that
capital is never redundant; and that because commodities may retain the same relative values, a glut
can only be partial, not general?

* Princ. of Polit. Econ. ch. xxi. p. 364. 2d edit.   f

Another fundamental error into which the writers above-mentioned and their followers appear to have fallen is, the not taking into consideration the influence of so general and important a principle in human nature, as indolence or the love of ease.

It has been supposed* that, if a certain number of farmers and a certain number of manufacturers had been exchanging their surplus food and clothing with each other, and their powers of production were suddenly so increased that both parties could, with the same labour, produce luxuries in addition to what they had before obtained, there could be no sort of difficulty with regard to demand, as part of the luxuries which the farmer produced would be exchanged against part of the luxuries produced by the manufacturer; and the only result would be, the happy one of both parties being better supplied and having more enjoyments.

But in this intercourse of mutual gratifications, two things are taken for granted, which are the very points in dispute. It is taken for granted that luxuries are always preferred to indolence, and that the profits of each party are consumed as revenue. What would be the effect of a desire to save under such circumstances, shall be considered presently. The effect of a preference of indolence to luxuries would evidently be to occasion a want of demand for the returns of the increased powers of production supposed, and to throw labourers out

* Edinburgh Review, No. LXIV. p. 471.

of employment. The cultivator, being now enabled
to obtain the necessaries and conveniences to which
he had been accustomed, with less toil and trouble,
and his tastes for ribands, lace and velvet not
being fully formed, might be very likely to indulge
himself in indolence, and employ less labour on
the land ; while the manufacturer, finding his velvets rather heavy of sale, would be led to discon-
tinue their manufacture, and to fall almost necessarily into the same indolent system as the farmer.
That an efficient taste for luxuries, that is, such a   a
taste as will properly stimulate industry, instead of
being ready to appear at the moment it is required, is
a plant of slow growth, the history of human society
sufficiently shews; and that it is a most important
error to take for granted, that mankind will produce
and consume all that they have the power to produce and consume, and will never prefer indolence
to the rewards of industry, will sufficiently appear
from a slight review of some of the nations with
which we are acquainted.   But I shall have occasion for a review of this kind in the next section ;
and to this I refer the reader.   b

A third very serious error of the writers above
referred to, and practically the most important of
the three, consists in supposing that accumulation
ensures demand ; or that the consumption of the
labourers employed by those whose object is to
save, will create such an effectual demand for commodities as to encourage a 'continued increase of
produce.

Mr. Ricardo observes, that " If 10,000*l.* were

given to a man having 100,000 *l.* per annum, he
would not lock it up in a chest, but would either
increase his expenses by 10,000*l.*, employ it himself
productively, or lend it to some other person for
that purpose; in either case demand would be increased, although it would be for different objects.
If he increased his expenses, his effectual demand
might probably be for buildings, furniture, or some
such enjoyment. If he employed his 10,000*l.* productively, his effectual demand would be for food,
clothing, and raw materials, which might set new
labourers to work. But still it would be *demand.*"*

Upon this principle it is supposed that if the
richer portion of society were to forego their accustomed conveniences and luxuries with a view
to accumulation, the only effect would be a direction of nearly the whole capital of the country to
the production of necessaries, which would lead to
a great increase of cultivation and population. But,
without supposing an entire change in the usual
motives to accumulation, this could not possibly
happen. The usual motives for accumulation are,
I conceive, either the future wealth and enjoyment
of the individual who accumulates, or of those to
whom he means to leave his property. And with
these motives it could never answer to the possessor
of land to employ nearly all the labour which the
soil could support in cultivation; as by so doing
he would necessarily destroy his neat rent, and
render it impossible for him, without subsequently
dismissing the greatest part of his workmen and

* Princ. of Polit. Econ. chap. xxi. p. 361. 2d edit.

occasioning the most dreadful distress, either to
give himself the means of greater enjoyment at a
future distant period, or to transmit such means to
his posterity.

The very definition of fertile land is, land that
will support a much greater number of persons
than are necessary to cultivate it; and if the landlord, instead of spending this surplus in conveniences, luxuries and unproductive consumers, were
to employ it in setting to work on the land as
many labourers as his savings could support, it is
quite obvious that, instead of being enriched, he
would be impoverished by such a proceeding, both
at first and in future. Nothing could justify such
a conduct but a different motive for accumulation;
that is, a desire to increase the population—not the
love of wealth and enjoyment; and till such a
change takes place in the passions and propensities
of mankind, we may be quite sure that the landlords and cultivators will not go on employing
labourers in this way.

What then would happen? As soon as the landlords and cultivators found that they could not
realize their increasing produce in some way which
would give them a command of wealth in future,
they would cease to employ more labour upon the
land;* and if the business of that part of the so-

* Theoretical writers in Political Economy, from the fear of appearing to attach too much importance to money, have perhaps
been too apt to throw it out of their consideration in their reasonings. It is an abstract truth that we want commodities, not
money. But, in reality, no commodity for which it is possible to

ciety which was not engaged in raising raw produce, consisted merely in preparing the other simple necessaries of life, the number required for this purpose being inconsiderable, the rest of those whom the soil could support would be thrown out of work. Having no means of legally demanding a portion of the raw produce, however plentiful it might be at first, they would gradually decrease in numbers; and the failure of effective demand for the produce of the soil would necessarily diminish cultivation, and throw a still greater number of persons out of employment. This action and re-action would thus go on till the balance of produce and consumption was restored in reference to the new tastes and habits which were established;

a and it is obvious that without an expenditure which
b will encourage commerce, manufactures, and un-
c productive consumers, or an Agrarian law calcu-
lated to change the usual motives for accumulation, the possessors of land would have no sufficient

sell our goods at once, can be an adequate substitute for a circulating medium, and enable us in the same manner to provide for children, to purchase an estate, or to command labour and provisions a year or two hence. A circulating medium is absolutely necessary to any considerable saving; and even the manufacturer would get on but slowly, if he were obliged to accumulate in kind all the wages of his workmen. We cannot therefore be surprized at his wanting money rather than other goods; and, in civilized countries, we may be quite sure that if the farmer or manufacturer cannot sell his products so as to give him a profit estimated in money, his industry will immediately slacken. The circulating medium bears so important a part in the distribution of wealth,

d and the encouragement of industry, that to set it aside in our reasonings may often lead us wrong.

stimulus to cultivate well; and a country such as our own, which had been rich and populous, would, with such parsimonious habits, infallibly become poor, and comparatively unpeopled.

The same kind of reasoning will obviously apply to the case noticed before. While the farmers were disposed to consume the luxuries produced by the manufacturers, and the manufacturers those produced by the farmers, all would go on smoothly; but if either one or both of the parties were disposed to save with a view of bettering their condition, and providing for their families in future, the state of things would be very different. The farmer, instead of indulging himself in ribands, lace, and velvets,* would be disposed to be satisfied with more simple clothing, but by this economy he would disable the manufacturer from purchasing the same amount of his produce; and for the returns of so much labour employed upon the land, and all greatly increased in productive power, there would evidently be no market. The manufacturer, in like manner, instead of indulging himself in sugar, grapes and tobacco, might be disposed to save with a view to the future, but would be totally unable to do so, owing to the parsimony of the farmers and the want of demand for manufactures.†

* Edinburgh Review, No. LXIV. p. 471.

† Of all the opinions advanced by able and ingenious men, which I have ever met with, the opinion of M. Say, which states that, *un produit consommé ou détruit est un débouché fermé* [l. i. ch.

An accumulation, to a certain extent, of common food and common clothing might take place on both sides ; but the amount must necessarily be extremely confined. It would be of no sort of use to the farmer to go on cultivating his land with a view merely to give food and clothing to his labourers. He would be doing nothing either for himself or family, if he neither consumed the surplus of what they produced himself, nor could realize it in a shape that might be transmitted to his descendants. If he were a tenant, such additional care and labour would be entirely thrown away ; and if he were a landlord, and were determined, without reference to markets, to cultivate his estate in such a way as to make it yield the greatest neat surplus with a view to the future, it is quite certain that the large portion of this surplus which was not required either for his own consumption, or to purchase clothing for himself and his labourers, would be absolutely wasted. If he did not choose to use it in the purchase of luxuries or the maintenance of unproductive labourers, it might as well be thrown into the sea. To save

a

b

c

15.) appears to me to be the most directly opposed to just theory, and the most uniformly contradicted by experience. Yet it directly follows from the new doctrine, that commodities are to be considered only in their relation to each other,—not to the consumers. What, I would ask, would become of the demand for commodities, if all consumption except bread and water were suspended for the next half year ?   What an accumulation of commodities !   Quels *débouchés* !   What a prodigious market would this event occasion !

it, that is to use it in employing more labourers
upon the land would, as I said before, be to im-
poverish both himself and his family.

It would be still more useless to the manufacturers to go on producing clothing beyond what
was wanted by the agriculturists and themselves.
Their numbers indeed would entirely depend upon
the demands of the agriculturists, as they would
have no means of purchasing subsistence, but in
proportion as there was a reciprocal want of their
manufactures. The population required to provide
simple clothing for such a society with the assistance
of good machinery would be inconsiderable, and
would absorb but a small portion of the proper surplus of rich and well cultivated land. There would
evidently therefore be a general want of demand,
both for produce and population; and while it is
quite certain that an adequate passion for consumption may fully keep up the proper proportion
between supply and demand, whatever may be the
powers of production, it appears to be quite as certain that a passion for accumulation must inevitably lead to a supply of commodities beyond
what the structure and habits of such a society
will permit to be consumed.*

But if this be so, surely it is a most important
error to couple the passion for expenditure and

* The reader must already know, that I do not share in the
apprehensions of Mr. Owen about the permanent effects of machinery. But I am decidedly of opinion, that on this point he
has the best of the argument with those who think that accumulation ensures effective demand.

the passion for accumulation together, as if they
were of the same nature; and to consider the
demand for the food and clothing of the labourer,
who is to be employed productively, as securing
such a general demand for commodities and
such a rate of profits for the capital employed in
producing them, as will adequately call forth the
powers of the soil, and the ingenuity of man in
procuring the greatest quantity both of raw and
manufactured produce.

a   Perhaps it may be asked by those who have
adopted Mr. Ricardo's view of profits,—what becomes of the division of that which is produced,
when population is checked merely by want of demand? It is acknowledged that the powers of production have not begun to fail; yet, if labour produces largely and yet is ill paid, it will be said that
profits must be high.

αb   I have already stated in a former chapter, that
the value of the materials of capital very frequently
do not fall in proportion to the fall in the value of
the produce of capital, and this alone will often
account for low profits.   But independently of
this consideration, it is obvious that in the production of any other commodities than necessaries,
the theory is perfectly simple.   From want of demand, such commodities may be very low in price,
and a large portion of the whole value produced
may go to the labourer, although in necessaries he
may be ill paid, and his wages, both with regard
to the quantity of food which he receives and the
labour required to produce it, may be decidedly low.

If it be said, that on account of the large portion   a
of the value of manufactured produce which on
this supposition is absorbed by wages, it may be
affirmed that the cause of the fall of profits is high
wages, I should certainly protest against so manifest an abuse of words. The only justifiable
ground for adopting a new term, or using an old
one in a new sense, is, to convey more precise information to the reader; but to refer to high
wages in this case, instead of to a fall of commodities, would be to proceed as if the specific inten-   b
tion of the writer were to keep his reader as much
as possible in the dark as to the real state of things.

In the production of necessaries however, it will   c
be allowed, that the answer to the question is not
quite so simple, yet still it may be made sufficiently
clear.   Mr. Ricardo acknowledges that there may   α
be a limit to the employment of capital upon the
land from the limited wants of society, independently of the exhaustion of the soil. In the case
supposed, this limit must necessarily be very narrow, because there would be comparatively no population besides the agriculturists to make an
effective demand for produce. Under such circumstances corn might be produced, which would
lose the character and quality of wealth; and, as I
before observed in a note, all the parts of the same   β
produce would not be of the same value. The actual labourers employed might be tolerably well
fed, as is frequently the case, practically, in those
countries where the labourers are fed by the far-

mers,* but there would be little work or food for
their grown up sons; and from varying markets
and varying crops, the profits of the farmer might
be the lowest at the very time when, according to
the division of the produce, it ought to be the
highest, that is, when there was the greatest proportionate excess of produce above what was paid
to the labourer.   The wages of the labourer cannot sink below a certain point, but a part of the
produce, from excess of supply, may for a time be
absolutely useless, and permanently it may so fall
from competition as to yield only the lowest profits.

a   I would observe further, that if in consequence
of a diminished demand for corn, the cultivators
were to withdraw their capitals so as better to
proportion their supplies to the quantity that could
be properly paid for; yet if they could not employ
the capital they had withdrawn in any other way,
which, according to the preceding supposition,
they could not, it is certain that, though they
might for a time make fair profits of the small

b   * In Norway and Sweden, particularly the former, where the
agricultural labourer either lives in the farmer's family or has a
portion of land assigned to him in lieu of wages, he is in general
pretty well fed, although there is but little demand for labour, and
considerable competition for such employment.   In countries so
circumstanced, (and there are many such all over the world,) it is
perfectly futile to attempt to estimate profits by the excess of the
produce above what is consumed in obtaining it, when for this
excess there may be often little or no market. All evidently
depends upon the exchangeable value of the disposable produce.

stock which they still continued to employ in agriculture, the consequences to them as cultivators
would be, to all intents and purposes, the same as
if a general fall had taken place on all their capital.

If, in the process of saving, all that was lost by
the capitalist was gained by the labourer, the
check to the progress of wealth would be but temporary, as stated by Mr. Ricardo; and the consequences need not be apprehended. But if the
conversion of revenue into capital pushed beyond
a certain point must, by diminishing the effectual demand for produce, throw the labouring
classes out of employment, it is obvious that the
adoption of parsimonious habits in too great a de- a
gree may be accompanied by the most distressing
effects at first, and by a marked depression of
wealth and population permanently. b

It is not, of course, meant to be stated that parsimony, or even a temporary diminution of consumption,* is not often in the highest degree useful, and sometimes absolutely necessary to the
progress of wealth. A state may certainly be
ruined by extravagance; and a diminution of the
actual expenditure may not only be necessary on
this account, but when the capital of a country is
deficient, compared with the demand for its products, a temporary economy of consumption is required, in order to provide that supply of capital

* Parsimony, or the conversion of revenue into capital, may
take place without any diminution of consumption, if the revenue
increases first.

which can alone furnish the means of an increased
consumption in future.   All that I mean to say is,
that no nation can *possibly* grow rich by an accumulation of capital, arising from a permanent diminution of consumption; because, such accumulation being greatly beyond what is wanted, in order to supply the effective demand for produce,
a part of it would very soon lose both its use and
its value, and cease to possess the character of
wealth.

   On the supposition indeed of a *given* consumption, the accumulation of capital beyond a certain
point must appear at once to be perfectly futile.
But, even taking into consideration the increased
consumption likely to arise among the labouring
classes from the abundance and cheapness of commodities, yet as this cheapness must be at the expense of profits, it is obvious that the limits to such
an increase of capital from parsimony, as shall not be
attended by a very rapid diminution of the motive
to accumulate, are very narrow, and may very
easily be passed.

   The laws which regulate the rate of profits and
the progress of capital, bear a very striking and
singular resemblance to the laws which regulate
the rate of wages and the progress of population.

   Mr. Ricardo has very clearly shewn that the
rate of profits must diminish, and the progress
of accumulation be finally stopped, under the
most favourable circumstances, by the increasing
difficulty of procuring the food of the labourer.
I, in like manner, endeavoured to shew in my

Essay on the Principle of Population that, under circumstances the most favourable to cultivation which could possibly be supposed to operate in the actual state of the earth, the wages of the la-   a
bourer would become more scanty, and the progress   b
of population be finally stopped by the increasing difficulty of procuring the means of subsistence.

But Mr. Ricardo has not been satisfied with proving the position just stated.   He has not been satisfied with shewing that the difficulty of pro-curing the food of the labourer is the only *abso-lutely necessary* cause of the fall of profits, in which I am ready fully and entirely to agree with him : but he has gone on to say, that there is *no other cause* of the fall of profits in the actual state of things that has any degree of permanence.   In   c
this latter statement he appears to me to have fallen into precisely the same kind of error as I should have fallen into, if, after having shewn that the unrestricted power of population was beyond comparison greater than the power of the earth to produce food under the most favourable circum-stances possible, I had allowed that population could not be redundant unless the powers of the earth to keep up with the progress of population had been tried to the uttermost.   But I all along said, that population might be redundant, and greatly redundant, compared with the demand for it and the actual means of supporting it, although it might most properly be considered as deficient, and greatly deficient, compared with the extent of terri-tory, and the powers of such territory to produce

additional means of subsistence; that, in such cases, notwithstanding the acknowledged deficiency of population, and the obvious desirableness of having it greatly increased, it was useless and foolish directly to encourage the birth of more children, as the effect of such encouragement, without a demand for labour and the means of paying it properly, could only be increased misery and mortality with little or no final increase of population.

a   Though Mr. Ricardo has taken a very different course, I think that the same kind of reasoning ought to be applied to the rate of profits and the progress of capital. Fully acknowledging that there is hardly a country in the four quarters of the globe where capital is not deficient, and in most of them very greatly deficient, compared with the territory and even the number of people; and fully allowing at the same time the extreme desirableness of an increase of capital, I should b   say that, where the demand for commodities was not such as to afford fair profits to the producer, and the capitalists were at a loss where and how to employ their capitals to advantage, the saving from revenue to add still more to these capitals would only tend prematurely to diminish the motive to accumulation, and still further to distress the capitalists, with little increase of a wholesome and effective capital.

c   The first thing wanted in both these cases of deficient capital and deficient population, is an effective demand for commodities, that is, a demand by those who are able and willing to pay an adequate price for them; and though high profits are not followed by an increase of capital, so certainly as high wages are by an increase of population, yet I believe that they are so followed more generally than they appear to be, because, in many countries, as I have before intimated, profits are often thought to be high, owing to the high interest of money, when they are really low; and because, universally, risk in employing capital has precisely the same effect in diminishing the motive to accumulate and the reward of accumulation, as low profits.   At the same time it will be allowed that determined extravagance, and a determined indisposition to save, may keep profits permanently high.   The most powerful stimulants may, under peculiar circumstances, be resisted; yet still it will not cease to be true that the natural and legitimate encouragement to the increase of capital is that increase of the power and will to save which is held out by high profits; and under circumstances in any degree similar, such increase of power and will to save must almost always be accompanied by a proportionate increase of capital.

One of the most striking instances of the truth of this remark, and a further proof of a singular resemblance in the laws that regulate the increase of capital and of population, is to be found in the rapidity with which the loss of capital is recovered during a war which does not interrupt commerce. The loans to government convert capital into revenue, and increase demand at the same time that they at first diminish the means of supply.* The necessary consequence must be an increase of profits. This naturally increases both the power and the reward of accumulation; and if only the same habits of saving prevail among the capitalists as before, the recovery of the lost stock must be rapid, just for the same kind of reason that the recovery of population is so rapid when, by some cause or other, it has been suddenly destroyed.

It is now fully acknowledged that it would be a gross error in the latter case, to imagine that, without the previous diminution of the population, the same rate of increase would still have taken place; because it is precisely the high wages occasioned by the demand for labour, which produce the effect of so rapid an increase of population. On the same principle it appears to me as gross an error to suppose that, without the previous loss of capital occasioned by the expenditure in question, capital should be as rapidly accumulated; because it is precisely the high profits of stock occasioned by the demand for commodities, and the consequent demand for

* Capital is withdrawn only from those employments where it can best be spared. It is hardly ever withdrawn from agriculture. Nothing is more common, as I have stated in the Chapter on Rent, than increased profits, not only without any capital being withdrawn from the land, but under a continual addition to it. Mr. Ricardo's assumption of constant prices would make it absolutely impossible to account theoretically for things as they are. If capital were considered as not within the pale of demand and supply, the very familiar event of the rapid recovery of capital during a war would be quite inexplicable.

the means of producing them, which at once give the power and the will to accumulate.

Though it may be allowed therefore that the laws which regulate the increase of capital are not quite so distinct as those which regulate the increase of population, yet they are certainly just of the same kind; and it is equally vain, with a view to the permanent increase of wealth, to continue converting revenue into capital, when there is no adequate demand for the products of such capital, as to continue encouraging marriage and the birth of children without a demand for labour and an increase of the funds for its maintenance.

SECTION IV.

Of the Fertility of the Soil, considered as a Stimulus to the continued Increase of Wealth.

In speaking of the fertility of the soil as not affording an adequate stimulus to the continued increase of wealth, it must always be recollected that a fertile soil gives at once the greatest natural capability of wealth that a country can possibly possess. When the deficient wealth of such a country is mentioned, it is not intended always to speak positively, but comparatively, that is with reference to its natural capabilites; and so understood, the proposition will be liable to few or no

376 ON THE IMMEDIATE CAUSES [CH. VII.

exceptions. Perhaps, indeed, it may be said that no instance has occurred, in modern times, of a large and very fertile country having made full use of its natural resources ; while there have been many instances of small and unfertile states having accumulated within their narrow limits, by means of foreign commerce, a degree of wealth very greatly exceeding the proportion which should belong to them, in reference to their physical capabilities.

If a small body of people were possessed of a rich and extensive inland territory, divided into large proportions, and not favourably situated with respect to markets, a very long period might elapse before the state became wealthy and populous, notwithstanding the fertility of the soil and the consequent facility of production. The nature of such a soil would make it yield a profit or rent to the owner in its uncultivated state. He would set a value therefore upon his property, as a source of profit as well as of power and -amusement ; and though it was capable of yielding much more raw produce than he and his immediate dependents could consume, he would by no means be disposed to allow others to seize on it, and divide it at their pleasure. He would probably let out considerable portions of it for small rents. But the tenant of these portions, if there were no foreign vent for the raw produce, and the commodities which contribute to the conveniences and luxuries of life were but little known, would have but small incitement to call forth the resources of his land, and give encouragement to a rapid increase of

population.   By employing ten families he might
perhaps, owing to the richness of the soil, obtain
food for fifty; but he would find no proportionate
market for this additional food, and would be soon
sensible that he had wasted his time and attention
in superintending the labour of so many persons.
He would be disposed therefore to employ a smaller
number; or if, from motives of humanity, or any
other reason, he was induced to keep more than
were necessary for the supply of the market, upon
the supposition of their being tolerably industrious,
he would be quite indifferent to their industry, and
his labourers would naturally acquire the most
indolent habits.   Such habits would naturally be
generated both in the masters and servants by such
circumstances, and when generated, a considerable
time and considerable stimulants are necessary to
get rid of them.

It has been said, that those who have food and
necessaries at their disposal will not be long in
want of workmen, who will put them in possession
of some of the objects most useful and desirable
to them.*   But this appears to be directly contradicted by experience.   If the establishment,
extension, and refinement of domestic manufactures were so easy a matter, our ancestors would
not have remained for many hundred years so ill
supplied with them; and been obliged to expend
the main part of their raw produce in the support
of idle retainers.   They might be very ready, when

* Ricardo's. Princ. of Polit. Econ. ch. xxi. p. 363. 2d. edit.

they had the opportunity, to exchange their surplus raw produce for the foreign commodities
with which they were acquainted, and which they
had learnt to estimate. But it would be a very
difficult thing, and very ill suited to their habits
and degree of information, to employ their power
of commanding labour in setting up manufactures on their own estates. Though the land
might be rich, it might not suit the production of
the materials most wanted; and the necessary machinery, the necessary skill in using it, and the necessary intelligence and activity of superintendance,
would all unavoidably be deficient at first, and
under the circumstances supposed, must be of
very slow growth; so that after those ruder and
more indispensable articles were supplied, which
are always wanted and produced in an early stage
of society, it is natural enough that a great lord
should prefer distinguishing himself by a few
splendid foreign commodities, if he could get
them, and a great number of retainers, than by a
large quantity of clumsy manufactures, which involved great trouble of superintendance.

It is certainly true, however, taking as an instance an individual workman, and supposing him
to possess a given degree of industry and skill,
that the less time he is employed in procuring food,
the more time will he be able to devote to the procuring of conveniences and luxuries; but to apply
this truth to whole nations, and to infer that the
greater is the facility of procuring food, the more
abundantly will the people be supplied with con-

veniences and luxuries would be one among the
many rash and false conclusions which are often
made from the want of due attention to the change
which the application of a proposition may make
in the premises on which it rests. In the present
case, all depends upon the supposition of a given
degree of industry and skill, and the means of employing them. But if, after the necessaries of life
were obtained, the workman should consider indolence as a greater luxury than those which he was
likely to procure by further labour, the proposition
would at once cease to be true. And as a matter
of fact, confirmed by all the accounts we have of
nations, in the different stages of their progress, it
must be allowed that this choice seems to be very
general in the early periods of society, and by no
means uncommon in the most improved states.

Few indeed and scanty would be the portion of
conveniences and luxuries found in society, if
those who are the main instruments of their production had no stronger motives for their exertions
than the desire of enjoying them. It is the want
of *necessaries* which mainly stimulates the labouring classes to produce luxuries; and were this
stimulus removed or greatly weakened, so that
the necessaries of life could be obtained with
very little labour, instead of more time being devoted to the production of conveniences, there is
every reason to think that less time would be so
devoted.

At an early period of cultivation, when only rich
soils are worked, as the quantity of corn is the

a

greatest, compared with the quantity of labour required to produce it, we ought always to find a
small portion of the population engaged in agriculture, and a large portion engaged in administer-
ing to the other wants of the society.   And there
can be little doubt that this is the state of things
which we really should see, were it true, that if
the means of maintaining labour be found, there
can be no difficulty in making it produce objects
of adequate value; or that when food can be obtained with facility, more time will be devoted to
the production of conveniences and luxuries.   But
in examining the state of unimproved countries,
what do we really see?—almost invariably, a much
larger proportion of the whole people employed on
the land than in those countries where the increase
of population has occasioned the necessity of resorting to poor soils; and less time instead of more
time devoted to the production of conveniences
and luxuries.

b

Of the great landed nations of Europe, and indeed of the world, England, with only one or two
exceptions, is supposed to have pushed its cultivation the farthest; and though the natural qualities
of its whole soil by no means stand very high in the
scale of comparative richness, there is a smaller proportion of the people employed in agriculture, and
a greater proportion employed in the production of
conveniences and luxuries, or living on monied incomes, than in any other agricultural country of
the world.   According to a calculation of Susmilch,
in which he enumerates the different proportions

of people in different states, who live in towns,
and are not employed in agriculture, the highest
is that of seven to three, or seven people living in
the country to three living in the towns :* whereas
in England, the proportion of those engaged in
agriculture, compared with the rest of the population, is less than as two to three.†

This is a very extraordinary fact, and affords a
striking proof how very dangerous it is, in political
economy, to draw conclusions from the physical
quality of the materials which are acted upon,
without reference to the moral as well as physical
qualities of the agents.

It is undoubtedly a physical quality of very rich
land, if worked by people possessing a given degree of industry and skill, to yield a large quantity
of produce, compared with the number of hands
employed; but, if the facility of production which
rich land gives has the effect, under certain circumstances, of preventing the growth of industry
and skill, the land may become practically less
productive, compared with the number of persons
employed upon it, than if it were not distinguished
for its richness.

Upon the same principle, the man who can procure the necessary food for his family, by two
days labour in the week, has the physical power of
working much longer to procure conveniences

a

b

α

β

* Susmilch, vol. iii. p. 60. Essay on Population, vol. i. p. 459.
edit.. 5th.   In foreign states very few persons live in the country
who are not engaged in agriculture ; but it is not so in England.

† Population Abstracts, 1811.

and luxuries, than the man who must employ four
days in procuring food; but if the facility of getting
food creates habits of indolence, this indolence
may make him prefer the luxury of doing little or
nothing, to the luxury of possessing conveniences
and comforts; and in this case, he may devote less
time to the working for conveniences and comforts,
and be more scantily provided with them than if
he had been obliged to employ more industry in
procuring food.

Among the crowd of countries which tend more
or less to illustrate and confirm by their present
state the truth of these positions, none perhaps
will do it more strikingly than the Spanish dominions in America, of which M. Humboldt has
lately given so valuable an account.

Speaking of the different plants which are cultivated in New Spain, he says of the banana, " Je
doute qu'il existe une autre plante sur le globe qui,
sur un si petit espace de terrain, puisse produire une
masse de substance nourrissante aussi considérable."*
He calculates in another place more particularly,
that " dans un pays éminemment fertile un demi
hectare, ou un arpent légal cultivé en bananes de la
grande espèce, peut nourrir plus de cinquantes individus, tandis qu'en Europe le même arpent ne don-
neroit par an, en supposant le huitième grain, que
576 kilogrammes de farine de froment, quantité
qui n'est pas suffisante pour la subsistance de deux
individus : aussi rien ne frappe plus l'Européen

* Essai Politique sur la Nouvelle Espagne, tom. iii. l. iv. c. ix.
p. 28.

récemment arrivé dans la zone torride que l'extrême petitisse des terrains cultivés autour d'une cabane qui renferme une famille nombreuse d'indigènes."*

It appears further, that the banana is cultivated with a very trifling quantity of labour, and " se perpétue sans que l'homme y mette d'autre soin que de couper les tiges dont le fruit a mûri, et de donner à la terre une ou deux fois par an un léger labour en piochant autour des racines."†

What immense powers of production are here described ! What resources for unbounded wealth, if effectively called into action ? Yet what is the actual state of things in this fertile region. M. Humboldt says, " On entend souvent répéter dans les colonies Espagnoles, que les habitans de la région chaude (tierra caliente) ne pourront sortir de l'état d'apathie dans lequel ils sont plongés depuis des siècles, que lorsqu'une *cedule royale* ordonnera la destruction des bananiers. Le remède est violent ; et ceux qui le proposent avec tant de chaleur ne déploient généralement pas plus d'activité que le bas-peuple qu'ils veulent forcer au travail en augmentant la masse de ses besoins. Il faut espérer que l'industrie fera des progrès parmi les Mexicains sans qu'on emploie des moyens de destruction. En considérant d'ailleurs la facilité avec laquelle l'homme se nourrit dans un climat où croissent les bananiers, on ne doit pas s'étonner que dans la région equinoctiale du nouveau con-

* Nouvelle Espagne, tom. iii. l. iv. c. ix. p. 36.
† Id. p. 28.

tinent la civilisation ait commencé dans les montagnes, sur un sol moins fertile, sous un ciel moins favorable au développement des êtres organisés où le besoin même réveille l'industrie.

" Au pied de la Cordillère dans les vallées humides des Intendances de Vera-Cruz, de Valladolid, ou de Guadalaxara, un homme qui employe seulement deux jours de la semaine à un travail peu pénible peut fournir de la subsistance à une famille entière."*

It appears then, that the extreme fertility of these countries, instead of affording an adequate stimulus to a rapid increase of wealth and population, has produced, under the actual circumstances in which they have been placed, a degree of indolence which has kept them poor and thinly peopled after the lapse of ages. Though the labouring classes have such ample time to work for conveniences and comforts, they are almost destitute of them. And, even in the necessary article of food, their indolence and improvidence prevent them from adopting those measures which would secure them against the effects of unfavourable seasons. M. Humboldt states that famines are common to almost all the equinoctial regions; and observes that, " sous la zone torride, où une main bienfaisante semble avoir répandu le germe de l'abondance, l'homme insouciant et phlegmatique éprouve périodiquement un manque de nourriture que l'in-

* Humboldt's Nouvelle Espagne, tom. iii. l. iv. c. ix. p. 38.

dustrie des peuples cultivés éloigne des régions les plus stériles du Nord.''*

It is possible, however, that the heat of the climate in these lower regions of New Spain, and an inferior degree of healthiness compared with the higher regions, though by no means such as to preclude a full population, may have assisted in keeping them poor and thinly peopled.   But when we ascend the Cordilleras, to climates which seem to be the finest in the world, the scene which presents itself is not essentially different.

The chief food of the lower classes of the inhabitants on the elevated plains of the Cordilleras, is maize ; and maize, though not so productive, compared with the labour employed upon it, as the banana, exceeds very greatly in productiveness the grains of Europe, and even of the United States. Humboldt states, that " La fécondité du *thaolli,* ou mais Mexicain, est au-delà de tout ce que l'on peut imaginer en Europe.   La plante, favorisée par de fortes chaleurs et par beaucoup d'humidité, aquiert une hauteur de deux à trois mètres.   Dans les belles plaines qui s'étendent depuis San Juan del Rio à Quiretaro, par exemple, dans les terres de la grande metairie de l'Esperanza, un fanègue de maïs en produit quelquefois huit cents ; des terreins fertiles en donnent, année commune, trois à quatre cents.   Dans les environs de Valladolid on regarde comme mauvaise une récolte qui ne donne que 130 ou 150 fois la semence.   Là où le sol est

* Essai Politique sur la Nouvelle Espagne, tom. i. l. ii. c. v. p. 358.

le plus stérile, on compte encore soixante ou quatre-vingt grains. On croit qu'en général le produit du maïs peut être évalué dans la région equinoctiale du royaume de la Nouvelle Espagne à cent cinquante pour un."*

This great fertility produces, as might be expected, its natural effect of making the maintenance of a family in ordinary times extremely easy.

In the town of Mexico itself, where provisions are very considerably dearer than in the country, on account of the badness of the roads, and the expense of carriage, the very dregs of the people are, according to Humboldt, able to earn their maintenance by only one or two days' labour in the week.† " Les rues de Mexico fourmillent de vingt à trente mille malheureux *(Saragates Guachinangos)*, dont la plûpart passent la nuit à la belle étoile, et s'étendent le jour au soleil, le corps tout nu enveloppé dans une couverture de flanelle. Cette lie du peuple, Indiens et Metis, présentent beaucoup d'analogie avec les Lazaronis de Naples. Paresseux, insoucians, sobres comme eux, les Guachinangos n'ont cependant aucune férocité dans le caractère ; ils ne demandent jamais l'aumône : s'ils travaillent un ou deux jours par semaine, ils gagnent ce qu'il leur faut pour acheter du pulque, ou de ces canards qui couvrent les lagunes Mexicaines, et que l'on rôtit dans leur propre graisse."

But this picture of poverty is not confined to

* Essai Politique sur la Nouvelle Espagne, tom. iii. l. iv. c. ix. p. 56.

† Tom. ii. l. ii. c. vii. p. 37.

the dregs of the inhabitants of a large town. " Les
Indiens Mexicains, en les considérant en masse,
présentent le tableau d'une grande misère. Re-
légués dans les terres les moins fertiles ; indolens
par caractère, et plus encore par suite de leur situation politique, les natifs ne vivent qu'au jour le
jour."*

With these habits they are little likely to make
provision against the occasional failures in the
crops of maize, to which these crops are peculiarly
liable ; and consequently, when such failures take
place, they are exposed to extreme distress.
Speaking generally of the obstacles to the progress of population in New Spain, Humboldt seems
to consider famine and the diseases which it produces, as the most cruel and destructive of all.
" Les Indiens Américains," (he says) " comme les
habitans de l'Indostan, sont accoûtumés à se con-
tenter de la moindre quantité d'alimens qu'exige
le besoin de la vie ; ils augmentent en nombre sans
que l'accroissement des moyens de subsistance soit
proportional à cette augmentation de population.
Indolens par caractère, et surtout à cause de la
position dans laquelle ils se trouvent sous un beau
climat, sur un sol généralement fertile, les indigènes ne cultivent en maïs, en pommes de terre, et
en froment que ce qu'il leur faut pour leur propre
nourriture, ou tout au plus ce que requiert la con-
sommation des villes et celle des mines les plus
voisines." And further on, he says, " le manque

* Tom. i. liv. ii. c. vi. p. 429.

de proportion qui existe entre les progrès de la population et l'accroissement de la quantité d'alimens
produite par la culture, renouvelle le spectacle
affligeant de la famine chaque fois qu'une grande
sécheresse ou quelque autre cause locale a gâté
la récolte du maïs."[*]

These accounts strikingly shew the indolence
and improvidence which prevail among the people.
Such habits must necessarily act as formidable
obstacles in the way of a rapid increase of
wealth and population. Where they have been
once fully established, they are not likely to
change, except gradually and slowly under a
course of powerful and effective stimulants. And
while the extreme inequality of landed property
continues, and no sufficient vent is found for the
raw produce in foreign commerce, these stimulants
will be furnished very slowly and inadequately.

That the indolence of the natives is greatly aggravated by their political situation, cannot for a
moment be doubted; but that, in spite of this situation, it yields in a great measure to the usual excitements is sufficiently proved by the rapid cultivation which takes place in the neighbourhood of
a new mine, where an animated and effective demand is created for labour and produce. " Bien-
tôt le besoin réveille l'industrie ; on commence à
labourer le sol dans les ravins, et sur les pentes des
montagnes voisines, par tout où le roc est couvert
de terreau : des fermes s'établissent dans le voisi-

[*] Nouvelle Espagne, tom. i, liv. ii. c. v. pp. 355 et 356.

nage de la mine : la cherté des vivres, le prix considérable auquel la concurrence des acheteurs
maintient tous les produits de l'agriculture, dé-
dommagent ·le cultivateur des privations aux-
quelles l'expose la vie pénible des montagnes."*

When these are the effects of a really brisk demand for produce and labour, we cannot be at a
loss for the main cause of the slow cultivation
which has taken place over the greatest part of
the country.   Except in the neighbourhood of the
mines and near the great towns, the effective demand for produce is not such as to induce the
great proprietors to bring their immense tracts of
land properly into cultivation : and the population,
which, as we have seen, presses hard against
the limits of subsistence, evidently exceeds in general the demand for labour, or the number of persons which the country can employ with regularity and constancy in the actual state of its agriculture and manufactures.

In the midst of an abundance of fertile land, it
appears that the natives are often very scantily supplied with it.   They would gladly cultivate portions of the extensive districts held by the great
proprietors, and could not fail of thus deriving an
ample subsistence for themselves and families ; but
in the actual state of the demand for produce in
many parts of the country, and in the actual state
of the ignorance and indolence of the natives, such
tenants might not be able to pay a rent equal to

a

* Nouvelle Espagne, tom. iii. liv. iv. c. ix. p. 12.

what the land would yield in its uncultivated state,
and in this case they would seldom be allowed to
intrude upon such domains ; and thus lands which
might be made capable of supporting thousands of
people, may be left to support a few hundreds of
cattle.

Speaking of a part of the Intendency of Vera
Cruz, Humboldt says, " Aujourd'hui des espaces
de plusieurs lieues carrées sont occupés par deux
ou trois cabanes, autour desquelles errent des bœufs
à demi-sauvages.   Un petit nombre de familles
puissantes, et qui vivent sur le plateau central,
possèdent la plus grande partie du littoral des Intendances de Vera Cruz, et de San Luis Potosi.
Aucune loi agraire ne force ces riches propriétaires
de vendre leurs majorats, s'ils persistent à ne pas
vouloir défricher eux-mêmes des terres immenses
qûi en dépendent."*

a   Among proprietors of this description, caprice
and indolence might often prevent them from
cultivating their lands. Generally, however, it
might be expected, that these tendencies would
yield, at least in a considerable degree, to the more
steady influence of self-interest.   But a vicious
division of territory prevents the motive of interest from operating so strongly as it ought to do
in the extension of cultivation. Without sufficient foreign commerce to give value to the raw
produce of the land ; and before the general introduction of manufactures had opened channels

* Tom. ii. l. iii. c. viii. p. 342.

for domestic industry, the demand of the great proprietors for labour would be very soon supplied; and beyond this, the labouring classes would have nothing to give them for the use of their lands. Though the landholders might have ample power to support an extended population on their estates, the very slender increase of enjoyments, if any, which they might derive from it, would rarely be sufficient to overcome their natural indolence, or overbalance the possible inconveniences or trouble that might attend the proceeding. Of that encouragement to the increase of population, which arises from the division and sub-division of land as new families are brought into being, the country is deprived by the original state of property, and the feudal customs and habits which it necessarily tends to generate. And under these circumstances, if a comparative deficiency of commerce and manufactures, which great inequality of property tends rather to perpetuate than to correct, prevents the growth of that demand for labour and produce, which can alone remedy the discouragement to population occasioned by this inequality, it is obvious that Spanish America may remain for ages thinly peopled and poor, compared with her natural resources.

And so, in fact, she has remained. For though the increase of population and wealth has been considerable, particularly of late years, since the trade with the mother-country has been more open, yet altogether it has been far short of what it would have been, even under a Spanish govern-

ment, if the riches of the soil had been called forth
by a better division of landed property, or a
greater and more constant demand for raw produce.

Humboldt observes that " Les personnes qui
ont réfléchi sérieusement sur la richesse du sol
Mexicain savent que, par le moyen d'une culture
plus soignée, et sans supposer des travaux extra-
ordinaires pour l'irrigation des champs, la portion de
terrain déjà défriché pourroit fournir de la subsistance pour une population huit à dix fois plus
nombreuse." He then adds, very justly, " Si les
plaines fertiles d'Atalisco, de Cholula et de Puebla
ne produisent pas des récoltes plus abondantes, la
cause principale doit être cherchée dans le manque
des consommateurs, et dans les entraves que les
inégalités du sol opposent au commerce intérieur
des grains, surtout à leur transport vers les côtes
qui sont baignées par la mer des Antilles."* In
the actual state of these districts, the main and
immediate cause which retards their cultivation is
indeed the want of consumers, that is, the want of
power to sell the produce at such a price as will at
once encourage good cultivation, and enable the
farmers to give the landlords something that they
want, for the use of their land. And nothing is
so likely to prevent this price from being obtained, as any obstacles natural or artificial to internal and external commerce.

That the slow progress of New Spain in wealth

* Tom. iii. l. iv. c. ix. p. 89.

and population, compared with its prodigious resources, has been more owing to want of demand
than want of capital, may fairly be inferred from
the actual state of its capital, which, according
to Humboldt, is rather redundant than deficient.
Speaking of the cultivation of sugar, which he
thinks might be successfully carried on in New
Spain, he says, " La Nouvelle Espagne, outre l'a-
vantage de sa population, en a encore un autre très
important, celui d'une masse énorme de capitaux
amoncelés chez les propriétaires des mines ou entre
les mains de négocians qui se sont retirés du commerce."*

Altogether the state of New Spain, as described
by Humboldt, clearly shews—

1st. That the power of supporting labour may
exist to a much greater extent than the will.

2dly. That the time employed in working for
conveniences and luxuries is not always great in
proportion as the time employed in working for
food is small.

3dly. That the deficient wealth of a fertile country may be more owing to want of demand than
want of capital.

And, in general, that fertility of soil alone is
not an adequate stimulus to the continued increase
of wealth.

It is not necessary, however, to go so far as the
Spanish dominions in America, to illustrate these
propositions. The state of the mother-country
itself, and of most of the countries of Europe,

* Tom. iii. l. iv. c. x. p. 178.

would furnish the same conclusions. We need not indeed go farther than Ireland to see a confirmation of them to a very considerable extent.

The cultivation of the potatoe, and its adoption as the general food of the lower classes of the people in Ireland, has rendered the land and labour necessary to maintain a family, unusually small, compared with most of the countries of Europe. The consequence of this facility of production, unaccompanied by such a train of fortunate circumstances as would give it full effect in the increase of wealth, is a state of things resembling, in many respects, countries less advanced in civilization and improvement.

The prominent feature of Ireland is, the power which it possesses and actually exercises, of supporting a much greater population than it can employ, and the natural and necessary effect of this state of things, is the very general prevalence of habits of indolence. The landed proprietors and principal tenants being possessed of food and necessaries, or at least of the ready means of procuring them, have found workmen in abundance at their command; but these workmen not finding sufficient employment in the farms on which they had settled, have rarely been able to put their landlords in possession of the objects " most useful and most desirable" to them. Sometimes, indeed, from the competition for land occasioned by an overflowing population, very high rents have been given for small portions of ground fit for the growth of potatoes; but as the power of paying such rents must depend, in a considerable degree, upon the power of getting work, the number of families upon an estate, who can pay high money rents, must have an obvious limit. This limit, there is reason to believe, has been often found in the inability of the Irish cottar to pay the rent which he had contracted for; and it is generally understood that the most intelligent Irish landlords, influenced both by motives of humanity and interest, are now endeavouring to check the progress of that redundant population upon their estates, which, while it generates an excessive degree of poverty and misery as well as indolence, seldom makes up to the employer, in the lowness of wages, for the additional number of hands which he is obliged to hire, or call upon for their appointed service in labour. He is now generally aware that a smaller number of more industrious labourers would enable him to raise a larger produce for the consumption of towns and manufacturers, and at the same time that they would thus contribute more largely to the general wealth of the country, would be in a more happy condition themselves, and enable him to derive a larger and more certain rent from his estates. It may fairly be said therefore, that the possessors of food and necessaries in Ireland have not been able to obtain the objects most useful and desirable to them in return.

a

The indolence of the country-labourers in Ireland has been universally remarked. And whether this arises from there being really little for them to do in the actual state of things, or from a natural tendency to idleness, not to be overcome by ordi-

b

nary stimulants; it is equally true that the large portion of time of which they have the command, beyond what is employed in providing themselves with necessaries, does not certainly produce the effect of making them abound in conveniences and luxuries. The poor clothing and worse lodging of the Irish peasant are as well known as the spare time which it might be expected would be the means of furnishing him amply with all kinds of conveniences.

In defence, however, of the Irish peasant, it may be truly said, that in the state of society in which he has been placed, he has not had a fair trial; he has not been subjected to the ordinary stimulants which produce industrious habits. In almost every part of the island, particularly in the south and west, the population of the country districts is greater than the actual business to be done on the land can employ. If the people, therefore, were ever so industriously inclined, it is not possible for them all to get regular employment in the occupations which belong to the soil. In the more hilly parts of the country which are devoted chiefly to pasture, this impossibility is more particularly striking. A small farm among the Kerry mountains may support perhaps a large family, among whom are a number of grown-up sons; but the business to be done upon the farm is a mere trifle. The greatest part of it falls to the share of the women. What remains for the men cannot occupy them for a number of hours equal to a single day in the week; and the consequence is, they are generally

a

seen loitering about, as if time was absolutely of no value to them.

They might, one should suppose, with all this leisure, employ themselves in building better houses, or at least in improving them, and keeping them neat and clean. But with regard to the first, some difficulties may occur in procuring materials; and with regard to the second, it appears from experience, that the object is either not understood, or not considered as worth the trouble it would cost.

They might also, one should suppose, grow or purchase the raw materials of clothing, and work them up at home; and this in fact is really done to a certain extent. Most of the linen and woollen *a* they wear is prepared by themselves. But the raw materials, when not of home growth, cannot be purchased without great difficulty, on account of the low money prices of labour; and in preparing them for wear, the temptations to indolence will generally be too powerful for human weakness, when the question is merely about a work which may be deferred or neglected, with no other effect than that of being obliged to wear old clothes a little longer, in a country where custom is certainly *b* in their favour.

If the Irish peasant could find such a market for the result of his in-door occupations as would give him constant employment at a fair money price, his habits might soon change; but it may be doubted whether any large body of people in any country ever acquired regular and industrious habits, where they were unable to get regular and

constant work, and when, to keep themselves constantly and beneficially employed, it was necessary
to exercise a great degree of providence, energy,
and self-command.

It may be said, perhaps, that it is capital alone
which is wanted in Ireland, and that if this want
were supplied, all her people might be easily employed.   That one of the great wants of Ireland is
capital will be readily allowed; but I conceive it
would be a very great mistake to suppose that the
importation of a large quantity of capital, if it
could be effected, would at once accomplish the
object required, and create a quantity of wealth
proportioned to the labour which seems ready to
be employed in its production.   The amount of
capital which could be laid out in Ireland in preparing goods for foreign sale, must evidently depend upon the state of foreign markets; and the
amount that could be employed in domestic manufactures, must as evidently depend upon the domestic demand.   An attempt to force a foreign
market by means of capital, must necessarily occasion a premature fall of profits, and might, after
great losses, be quite ineffectual; and with regard
to the domestic demand, while the habits of the
great mass of the people are such as they are at
present, it must be quite inadequate to take off the
products of any considerable mass of new capital.
In a country, where the necessary food is obtained
with so little labour, and the population is still
equal or nearly equal to the produce, it is perhaps
impossible that the time not devoted to the produc-

tion of food should create a proportionate quantity of wealth, without a very decided taste for conveniences and luxuries among the lower classes of society, and such a power of purchasing as would occasion an effective demand for them. But it is well known, that the taste of the Irish peasant for articles of this description is yet to be formed. His wants are few, and these wants he is in the habit of supplying principally at home. Owing to the cheapness of the potatoe, which forms the principal food of the lower classes of the people, his money wages are low; and the portion which remains, after providing absolute necessaries, will go but a very little way in the purchase of conveniences. All these circumstances are most unfavourable to the increase of wealth derived from manufactures destined for home consumption. But the tastes and habits of a large body of people are extremely slow in changing; and in the mean time the application of capital in larger quantities than was suited to the progress of the change, would certainly fail to yield such profits as would encourage its continued accumulation and application in the same way. In general it may be said that demand is quite as necessary to the increase of capital as the increase of capital is to demand. They mutually act upon and encourage each other, and neither of them can proceed with vigour if the other be left far behind.

In the actual state of Ireland, I am inclined to believe, that the check which the progress of her manufactures has received, has been owing to a want of demand rather than a want of capital.

a

Her peculiar distress upon the termination of the late war had unquestionably this origin, whatever might have been the subsequent destruction of capital. And the great checks to her manufactures formerly were the unjust and impolitic restrictions imposed by England which prevented, or circum-
a scribed the demand for them. When, however, a brisk demand for any manufacture has existed, few instances I believe have occurred of its being allowed to languish through the want of capital; though there is reason to think that advances of capital have been sometimes made, which have failed to create an adequate market.

b The state of Ireland in respect to the time and labour necessary to the production of her food is such, that her capabilities for manufacturing and
c commercial wealth are prodigious. If an im-proved system of agriculture were to raise the food and raw materials required for the population with the smallest quantity of labour necessary to do it in the best manner, and the remainder of the people, instead of loitering about upon the land, were engaged in manufactures and commerce car-ried on in great and flourishing towns, Ireland would be beyond comparison richer than England. This is what is wanted to give full scope to her great natural resources; and to attain this state of things an immense capital is undoubtedly required; but it can only be employed to advantage as it is gradually called for; and a premature supply of it would be much less beneficial and less permanent in its effects, than such a change in the tastes and

habits of the lower classes of people, and such an   a
alteration in the mode of paying their labour, as
would give them both the will and the power to
purchase domestic manufactures and foreign commodities.

The state of Ireland then may be said to lead to
nearly the same conclusions as that of New Spain,
and to shew—

That the power of supporting labour may often   b
exist to a much greater extent than the will;

That the necessity of employing only a small   c
portion of time in producing food does not always
occasion the employment of a greater portion of
time in procuring conveniences and luxuries ;

That the deficiency of wealth in a fertile country may be more owing to want of demand than
to want of capital;

And, in general, that the fertility of the soil
alone is not an adequate stimulus to the permanent
increase of wealth.

SECTION V.

*Of Inventions to save Labour, considered as a Stimulus to
the continued Increase of Wealth.*

Inventions to save labour seldom take place to any
considerable extent, except when there is a decided
demand for them.   They are the natural products   d

of improvement and civilization, and, in their more perfect forms, generally come in aid of the failing powers of production on the land.   The fertility of the soil, being a gift of nature, exists whether it is wanted or not ; and must often therefore exceed for many hundred years the power of fully using it.   Inventions, which substitute machinery for manual exertions, being the result of the ingenuity of man, and called forth by his wants, will, as might be expected, seldom greatly exceed those wants.

But the same laws apply to both.   They both come under the head of facilities of production ; and in both cases a full use cannot be made of this facility, unless the power of supply which it furnishes be accompanied by an adequate extension of the market.

When a machine is invented, which, by saving labour, will bring goods into the market at a much cheaper rate than before, the most usual effect is such an extension of the demand for the commodity, by its being brought within the power of a much greater number of purchasers, that the value of the whole mass of goods made by the new machinery greatly exceeds their former value; and, notwithstanding the saving of labour, more hands, instead of fewer, are required in the manufacture.

This effect has been very strikingly exemplified in the cotton machinery of this country.   The consumption of cotton goods has been so greatly extended both at home and abroad, on account of their cheapness, that the value of the whole of

the cotton goods and twist now made exceeds, beyond comparison, the former value; while the   a
rapidly increasing population of the towns of Manchester, Glasgow, &c. during the last thirty years, amply testifies that, with a few temporary exceptions, the demand for the labour concerned in the cotton manufactures, in spite of the machinery used, has been increasing very greatly.

When the introduction of machinery has this effect, it is not easy to appreciate its enriching power, or its tendency to increase both the value and quantity of domestic and foreign commodities.

When however the commodity to which machinery is applied is not of such a nature, that its consumption can extend with its cheapness, the increase of wealth derived from it is neither so great nor so certain. Still however it may be highly beneficial; but the extent of this benefit   b
depends upon a contingency. Let us suppose a   c
number of capitalists in the habit of employing 20,000l. each in a manufacture of limited con-   d
sumption, and that machines were introduced which, by the saving of labour, would enable them to supply the actual demand for the commodity with capitals of ten thousand pounds each, instead of   e
twenty. There would, in this case, be a certain number of ten thousand pounds, and the men employed by these capitals, thrown out of employment. On the other hand, there would be a portion of revenue set free for the purchase of fresh commodities; and this demand would undoubtedly be of the greatest advantage in encouraging the

employment of the vacant capitals in other directions.   At the same time it must be recollected
that this demand is not a new one, and, even when
fully supplied, could only replace the diminution
of capital and profits in one department, occasioned by the employment of so many ten thousands, instead of twenty thousands.   But in withdrawing capital from one employment and placing
it in another, there is almost always a considerable loss.   Even if the whole of the remainder
were directly employed, it would be less in
amount.   Though it might yield a greater produce, it would not command the same quantity of
labour as before; and, unless more menial servants
were used, many persons would be thrown out of
work; and thus the power of the whole capital to
command the same quantity of labour would evidently depend upon the contingency of the vacant
capitals being withdrawn undiminished from their
old occupations, and finding immediately equivalent employment in others.

   If, in order to try the principle, we were to push it
farther, and to suppose that, without any extension
of the foreign market for our goods, we could by
means of machinery obtain all the commodities at
present in use, with one third of the labour now
applied, is it in any degree probable that the mass
of vacant capitals could be advantageously employed, or that the mass of labourers thrown out
of work could find the means of commanding an
adequate share of the national produce?   If there
were other foreign trades which, by means of the

capital and labour thrown out of employment,
might be greatly extended, the case would be at
once quite altered, and the returns of such trades
might furnish stimulants sufficient to keep up the
value of the national income.   But, if only an
increase of domestic commodities could be obtained, there is every reason to fear that the exertions of industry would slacken.   The peasant,
who might be induced to labour an additional
number of hours for tea or tobacco, might prefer
indolence to a new coat.   The tenant or small
owner of land, who could obtain the common conveniences and luxuries of life at one third of their
former price, might not labour so hard to procure
the same amount of surplus produce from the
land.   And the trader or merchant, who would
continue in his business in order to be able to
drink and give his guests claret and champagne,
might think an addition of homely commodities
by no means worth the trouble of so much constant attention.

It has been said that, when there is an income
ready for the demand, it is impossible that there
should be any difficulty in the employment of
labour and capital to supply it, as the owner
of such an income, rather than not spend it,
would purchase a table or chair that had cost the
labour of a hundred men for a year.   This may
be true, in cases of fixed monied revenues, obtained by inheritance, or with little or no trouble.
We well know that some of the Roman nobles,
who obtained their immense wealth chiefly by the

a   easy mode of plunder, sometimes gave the most enormous prices for fancied luxuries. A feather will weigh down a scale when there is nothing in the opposite one. But where the amount of the

b   incomes of a country depend, in a considerable degree, upon the exertion of labour, activity and attention, there must be something in the commodities to be obtained sufficiently desirable to balance this exertion, or the exertion will cease. And experience amply shews, by the number of persons who daily leave off business, when they might certainly have continued to improve their fortunes, that most men place some limits, however variable, to the quantity of conveniences and luxuries which they will labour for; and that very few indeed would attend a counting-house six or eight hours a day, in order to purchase commodities which have no other merit than the quantity of labour which has been employed upon them.

c   Still however it is true that, when a great income has once been created in a country, in the shape of a large mass of rents, profits and wages, a considerable resistance will be made to any essential fall in its value. It is a very just remark of

α   Hume,* that when the affairs of a society are brought to this situation; that is, when, by means of foreign trade, it has acquired the tastes necessary to give value to a great quantity of labour not employed upon actual necessaries, it may lose most of this trade, and yet continue great and

* Essays, vol. i. p. 293.

powerful, on account of the extraordinary efforts which would be made by the spare capital and ingenuity of the country to refine home manufactures, in order to supply the tastes already formed, and the incomes already created. But if we were to allow that the income of such a nation might, in this way, by possibility be maintained, there is little chance of its increasing; and it is almost certain that it would not have reached the same amount, without the market occasioned by foreign commerce.

a

Of this I think we shall be convinced, if, in our own country, we look at the quantity of goods which we export chiefly in consequence of our machinery, and consider the nature of the returns obtained for them. In the accounts of the year ended the 5th of January 1818, it appears that the exports of three articles alone in which machinery is used—cottons, woollen and hardware, including steel goods, &c. are valued at above 29 millions. And among the most prominent articles of the imports of the same year, we find coffee, indigo, sugar, tea, silks, tobacco, wines, and cotton-wool, amounting in value all together to above 18 millions out of thirty! Now I would ask how we should have obtained these valuable imports, if the foreign markets for our cottons, woollens, and hardware had not been extended with the use of machinery? And further, where we could have found substitutes at home for such imports, which would have been likely to have produced the same effects, in stimulating the cultivation of the land, the accumulation

α

b

of capital, and the increase of population? And
when to these considerations we add the fortunes
which have been made in these manufactures, the
market for which has been continually extending,
and continually requiring more capital and more
people to be employed in them; and contrast with
this state of things the constant necessity of looking out for new modes of employing the same
capital and the same people, a portion of which
would be thrown out of their old occupations by
every new invention;—we must be convinced that
the state of this country would have been totally
different from what it is, and that it would not
a   certainly have acquired the same income in rents,
profits and wages, if the same ingenuity had been
exercised in the invention of machinery, without
the same extension of the market for the commodities produced.

It may justly be doubted, whether, at the present moment, upon the supposition of our foreign
intercourse being interrupted, we should be likely
to find efficient substitutes for teas, coffee, sugar,
wines, silks, indigo, cottons, &c. so as to keep up the
b   value of our present income; but it cannot well be
doubted, that if, from the time of Edward the First,
and setting out with the actual division of landed
property which then prevailed, the foreign vent
for our commodities had remained stationary, our
revenue from the land alone would not have approached to what it is at present, and still less, the
revenue from trade and manufactures.

Even under the actual division of the landed

property in Europe, which is very much better than it was 500 years ago, most of the states of which it is composed would be comparatively un-peopled, if it were not for trade and manufactures. Without the excitements arising from the results of this sort of industry, no sufficient motives could be presented to them either to divide their great   ab
estates by sale, or to take care that they were well cultivated.

According to Adam Smith, the most important manufactures of the northern and western parts of Europe were established either in imitation of fo-reign articles, the tastes for which had been already formed by a previous foreign trade, or by the gra-dual refinement of domestic commodities till they were fit for exportation.*   In the first case, the very origin of the manufacture is made to depend upon a previous extension of market, and the im-portation of foreign articles; and in the second case, the main object and use of refining the do-mestic commodities in an inland country, appears to be the fitting them for an extensive market, without which the local advantages enjoyed would be in a great measure lost.

In carrying on the late war, we were powerfully assisted by our steam-engines, which enabled us to command a prodigious quantity of foreign pro-duce and foreign labour.   But how would their efficacy have been weakened if we could not have exported our cottons, cloths and hardware?

* Wealth of Nations, Vol. ii. B. iii. ch. iii. p. 115. 6th edit.   α

If the mines of America could be successfully worked by machinery, and the King of Spain's tax could be-increased at will, so as to make the most of this advantage, what a vast revenue might they not be made to afford him ! But it is obvious that the effects of such machinery would sink into insignificance, if the market for the precious metals were confined to the adjacent countries, and the principal effect of it was to throw capital and labour out of employment.

In the actual state of things in this country, the population and wealth of Manchester, Glasgow, Leeds, &c. have been greatly increasing; because, on account of the extending demand for their goods, more people have been continually required to work them up ; but if a much smaller number of people had been required, on account of a saving of labour from machinery, without an adequate extension of the market, it is obvious that these towns would have been comparatively poor, and thinly peopled. To what extent the spare capital and labour thrown out of employment in one district would have enriched others, it is impossible to say; and on this subject any assertion may be made, as we cannot be set right by an appeal to facts. But I would ask, whether there are any grounds in the slightest degree plausible for saying, that not only the capital spared at any time from these manufactures would be preserved and employed elsewhere; but that it would be employed as profitably, and create as much exchangeable value in other places as it would have done in

Manchester and Glasgow, with an extending market? In short, are there any plausible grounds whatever for stating that, if the twenty millions worth of cottons which we now export, were entirely stopped, either by successful foreign competition or positive prohibitions, we should have no difficulty in finding employment for our capital and labour equally advantageous to individuals in point of profit, and equally enriching to the country with respect to the exchangeable value of its revenue?

Unquestionably any country has the power of consuming all that it produces, however great in quantity; and every man in health has the *power* of applying his mind and body to productive labour for ten or twelve hours of the day. But these are dry assertions respecting the powers of a country, which do not necessarily involve any practical consequences relating to the increase of wealth. If we could not export our cottons, it is quite certain that, though we might have the power, we should not have the will, to consume them all in kind at home; and the maintenance of our national wealth and revenue would depend entirely upon the circumstance whether the capital thrown out of the cotton trade could be so applied as to produce commodities which would be estimated as highly and consumed as eagerly as the foreign goods before imported. There is no magic in foreign markets. The final demand and consumption must always be at home; and if goods could be produced at home, which would excite people to work as many hours in the day, would communicate the same enjoyments, and create a consumption of the same *value*, foreign markets would be useless. We know however from experience, that very few countries are capable of producing commodities of the same efficacy, in this respect, as those which may be obtained by a trade to various climates and soils. Without such a trade, and with a great increase in the power of production, there is no inconsiderable danger that industry, consumption, and exchangeable value would diminish; and this danger would most unquestionably be realized if the cheapness of domestic commodities occasioned by machinery, were to lead to increased saving rather than to increased expenditure.

But it is known that facilities of production have the strongest tendency to open markets, both at home and abroad. In the actual state therefore of most countries, there is little reason to apprehend any permanent evil from the introduction of machinery. The presumption always is, that it will lead to a great extension of wealth and value. But still we must allow that the pre-eminent advantages derived from the substitution of machinery for manual labour, depend upon the extension of the market for the commodities produced, and the increased stimulus given to consumption; and that, without this extension of market and increase of consumption, they must be in a great degree lost. Like the fertility of land, the invention of good machinery confers a prodigious power of production. But neither of these great powers can be called fully into action, if the situation and circumstances, or the habits and tastes of the society prevent the opening of a sufficient market, and an adequate increase of consumption.

The three great causes most favourable to production are, accumulation of capital, fertility of soil, and inventions to save labour. They all act in the same direction; and as they all tend to facilitate supply, without reference to demand, it is not probable that they should either separately or conjointly afford an adequate stimulus to the continued increase of wealth, which can only be   a
kept up by a continued increase of the demand for commodities.

SECTION VI.

Of the Necessity of a Union of the Powers of Production with the Means of Distribution, in order to ensure a continued Increase of Wealth.

We have seen that the powers of production, to whatever extent they may exist, are not alone sufficient to secure the creation of a proportionate degree of wealth. Something else seems to be necessary in order to call these powers fully into action; and this is, such a distribution of produce,   b
and such an adaptation of this produce to the wants of those who are to consume it, as constantly to increase the exchangeable value of the whole mass.   c

In individual cases, the power of producing particular commodities is called into action, in proportion to the effective demand for them ; and the greatest stimulus to their production is a high market price, or an increase of their exchangeable value, before more capital and labour have been employed upon them.

In the same manner, the greatest stimulus to the continued production of commodities, taken all together, is an increase in the exchangeable value of the whole mass, before more labour and capital have been employed upon them.   And this increase of value is effected by such a distribution of the actual produce as is best adapted to gratify the existing wants of society, and to inspire new ones.

It has been stated in a preceding section, that if all the roads and canals of the country were broken up, and the means of distributing its produce were essentially impeded, the whole value of the produce would greatly fall; indeed, it is obvious that if it were so distributed as not to be suited to the wants, tastes, and powers of the actual population in different situations, its value might sink to such a degree as to be comparatively quite inconsiderable.   Upon the same principle, if the means of distributing the produce of the country were still further facilitated, and if the adaptation of it to the wants, tastes and powers of the consumers were more complete than at present, there can be no doubt that a great increase in the value of the whole produce would follow.

But to illustrate the power of distribution in in-

creasing the mass of exchangeable value, we need
only refer to experience. Before the introduction
of good roads and canals in England, the prices   a
of produce in many country districts were extremely low compared with the same kind of produce in the London markets. After the means of
distribution were facilitated, the price of country   b
produce, and of some sorts of London produce
which were sent into the country in exchange for
it, rose; and rose in a greater degree than the
country produce fell in the London markets, or the
London produce fell in the country markets; and
consequently the value of the whole produce, or
the supplies of London and the country together,   c
was greatly increased; and while encouragement   d
was thus given to the employment of a greater
quantity of capital by the extension of demand,
the temporary rise of profits, occasioned by this
extension, would greatly contribute to furnish the
additional capital required.   ef
    It will be asked, perhaps, how an increase in   g
the exchangeable value of the whole produce of a
country is to be estimated? It has before been
stated that real value in exchange, from its very
nature, admits of no accurate and standard measure; and consequently, in the present case, no
measure can be mentioned which is perfectly satisfactory.   Yet even bullion, our most common   h
measure of value, might, in general, and for short
periods, be referred to; and though abstractedly   i
considered, wealth is nearly independent of money;
yet in the actual state of the relations of the dif-

ferent countries of the world with each other, it
rarely happens that any great increase or decrease
in the bullion value of all the commodities of a
country takes place, without an increase or decrease
of demand for commodities, compared with the
supply of them.

a   It happens however, undoubtedly, sometimes,
that the value of bullion alters, not only generally,
but in particular countries; and it is not meant to
b   be said that a country cannot possibly be stimulated to an increase of wealth after a fall has taken
place in the money-price of all its commodities.

c   As the best approximation to a measure of real
value in exchange, in application to the commodities of different countries and different times, I
before proposed a mean between corn and labour;*
and to this measure I should be disposed always
to refer, when any commodities are to be estimated,
with the exception of corn and labour themselves.
But as, in speaking of national wealth, it is necessary to include the exchangeable value of food; and
as food cannot well be the measure of food, I shall
refer generally to the labour, domestic and foreign,
which the bullion-price of the produce will command, or the sacrifices which people are willing
and able to make of their own or other persons
exertions in order to obtain it, as the best practical
measure of value that can be applied; and though
undoubtedly not accurate, yet sufficiently so for
the present purpose.

* Chap. ii, sect. vii.

General wealth, like particular portions of it, will always follow effective demand. Whenever there is a great demand for commodities, that is, whenever the exchangeable value of the whole mass will command more labour than usual at the same price, there is the same kind of reason for expecting a general increase of commodities, as there is for expecting an increase of particular commodities when their market-prices rise. And on the other hand, whenever the produce of a country estimated in the labour which it will command falls in value, it is evident that with it the power and will to purchase the same quantity of labour must be diminished, and the effective demand for an increase of produce must, for a time, be checked.

Mr. Ricardo, in his chapter on Value and Riches, has stated that " a certain quantity of clothes and provisions will maintain and employ the same number of men, and will therefore procure the same quantity of work to be done, whether they be produced by the labour of a hundred or of two hundred men; but they will be of twice the value, if two hundred have been employed in their production."* But, even taking his own peculiar estimate of value, this statement would very rarely indeed be true.   The clothes and provisions which had cost only one hundred days' labour would never, but in the most unnatural state of things, be able to procure the same quantity of work to

* Princ. of Polit. Econ. ch. xx. p. 349.

a

be done as if they had cost two hundred days'
labour. To suppose it, is to suppose that the price
of labour, estimated in necessaries, is the same at
all times and in all countries, and does not depend
upon the plenty or scarcity of necessaries compared with labour, a supposition contradicted by
universal experience. Nine quarters of wheat
will perhaps command a year's labour in England;

b

but sixteen quarters will hardly procure the same

c

quantity of work to be done in America. And in
the case either of a sudden increase of productive
labour, by a rapid conversion of revenue into capital, or a sudden increase of the productiveness of
the same quantity of labour, there is not the
slightest doubt that a given portion of necessaries
would be quite unable to set in motion the same
quantity of labour; and, if the exchangeable value
of the produce should fall in a greater ratio than
its quantity increases, (which may very easily
happen,) then the same quantity of labour would
not be set in motion by the increased quantity of
necessaries, and the progress of wealth would receive a decided check.

d

Such a check would still more obviously be the
consequence of a diminished demand for produce,
owing to the decline of foreign commerce, or any
other cause. Under these circumstances, both the
quantity and value of produce would soon be diminished; and though labour, from the want of
demand, would be very cheap, the capitalists
would soon lose both the will and the power to
employ it in the same quantity as before.

In every case, a continued increase in the value
of produce estimated in labour seems to be absolutely necessary to a continued and unchecked
increase of wealth; because without such an increase of value it is obvious that no fresh labour
can be set in motion. And in order to support this
value it is necessary that an effective distribution
of the produce should take place, and a due proportion be maintained between the objects to be
consumed and the number, wants, and powers of
the consumers, or, in other words, between the sup
ply of commodities and the demand for them.

It has already been shewn that this value cannot
be maintained in the case of a rapid accumulation
of capital occasioned by an actual and continued
diminution in the expenditure and consumption of
the higher classes of society.* Yet it will be
most readily allowed that the saving from revenue
to add to capital is an absolutely necessary step in
the progress of wealth. How then is this saving
to take place without producing the diminution of
value apprehended?

It may take place, and practically almost always
does take place, in consequence of a previous increase of value, or of revenue, in which case a
saving may be effected, not only without any diminution of demand and consumption, but under
an actual increase of demand, consumption and
value during every part of the process. And it is
in fact this previous increase of value and revenue

* Sect. III. of this chapter.

which both gives the great stimulus to accumulation, and makes that accumulation effective in the continued production of wealth.

M. Sismondi, in his late work, speaking of the limits of accumulation, observes, " On ne fait jamais après tout qu'échanger la totalité de la production de l'année contre la totalité de la production de l'année précédente."* If this were really the case, it would be difficult to say how the value of the national produce could ever be increased. But in

* Nouveaux Principes d'Economie Politique, tom. i. p. 120.
I quite agree with M. Sismondi in many of his principles respecting consumption and demand; but I do not think that the view which he takes of the formation of national revenue, on which all increase of consumption and demand depends, is just; and I can by no means go with him in the fears which he expresses about machinery, and still less in the opinion which he holds respecting the necessity of a frequent interference on the part of government to protect individuals, and classes, from the consequences of competition. With regard to population, he has misunderstood my work more than I could have expected from so able and distinguished a writer. He says, that my reasoning is completely sophistical, because I have compared the *virtual* increase of population with the *positive* increase of food. But surely I have compared the *virtual* increase of population with the *virtual* increase of food; and the *positive* increase of population with the *positive* increase of food; and the greater part of my book is taken up with the latter comparison. Practically M. Sismondi goes much farther than I do in his apprehensions of a redundant population, and proposes to repress it by all sorts of strange means. I never have recommended, nor ever shall, any other means than those of explaining to the labouring classes the manner in which their interests are affected, by too great an increase of their numbers, and of removing or weakening the positive laws which tend to discourage habits of prudence and foresight.

fact a great increase of productions may immediately find an adequate market, and experience consequently a great increase of exchangeable value, if they are so well distributed and so well adapted to the tastes and wants of the society as to excite the desire of making an adequate sacrifice in order to procure and consume them. All increase   a
of commodities shews itself first in increased revenue; and as long as they increase in value as well as in quantity by being properly distributed and the consumption properly proportioned to the supply, it is obvious that a yearly saving may take place consistently with a yearly increase of revenue and a yearly increase of expenditure and demand.

The fortune of a country, though necessarily made more slowly, is made in the same way as the   b
fortunes of individuals in trade are generally made, —by *savings*, certainly ; but by savings which are furnished from increased gains, and by no means involve a diminished expenditure on objects of luxury and enjoyment.

Many a merchant has made a large fortune although, during the acquisition of this fortune, there was perhaps hardly a single year in which he did not rather increase than diminish his expenditure in objects of luxury, enjoyment, and liberality.   The amount of capital in this country is immense, and it certainly received very great additions during the last twenty-five years;   c
but on looking back, few traces are to be found of a diminished expenditure in the maintenance of   d

unproductive labour. If some such traces however are to be found, they will be found in exact
conformity to the theory here laid down; they
will be found during a period, when, from particular circumstances, the value of the national produce
was not maintained, and there was in consequence
a great diminution of the power of expenditure,
and a great check to the production of wealth.

Perhaps it will be said, that to lay so much
stress on distribution, and to measure demand by
the exchangeable value of the whole produce, is to
exalt the gross revenue at the expense of the neat
revenue of a country, and to favour that system of
cultivation and manufacturing which employs on
each object the greatest number of hands. But I
have already shewn that the saving of labour, and
the increase of skill, both in agriculture and manufacturing industry, by enabling a country to push
its cultivation over poorer lands, without diminution of profits, and to extend far and wide the
markets for its manufactures, must tend to increase
the exchangeable value of the whole; and there
cannot be a doubt that in this country they must
have been the main sources of that rapid and as-
tonishing increase in the value of the national
wealth, which has taken place during the last
thirty or forty years.

To dwell therefore mainly on the gross revenue
of a country rather than on its neat revenue is in no
respect to under-rate the prodigious advantage derived from skill and machinery, but merely to give
that importance to the value of the whole produce

to which it is so justly entitled. No description
of national wealth, which refers only to neat revenue, can ever be in any degree satisfactory. The
Economists destroyed the practical utility of their   a
works by referring exclusively to the neat produce
of the land. And the writers who make wealth consist of rents and profits, to the exclusion of wages,
commit an error exactly of the same kind though
less in degree. Those who live upon the wages of
labour, unproductive as well as productive, re-   b
ceive and expend much the greatest part of the
annual produce, pay a very considerable sum in
taxes for the maintenance of the government,
and form by far the largest portion of its physical
force. Under the prevalence of habits of prudence, the whole of this vast mass might be nearly
as happy as the individuals of the other two classes,
and probably a greater number of them, though
not a greater proportion of them, happier. In
every point of view therefore, both in reference
to the part of the annual produce which falls to
their share, and the means of health and happiness
which it may be presumed to communicate, those
who live on the wages of labour must be considered as the most important portion of the society; and any definition of wealth which should
involve such a diminution of their numbers, as
to require for the supply of the whole population
a smaller annual produce, must necessarily be
erroneous.

In the First Chapter of this Work, having defined
wealth to be "the material objects which are ne-

α cessary, useful, and agreeable to mankind," I stated as a consequence that a country was rich or poor according to the abundance or scantiness in which these objects were supplied, compared with the extent of territory. It will be readily allowed that this definition does not include the question of what may be called the amount of disposable a produce, or the fund for taxation; but still I must consider it as a much more correct definition of the wealth of a country than any that should refer to this disposable part alone. What should we say of the wealth of this country, if it were possible that its rents and profits could remain the same, while its population and produce were reduced two-thirds? Certainly it would be much b poorer according to the above definition; and there are not many that would dissent from such a conclusion.

That it would be desirable, in a definition of national wealth, to include the consideration of disposable produce, as well as of actual quantity and value, cannot be doubted; but such a definition seems to be in its nature impossible, because in each individual case it must depend upon opinion, what increase of disposable produce should be accounted equivalent to a given diminution of gross produce.

We must content ourselves therefore with referring generally to the amount and value of national produce; and it may be subsequently stated as a separate, though very important consideration, that particular countries, with the same amount and

value of produce, have a larger or smaller proportion of that produce disposable. In this respect,
no doubt, a country with a fertile territory will
have a prodigious advantage over those whose
wealth depends almost entirely on manufactures.
With the same population, the same rate of profits,   a
and the same amount and value of produce, the
landed nation would have much the largest por-   b
tion of its wealth disposable.

Fortunately, it happens but seldom that we have
to determine the amount of advantage or disadvantage occasioned by the increase of the neat,
at the expense of the gross revenue. The interest
of individual capitalists uniformly prompts them
to the saving of labour, in whatever business they
are engaged; and both theory and experience com-
bine to shew that their successful efforts in this
direction, by increasing the powers of production,
afford the means of increasing, in the greatest
practicable degree, the amount and value of the
gross produce,* provided always that such a dis-

---

* From what has been here said, the reader will see that I can
by no means agree with Mr. Ricardo, in his chapter *On Gross and*   α
Net Revenue. I should not hesitate a moment in saying, that a
country with a neat revenue from rents and profits, consisting of
food and clothing for five millions of men, would be decidedly
richer and more powerful, if such neat revenue were obtained
from seven millions of men, rather than five, supposing them to
be equally well supported. The whole produce would be greater;
and the additional two millions of labourers would some of them
unquestionably have a part of their wages disposable. But I   c
would further ask what is to become of the capital as well as the
people in the case of such a change? It is obvious that a con-

tribution and consumption of the increased supply of commodities takes place as constantly to increase their exchangeable value.

In general, an increase of produce and an increase of value go on together; and this is that natural and healthy state of things, which is most favourable to the progress of wealth. An increase in the quantity of produce depends chiefly upon the power of production, and an increase in the value of produce upon its distribution. Production and distribution are the two grand elements of wealth, which, combined in their due proportions, are capable of carrying the riches and population of the earth in no great length of time to the utmost limits of its possible resources; but which taken separately, or combined in undue proportions, produce only, after the lapse of many thousand years, the scanty riches and scanty population, which are at present scattered over the face of the globe.

siderable portion of it must become redundant and useless. I quite agree with Mr. Ricardo, however, in approving all saving of labour and inventions in machinery; but it is because I think that their tendency is to increase the gross produce and to make room for a larger population and a larger capital. If the saving of labour were to be accompanied by the effects stated in Mr. Ricardo's instance, I should agree with M. Sismondi and Mr. Owen in deprecating it as a great misfortune.

SECTION VII.

*Of the Distribution occasioned by the Division of landed
Property considered as the Means of increasing the exchangeable Value of the whole Produce.*

The causes most favourable to that increase of
value which depends upon distribution are, 1st,
the division of landed property ; 2dly, internal and
external commerce; 3dly, the maintenance of un-   a
productive consumers.

In the first settlement and colonization of new
countries, an easy division and subdivision of the
land is a point of the very highest importance.
Without a facility of obtaining land in small portions by those who have accumulated small capitals, and of settling new proprietors upon the   b
soil, as new families branch off from the parent
stocks, no adequate effect can be given to the principle of population.   This facility of settling the   c
rising population upon the soil is still more im-
periously necessary in inland countries, which are
not favourably situated for external and internal
commerce.   Countries of this description, if, from
the laws and customs relating to landed property,
great difficulties are thrown in the way of its distribution, may remain for ages very scantily peopled, in spite of the principle of population; while
the easy division and subdivision of the land as

new families arise to be provided for, might, with comparatively little commerce, furnish an effective demand for population, and create a produce which would have no inconsiderable value in exchange. Such a country would probably have a small neat produce compared with its gross produce; it would also be greatly deficient in the amount of its manufactures and mercantile products; yet still its actual produce and population might be respectable; and for the increase of exchangeable value which had produced these effects, it would be mainly indebted to that distribution of the produce which had arisen from the easy division of land.

The rapid increase of the United States of America, taken as a whole, has undoubtedly been aided very greatly by foreign commerce, and particularly by the power of selling raw produce, obtained with little labour, for European commodities which have cost much labour. But the cultivation of a great part of the interior territory has depended in a considerable degree upon the cause above stated; and the facility with which even common workmen, if they were industrious and economical for some years, could become new settlers and small proprietors of land, has given prodigious effect to that high money price of labour, which could not have taken place without foreign commerce; and together they occasioned yearly that extraordinary increase of exchangeable value, which so distinguished the progress of the establishments in North

America, compared with any others with which we are acquainted.

Over almost all Europe a most unequal and vicious division of landed property was established   a
during the feudal times. In some states the laws, which protected and perpetuated this division, have been greatly weakened, and by the aids of commerce and manufactures have been rendered comparatively inefficient. But in others these laws still remain in great force, and throw very great obstacles in the way of increasing wealth and population. A very large proprietor, surrounded by very poor peasants, presents a distribution of property most unfavourable to effective demand.   b

Adam Smith has well described the slack kind   α
of cultivation which was likely to take place, and did in fact take place, among the great proprietors of the middle ages. But not only were they bad cultivators and improvers ; and for a time perhaps deficient in a proper taste for manufactured products; yet, even if they had possessed these tastes in the degree found to prevail at present, their inconsiderable numbers would have prevented their demand from producing any important mass of such wealth. We hear of great splendour among princes and nobles in every period of history. The difficulty was not so much to inspire the rich with a love of finery, as to break down their immense properties, and to create a greater number of demanders who were able and willing to pur-   c
chase the results of productive labour. This, it is obvious, could only be effected very gradually.

a   That the increasing love of finery might have assisted considerably in accomplishing this object is
highly probable; but these tastes alone, unaccom-
b   panied by a better distribution of property, would
have been quite inefficient. The possessor of
numerous estates, after he had furnished his man-
sion or castle splendidly, and provided himself
with handsome clothes and handsome carriages,
would not change them all every two months,
merely because he had the power of doing it.
Instead of indulging in such useless and trouble-
some changes, he would be more likely to keep a
number of servants and idle dependants, to take
lower rents with a view of having a greater command over his tenants, and perhaps to sacrifice the
produce of a considerable portion of his land in
order to encourage more game, and to indulge,
with more effect and less interruption, in the plea-
sures of the chase. Thirty or forty proprietors,
with incomes answering to between one thousand
and five thousand a year, would create a much
c   more effective demand for wheaten bread, good
meat, and manufactured products, than a single
proprietor possessing a hundred thousand a year.

      It is physically possible indeed for a nation,
with a comparatively small body of very rich proprietors, and a large body of very poor workmen, to
d   push both the produce of the land and manufactures to the greatest extent, that the resources and
e   ingenuity of the country would admit. Perhaps
under such a division of property the powers of
production might be rendered the greatest possible;

but, in order to call them forth, we must suppose a
passion among the rich for the consumption of manufactures, and the results of productive labour,
much more excessive than has ever been witnessed
in human society. And the consequence is, that no
instance has ever been known of a country which
has pushed its natural resources to a great extent,
with a small proportionate body of persons of property, however rich and luxurious they might be.
Practically it has always been found that the excessive wealth of the few is in no respect equivalent, with regard to effective demand, to the more   a
moderate wealth of the many. A large body of
manufacturers and merchants can only find a market for their commodities among a numerous class
of consumers above the rank of mere workmen and   b
labourers. And experience shews us that manufacturing wealth is at once the consequence of a better distribution of property, and the cause of further
improvements in such distribution, by the increase
in the proportion of the middle classes of society,
which the growth of manufacturing and mercantile
capital cannot fail to create.

But though it be true that the division of landed
property, and the diffusion of manufacturing and
mercantile capital to a certain extent, are of the
utmost importance to the increase of wealth; yet
it is equally true that, beyond a certain extent,
they would impede the progress of wealth as much
as they had before accelerated it. There is a certain elevation at which the projectile will go the

farthest; but if it be directed either higher or lower, it will fall short. With a comparatively small proportion of rich proprietors, who would prefer menial service and territorial influence to an excessive quantity of manufactured and mercantile products, the power of supplying the results of productive labour would be much greater than the will to consume them, and the progress of wealth would be checked by the want of effective demand.* With an excessive proportion of small proprietors both of land and capital, all great improvements on the land, all great enterprizes in commerce and manufactures, and all the wonders described by Adam Smith, as resulting from the division of labour, would be at an end; and the progress of wealth would be checked by a failure in the powers of supply.

It will be found, I believe, true that all the great results in political economy, respecting wealth, depend upon *proportions*; and it is from overlooking this most important truth, that so many errors have prevailed in the prediction of consequences; that nations have sometimes been enriched when it was expected that they would be impoverished, and impoverished when it was ex-

* It is perhaps just possible to conceive a passion for menial service, which would stimulate landlords to cultivate lands in the best way, in order to support the greatest quantity of such attendants. This would be the same thing as the passion for population adverted to in a former section. Such a passion, to the extent here supposed, may be *possible*; but scarcely any supposition can be less probable.

pected that they would be enriched ; and that such
contradictory opinions have occasionally prevailed
respecting the most effective encouragements to
the increase of wealth. But there is no part of the
whole subject, where the efficacy of proportions in
the production of wealth is so strikingly exemplified, as in the division of landed and other property;
and where it is so very obvious that a division to a
certain extent must be beneficial, and beyond a
certain extent prejudicial to the increase of wealth.

On the effects of a great sub-division of property,
a fearful experiment is now making in France.
The law of succession in that country divides property of all kinds among all the children equally,
without right of primogeniture or distinction of
sex, and allows but a small portion of it to be disposed of by will.

This law has not yet prevailed long enough
to shew what its effects are likely to be on the
national wealth and prosperity. If the state of
property in France appears at present to be favourable to industry and demand, no inference
can thence be drawn that it will be favourable in future. It is universally allowed that
a division of property to a certain extent is extremely desirable; and so many traces yet remain almost all over Europe of the vast landed
possessions which have descended from the feudal
times, that there are not many states in which
such a law as that of France might not be of use,
with a view to wealth, for a certain number of
years. But if such a law were to continue per-

manently to regulate the descent of property in
France; if no modes of evading it should be invented, and if its effects should not be weakened
by the operation of an extraordinary degree of prudence in marriage, which prudence such a law
would certainly tend to discourage, there is every
reason to believe that the country, at the end of a
century, will be quite as remarkable for its extraordinary poverty and distress, as for its unusual
equality of property. The owners of the minute
divisions of landed property will be, as they always
are, peculiarly without resource, and must perish
in great numbers in every scarcity. Scarcely any
will be rich but those who receive salaries from the
government.

In this state of things, with little or none of the
natural influence of property to check at once the
power of the crown and the violence of the people,
it is not possible to conceive that such a mixed
government as France has now established can
be maintained. Nor can I think that a state of
things, in which there would be so much poverty,
could be favourable to the existence and duration
of a republic. And when, in addition to this, we
consider how extremely difficult it is, under any
circumstances, to establish a well-constituted republic, and how dreadfully the chances are against
its continuance, as the experience of all history
shews; it is not too much to say, that no well-
grounded hope could be entertained of the permanent prevalence of such a form of government.

But the state of property above described would
be the very soil for a military despotism. If the

government did not adopt the Eastern mode of considering itself as sole territorial proprietor, it might at least take a hint from the Economists, and declare itself co-proprietor with the landlords, and from this source, (which might still be a fertile one, though the landlords, on account of their numbers, might be poor,) together with a few other taxes, the army might easily be made the richest part of the society; and it would then possess an overwhelming influence, which, in such a state of things, nothing could oppose. The despot might now and then be changed, as under the Roman emperors, by the Prætorian guards; but the despotism would certainly rest upon very solid foundations.

It is hardly necessary to enter into the question, whether the wealth of the British empire would be essentially increased by that division of landed property which would be occasioned by the abolition of the right of primogeniture, and the law of entails, without any interference with testamentary dispositions. It is generally acknowledged that the country, in its actual state and under its actual laws, presents a picture of greater wealth, especially when compared with its natural resources, than any large territorial state of modern times. By the natural extinction of some great families, and the natural imprudence of some others, but, above all, by the extraordinary growth of manufactures and commerce, the immense landed properties which formerly prevailed all over the country have been in a great degree broken down, notwithstanding the right of primogeniture. And the few

a

b

which remain may perhaps be of use in furnishing motives to the merchant and master-manufacturer, to continue the exercise of their skill and powers till they have acquired large capitals, and are able to contend in wealth with the great landlords. If, from the abolition of the right of primogeniture, the landed fortunes were all very inconsiderable, it is not probable that there would be many large capitals among merchants; and in this case, much productive power would unquestionably be lost.

But however this may be, it is certain that a very large body of what may be called the middle classes of society has been established in this country; while the right of primogeniture, by forcing the younger sons of the nobility and great landed proprietors into the higher divisions of these classes, has, for all practical purposes, annihilated the distinctions founded on rank and birth, and opened the fairest *arena* for the contests of personal merit in all the avenues to wealth and honours. It is probable that the obligation generally imposed upon younger sons to be the founders of their own fortunes, has infused a greater degree of energy and activity into professional and commercial exertions than would have taken place if property in land had been more equally divided. Altogether, the country possesses a very large class of effective demanders, who derive their power of purchasing from the various professions, from commerce, from manufactures, from wholesale and retail trade, from salaries of different kinds, and from the interest of public and private debts; and these demanders are likely, perhaps, to acquire tastes more favourable to the encouragement of wealth than the owners of small properties on the land.

Under these circumstances, which, to the extent in which they prevail, it must be allowed are almost peculiar to this country, it might be rash to conclude that the nation would be richer if the right of primogeniture were abolished. But even if we were able to determine the question in the affirmative, it would by no means determine the policy of such a change. In all cases of this kind there are higher considerations to be attended to than those which relate to mere wealth.

It is an historical truth which cannot for a moment be disputed, that the first formation, and subsequent preservation and improvement, of our present constitution, and of the liberties and privileges which have so long distinguished Englishmen, are mainly due to a landed aristocracy. And we are certainly not yet warranted by any experience to conclude that without an aristocracy, which cannot certainly be supported in an effective state but by the law of primogeniture, the constitution and liberties so established can be in future maintained. If then we set a value upon the British Constitution; if we think that, whatever may be its theoretical imperfections, it has practically given a better government, and more liberty to a greater mass of people for a longer time than any which history records, it would be most unwise to venture upon any such change as would risk the whole structure, and throw us upon a wide sea of experi-

a

b

ment, where the chances are so dreadfully against
our attaining the object of our search.

It is not perhaps easy to say to what extent the
abolition of the law of primogeniture and entails
would divide the landed property of this country.
If the power of testamentary bequest were left un-
touched, it is possible that past habits might still
keep many estates together for a time; but the probabilities are, that by degrees a considerable subdivision of land would take place; and if there
were few estates of above a thousand a year, the
mercantile classes would either be induced to moderate their exertions in the acquisition of wealth,
from the absence of the motive of competition with
the landlords, as I stated above; or, if the merchants and manufacturers were still to acquire great
wealth, excited either by a competition with each
other or by political ambition, they would be the
only persons who could possess great influence in
the state; and the government of the country
would fall almost wholly into their hands. In
neither case, probably, could our present constitution be maintained. In the first, where the property of individuals would be so inconsiderable,
and so equal, the tendencies would be either to
democracy or military despotism, with the chances
greatly in favour of the latter. And in the second
case, whatever might be the form of government,
the merchants and manufacturers would have the
greatest influence in its councils; and it is justly observed by Adam Smith, that the interests of these

classes do not always prepare them to give the most salutary advice.

Although therefore it be true that a better distribution of landed property might exist than that which actually prevails in this country at present; and although it be also true, that to make it better, the distribution should be more equal; yet it may by no means be wise to abolish the law of primogeniture, which would be likely to lead to a subdivision of land greater probably than would be favourable even to the wealth of the country; and greater certainly than would be consistent with those higher interests, which relate to the protection of a people equally from the tyranny of despotic rulers, and the fury of a despotic mob.

But, whatever conduct the wisdom and policy of a legislature may dictate respecting the laws of succession, the principle will still be true, that the division of landed property is one of the great means of the distribution of wealth, which tends to keep up and increase its exchangeable value, and to encourage further production; and that the distribution so occasioned will, as it extends, continue to produce a more favourable effect on wealth, till it meets its antagonist principle, and begins to interfere with the power of production. This will take place sooner or later, according to circumstances, depending chiefly upon the activity of foreign and domestic commerce, and the mass of effective demanders besides the landlords. If the demand be great, independently of the land, a slight diminution in the power of production may turn the scale; and any change which is unfavourable to accumulation, enterprize, and the division of labour, will be unfavourable to the progress of wealth. But if the country be ill situated for foreign commerce, and its tastes, habits, and internal communications be such as not to encourage an active home trade, nothing can occasion an adequate demand for produce, but an easy subdivision of landed property; and without such a subdivision, a country with great natural resources might slumber for ages with an uncultivated soil, and a scanty yet starving population.

SECTION VIII.

Of the Distribution occasioned by Commerce, internal and external, considered as the Means of increasing the exchangeable Value of Produce.

The second main cause favourable to that increase of exchangeable value, which depends upon distribution, is internal and external commerce.

Every exchange which takes place in a country, effects a distribution of its produce better adapted to the wants of the society. It is with regard to both parties concerned, an exchange of what is wanted less for what is wanted more, and must therefore raise the value of both the products. If two districts, one of which possessed a rich copper mine, and the other a rich tin mine, had always been separated by an impassable river or mountain, there can be no doubt that on the opening of a communication, a greater demand would take place, and a greater price be given both for tin and copper; and this greater price of both metals, though it might only be temporary, would alone go a great way towards furnishing the additional capital wanted to supply the additional demand; and the capitals of both districts, and the products of both mines, would be increased both in quantity and value to a degree which could not have taken place without this new distribution of the produce, or some event equivalent to it.

The Economists, in their endeavours to prove the unproductive nature of trade, always insisted that the effect of it was merely to equalize prices, which were in some places too high and in others too low, but in their amount the same as they would be after the exchange had taken place. This position must be considered as unfounded, and capable of being contradicted by incontrovertible facts. The increase of price at first, from the extension of the market, is unquestionable. And when to this we add the effect occasioned by the demand for further produce, and the means thus afforded of rapid accumulation for the supply of this demand, it is impossible to doubt for a moment the direct tendency of all internal trade to increase the value of the national produce.

If indeed it did not tend to increase the value of the national produce, it would not be carried on. It is out of this increase that the merchants concerned are paid; and if some London goods are not more valued in Glasgow than in London, and some Glasgow goods more valued in London than in Glasgow, the merchants who exchange the articles in which these towns trade, would neither be doing themselves any good, nor any one else. It is a mere futile process to exchange one set of commodities for another, if the parties, after this new distribution of goods has taken place, are not better off than they were before. The giving one article for another has nothing to do with effectual demand, unless the commodity received so far exceeds in value the labour employed on the commodity parted with, as to yield adequate profits to the capitalists concerned, and to give them both the power and the will to set fresh labour to work in the same trade.

It has been said that the industry of a country is measured by the extent of its capital, and that the manner in which this capital is employed, though it may make some difference to the enjoyment of the inhabitants, makes very little in the *value* of the national revenue. This would be true on one supposition, and on one supposition only ; namely, that the inhabitants could be persuaded to estimate their confined productions just as highly, to be as eager to obtain and consume them, and as willing to work hard for them, and to make great sacrifices for them, as for the commodities which they obtain from a distance. But are we at liberty to make such a supposition? It is specifi-

cally to overcome the want of eagerness to purchase domestic commodities that the merchant
exchanges them for others more in request. Could
we but so alter the wants and tastes of the people
of Glasgow as to make them estimate as highly
the profusion of cotton goods which they produce,
as any articles which they could receive in return
for them under a prosperous trade, we should hear
no more of their distresses. It may be allowed
that the quantity of productive industry maintained in a country is nearly proportioned to the
quantity of capital employed; but the value of the
revenue will be greater or less, according to the
market prices of the commodities produced. These
market prices must obviously depend upon the
interchange of goods ; and consequently the value
of the revenue, and the power and will to increase
it, must depend upon that distribution of commodities which best adapts them to the wants and
tastes of the society.

The whole produce of a nation may be said to
have a market price in money and labour. When
this market price is high, that is, when the prices
of commodities rise so as to command a greater
excess of labour above what they had cost in
production than before, while the same capital
and number of people had been employed upon
them, it is evident that more fresh labour will
be set in motion every year, and the increase of
wealth will be certain and rapid. On the other
hand, when the market prices of commodities are
such as to be able to command very little more

labour than the production of them has cost, it is as evident that the national wealth will proceed very slowly, or perhaps be quite stationary.

In the distribution of commodities, the circulating medium of every country bears a most important part; and, as I intimated before in a note, we are much more likely to obscure our reasonings than to render them clearer, by throwing it out of our consideration. It is not easy indeed, without reference to a circulating medium, to ascertain whether the commodities of a country are so distributed as to give them their proper value.

It may be said, perhaps, that if the funds for the maintenance of labour are at any time in unusual abundance, it may fairly be presumed that they will be able to command a more than usual quantity of labour. But they certainly will not be able to command more labour, nor even so much, if the distribution of them be defective; and in a country which has a circulating medium, the specific proof of the distribution being defective is, that the whole produce does not exchange for so large an amount of circulating medium as before, and that consequently the producers have been obliged to sell at a great diminution of money profits, or a positive money loss.

From the harvest of 1815 to the harvest of 1816, there cannot be a doubt that the funds for the maintenance of labour in this country were unusually abundant. Corn was particularly plentiful, and no other necessaries were deficient; yet it is an acknowledged fact, that great numbers were

thrown out of employment, partly from the want
of power, and partly from the want of will to employ the same quantity of labour as before. How is
this fact to be accounted for? As I have said before, a
it would not be easy to account for it without
referring to a circulating medium; because, without such reference, the proof of a defective distribution would be extremely difficult. But the moment we refer to a circulating medium, the theory
of the fact observed becomes perfectly clear. It is
acknowledged that there was a fall in the money
value of the raw produce, to the amount of nearly
one third. But if the farmer sold his produce for
only two thirds of the price at which he had
before sold it, it is evident that he would be quite b
unable to command the same quantity of labour,
and to employ the same quantity of capital on his
farm as he did the year before. And when afterwards a great fall of money price took place in all cd
manufactured products, occasioned in a considerable degree by this previous fall of raw produce,
it is as evident that the manufacturers would be e
unable to command the labour of the same number
of workmen as before. In the midst of the plenty
of necessaries, these two important classes of society
would really have their power of employing labour
diminished, while all those who possessed fixed
incomes would have their power of employing
labour increased, with very little chance of an increase of will to extend their demand in proportion; and the general result would resemble the
effects of that partial distribution of products which

a would arise from the interruption of accustomed communications. The same, or a greater quantity of commodities might be produced for a short time; but the distribution not being such as to proportion the supply in each quarter to the demand, the whole would fall in exchangeable value, and a

b very decided check to production would be experienced in reference to the whole country. It follows, that the labouring classes of society may be thrown out of work in the midst of an abundance of necessaries, if these necessaries are not in the hands of those who are at the same time both able and willing to employ an adequate quantity of labour.

c It is of no use therefore to make suppositions about a great increase of produce, and, rejecting all reference to a circulating medium, to conclude that this great increase will be properly distributed and effectively consumed. It is a conclusion which we have no right whatever to make. We know, both from theory and experience, that if the whole produce falls in money value, the distribution must be such as to discourage production. As long as this fall in the money price of produce continues

d to diminish the power of commanding domestic

e and foreign labour, a great discouragement to production must obviously continue; and if, after labour has adjusted itself to the new level of prices, the permanent distribution of the produce and the permanent tastes and habits of the people should

f not be favourable to an adequate degree of consumption, the clearest principles of political eco-

nomy shew that the profits of stock might be lower
for any length of time than the state of the land
rendered necessary ; and that the check to produc-   a
tion might be as permanent as the faulty distribution of the produce and the unfavourable tastes
and habits which had occasioned it.

It is scarcely possible for any essential change   b
to take place in the value of the circulating medium of a country without occasioning an alteration in the distribution of its produce. The impru-
dent use of paper money must be allowed to be the
principal cause of these changes. But even without a paper currency, or with one always maintaining the same value as bullion, every country is
liable to changes in the value of its produce, compared with its money; and as such changes must
have a great effect on the distribution of produce,
partly temporary, and partly permanent, a determination to reason on these subjects, without taking
into account the effects of so powerful an agent,
would be purposely to shut our eyes to the truth.
Referring therefore ultimately to the command over
labour, domestic and foreign, as the best practical   c
measure of the value of the whole produce, it will
be useful to refer previously to its bullion value,
in order to ascertain whether the distribution of
the produce is such as to enable it to command
labour in some proportion to the increase of its   d
quantity. If the bullion value of a country's products so increases as to command yearly an in-   e
creased quantity of domestic and foreign labour,
we may feel pretty well assured that it is pro-

ceeding without check in wealth and prosperity. But, if there is merely an increase of commodities, it is impossible to say, without further inquiry, that they may not be so distributed as

a   to retard, instead of promote, the progress of national wealth.

It has been fully stated and allowed, that a period

b   of stagnation must finally arrive in every country

c   from the difficulty of procuring subsistence. But an indisposition to consume in large quantities the goods produced at home, and a want of the means of advantageous barter may occasion, and has often occasioned, a similar stagnation at a very early period of a nation's progress. No country with a very confined market, internal as well as external, has ever been able to accumulate a large capital, because such a market prevents the formation of those wants and tastes, and that desire to consume, which are absolutely necessary to keep

d   up the market prices of commodities, and to occasion an increasing demand for them, and for the capital which is to produce them. The distribution of commodities occasioned by internal trade is the first step towards any considerable increase of wealth and capital ; and if no exchanges could have taken place in this country, at a greater distance than five miles, it is probable that not a fifth part of our present capital could have been employed before the effective encouragement to accumulation and the further progress of wealth

e   had ceased.

The motives which urge individuals to engage

in foreign commerce are precisely the same as those which lead to the interchange of goods between the more distant parts of the same country, namely, an increase in the market price of the   a
local products; and the increase of profits thus made by the individual, or the prevention of that fall of profits which would have taken place if the capital had been employed at home, must be considered as a proportionate increase in the value of   b
the national produce.

Mr. Ricardo begins his Chapter on Foreign Trade   α
by stating that "No extension of foreign trade will immediately increase the amount of value in a country although it will very powerfully contribute to increase the mass of commodities and therefore the sum of enjoyments." This statement is quite consistent with his peculiar view of value, as depending solely upon the labour which a commodity has cost. However abundant may be the returns of the merchant, or however greatly they may exceed his exports in value according to the common acceptation of the term, it is certain that the labour employed in procuring these exports will at first remain the same. But, as it is so glaring and undeniable a fact that the returns from an unusually favourable trade will exchange for an unusual quantity of money, labour and domestic commodities; as this increased power of commanding money, labour and commodities is in reality what is meant by the merchant when he talks of the extension of the foreign market and a favourable trade, it appears to me that such   c

a state of things which may, and often does last a
sufficient time to produce the most important results, is alone, and at once, a decisive proof that
the view of exchangeable value, which makes it
depend exclusively upon the cost of production, is
essentially incorrect, and utterly useless in solving
the great phenomena which attend the progress of
wealth.

Mr. Ricardo seems to think that value cannot
increase in one department of produce without diminishing it in some other.* This again may be
true according to his view of value, but is utterly
unfounded according to that more enlarged view
of exchangeable value which is established and
confirmed by experience. If any foreign power
were to send to a particular merchant commodities
of a new description which would sell in the
London market for fifty thousand pounds, the
wealth of such merchant would be increased to
that extent; and who, I would ask, would be the
poorer for it? It is no doubt true that the purchasers of these commodities may be obliged to
forego the use of some of the articles which they
had before been in the habit of buying, † and so

* It appears to me that if the two first sentences in Mr. Ricardo's Chapter on Foreign Trade were well founded, there
would be no such intercourse between nations.

† This, however, will not necessarily happen. The greater
temptation offered to consumption may induce some persons to
spend what they otherwise would have saved, and in many cases
the wealth of the country, instead of suffering by this change, will
gain by it. The increased consumption, as far as it goes, will occasion an increase of market prices and profits. The increase of

far in some quarters may diminish demand; but,   a
to counterbalance this diminution, the enriched
merchant will become a purchaser of additional
goods to the amount perhaps of the whole fifty
thousand pounds, and thus prevent any general
fall in the value of the native produce consumed
in the country, while the value of the foreign produce so consumed has increased to the amount of
the whole of the new produce imported.   I see no
difference between a present from abroad, and the
unusual profits of a new foreign trade, in their
effects upon the wealth of a state.   They are
equally calculated to increase the wealth of the
community, by an increase both of the quantity
and *value* of the produce obtained.

It will be said perhaps that, neither the people   b
nor the money of the country having been by
supposition increased, the value of the whole produce estimated in labour or money cannot be
increased.

With regard to labour I would observe that,   c
when I speak of the value of the whole produce
of a country being able to command more labour
than before, I do not mean to refer specifically to
a greater *number* of labourers, but to say that it
could either purchase more at the old price, or pay
the actual labourers higher; and such a state of
things, with a population which cannot imme-

profits will soon restore the capital which for a short time had
been diverted from its destined office; and the country will be left   d
with habits of greater consumption, and at the same time with
proportionate means of supplying them.

diately be increased, always occasions that demand for labour, which so powerfully encourages the exertions of those who were before perhaps only half paid and half employed ; and is at once the surest sign and most effective stimulus of increasing wealth. It is the natural consequence of the value of the produce estimated in labour increasing faster than the population, and forms the true and healthy encouragement to the further increase of numbers.

a   With regard to money, this most useful measure of value would perform its functions very indifferently, if it could in no respect accommodate itself to cases of this kind ; and if the importation of a valuable commodity always proportionably reduced the price of the other parts of the national produce. But this is far from being the case, even if we do not suppose any fresh importation of the precious metals. The occurrence of such an event is precisely the period, when a greater velocity is given to the circulation of the money actually in use, and when fresh paper may be issued without a fall in the rate of foreign exchanges, or a rise in the price of bullion and of goods. One or other, or both of these resources will be applied, except in the most barbarous countries ; and though undoubtedly, in the case of the importation of foreign commodities which come directly into competition with domestic goods, such goods will fall in price, and the producers of them be for a time rendered poorer, yet it will very rarely indeed happen that

other goods not affected by such competition will
fall in money value; and altogether no fall will
take place in particular commodities sufficient
to prevent a rise in the money price of the whole
produce.

It may naturally be expected however that more   a
money will be imported; and, in fact, a successful
extension of foreign trade is exactly that state of
things which most directly leads to the importation
of bullion. For what is it that the merchant ex-   b
porter specifically considers as a successful extension of foreign commerce in dealing with civilized
nations? Undoubtedly the power of selling his
exports abroad for a greater value than usual, estimated in bullion; and of course, if the goods
which he would import in return will not sell at
home so much higher as to warrant their importation, a part or the whole of the returns will be im-   c
ported in money. But if only such an amount be   d
imported as shall bear the same proportion to the
returns in goods as the whole of the currency of
the country does to the whole of its produce, it is
obvious that no difficulty whatever can occur in
the circulation of the commodities of the country
at their former prices, with the single exception of
those articles with which the foreign goods might
directly enter into competition, which in this case
would never be sufficient to prevent a general increase of value in the whole produce.

I distinctly therefore differ from Mr. Ricardo in   e
the conclusion implied in the following passage.   f
" In all cases the demand for foreign and home

commodities together, as far as regards value, is limited by the revenue and capital of the country. If one increases, the other must diminish."* It appears to me that in almost every case of successful foreign trade, it is a matter of unquestionable fact that the demand for foreign and home commodities taken together decidedly increases; and that the increase in the value of foreign produce does not occasion a proportionate diminution in the value of home produce.

I would still however allow that the demand for foreign and home commodities together, as far as regards value, is limited by the revenue and capital of the country; but, according to my view of the subject, the national revenue, which consists of the sum of rents, profits, and wages, is at once decidedly increased by the increased profits of the foreign merchant, without a proportionate diminution of revenue in any other quarter; whereas Mr. Ricardo is evidently of opinion that, though the abundance of commodities is increased, the revenue of the country, as far as regards value, remains the same; and it is because I object rather to the conclusion *intended* to be conveyed, than to the actual terms of the passage quoted, that I have used the word *implied* rather than *expressed*.

It will readily be allowed that an increase in the *quantity* of commodities is one of the most desirable effects of foreign commerce; but I wish particularly to press on the attention of the reader

* Princ. of Polit. Econ. c. vii. p. 138. 2d edit.

that in almost all cases, another most important effect accompanies it, expressly rejected by Mr. Ricardo, namely, an increase in the amount of exchangeable value. And that this latter effect is so necessary, in order to create a continued stimulus to productive industry, and keep up an abundant supply of commodities, that in the few cases in which it does not take place, a stagnation in the demand for labour is immediately perceptible, and the progress of wealth is checked. An extension of foreign commerce, according to the view which Mr. Ricardo takes of it, would, in my opinion, place us frequently in the situation in which this country was in the early part of 1816, when a sudden abundance and cheapness of corn and other commodities, from a great supply meeting a deficient demand, so diminished the value of the income of the country, that it could no longer command the same quantity of labour at the same price; the consequence of which was that, in the midst of plenty, thousands upon thousands were thrown out of employment—a most painful but almost unavoidable preliminary to a fall in the money wages of labour, which it is obvious could alone enable the general income of the country to employ the same number of labourers as before, and, after a period of severe check to the increase of wealth, to recommence a progressive movement.

Mr. Ricardo always seems to think that it is quite the same to the labourer, whether he is able to command more of the necessaries of life by a rise in the money price of labour, or by a fall in

the money price of provisions; but these two
events, though apparently similar in their effects,
may be, and in general are, most essentially different. An increase in the wages of labour, both
nominal and real, invariably implies such a distribution of the actual wealth as to give it an increasing value, to ensure full employment to all the
labouring classes, and to create a demand for further
produce, and for the capital which is to obtain it.
In short, it is the infallible sign of health and
prosperity. Whereas a general fall in the money
price of necessaries often arises from so defective
a distribution of the produce of the country, that
the general amount of its value cannot be kept up;
in which case, under the most favourable circumstances, a temporary period of want of employment
and distress is unavoidable ; and in many cases, as
may be too frequently observed in surveying the
different countries of the globe, this fall in the
money price of necessaries is the accompaniment of
a permanent want of employment, and the most
abject poverty, in consequence of retrograde and
permanently diminished wealth.

The reader will be fully aware that a great fall
in the price of particular commodities, either from
improved machinery or foreign commerce, is perfectly compatible with a continued and great increase, not only in the exchangeable value of the
whole produce of the country, but even in the exchangeable value of the whole produce of these
particular articles themselves. It has been repeatedly stated that the whole value of the cotton

produced in this country has been prodigiously increased, notwithstanding the great fall in their price. The same may be said of the teas, although   a
when they were first imported, the price per pound was greatly higher than at present; and there can be little doubt, that if we were to attempt to make our own wines by means of hot-houses, they would altogether be worth much less money, and would give encouragement to much less industry than at present.

Even when the commodity is of such a nature   b
as not to admit of an extension of the market for it from reduced price, which very rarely happens, yet the capital and labour, which in this case will be thrown out of employment, will generally, in enterprising and commercial countries, find other channels into which they may be directed, with such profit as to keep up, and often more than keep up, the value of the national income. At the same time it should be observed, and it is a point of great importance, that it is precisely among cases of this description, where the few exceptions occur to the general and powerful tendency of foreign commerce, to raise the value of the national income; and whenever these exceptions do take place, that is, whenever the value of the national income is diminished, estimated even in money, a temporary distress from a defective distribution of the produce cannot fail to take place. If this diminished value be estimated in labour, the distress among the labouring classes, and check to the progress of wealth, will continue as long as the

diminished value so estimated lasts: and if it could be proved that, under particular circumstances, any species of foreign trade tended permanently to diminish the power of the national produce in the command of domestic and foreign labour, such trade would certainly have the effect of checking permanently the progress of wealth and population.

a   The causes of an increase in the effective demand for particular commodities are of very easy explanation; but it has been considered, and with reason, as not very easy to explain the cause of that general briskness of demand which is sometimes so very sensibly felt throughout a whole country, and is so strikingly contrasted with the feeling which gives rise to the expression of trade being universally very dead. As the specific and immediate cause of this general increase of effective demand, I should decidedly point to such a distribution of the produce, and such an adaptation of it to the wants and tastes of the society as will give the money price for which it sells an

b   increased command of domestic and foreign labour; and I am inclined to think that, if this test be applied to all the striking cases that have occurred, it will rarely or never be found to fail.

It cannot for a moment be doubted, for instance, that the annual increase of the produce of the United States of America, estimated either in bul-

c   lion or in domestic and foreign labour, has been greater than that of any country we are acquainted with, and that this has been greatly owing to their foreign commerce, which, notwithstanding their facility of production, has given a value to their corn and raw produce equal to what they bear in   a many of the countries of Europe, and has consequently given to them a power in commanding   b the produce and labour of other countries quite   c extraordinary, when compared with the quantity of labour which they have employed. It can as little be doubted that in this country, from 1793 to 1814, the whole exchangeable value of the produce, estimated either in domestic and foreign   d labour, or in bullion, was greatly augmented every year. In this increase of value, as well as riches,   e the extension of our foreign commerce has been considered, almost without a dissentient opinion, as a most powerful agent; and certainly till 1815, no appearances seemed to indicate, that the increasing value of our imports had the slightest tendency to diminish the value of our domestic produce. They both increased, and increased greatly,   f together, estimated either in bullion or labour.

But while in every country to which it seems possible to refer, an increase of value will be found to accompany increasing prosperity and riches, I   g am inclined to think that no single instance can be produced of a country engaged in a successful commerce, and exhibiting an increasing plenty of commodities, where the value of the whole produce estimated in domestic and foreign labour   h was retrograde or even stationary. And of the two ways in which capital may be accumulated, as stated by Mr. Ricardo in his chapter on Fo-

a   reign Commerce, namely an increase of revenue
b   from increased profits, or a diminished expendi-
c   ture, arising from cheap commodities,* I believe
the latter never has been, nor ever will be, experienced as an effective stimulus to the permanent and continued production of increasing
wealth.

d   Mr. Ricardo will perhaps say, and say truly, that
according to his own view of value, foreign commerce will increase it, as soon as more labour has
been employed in the production of all the commodities taken together, which the country obtains;
and that the plenty produced by foreign trade will
e   naturally encourage this employment. But what
I wish specifically to state is, that the natural tendency of foreign trade, as of all sorts of exchanges
by which a distribution is effected better suited to
the wants of society, is *immediately* to increase the
value of that part of the national revenue which
f   consists of profits, without any proportionate dimi-
g   nution elsewhere, and that it is precisely this *immediate* increase of national income arising from
the exchange of what is of less value in the country, for what is of more value, that furnishes both
the power and will to employ more labour, and
occasions the animated demand for labour, produce
and capital, which is a striking and almost universal accompaniment of successful foreign commerce; whereas, a mere abundance of commodities
h   falling very greatly in value compared with labour,

i   * Princ. of Pol. Econ. ch. vii. p. 139. 2d edit.

would obviously at first diminish the power of employing the same number of workmen, and a temporary glut and general deficiency of demand could not fail to ensue in labour, in produce, and in capital, attended with the usual distress which a glut must occasion.

a

Mr. Ricardo always views foreign trade in the light of means of obtaining *cheaper* commodities. But this is only looking to one half of its advantages, and I am strongly disposed to think, not the larger half. In our own commerce at least, this part of the trade is comparatively inconsiderable. The great mass of our imports consists of articles as to which there can be no kind of question about their comparative cheapness, as raised abroad or at home. If we could not import from foreign countries our silk, cotton and indigo, our tea, sugar, coffee and tobacco, our port, sherry, claret and champagne, our almonds, raisons, oranges and lemons, our various spices and our various drugs, with many other articles peculiar to foreign climates, it is quite certain that we should not have them at all. To estimate the advantage derived from their importation by their cheapness, compared with the quantity of labour and capital which they would have cost, if we had attempted to raise them at home, would be perfectly preposterous. In reality, no such attempt would have been thought of. If we could by possibility have made fine claret at ten pounds a bottle, few or none would have drunk it; and the actual quantity of labour and capital employed in obtaining these

b

c

foreign commodities is at present beyond comparison greater than it would have been if we had not imported them.

We must evidently therefore estimate the advantage which we derive from such a trade upon a very different principle. This is the simple and obvious one often adverted to as the foundation of every act of barter, whether foreign or domestic, namely, the increased value which results from exchanging what is wanted less for what is wanted more. After we had, by our exports of home commodities, obtained in return all the foreign articles above-mentioned, we might be very much puzzled to say whether we had increased or decreased the *quantity* of our commodities, but we should feel quite certain that the new distribution of produce which had taken place, by giving us commodities much better suited to our wants and tastes than those which had been sent away, had decidedly increased the exchangeable value of our possessions, our means of enjoyment, and our wealth.

a

Taking therefore a very different view of the effects of foreign commerce on exchangeable value from Mr. Ricardo, I should bring forwards the extension of markets as being, in its general tendency, pre-eminently favourable to that increase of value and wealth which arises from distribution.

SECTION IX.

Of the Distribution occasioned by unproductive Consumers,   a
considered as the Means of increasing the exchangeable
Value of the whole Produce.

The third main cause which tends to keep up and
increase the value of produce by favouring its distribution is the employment of unproductive la-   b
bour, or the maintenance of an adequate proportion of unproductive consumers.   c

It has been already shewn that, under a rapid
accumulation of capital, or, more properly speak-   d
ing, a rapid conversion of unproductive into pro-   e
ductive labour, the demand, compared with the
supply of material products, would prematurely
fail, and the motive to further accumulation be
checked, before it was checked by the exhaustion
of the land. It follows that, without supposing
the productive classes to consume much more than
they are found to do by experience, particularly
when they are rapidly saving from revenue to add
to their capitals, it is absolutely necessary that a   f
country with great powers of production should
possess a body of unproductive consumers.   gα

In the fertility of the soil, in the powers of man
to apply machinery as a substitute for labour, and
in the motives to exertion under a system of private
property, the great laws of nature have provided   h
for the leisure of a certain portion of society; and   i

if this beneficent offer be not accepted by an adequate number of individuals, not only will a positive good, which might have been so attained, be lost, but the rest of the society, so far from being benefited by such self-denial, will be decidedly injured by it.

a   What the proportion is between the productive and unproductive classes of a society, which affords the greatest encouragement to the continued increase of wealth, it has before been said that the resources of political economy are unequal to determine. It must depend upon a great b   variety of circumstances, particularly upon fertility of soil and the progress of invention in machinery. A fertile soil and an ingenious people can c   not only support a considerable proportion of unproductive consumers without injury, but may absolutely require such a body of demanders, in d   order to give effect to their powers of production. While, with a poor soil and a people of little ingenuity, an attempt to support such a body would throw land out of cultivation, and lead infallibly to impoverishment and ruin.

Another cause, which makes it impossible to e   say what proportion of the unproductive to the productive classes is most favourable to the in- f   crease of wealth, is the difference in the degrees of consumption which may prevail among the producers themselves.

Perhaps it will be said that there can be no occasion for unproductive consumers, if a consumption sufficient to keep up the value of the produce takes place among those who are engaged in production.

With regard to the capitalists who are so engaged, they have certainly the power of consuming their profits, or the revenue which they make by the employment of their capitals; and if they were to consume it, with the exception of what could be beneficially added to their capitals, so as to provide in the best way both for an increased production and increased consumption, there might be little occasion for unproductive consumers. But such consumption is not consistent with the actual habits of the generality of capitalists. The great object of their lives is to save a fortune, both because it is their duty to make a provision for their families, and because they cannot spend an income with so much comfort to themselves, while they are obliged perhaps to attend a counting-house for seven or eight hours a day.

It has been laid down as a sort of axiom among some writers that the wants of mankind may be considered as at all times commensurate with their powers; but this position is not always true, even in those cases where a fortune comes without trouble; and in reference to the great mass of capitalists, it is completely contradicted by experience. Almost all merchants and manufacturers save, in prosperous times, much more rapidly than it would be possible for the national capital to increase, so as to keep up the value of the produce. But if this be true of them as a body, taken one with another, it is quite obvious that, with their actual habits, they could not afford an adequate market to each other by exchanging their several products.

There must therefore be a considerable class of other consumers, or the mercantile classes could not continue extending their concerns, and realizing their profits. In this class the landlords no doubt stand pre-eminent; but if the powers of production among capitalists are considerable, the consumption of the landlords, in addition to that of the capitalists themselves and of their workmen, may still be insufficient to keep up and increase the exchangeable value of the whole produce, that is, to make the increase of quantity more than counterbalance the fall of price. And if this be so, the capitalists cannot continue the same habits of saving. They must either consume more, or produce less; and when the mere pleasure of present expenditure, without the accompaniments of an improved local situation and an advance in rank, is put in opposition to the continued labour of attending to business during the greatest part of the day, the probability is that a considerable body of them will be induced to prefer the latter alternative, and produce less. But if, in order to balance the demand and supply, a permanent diminution of production takes place, rather than an increase of consumption, the whole of the national wealth, which consists of what is produced and consumed, and not of the excess of produce above consumption, will be decidedly diminished.

Mr. Ricardo frequently speaks, as if saving were an end instead of a means. Yet even with

(margin notes: ab, c, d, e, f)

regard to individuals, where this view of the subject is nearest the truth, it must be allowed that
the final object in saving is expenditure and enjoyment. But, in reference to national wealth, it can
never be considered either immediately or permanently in any other light than as a means. It   a
may be true that, by the cheapness of commodities, and the consequent saving of expenditure in
consumption, the same surplus of produce above
consumption may be obtained as by a great rise of
profits with an undiminished consumption; and, if
saving were an end, the same end would be accomplished. But saving is the means of furnishing an increasing supply for the increasing national wants. If however commodities are already
so plentiful that an adequate portion of them is
not consumed, the capital so saved, the office of   bc
which is still further to increase the plenty of
commodities, and still further to lower already low
profits, can be comparatively of little use. On   d
the other hand, if profits are high, it is a sure sign
that commodities are scarce, compared with the
demand for them, that the wants of the society
are clamorous for a supply, and that an increase in
the means of production, by saving a considerable
part of the new revenue created by the high profits, and adding it to capital, will be specifically
and permanently beneficial.

National saving, therefore, considered as the
means of increased production, is confined within
much narrower limits than individual saving.
While some individuals continue to spend, other

a individuals may continue to save to a very great extent; but the national saving, or the balance of produce above consumption, in reference to the whole mass of producers and consumers, must necessarily be limited by the amount which can be advantageously employed in supplying the demand for produce; and to create this demand, there

b must be an adequate consumption either among the producers themselves, or other classes of consumers.

Adam Smith has observed "that the desire of food is limited in every man by the narrow capacity of the human stomach; but the desire of the conveniences and ornaments of building, dress, equipage, and household furniture, seems to have no limit or certain boundary." That it has no *certain* boundary is unquestionably true; that it has no limit must be allowed to be too strong an expression, when we consider how it will be practically limited by the countervailing luxury of indolence, or by the general desire of mankind to better their condition, and make a provision for a family; a principle which, as Adam Smith himself states, is on the whole stronger than the principle which prompts to expense.* But surely it is a glaring misapplication of this statement in any sense in which it can be reasonably understood, to say, that there is no limit to the saving and employment of capital except the difficulty of procuring food. It is to

c found a doctrine upon the unlimited desire of man-

* Wealth of Nations, Vol. ii. B. ii. ch. ii. p. 19. 6th edit.

kind to consume; then to suppose this desire li-   a
mited in order to save capital, and thus completely
alter the premises; and yet still to maintain that
the doctrine is true.   Let a sufficient consumption
always take place, whether by the producers or
others, to keep up and increase most effectually   b
the exchangeable value of the whole produce;
and I am perfectly ready to allow that, to the employment of a national capital, increasing only at
such a rate, there is no other limit than that which
bounds the power of maintaining population.   But
it appears to me perfectly clear in theory, and universally confirmed by experience, that the employ-   c
ment of a capital, too rapidly increased by parsimonious habits, may find a limit, and does, in fact,
often find a limit, long before there is any real
difficulty in procuring the means of subsistence;
and that both capital and population may be at the
same time, and for a period of great length, redun-   d
dant, compared with the effective demand for   e
produce.

Of the wants of mankind in general, it may be
further observed, that it is a partial and narrow
view of the subject, to consider only the propensity to spend what is actually possessed.   It forms
but a very small part of the question to determine
that if a man has a hundred thousand a year, he
will not decline the offer of ten thousand more; or
to lay down generally that mankind are never disposed to refuse the means of increased power and
enjoyment.   The main part of the question respecting the wants of mankind, relates to their

power of calling forth the exertions necessary to acquire the means of expenditure. It is unquestionably true that wealth produces wants; but it is a still more important truth, that wants produce wealth. Each cause acts and re-acts upon the other, but the order, both of precedence and of importance, is with the wants which stimulate to industry; and with regard to these, it appears that, instead of being always ready to second the physical powers of man, they require for their de-

α velopement, "all appliances and means to boot." The greatest of all difficulties in converting uncivilized and thinly peopled countries into civilized and populous ones, is to inspire them with the wants best calculated to excite their exertions in the production of wealth. One of the greatest benefits which foreign commerce confers, and the reason why it has always appeared an almost necessary ingredient in the progress of wealth, is, its tendency to inspire new wants, to form new tastes, and to furnish fresh motives for industry. Even civilized and improved countries cannot afford to lose any of these motives. It is not the most pleasant employment to spend eight hours a day in a counting-house. Nor will it be submitted to after the common necessaries and conveniences of life are attained, unless adequate motives are presented to the mind of the man of business. Among these motives is undoubtedly the desire of advancing his rank, and contending with the landlords in the enjoyment of leisure, as well as of foreign and domestic luxuries.

But the desire to realize a fortune as a permanent provision for a family is perhaps the most general motive for the continued exertions of those whose incomes depend upon their own personal skill and efforts. Whatever may be said of the virtue of parsimony or saving, as a *public* duty, there cannot be a doubt that it is, in numberless cases, a most sacred and binding *private* duty; and were this legitimate and praiseworthy motive to persevering industry in any degree weakened, it is impossible that the wealth and prosperity of the country should not most materially suffer. But if, from the want of other consumers, the capitalists   a were obliged to consume all that could not be advantageously added to the national capital, the   b motives which support them in their daily tasks must essentially be weakened, and the same powers of production would not be called forth.

It has appeared then that, in the ordinary state of society, the master producers and capitalists, though they may have the power, have not the will, to consume to the necessary extent. And   c with regard to their workmen, it must be allowed that, if they possessed the will, they have not the power. It is indeed most important to observe that no power of consumption on the part of the labouring classes can ever, according to the common motives which influence mankind, alone furnish an encouragement to the employment of capital. As I have before said, nobody will ever   d employ capital merely for the sake of the demand occasioned by those who work for him. Unless they produce an excess of value above what they consume, which he either wants himself in kind, or which he can advantageously exchange for something which he desires, either for present or future use, it is quite obvious that his capital will not be employed in maintaining them. When indeed this further value is created and affords a sufficient excitement to the saving and employ-

a   ment of stock, then certainly the power of consumption possessed by the workmen will greatly add to the whole national demand, and make room for the employment of a much greater capital.

It is most desirable that the labouring classes should be well paid, for a much more important reason than any that can relate to wealth; namely,

b   the happiness of the great mass of society. But to those who are inclined to say that unproductive consumers cannot be necessary as a stimulus to the increase of wealth, if the productive classes do but consume a fair proportion of what they produce, I would observe that as a great increase of consumption among the working classes must greatly increase the cost of production, it must lower profits, and diminish or destroy the motive to accumulate, before agriculture, manufactures, and commerce have reached any considerable degree of prosperity. If each labourer were actually to consume double the quantity of corn which he does at present, such a demand, instead

c   of giving a stimulus to wealth, would probably throw a great quantity of land out of cultivation, and greatly diminish both internal and external commerce.

a

There is certainly however very little danger
of a diminution of wealth from this cause. Owing
to the principle of population, all the tendencies are
the other way; and there is much more reason to
fear that the working classes will consume too
little for their own happiness, than that they will
consume too much to allow of an adequate increase of wealth. I only adverted to the circumstance to shew that, supposing so impossible a
case as a very great consumption among the working producers, such consumption would not be of
the kind to push the wealth of a country to its
greatest extent.

b

It may be said, perhaps, that though, owing to
the laws which regulate the increase of population, it is in no respect probable that the corn
wages of labour should continue permanently
very high, yet the same consumption would take
place if the labouring classes did not work so
many hours in the day, and it was necessary to
employ a greater number in each occupation. I
have always thought and felt that many among
the labouring classes in this country work too hard
for their health, happiness, and intellectual improvement; and, if a greater degree of relaxation
from severe toil could be given to them with a
tolerably fair prospect of its being employed in
innocent amusements and useful instruction, I
should consider it as very cheaply purchased, by
the sacrifice of a portion of the national wealth

c

and populousness. But I see no probability, or even possibility, of accomplishing this object. To interfere generally with persons who are arrived at years of discretion in the command of the main property which they possess, namely their labour, would be an act of gross injustice; and the attempt to legislate directly in the teeth of one of the most general principles by which the business of society is carried on, namely, the principle of competition, must inevitably and necessarily fail. It is quite obvious that nothing could be done in this way, but by the labouring classes themselves; and even in this quarter we may perhaps much more reasonably expect that such a degree of prudence will prevail among them as to keep their wages permanently high, than that they should not enter into a competition with each other in working. A man who is prudent before marriage, and saves something for a family, reaps the benefit of his conduct, although others do not follow his example; but, without a simultaneous resolution on the part of all the labouring classes to work fewer hours in the day, the individual who should venture so to limit his exertions would necessarily reduce himself to comparative want and wretchedness. If the supposition here made were accomplished, not by a simultaneous resolution, which is scarcely possible, but by those general habits of indolence and ignorance, which so frequently prevail in the less improved stages of society, it is well known that such leisure would be of little value; and that while these habits would pre-

maturely check the rate of profits and the progress
of population, they would bring with them nothing to compensate the loss.

It is clear therefore that, with the single exception of the increased degree of prudence to be
expected among the labouring classes of society
from the progress of education and general improvement, which may occasion a greater consumption among the working producers, all the
other tendencies are precisely in an opposite direction; and that, generally, all such increased consumption, whether desirable or not on other
grounds, must always have the specific effect of
preventing the wealth and population of a country,
under a system of private property, from being
pushed so far, as it might have been, if the costs
of production had not been so increased.

It may be thought perhaps that the landlords
could not fail to supply any deficiency of demand
and consumption among the producers, and that
between them there would be little chance of any
approach towards redundancy of capital. What
might be the result of the most favourable distribution of landed property it is not easy to say from
experience; but experience certainly tells us that,
under the distribution of land which actually takes
place in most of the countries in Europe, the demands of the landlords, added to those of the producers, have not always been found sufficient to
prevent any difficulty in the employment of capital. In the instance alluded to in a former chapter,
which occurred in this country in the middle of

last century, there must have been a considerable difficulty in finding employment for capital, or the national creditors would rather have been paid off than have submitted to a reduction of interest from 4 per cent. to 3½, and afterwards to 3. And that this fall in the rate of interest and profits arose from a redundancy of capital and a want of demand for produce, rather than from the difficulty of production on the land, is fully evinced by the low price of corn at the time, and the very different state of interest and profits which has occurred since.

A similar instance took place in Italy in 1685, when, upon the Pope's reducing the interest of his debts from 4 to 3 per cent., the value of the principal rose afterwards to 112; and yet the Pope's territories have at no time been so cultivated as to occasion such a low rate of interest and profits from the difficulty of procuring the food of the labourer. Under a more favourable distribution of property, there cannot be a doubt that such a demand for produce, agricultural, manufacturing, and mercantile, might have been created, as to have prevented for many many years the interest of money from falling below 3 per cent. In both these cases, the demands of the landlords were added to those of the productive classes.

But if the master-producers, from the laudable desire they feel of bettering their condition, and providing for a family, do not consume sufficiently to give an adequate stimulus to the increase of wealth; if the working producers, by increasing their consumption, supposing them to have the means of so doing, would impede the growth of wealth more by diminishing the power of production, than they could encourage it by increasing the demand for produce; and if the expenditure of the landlords, in addition to the expenditure of the two preceding classes, be found insufficient to keep up and increase the value of that which is produced, where are we to look for the consumption required but among the unproductive labourers of Adam Smith?

Every society must have a body of unproductive labourers; as every society, besides the menial servants that are required, must have statesmen to govern it, soldiers to defend it, judges and lawyers to administer justice and protect the rights of individuals, physicians and surgeons to cure diseases and heal wounds, and a body of clergy to instruct the ignorant, and administer the consolations of religion. No civilized state has ever been known to exist without a certain portion of all these classes of society in addition to those who are directly employed in production. To a certain extent therefore they appear to be absolutely necessary. But it is perhaps one of the most important practical questions that can possibly be brought under our view, whether, however necessary and desirable they may be, they must be considered as detracting so much from the material products of a country, and its power of supporting an extended population; or whether they furnish fresh motives to production, and tend to push the wealth of a country farther than it would go without them.

The solution of this question evidently depends, first, upon the solution of the main practical question, whether the capital of a country can or cannot be redundant; that is, whether the motive to accumulate may be checked or destroyed by the want of effective demand long before it is checked by the difficulty of procuring the subsistence of the labourer. And secondly, whether, allowing the *possibility* of such a redundance, there is sufficient reason to believe that, under the actual habits of mankind, it is a probable occurrence.

In the Chapter on Profits, but more particularly in the Third Section of the present Chapter, where I have considered the effect of accumulation as a stimulus to the increase of wealth, I trust that the first of these questions has been satisfactorily answered. And in the present Section it has been shewn that the actual habits and practice of the productive classes, in the most improved societies, a do not lead them to consume so large a proportion of what they produce, even though assisted by the landlords, as to prevent their finding frequent difficulties in the employment of their capitals. We may conclude therefore, with little danger of error, that such a body of persons as I have described is not only necessary to the government, protection, health, and instruction of a country, but is also necessary to call forth those exertions which are required to give full play to its physical resources.

b With respect to the persons constituting the unproductive classes, and the modes by which they should be supported, it is probable that those which are paid voluntarily by individuals, will be allowed by all to be the most likely to be useful in exciting industry, and the least likely to be prejudicial by interfering with the costs of production. It may be presumed that a person will not take a menial servant, unless he can afford to pay him; and that he is as likely to be excited to industry by the prospect of this indulgence, as by the prospect of buying ribands and laces. Yet to shew how much the wealth of nations depends upon the proportion of parts, rather than on any positive rules respecting the advantages of productive or unproductive labour generally, it may be worth while to remind the reader that, though the employment of a certain number of persons in menial service is in every respect desirable, there could hardly be a taste more unfavourable to the progress of wealth than a strong preference of menial service to material products.* We may however, for the most part, trust to the inclinations of individuals in this respect; and it will be allowed generally, that there is little difficulty in reference to those classes which are supported voluntarily, though there may be much with regard to those which must be supported by taxation.

With regard to these latter classes, such as statesmen, soldiers, sailors, and those who live upon the interest of a national debt, it cannot be denied that they contribute powerfully to distribution and de-

* See Ch. i. p. 35.

a

mand; they frequently occasion a division of property more favourable to the progress of wealth than would otherwise have taken place; they ensure that consumption 'which is necessary to give the proper stimulus to production; and the desire to pay a tax, and yet enjoy the same means of gratification, must often operate to excite the exertions of industry quite as effectually as the desire to pay a lawyer or physician. Yet to counterbalance these advantages, which so far are unquestionable, it must be acknowledged that injudicious taxation might stop the increase of wealth at almost any period of its progress, early or late;* and that the most judicious taxation might ultimately be so heavy as to clog all the channels of foreign and domestic trade, and almost prevent the possibility of accumulation.

b

The effect therefore on national wealth of those classes of unproductive labourers which are supported by taxation, must be very various in different countries, and must depend entirely upon the powers of production, and upon the manner in

* The effect of obliging a cultivator of a certain portion of rich land to maintain two men and two horses for the state, might in some cases only induce him to cultivate more, and create more wealth than he otherwise would have done, while it might leave him personally as rich as before, and the nation richer; but if the same obligation were to be imposed on the cultivator of an equal quantity of poor land, the property might be rendered at once not worth working, and the desertion of it would be the natural consequence. An indiscriminate and heavy tax on gross produce might immediately scatter desolation over a country, capable, under a better system, of producing considerable wealth.

which the taxes are raised in each country. As
great powers of production are neither likely to be
called into action, or, when once in action, kept in
activity without great consumption, I feel very   a
little doubt that instances have practically occurred
of national wealth being greatly stimulated by the   b
consumption of those who have been supported
by taxes. Yet taxation is a stimulus so liable in
every way to abuse, and it is so absolutely necessary for the general interests of society to consider
private property as sacred, that one should be ex-   c
tremely cautious of trusting to any government,
the means of making a different distribution of
wealth, with a view to the general good. But
when, either from necessity or error, a different distribution has taken place, and the evil, as far as it
regards private property, has actually been committed, it would surely be most unwise to attempt,   d
at the expense of a great temporary sacrifice, a
return to the former distribution, without very   e
fully considering whether, if it were effected, it
would be really advantageous ; that is, whether, in
the actual circumstances of the country, with reference to its powers of production, more would
not be lost by the want of consumption than   f
gained by the diminution of taxation.

If there could be no sort of difficulty in finding
employment for capital, provided the price of la-   g
bour were sufficiently low, the way to national
wealth, though it might not always be easy, would
be quite straight, and our only object need be to
save from revenue, and repress unproductive con-

sumers. But, if it has appeared that the greatest
powers of production are rendered comparatively

abc   unless without adequate consumption, and that a
proper distribution of the produce is as necessary
to the continued increase of wealth as the means
of producing it, it follows that, in cases of this
kind, the question depends upon proportions ; and
it would be the height of rashness to determine,

d   under all circumstances, that the diminution of a
national debt and the removal of taxation must
necessarily tend to increase the national wealth,
and provide employment for the labouring classes.

e   If we were to suppose the powers of production
in a rich and well peopled country to be so increased that the whole of what it produced could
be obtained by one third of the labour before applied, can there be a reasonable doubt that the
principal difficulty would be to effect such a distribution of the produce, as to call forth these great
powers of production? To consider the gift of
such powers as an evil would indeed be most
strange; but they would be an evil, and practically a great and grievous one, if the effect were
to be an increase of the neat produce at the expense of the gross produce, and of the population.
But if, on the other hand, a more favourable distribution of the abundant produce were to take
place; if the more intelligent among the working
classes were raised into overseers of works, clerks
of various kinds, and retail dealers, while many
who had been in these situations before, together
with numerous others who had received a tolerable

education, were entitled to an income from the general produce, and could live nearly at leisure upon their mortgages; what an improved structure of society would this state of things present; while the value of the gross produce, and the numbers of the people would be increasing with rapidity! As I have before said, it would not be possible, under the principle of competition, (which can never be got rid of,) to secure much more leisure to those actually engaged in manual labour; but the very great increase in the number of prizes which would then be attainable by industrious and intelligent exertion, would most essentially improve their condition; and, on the whole, the society would have gained a great accession of comfort and happiness. It is not meant to be stated that such a distribution of the produce could be easily effected; but merely that, *with* such a distribution, the powers supposed would confer a prodigious benefit on the society, and *without* such a distribution, or such a change of tastes as would secure an equivalent consumption, the powers supposed might be worse than thrown away.

Now the question is, whether this country, in its actual state, with the great powers of production which it unquestionably possesses, does not bear some slight resemblance to the case here imagined; and whether, without such a body of unproductive consumers as these who live upon the interest of the national debt, the same stimulus would have been given to production, and the same powers would have been called forth. Under the actual

division of landed property which now takes place
in this country, I feel no sort of doubt that the
incomes which are received and spent by the national creditors are more favourable to the demand
for the great mass of manufactured products, and
tend much more to increase the happiness and intelligence of the whole society, than if they were
returned to the landlords.

a   I am far, however, from being insensible to the
evils of a great national debt. Though, in many
respects, it may be a useful instrument of distribution, it must be allowed to be a very cumbersome
and very dangerous instrument. In the first place,
the revenue necessary to pay the interest of such
a debt can only be raised by taxation; and, as this
taxation, if pushed to any considerable extent, can
hardly fail of interfering with the powers of production, there is always danger of impairing one
element of wealth, while we are improving another.
A second important objection to a large national
debt, is the feeling which prevails so very generally among all those not immediately concerned in
it, and consequently among the great mass of the
population, that they would be immediately and
greatly relieved by its extinction; and, whether
this impression be well founded or not, it cannot
b   exist without rendering such revenue in some
degree insecure, and exposing a country to the
c   risk of a great convulsion of property. A third
objection to such a debt is, that it greatly aggra-
vates the evils arising from changes in the value of
money. When the currency falls in value, the an-

nuitants, as owners of fixed incomes, are most unjustly deprived of their proper share of the national
produce; when the currency rises in value, the
pressure of the taxation necessary to pay the in-   a
terest of the debt, may become suddenly so heavy
as greatly to distress the productive classes;* and
this kind of sudden pressure must very much en-
hance the insecurity of property vested in public
funds.

On these and other accounts it might be desir-   b
able slowly to diminish the debt, and to discourage
the growth of it in future, even though it were
allowed that its past effects had been favourable
to-wealth, and that the advantageous distribution
of produce which it had occasioned, had, under the
actual circumstances, more than counterbalanced
the obstructions which it might have given to commerce. Security with moderate wealth is a wiser   c
choice, and better calculated for peace and happiness than insecurity with greater wealth. But,

* In a country with a large public debt, there is no duty which
ought to be held more sacred on the part of the administrators of
the government than to prevent any variations of the currency beyond those which necessarily belong to the varying value of the
precious metals. I am fully aware of the temporary advantages
which may be derived from a fall in the value of money; and
perhaps it may be true that a part of the distress during the last
year, though I believe but a small part, was occasioned by the
measure lately adopted, for the restoration of the currency to its
just value. But some such measure was indispensably necessary;
and Mr. Ricardo deserves the thanks of his country for having   α
suggested one which has rendered the transition more easy than
could reasonably have been expected.   d

unfortunately, a country accustomed to a distribution of produce which has at once excited and
given full play to great powers of production, cannot withdraw into a less ambitious path without
passing through a period of very great distress.

a   It is, I know, generally thought that all would
be well, if we could but be relieved from the
heavy burden of our debt. And yet I feel perfectly convinced that, if a spunge could be applied
to it to-morrow, and we could put out of our consideration the poverty and misery of the public
creditors, by supposing them to be supported com-
fortably in some other country, the rest of the
society, as a nation, instead of being enriched,
would be impoverished. It is the greatest mistake
to suppose that the landlords and capitalists would
either at once, or in a short time, be prepared for
so great an additional consumption as such a
change would require; and if they adopted the
alternative suggested by Mr. Ricardo in a former
instance, of saving, and lending their increased incomes, the evil would be aggravated tenfold. The
new distribution of produce would diminish the
demand for the results of productive labour; and
if, in addition to this, more revenue were converted
into capital, profits would fall to nothing, and a
much greater quantity of capital would emigrate,
or be destroyed at home, and a much greater number of persons would be starving for want of employment, than before the extinction of the debt.
It would signify little to be able to export cheap
goods. If the distribution of property at home were

not such as to occasion an adequate power and will to purchase and consume the returns for these goods, the quantity of capital which could be employed in the foreign trade of consumption would be diminished instead of increased. Of this we may be convinced if we look to India, where low wages appear to be of little use in commerce, while there are no middle classes of society to afford a market for any considerable quantity of foreign goods.

The landlords, in the event supposed, not being   a
inclined to an adequate consumption of the results of productive labour, would probably employ a greater number of menial servants; and perhaps, in the actual circumstances, this would be the best thing that could be done, and indeed the only way of preventing great numbers of the labouring classes from being starved for want of work. It is by no means likely, however, that it should soon take place to a sufficient extent; but if it were done completely, and the landlords paid as much in wages to menial servants as they had before paid to the national creditors, could we for a moment compare the state of society which would ensue to that which had been destroyed?

With regard to the capitalists, though they would   b
be relieved from a great portion of their taxes, yet there is every probability that their habits of saving, combined with the diminution in the number of effective demanders, would occasion such a fall in the prices of commodities as greatly to diminish that part of the national income which depends

upon profits; and I feel very little doubt that, in five years from the date of such an event, not only would the exchangeable value of the whole produce, estimated in domestic and foreign labour, be decidedly diminished, but a smaller absolute quantity of corn would be grown, and fewer manufactured and foreign commodities would be brought to market than before.

a   It is not of course meant to be said that a country with a large quantity of land, labour, and capital, has not the means of gradually recovering itself from any shock, however great, which it may experience; and after such an event, it might certainly place itself in a situation in which its property would be more secure than with a large national debt. All that I mean to say is, that it would pass through a period, probably of considerable duration, in which the diminution of effective demand from an unfavourable distribution of the produce would more than counterbalance the increased power of production occasioned by the relief from taxation; and it may fairly be doubted whether finally it would attain a great degree of wealth, or call forth, as it ought, a great degree of skill in agriculture, manufactures, and commerce, without possessing, in some way or other, a large body of unproductive consumers, or supplying this deficiency by a much greater tendency to consume the results of productive labour than is generally observed to prevail in society.

b   It has been repeatedly conceded, that the pro-

ductive classes have the power of consuming all
that they produce; and, if this power were adequately exercised, there might be no occasion, with
a view to wealth, for unproductive consumers. But
it is found by experience that, though there may
be the power, there is not the will; and it is to
supply this will that a body of unproductive consumers is necessary. Their specific use in encou-   a
raging wealth is, to maintain such a balance between produce and consumption as to give the
greatest exchangeable value to the results of the
national industry. If unproductive labour were   b
to predominate, the comparatively small quantity
of material products brought to market would keep
down the value of the whole produce, from the
deficiency of quantity. If the productive classes   c
were in excess, the value of the whole produce
would fall from excess of supply. It is obviously   d
a certain proportion between the two which will
yield the greatest value, and command the greatest   e
quantity of domestic and foreign labour; and we
may safely conclude that, among the causes necessary to that distribution, which will keep up and   f
increase the exchangeable value of the whole produce, we must place the maintenance of a certain
body of unproductive consumers. This body, to   gh
make it effectual as a stimulus to wealth, and to
prevent it from being prejudicial, as a clog to it,
should vary in different countries, and at different
times, according to the powers of production; and
the most favourable result evidently depends upon

a the proportion between productive and unproductive consumers, being best suited to the natural
b resources of the soil, and the acquired tastes and
habits of the people.

SECTION X.

*Application of some of the preceding Principles to the
Distresses of the Labouring Classes since 1815, with
General Observations.*

It has been said that the distresses of the labouring
classes since 1815 are owing to a deficient capital,
which is evidently unable to employ all that are
c in want of work.   That the capital of the country
does not bear an adequate proportion to the population ; that the capital and revenue together do
not bear so great a proportion as they did before
1815 ; and that such a disproportion will at once
account for very great distress among the labouring classes, I am most ready to allow.   But it is a
very different thing to allow that the capital is
deficient compared with the population ; and to
allow that it is deficient compared with the demand
for it, and the demand for the commodities pro-
d cured by it.   The two cases are very frequently
confounded, because they both produce distress
among the labouring classes; but they are essentially
distinct.   They are attended with some very dif-

ferent symptoms, and require to be treated in a very different manner.

If one fourth of the capital of a country were suddenly destroyed, or entirely transferred to a different part of the world, without any other cause occurring of diminished demand, this scantiness of capital would certainly occasion great distress among the working classes; but it would be attended with great advantages to the remaining capitalists. Commodities, in general, would be scarce, and bear a high price on account of the deficiency in the means of producing them. Nothing would be so easy as to find a profitable employment for stock; but it would by no means be easy to find stock for the number of employments in which it was deficient; and consequently the rate of profits would be very high. In this state of things, there would be an immediate and pressing demand for capital, on account of there being an immediate and pressing demand for commodities; and the obvious remedy would be, the supply of the demand in the only way in which it could take place, namely, by saving from revenue to add to capital. This supply of capital would, as I stated in a former section, take place just upon the same principle as a supply of population would follow a great destruction of people on the supposition of there being an immediate and pressing want of labour evinced by the high real wages given to the labourer.

On the other hand, if the capital of the country were diminished by the failure of some branches of trade, which had before been very prosperous, and absorbed a great quantity of stock; or even if capital were suddenly destroyed, and from peculiar circumstances a period were to succeed of diminished consumption and slack demand, the state of things, with the exception of the distresses of the poor, would be almost exactly reversed. The remaining capitalists would be in no respect benefited by events which had diminished demand in a still greater proportion than they had diminished capital. Commodities would be every where cheap. Capital would be seeking employment, but would not easily find it; and the profits of stock would be low. There would be no pressing and immediate demand for capital, because there would be no pressing and immediate demand for commodities; and, under these circumstances, the saving from revenue to add to capital, instead of affording the remedy required, would only aggravate the distresses of the capitalists, and fill the stream of capital which was flowing out of the country. The distresses of the capitalists would be aggravated, just upon the same principle as the distresses of the labouring classes would be aggravated, if they were encouraged to marry and increase, after a considerable destruction of people, although accompanied by a still greater destruction of capital which had kept the wages of labour very low. There might certainly be a great deficiency of population, compared with the territory and powers of the country, and it might be very desirable that it should be greater; but if the wages of labour

were still low, notwithstanding the diminution of
people, to encourage the birth of more children
would be to encourage misery and mortality rather
than population.

Now I would ask, to which of these two suppositions does the present state of this country bear
the nearest resemblance? Surely to the latter.
That a great loss of capital has lately been sustained, is unquestionable. During nearly the whole
of the war, owing to the union of great powers of
production with great consumption and demand,
the prodigious destruction of capital by the government was much more than recovered. To doubt
this would be to shut our eyes to the comparative
state of the country in 1792 and 1813. The two
last years of the war were, however, years of extraordinary expense, and being followed immediately
by a period marked by a very unusual stagnation
of demand, the destruction of capital which took
place in those years was not probably recovered.
But this stagnation itself was much more disastrous
in its effects upon the national capital, and still
more upon the national revenue, than any previous
destruction of stock. It commenced certainly with
the extraordinary fall in the value of the raw produce of the land, to the amount, it is supposed, of
nearly one third. When this fall had diminished
the capitals of the farmers, and still more the revenues both of landlords and farmers, and of all those
who were otherwise connected with the land, their
power of purchasing manufactures and foreign
products was of necessity greatly diminished. The

failure of home demand filled the warehouses of the manufacturers with unsold goods, which urged them to export more largely at all risks. But this excessive exportation glutted all the foreign markets, and prevented the merchants from receiving adequate returns; while, from the diminution of the home revenues, aggravated by a sudden and extraordinary contraction of the currency, even the comparatively scanty returns obtained from abroad found a very insufficient domestic demand, and the profits and consequent expenditure of merchants and manufacturers were proportionably lowered. While these unfavourable changes were

a   taking place in rents and profits, the powerful stimulus which had been given to population during the war continued to pour in fresh supplies of labour, and, aided by the disbanded soldiers and sailors and the failure of demand arising from the losses of the farmers and merchants, reduced gene-

b   rally the wages of labour, and left the country

c   with a generally diminished capital and revenue;— not merely in proportion to the alteration of the value of the currency, but in reference to the bullion value of its produce, and the command of this

d   bullion value over domestic and foreign labour. For the four or five years since the war, on account of the change in the distribution of the national

e   produce, and the want of consumption and demand

f   occasioned by it, a decided check has been given

g   to production, and the population, under its former impulse, has increased, not only faster than the demand for labour, but faster than the actual pro-

duce; yet this produce, though decidedly deficient,   a
compared with the population, and compared with   b
past times, is redundant, compared with the effectual demand for it and the revenue which is to
purchase it. Though labour is cheap, there is
neither the power nor the will to employ it all;
because not only has the capital of the country
diminished, compared with the number of labourers, but, owing to the diminished revenues of
the country, the commodities which those labourers
would produce are not in such request as ensure   c
tolerable profits to the reduced capital.

But when profits are low and uncertain, when
capitalists are quite at a loss where they can safely
employ their capitals, and when on these accounts
capital is flowing out of the country; in short,
when all the evidence which the nature of the
subject admits, distinctly proves that there is no
effective demand for capital at home, is it not contrary to the general principles of political economy,
is it not a vain and fruitless opposition to that
first, greatest, and most universal of all its principles, the principle of supply and demand, to recommend saving, and the conversion of more
revenue into capital?   Is it not just the same sort
of thing as to recommend marriage when people
are starving and emigrating ?

I am fully aware that the low profits of stock,
and the difficulty of finding employment for it,
which I consider as an unequivocal proof that the
immediate want of the country is not capital, has
been attributed to other causes; but to whatever

causes they may be attributed, an increase in the proportion of capital to revenue must aggravate them. With regard to these causes, such as the cultivation of our poor soils, our restrictions upon commerce, and our weight of taxation, I find it very difficult to admit a theory of our distresses so

a inconsistent with the theory of our prosperity. While the greatest quantity of our poor lands were in cultivation; while there were more than usual restrictions upon our commerce, and very little corn was imported; and while taxation was at its height, the country confessedly increased in wealth with a rapidity never known before. Since some of our poorest lands have been thrown out of cultivation; since the peace has removed many of the restrictions upon our commerce, and, notwithstanding our corn laws, we have imported a great quantity of corn; and since seventeen millions of taxes have been taken off from the people, we have

b experienced a degree of distress, the pressure of which has been almost intolerable.

c I am very far from meaning to infer from these striking facts that restrictions upon commerce and

d heavy taxation are likely in general to be beneficial to a country. But the facts certainly shew that, whatever may be the future effect of the causes above alluded to in checking the progress of our wealth, we must look elsewhere for the immediate sources of our present distresses. How far our artificial system, and particularly the changes in the value of our currency operating upon a large national debt, may have aggravated the evils we have experienced, it would be extremely difficult to say. But I feel perfectly convinced that a very considerable portion of these evils might be experienced by a nation without poor land in cultivation, without taxes, and without any fresh restrictions on trade.

If a large country, of considerable fertility, and sufficient inland communications, were surrounded by an impassable wall, we all agree that it might be tolerably rich, though not so rich as if it enjoyed the benefit of foreign commerce. Now, supposing such a country gradually to indulge in a considerable consumption, to call forth and employ a great quantity of ingenuity in production, and to save only yearly that portion of its revenue which it could most advantageously add to its capital, expending the rest in consumable commodities and unproductive labour, it might evidently, under such a balance of produce and consumption, be increasing in wealth and population with considerable rapidity. But if, upon the principle laid down by M. Say, that the consumption of a commodity is a diminution of demand, the society were greatly and generally to slacken their consumption, and add to their capitals, there cannot be the least doubt, on the great principles of demand and supply, that the profits of capitalists would soon be reduced to nothing, though there were no poor land in cultivation ; and the population would be thrown out of work and would be starving, although without a single tax, or any restrictions on trade.

The state of Europe and America may perhaps be said, in some points, to resemble the case here supposed; and the stagnation which has been so generally felt and complained of since the war, appears to me inexplicable upon the principles of those who think that the power of production is the only element of wealth, and who consequently

a   infer that if the powers of production be in-creased, wealth will certainly increase in propor-

b   tion. Now it is unquestionable that the powers of production were increased by the cessation of war, and that more people and more capital were ready to be employed in productive labour; but not-

c   withstanding this obvious increase in the powers of production, we hear every where of difficulties and distresses, instead of ease and plenty. In the United States of America in particular, a country of extraordinary physical resources, the difficulties which have been experienced are very striking, and such certainly as could hardly have been ex-pected. These difficulties, at least, cannot be at-tributed to the cultivation of poor land, restric-tions upon commerce, and excess of taxation. Altogether the state of the commercial world, since the war, clearly shews that something else is ne-cessary to the continued increase of wealth be-

d   sides an increase in the power of producing.

That the transition from war to peace, of which so much has been said, is a main cause of the effects observed, will be readily allowed, but not as the operation is usually explained. It is gene-rally said that there has not been time to transfer capital from the employments where it is redundant to those where it is deficient, and thus to restore the proper equilibrium.   But I cannot bring myself to believe that this transfer can require so much time as has now elapsed since the war ; and I would again ask, where are the under-stocked employments, which, according to this theory, ought to be numerous, and fully capable of absorbing all the redundant capital, which is confessedly glutting the markets of Europe in so many different branches of trade ? It is well known by the owners of floating capital, that none such are now to be found ; and if the transition in question is to account for what has happened, it must have produced some other effects besides that which arises from the difficulty of moving capital.   This I conceive to be a great diminution of the whole amount of consumption and demand.   The necessary changes in the channels of trade would be effected in a year or two ; but the general diminution of consumption and demand, occasioned by the transition from such a war to a peace, may last for a very considerable time.   The returned taxes, and the excess of individual gains above expenditure, which were so largely used as revenue during the war, are now in part, and probably in no inconsiderable part, saved. I cannot doubt, for instance, that in our own country very many persons have taken the opportunity of saving a part of their returned property-tax, particularly those who have only life-incomes, and who, contrary to the principles of just taxation,

a

b

c

d

had been assessed at the same rate with those
whose incomes were derived from realized property. This saving is quite natural and proper,
and forms no just argument against the removal
of the tax; but still it contributes to explain the
cause of the diminished demand for commodities,
compared with their supply since the war. If
some of the principal governments concerned
spent the taxes which they raised in a manner to
create a greater and more certain demand for labour and commodities, particularly the former, than
the present owners of them, and if this difference
of expenditure be of a nature to last for some
time, we cannot be surprised at the duration of the
effects arising from the transition from war to
peace.

a   The diminished consumption however, which
has taken place so generally, must have operated
very differently upon the different countries of the
commercial world, according to the different circumstances in which they were placed; and it
will be found generally, as the principles which
have been laid down would lead us to expect, that
those states which have suffered the most by the
war have suffered the least by the peace. In the
countries where a great pressure has fallen upon
moderate or scanty powers of production, it is hardly
possible to suppose that their wealth should not
have been stopped in its progress during the war,
or perhaps rendered positively retrograde. Such
b   countries must have found relief from that diminution of consumption, which now allows them to

accumulate capital, without which no state can permanently increase in wealth.   But in those countries, where the pressure of the war found great powers of production, and seemed to create much greater; where accumulation, instead of being   a
checked, was accelerated, and where the vast consumption of commodities was followed by supplies which occasioned a more rapid increase of wealth than was ever known before, the effect of peace   b
would be very different.   In such countries it is natural to suppose that a great diminution of con-   c
sumption and demand would decidedly check the progress of wealth, and occasion very general and severe distress, both to capitalists and the labouring classes.   England and America come the nearest to the countries of this latter description. They suffered the least by the war, or rather were enriched by it, and they are now suffering the most by the peace.

I cannot but consider it as a very unfortunate   d
circumstance that any period should ever have occurred in which peace should appear to have been, in so marked a manner, connected with distress; but it should always be recollected that it is owing   e
to the very peculiar circumstances attending the late war that the contrast has been so striking. It was very different in the American and former   f
wars; and, if the same exertions had been attempted, without the same powers of supporting them, that is, without the command of the greatest part of the commerce of the world, and a more rapid and successful progress in the use of machi-

nery than was ever before known, we might have
been in a state to have felt the greatest relief at
the cessation of hostilities.   When Hume and
Adam Smith prophesied that a little increase of
national debt beyond the then amount of it,
would probably occasion bankruptcy; the main
cause of their error was the very natural one, of
not being able to see the vast increase of productive power to which the nation would subsequently attain.   An expenditure, which would
have absolutely crushed the country in 1770, might
be little more than what was necessary to call
forth its prodigious powers of production in 1816.
But just in proportion to this power of production,
and to the facility with which a vast consumption
could be supplied, consistently with a rapid accumulation of capital, would be the distress felt
by capitalists and labourers upon any great and
sudden diminution of expenditure.

On this account, there is reason to doubt the
policy of raising the supplies of a long and expensive war within the year, a policy which has
been recommended by very able writers.   If the
country were poor, such a system of taxation
might completely keep down its efforts.   It might
every year positively diminish its capital, and
render it every year more ruinous to furnish the
same supplies; till the country would be obliged
to submit to its enemies from the absolute inability of continuing to oppose them with effect.
On the other hand, if the country were rich, and
had great powers of production, which were likely

α
β

to be still further called forth by the stimulus of a great consumption, it might be able to pay the a heavy taxes imposed upon it, out of its revenue, and yet find the means of adequate accumulation ; but if this process were to last for any time, and the habits of the people were accommodated to this scale of public and private expenditure, it is scarcely possible to doubt that, at the end of the war, when so large a mass of taxes would at once be restored to the payers of them, the just balance of produce and consumption would be completely destroyed, and a period would ensue, longer or shorter, according to circumstances, in which a very great stagnation would be felt in every branch of productive industry, attended by its usual concomitant general distress.   The evil occasioned by imposing a tax is very rarely compensated by the taking it off.   We should constantly keep in mind that the tendency to expenditure in individuals has most formidable antagonists in the love of indolence, and in the desire of saving, in order to better their condition and provide for a family ; and that all theories founded upon the assumption that mankind always produce and consume as much as they have the power to produce and consume, are founded upon a want of knowledge of the human character and of the motives by which it is usually influenced.

It will be said, perhaps, that as it is acknowledged b that the capital of this country compared with the population has been diminished since the

war, partly by the unrecovered destruction which
it sustained during the last two years of the contest, but still more by the sudden want of consumption and demand which occurred on its termination; how is the lost capital ever to be recovered, if we are' not active in accumulation? I
am very far indeed from saying that we must not
accumulate. It is perfectly true that there is no
other possible way of recovering our lost capital
than by accumulation. All that I mean to say is,
that, in looking to this most desirable object, the
recovery and increase of our capital, we should
listen to the dictates of those great general laws
which do not often fail to direct us in the right
course. If population were ever so deficient in a
state compared with its territory, yet, if the wages
of labour still continued very scanty, and the
people were emigrating, the great general laws of
demand and supply would instruct us that some
previous change in the state of things was necessary, before we ought to wish for an increased
proportion of marriages, which in fact, under the
actual circumstances, would not accomplish the
object aimed at. In the same manner, if a portion
of our profits be destroyed, and yet the profits of
the remainder are low, and its employment attended
with such frequent losses as, joined to its tendency to emigrate, make it stationary or even retrograde; surely the great general laws of demand
and supply cannot more clearly shew us that something else is wanted before we can accumulate
with effect.

What is now wanted in this country is an increased national revenue,—an increase in the exchangeable value of the whole produce estimated in bullion,—and in the command of this bullion over domestic and foreign labour.   When we have   a attained this, which can only be attained by increased and steady profits, we may then begin again to accumulate, and our accumulation will then be effectual.   But if, instead of saving from increased profits, we save from diminished expenditure; if, at the very time that the supply of commodities compared with the demand for them, clearly admonishes us that the proportion of capital to revenue is already too great, we go on saving from our revenue to add still further to our capital, all general principles concur in shewing that we must of necessity be aggravating instead of alleviating our distresses.

But how, it will be asked, are we to obtain this increase of revenue?   What steps are we to take in order to raise the exchangeable value of the whole produce, and prepare the way for the future saving which is acknowledged to be necessary? These questions I have endeavoured to answer in the latter Section of this very long Chapter *On*   b *the immediate Causes of the Progress of Wealth*, where it has appeared that a union of the means of distribution with the powers of production is absolutely necessary to create an adequate stimulus to the continued increase of wealth; and that the three causes, which, by favouring distribution, tend most to keep up and increase the exchangeable value of the whole produce, are, the division of landed property, the extension of domestic and foreign trade, and the maintenance of unproductive labourers.

The mention of these causes is alone sufficient to shew that they are much less within our immediate controul than the common process of accumulation. If it were true that, in order to employ all that are out of work, and to create at the same time a sufficient market for what they produce, it is only necessary that a little more should be saved from the revenue and added to the capital of the country, I am fully persuaded that this species of charity would not want contributors, and that a change would soon be wrought in the condition of the labouring classes. But when we know, both from theory and experience, that this proceeding will not afford the relief sought for, and are referred to an increase in the exchangeable value of the whole produce as the only cause which can restore a healthy and effective demand for labour, it must be allowed that we may be at a loss with respect to the first steps which it would be advisable to take, in order to accomplish what we wish.

Still, however, it is of the utmost importance to know the immediate object which ought to be aimed at; that if we can do but little actually to forward it, we may not, from ignorance, do much to retard it. With regard to the first main cause which I have mentioned, as tending to increase the exchangeable value of the national produce, namely the division of landed property, I have given my reasons for thinking that, in the actual and peculiar state of this country, the abolition of the law of primogeniture would produce more evil than good; and there is no other way in which a different division of land could be effected, consistently with an adequate respect for the great fundamental law of property, on which all progress in civilization, improvement, and wealth, must ever depend.   But if the *distribution* of wealth to a certain extent be one of the main causes of its increase, while it is unadvisable directly to interfere with the present division of land in this country, it may justly become a question, whether the evils attendant on the national debt are not more than counterbalanced by the distribution of property and increase of the middle classes of society, which it must necessarily create; and whether by saving, in order to pay it off, we are not submitting to a painful sacrifice, which, if it attains its object, whatever other good it may effect, will leave us with a much less favourable distribution of wealth?   By greatly reducing the national debt, if we are able to accomplish it, we may place ourselves perhaps in a more safe position, and this no doubt is an important consideration; but grievously will those be disappointed who think that, either by greatly reducing or at once destroying it, we can enrich ourselves, and employ all our labouring classes.

a

With regard to the second main cause of an increase in the exchangeable value of the whole produce—namely, the extension of domestic and foreign trade, it is well known that we can by no means command either of these at pleasure, but we may do much to impede both.   We cannot indeed reasonably attribute any sudden deficiency of trade to causes which have been of long duration; yet there can be little doubt that our commerce has been much impaired by unnecessary restraints, and that much benefit might be derived from the removal of them.   While it is necessary to raise a large sum by taxation for the expenses of the government and the payment of the interest of the national debt, it would by no means be advisable to neglect so fair and fruitful a resource as the customs.   In regulating these taxes, it is also natural that those foreign commodities should be taxed the highest, which are either of the same kind as the native commodities which have been taxed, or such as, for special reasons of health, happiness, or safety, it is desirable to grow largely at home.   But there seems to be no reason for the absolute prohibition of any commodities whatever; and there is little doubt that, upon this principle, a much greater freedom might be given to foreign commerce, at the same time that a greater revenue might be derived from the customs.   I have already stated, in more places than one, why, under all the circumstances of the case, I think it desirable that we should permanently grow nearly our own consumption of corn.   But I see no sufficient cause why we should permanently prefer the wines of Portugal and the silks of London to the wines and silks of France.   For the same reason that more British capital and labour is even now employed in purchasing claret than would be employed in attempting to make it at home, we might fairly expect that, in the case of an extended trade with France, more British capital would be employed in purchasing the wines and silks of France, than is now employed in purchasing the wines of Portugal and making the silks of Spitalfields and Derby.

At the same time it should be remarked that, in looking forward to changes of this kind, it is always incumbent upon us, particularly in the actual situation of our people, to attend to the wise caution suggested by Adam Smith.   Fully convinced of the benefits of unrestrained trade, he observes, that " The case in which it may sometimes be a matter of deliberation how far, and in what manner, it is proper to restore the free importation of foreign goods, after it has been for some time interrupted, is, when particular manufactures, by means of high duties and prohibitions upon all foreign goods which can come into competition with them, have been so far extended as to employ a great multitude of hands.   Humanity may in this case require that the freedom of trade should be restored only by slow gradations, and with a good deal of reserve and circumspection.   Were these high duties and prohibitions taken away all at once, cheaper foreign goods of the same kind might be poured so fast into the home market as to deprive all at once many thousands of their ordinary employment and means of subsistence."* The caution here given by Adam Smith certainly applies in a very marked manner to the silk trade; and, however desirable it may be (and it is so most unquestionably) to open the trade with France, a sudden and incautious admission of a large quantity of French silks would tend to aggravate, instead of to relieve the present distresses of our working classes.

In all cases where, under peculiar circumstances, the distress of the country would be aggravated by the opening of certain trades, which had before been subject to restrictions, the exchangeable value of the whole produce estimated in domestic and foreign labour would for a time be diminished. But, in general, as I have endeavoured to shew in the 8th Section of this Chapter, the natural and permanent tendency of all extension of trade both domestic and foreign, is to increase the exchangeable value of the whole produce. This is more especially the case when, instead of changing the channels of commerce, we are able to make large and distinct additions to them. The good is then unallayed by partial and temporary evil. This better distribution of the produce of the country, this better adaptation of it to the wants and tastes of the consumers, will at once give it a greater market value, and at once increase the national revenue, the rate of steady profits, and the wages of labour.

* Wealth of Nations, Book iv. ch. vii. p. 202. 6th edit.

With regard to the third cause of an increase in the exchangeable value of the whole produce, the maintenance of unproductive consumers—though many have no power to be of use in this respect, others may do something; and it must certainly be advantageous that the truth, whatever it may be, relating to the effects of unproductive   a labour, should be fully known, that we may not aim at what will obstruct the progress of wealth, and clamour at what is calculated to advance it. Whatever it may be thought advisable to do respecting the diminution of unproductive consumers, with a view to the placing ourselves in a safer position, we shall be led to proceed with more deliberation, if we are not hurried on by the impression that, by this diminution, we are affording immediate relief to the labouring classes.

It is also of importance to know that, in our endeavours to assist the working classes in a period like the present, it is desirable to employ them in unproductive labour, or at least in labour, the   b results of which do not come for sale into the market, such as roads and public works. The objection to employing a large sum in this way, raised by taxes, would not be its tendency to diminish the capital employed in productive labour; because this, to a certain extent, is exactly what is wanted; but it might, perhaps, have the effect of concealing too much the failure of the national demand for labour, and prevent the population from gradually accommodating itself to a reduced demand. This however might be, in a considerable degree, corrected by the wages given. And altogether I should say, that the employment of the poor in roads and public works, and a tendency among landlords and persons of property to build, to improve and beautify their grounds, and to employ workmen and menial servants, are the means most within our power and most directly calculated to remedy the evils arising from that disturbance in the balance of produce and consumption, which has been occasioned by the sudden conversion of soldiers, sailors, and various other classes which the war employed, into productive labourers.

a

If by the operation of these three causes, either separately or conjointly, we can make the supply and consumption bear a more advantageous proportion to each other, so as to increase the exchangeable value of the whole produce, the rate of profits may then permanently rise as high as the quality of the soil in cultivation combined with the actual skill of the cultivators will allow,* which is far from being the case at present. And as soon

b

as the capitalist can begin to save from steady and improving profits, instead of from diminished expenditure, that is, as soon as the national revenue,

c

* The profits of stock cannot be higher than the state of the land will allow, but they may be lower in any degree. (see p. 300.) The great difference between Mr. Ricardo and me on this point is, that Mr. Ricardo thinks profits are *regulated* by the state of the land; I think they are only *limited* by it one way, and that if capital be abundant, compared with the demand for commodities, profits may be low in any degree, in spite of the fertility of the land.

estimated in bullion, and in the command of this bullion over domestic and foreign labour, begins yearly and steadily to increase, we may then begin safely and effectively to recover our lost capital by the usual process of saving a portion of our increased revenue to add to it.

It is, I believe, the opinion of many persons, particularly among the mercantile classes, that nothing would so soon and so effectively increase the revenue and consumption of the country as a free issue of paper. But in holding this opinion, they have mistaken the nature of the great advantage which the national wealth may sometimes unquestionably derive from a fall in the value of the currency. The specific effect of this fall is to take away property from those who have fixed incomes, and give a greater command over the pro] duce of the country to those who buy and sell. When the state of the national expenditure is such that there is a difficulty of supplying it, then whatever tends to throw a greater proportion of the produce into the hands of capitalists, as it must increase the power of production, must be just calculated to supply what is wanted. And, though the continuation of the act of restriction beyond the immediate necessity of the case, can hardly be considered in any other light than as an act of positive injustice towards the possessors of fixed incomes; yet I can feel very little doubt that the fall in the value of money, and the facility of credit which it occasioned, acting in the way described, must have contributed greatly to that rapid recovery of vast capital destroyed, which, in the same degree, never probably occurred in the history of any nation before.

But, if we were now to make similar issues of paper, the effect would be very different. Perhaps a sudden increase of currency and a new facility of borrowing might, under any circumstances, give a temporary stimulus to trade, but it would only be temporary. Without a large expenditure on the part of the government, and a frequent conversion of capital into revenue, the great powers of production acquired by the capitalists, operating upon the diminished power of purchasing possessed by the owners of fixed incomes, could not fail to occasion a still greater glut of commodities than is felt at present; and experience has sufficiently shewn us, that paper cannot support prices under such circumstances. In the history of our paper transactions, it will be found that the abundance or scantiness of currency has followed and aggravated high or low prices, but seldom or never led them; and it is of the utmost importance to recollect that, at the end of the war, the prices failed before the contraction of the currency began. It was, in fact, the failure of prices, which destroyed the country banks, and shewed us the frail foundations on which the excess of our paper-currency rested. This sudden contraction no doubt aggravated very greatly the distresses of the merchants and of the country; and for this very reason we should use our utmost endeavours to avoid such an event in future; not, how-

ever, by vain efforts to keep up prices by forcible
issues of paper, in defiance at once of the laws of
justice and the great principles of supply and demand, but by the only effectual way, that of
steadily maintaining our paper of the same value
with the coin which it professes to represent, and
subjecting it to no other fluctuations than those
which belong to the precious metals.

In reference to the main doctrine inculcated in
the latter part of this work, namely, that the progress of wealth depends upon proportions; it will be
objected, perhaps, that it necessarily opens the way
to differences of opinion relating to these proposi-   a
tions, and thus throws a kind of uncertainty over
the science of political economy which was not supposed to belong to it.   If, however, the doctrine
should be found, upon sufficient examination, to be
true; if it adequately accounts for things as they
are, and explains consistently why frequent mistakes have been made respecting the future, it will
be allowed that such objectors are answered.   We
cannot make a science more certain by our wishes
or opinions; but we may obviously make it much
more uncertain in its application, by believing it to
be what it is not.

Though we cannot, however, lay down a certain
rule for growing rich, and say that a nation will
increase in wealth just in the degree in which it
saves from its revenue, and adds to its capital:
yet even in the most uncertain parts of the science,
even in those parts which relate to the proportions
of production and consumption, we are not left   b

without guides; and if we attend to the great
laws of demand and supply, they will generally
direct us into the right course. It is justly observed by Mr. Ricardo that " the farmer and
manufacturer can no more live without profit than
the labourer without wages. Their motive for
accumulation will diminish with every diminution
of profit, and will cease altogether when their
profits are so low as not to afford them an adequate compensation for their trouble, and the
risk which they must necessarily encounter in
employing their capital productively."* Mr. Ricardo applies this passage to the final and necessary fall of profits occasioned by the state of the
land. I would apply it at all times, throughout all
the variable periods which intervene between the
first stage of cultivation and the last. Whenever
capital increases too fast, the motive to accumula-
lation diminishes, and there will be a natural tendency to spend more and save less. When profits
rise, the motive to accumulation will increase,
and there will be a tendency to spend a smaller
proportion of the gains, and to save a greater.
These tendencies, operating on individuals, direct
them towards the just mean, which they would
more frequently attain if they were not interrupted by bad laws or unwise exhortations. If
every man who saves from his income is necessarily a friend to his country, it follows that all
those who spend their incomes, though they may

α

* Princ. of Polit. Econ. ch. vi. p. 127.

not be absolute enemies, like the spendthrift, must be considered as failing in the duty of benefiting their country, and employing the labouring classes, when it is in their power; and this cannot be an agreeable reflection to those whose scale of expenditure in their houses, furniture, carriages and table, would certainly admit of great retrenchment, with but little sacrifice of real comfort. But if, in reality, saving is a national benefit, or a national disadvantage, according to the circumstances of the period; and, if these circumstances are best declared by the rate of profits, surely it is a case in which individual interest needs no extraneous assistance.

Saving, as I have before said, is, in numerous instances, a most sacred private duty. How far a just sense of this duty, together with the desire of bettering our condition so strongly implanted in the human breast, may sometimes, and in some states of society, occasion a greater tendency to parsimony than is consistent with the most effective encouragement to the growth of public wealth, it is difficult to say; but whether this tendency, if let alone, be ever too great or not, no one could think of interfeing with it, even in its caprices. a There is no reason, however, for giving an additional sanction to it, by calling it a public duty. The market for national capital will be supplied, like other markets, without the aid of patriotism. And in leaving the whole question of saving to the uninfluenced operation of individual interest and individual feelings, we shall best conform to that great principle of political economy laid down by Adam Smith, which teaches us a general maxim, liable to very few exceptions, that the wealth of nations is best secured by allowing every person, as long as he adheres to the rules of justice, to pursue his own interest in his own way.

Still it must be allowed that this very doctrine, and the main doctrines of the foregoing work, all tend to shew, as was stated in the Introduction, that the science of political economy bears a nearer resemblance to the sciences of morals and politics, than to the science of mathematics. But this truth, though it detracts from its certainty, does not detract from its importance. While the science of political economy involves some of the questions which have the nearest connection with the well-being of society, it must always be a subject of the highest interest. The study of it is calculated to be of great practical use, and to prevent much positive evil. And if its principles be carefully founded on an experience sufficiently extended, we have good reason to believe, from what they have already done, that, when properly applied, they will rarely disappoint our just expectations.

There is another objection which will probably be made to the doctrines of the latter part of this work, which I am more anxious to guard against. If the principles which I have laid down be true, it will certainly follow that the sudden removal of taxes will often be attended with very different effects, particularly to the labouring classes of so- ciety, from those which have been generally expected. And an inference may perhaps be drawn from this conclusion in favour of taxation. But the just inference from it is, that taxes should never be imposed, nor to a greater amount, than the necessity of the case justifies, and particularly that every effort should be made, consistently with national honour and security, to prevent a scale of expenditure so great that it cannot proceed without ruin, and cannot be stopped without distress.

Even if it be allowed that the excitement of a prodigious public expenditure, and of the taxation necessary to support it, operating upon extraordinary powers of production, might, under peculiar circumstances, increase the wealth of a country in a greater degree than it otherwise would have increased; yet, as the greatest powers of production must finally be overcome by excessive borrowing, and as increased misery among the labouring classes must be the consequence, whether we go on or attempt to return, it would surely have been much better for the society if such wealth had never existed. It is like the unnatural strength occasioned by some violent stimulant, which, if not absolutely necessary, should be by all means avoided, on account of the exhaustion which is sure to follow it.

In the Essay on Population I have observed, that " In the whole compass of human events, I doubt if there be a more fruitful source of misery, or one more invariably productive of disastrous consequences, than a sudden start of population from two or three years of plenty, which must

α

a

necessarily be repressed by the first return of scarcity, or even by average crops." *   The great
demand for labour which took place during the
war must have had an effect precisely of a
similar kind, and only aggravated by duration;
and as this is a state of things which cannot in its
nature continue, it is obviously the duty of all
governments, if they have any regard for the happiness of their subjects, to avoid all wars and excessive expenditure as far as it is possible; but if
war be unavoidable, so to regulate the necessary
expenditure as to occasion the least pressure upon
the people during the contest, and the least convulsion in the state of the demand at the termination of it. We may have good reason to lament
that such taxation and consumption should ever
have taken place, and that so great an impetus,
which could only be temporary, should have been
given to the wealth and population of the country;
but it is a very different question, what is the best

b   remedy now that the evil is incurred? If the population had made a start during a few years of
plenty, we should surely make great efforts to prevent, by importation, the misery which would be
occasioned by the sudden return of average crops.
If the human body had been subjected to a very
powerful stimulus, we should surely be cautious
not to remove it too suddenly. And, if the country had been unfortunately subjected to the excitement of a long continuance of excessive ex-

* Vol. ii. p. 170. 4th edit.

penditure, it surely must be against all analogy and all general principles, to look for the immediate remedy of it in a great and sudden contraction of consumption.

There is every reason to believe that the working classes of society would be severely injured by attaining the object which they seem so ardently to wish for. To those who live upon fixed incomes, the relief from taxation is a great and unmixed good; to the mercantile and trading classes it is sometimes a good and sometimes an evil, according to circumstances; but to the working classes, no taking off of taxes, nor any degree of cheapness of corn, can compensate a want of demand for labour. If the general demand for labour fail, particularly if the failure be sudden, the labouring classes will be wretched in the midst of cheapness; if the demand for labour be considerable, they will be comparatively rich in the midst of dearness.

a

To state these facts is not to favour taxes; but to give one of the strongest reasons against them; namely, that they are not only a great evil on their first imposition, but that the attempt to get rid of them afterwards, is often attended with fresh suffering. They are like those injudicious regulations of the mercantile system noticed by Adam Smith, which, though acknowledged to be pernicious, cannot be removed without producing a greater evil for an interval of considerable length.

α

Theoretical writers are too apt, in their calculations, to overlook these intervals; but eight or ten

years, recurring not unfrequently, are serious spaces
in human life.   They amount to a serious sum of
happiness or misery, according as they are prosperous or adverse, and leave the country in a very
different state at their termination.   In prosperous
times the mercantile classes often realize fortunes,
which go far towards securing them against the
future; but unfortunately the working classes,
a   though they share in the general prosperity, do
not share so largely as in the general adversity.
They may suffer the greatest distress in a period
of low wages, but cannot be adequately compensated by a period of high wages.   To them fluctuations must always bring more evil than good;
and, with a view to the happiness of the great
mass of society, it should be our object, as far as
possible, to maintain peace, and an equable expenditure.

SUMMARY

a

OF THE CONTENTS OF THE FOREGOING WORK.

INTRODUCTION.

CHAPTER I.

ON THE DEFINITIONS OF WEALTH AND PRODUCTIVE LABOUR.

α

CHAP. II.
OF THE NATURE AND MEASURES OF VALUE.

a

b

SECT. II.—*Of Demand and Supply as they affect Exchangeable Value.*

SECT. III.—*Of the Cost of Production as it affects Exchangeable
Value.*

Sect. V.—*Of Money, when uniform in its Cost, considered as a
Measure of value.*

CHAPTER III.
OF THE RENT OF LAND.

SEC. III.—*Of the Causes which tend to raise Rents in the ordinary Progress of Society.*

SECT. V.—*On the Dependance of the Actual Quantity of Produce
obtained from the Land upon the existing Rents, and the existing
Prices.*

Sect. VIII.— *On the strict and necessary Connection of the Interests of the Landlord and of the State, in a Country which supports its own Population.*

It is allowed that if a most extraordinary degree of fertility

SECT. IX.—*On the Connection of the Interests of the Landlord and
of the State, in Countries which import Corn.*

PAGE

CHAPTER IV.
OF THE WAGES OF LABOUR.

a

CHAPTER V.

OF THE PROFITS OF CAPITAL.

SECT. I.—*Of Profits as affected by the increasing Difficulty of procuring the Means of Subsistence.*

SECT. II.—*Of Profits as affected by the Proportion which Capital
bears to Labour.*

The second main cause which, by increasing the amount of

SECT. IV.—*Remarks on Mr. Ricardo's Theory of Profits.*

CHAPTER VI.

OF THE DISTINCTION BETWEEN WEALTH AND VALUE.

CHAPTER VII.

ON THE IMMEDIATE CAUSES OF THE PROGRESS OF WEALTH.

SECT. I.—*Statement of the particular Object of Inquiry.*

SECT. IV.—*Of the Fertility of the Soil considered as a Stimulus to the continued Increase of Wealth.*

α SECT. V.—*Of Inventions to abridge Labour, considered as a Stimulus to the continued Increase of Wealth.*

But the same laws apply to machinery as to fertile land: a

SECT. VII.—*Of the Distribution occasioned by the Division of
Landed Property considered as the means of increasing the Exchangeable Value of the whole Produce.*

a

Sect. IX.—*Of the Distribution occasioned by unproductive Consumers, considered as the Means of increasing the exchangeable Value of the whole Produce.*

a

α

INDEX.

598   INDEX.

486—probable effects of annihilating the public debt, 486—particularly on landlords, 487—and on capitalists, ib. 488, 489.

New Spain. See *Mexico*.

Non-interference, the principle of necessarily limited in practice; *first*, by some duties connected with political economy, which it is universally acknowledged belong to the sovereign, 18; *secondly*, by the almost universal prevalence of bad regulations, which require to be amended or removed, 19; and *thirdly*, by the necessity of taxation, ib.—the propriety of interfering but little does not supersede in any degree the use of the most extensive professional knowledge, 20.

O.

Oats, unfavourable operation of prohibitory laws, and of bounty on the growth of, 255, 256.

P.

Political Economy, importance and nature of the science of, 1, 2—strictures on the differences between the Economists and Adam Smith, 2, 3, 5—causes of the differences in opinion among the principal writers on political economy, 5—21—motives and design of the present work, 21—24.

Population and cultivation do not always proceed with equal steps, 127—influence of the increase of population on rents, 161, 162—cause of the increase of the population of Ireland, 232, 252—why the population of England did not increase in proportion to that of Ireland, during the same period, 253, 290—causes of the increase of population in Scotland, 254—of the causes which principally influence the increase of population, 257—266—the increase of population, considered as a stimulus to the continued increase of wealth, 347—351—the thin population of some parts of New Spain accounted for, 385—obstacles to the progress of population in that country, 387.

Potatoes, the culture of in Ireland a cause of the increased population of that island, 232, 252.

Prices of commodities, how influenced by demand and supply, 64—72—by the cost of production, 72—84—by the labour, which a commodity

has actually cost, 84—108—and by the labour which it will command, 118—126—prices of commodities, how influenced by money, when uniform in its value, 108—118—natural or necessary price, what, 83, 84—the causes of the excess of the price of raw produce above the costs of production, 139—150—the dependence of the actual quantity of produce obtained from the land upon the existing price, illustrated, 183—191—a temporary rise of prices, not sufficient to warrant an increase of rent, 200—rent ought always to be a little behind prices, 201—the natural price of labour, what, 247—and what the market price, ib. 248—prices of wheat in the 15th and 16th centuries, 271, 272, 273—in the 17th century, 277—in the 18th century, 279—and in the former part of the 19th century, 280—general observations on the prices of corn during the last five centuries, 281—292—particularly as affected by the seasons, 284—286.

Primogeniture, right of, ought not to be abolished in this country, and why, 437—440.

Produce (agricultural), influence of the increase of price in, on raising rents, 166—178—and also in diminishing them, 181, 182—on the dependence of the actual quantity of produce obtained from the land upon the existing rents and existing prices, 183—191—the connexion between great comparative wealth, and a high comparative price of raw produce, 192—199—of the distribution occasioned by the division of landed property, considered as the means of increasing the exchangeable value of the whole produce, 427—440—of the distribution occasioned by commerce, considered as the means of increasing the exchangeable value of produce, 440—462—the distribution occasioned by unproductive consumers, considered as a means of increasing the exchangeable value of the whole produce, 463—490—an increase in the exchangeable value of the whole produce, necessary to extricate the labouring classes of this country from their present distresses, 505, 508—520.

Production, cost of, considered as it affects exchangeable value, 72—76

THE END.

London: Printed by C. Roworth,
Bell-yard. Temple-bar.